W9-ALV-200

American Foreign Policy
Since World War II

American Foreign Policy Since World War II

FIFTEENTH EDITION

STEVEN W. HOOK
Kent State University

JOHN SPANIER
University of Florida

CQ PRESS

A DIVISION OF CONGRESSIONAL QUARTERLY INC.
WASHINGTON, D.C.

CQ Press
A Division of Congressional Quarterly Inc.
1414 22nd Street, N.W.
Washington, D.C. 20037

(202) 822-1475; (800) 638-1710

www.cqpress.com

Cover designer: Ed Atkeson

Book and map design: Kachergis Book Design, Pittsboro, North Carolina

Printed and bound in the United States of America.

04 03 02 01 00   5 4 3 2 1

Library of Congress Cataloging-in-Publication Data

Hook, Steven W.
American foreign policy since World War II / Steven W. Hook, John Spanier.—15th ed.
p. cm.
Spanier's name appears first on the earlier edition.
Includes bibliographical references and index.
ISBN 1-56802-578-5 (alk. paper)
1. United States—Foreign relations—1945–1989. 2. United States—Foreign relations—1989–. I. Spanier, John W. II. Title.
E744.S8 2000
327.73'009'045—dc21   00-040384

Illustration credits and acknowledgments appear on page 408, which is to be considered a continuation of the copyright page.

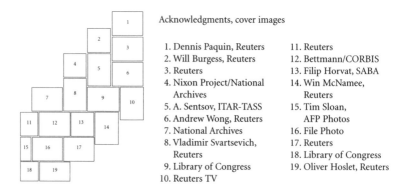

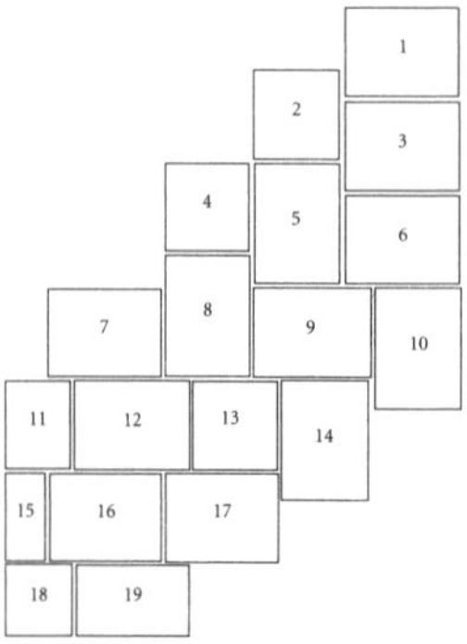

Acknowledgments, cover images

1. Dennis Paquin, Reuters
2. Will Burgess, Reuters
3. Reuters
4. Nixon Project/National Archives
5. A. Sentsov, ITAR-TASS
6. Andrew Wong, Reuters
7. National Archives
8. Vladimir Svartsevich, Reuters
9. Library of Congress
10. Reuters TV
11. Reuters
12. Bettmann/CORBIS
13. Filip Horvat, SABA
14. Win McNamee, Reuters
15. Tim Sloan, AFP Photos
16. File Photo
17. Reuters
18. Library of Congress
19. Oliver Hoslet, Reuters

For Peg Hook

and

For Joshua and Jacob Vayle

Contents

Maps and Featured Figures

MAPS

IMPACT AND INFLUENCE

Preface

American foreign policy has returned to form. As in the days before the United States became a world power, many Americans today are openly questioning what obligations, if any, the nation has beyond its shores. Public opinion polls consistently register a widespread belief that domestic problems should take priority over transnational concerns. To many, American activism in world politics imposes unacceptable burdens on the nation and threatens its own democratic values and institutions. Such fundamental questions were set aside during the two world wars and remained dormant for much of the Cold War, when the containment of communism served as a unifying thread for foreign policy makers.

An unending sequence of regional crises in the 1990s rekindled old debates about America's world role. Some believed these crises should be allowed to run their course whatever the cost in human lives and material devastation. Others called for the United States to take the lead in ending regional conflicts, preserving democratic reforms, and tackling global problems such as environmental decay. Still others insisted that U.S. "primacy" be upheld as a principal foreign policy goal. A final group favored a pragmatic policy of selective engagement that was based on realism but ran counter to America's traditional approach to foreign affairs.

Given the lack of national consensus, the United States pursued all these courses at various times after the collapse of the Soviet Union in 1991. Consequently, American foreign policy remained in perpetual flux as turmoil in places such as Iraq, Somalia, Rwanda, Haiti, East Timor, and the former Yugoslavia overwhelmed the agendas of policy makers and produced erratic, often contradictory responses. By the turn of the century, the triumphalism of the immediate post–Cold War years had yielded to pervasive doubts about America's capacity and willingness to lead. This unease was paradoxical at a time when the United States maintained global military superiority, a widely emulated political system, and a booming economy.

A unipolar world, however, is inherently fraught with risk and potential dangers.[1] In this respect, it is doubtful that the United States is more

1. For elaboration, see Ethan B. Kapstein and Michael Mastanduno, eds., *Unipolar Politics: Realism and State Strategies after the Cold War* (New York: Columbia University Press, 1999).

secure today than it was when its primary rival, the Soviet Union, self-destructed in 1991. Relations between the United States and the Russian government steadily deteriorated during the 1990s, while U.S. efforts to "engage" China only produced greater defiance from Beijing. India and Pakistan joined the nuclear club, while North Korea, Iran, and Iraq pursued their own nuclear ambitions. Peace in the Middle East remained elusive, civil wars engulfed many African nations, and the bitter ethnic conflicts in the Balkan peninsula were restrained only by the presence of foreign peacekeepers. Meanwhile, the gap widened between the world's richest and poorest peoples, the global population continued to grow at an alarming pace, and cooperative efforts to protect the environment remained frustrated.

For all of these reasons, national prosperity failed to subdue uncertainties about America's mission overseas. President Bill Clinton, who sought to implement a "neo-Wilsonian" foreign policy based on solving transnational problems, neared the end of his second term without recording a major breakthrough in foreign policy. As one critic observed, "Clinton may not leave a legacy in foreign affairs, but what he will leave is a void: no clear priorities, no consistency or thoroughness in the implementation of strategies, and no true commitment to building a domestic consensus in support of internationalism." [2]

This lack of leadership contributed to a bitter division between the White House and Congress. A united front in foreign policy became impossible after January 1995, when the Republican Party assumed control of both houses of Congress. Republican leaders quickly challenged the president's foray into liberal internationalism and called for a modest world role, limited largely to protecting national self-interests. Using its power of the purse and other constitutional levers, Congress slashed foreign aid spending, refused to pay back dues to the United Nations, blocked key presidential appointments, and rejected several arms control treaties, most notably the Comprehensive Test Ban Treaty in 1999. Clinton, whose energies in his second term were consumed by a sex scandal for which he was impeached by the House of Representatives, lashed out at the "new isolationists" in Congress. But he could not overcome the challenge from Capitol Hill. Although Clinton remained in office, he was left crippled as a national and world leader for the remainder of his presidency.

These turbulent developments provide the context for this fifteenth edition of *American Foreign Policy Since World War II*. As in the past, our primary concern is with the *conduct* of American foreign policy

2. Richard N. Haass, "The Squandered Presidency," *Foreign Affairs* (May–June 2000):139.

rather than its *formulation,* which remains the focus of most textbooks. Detailed knowledge of the policy-making process is essential but ultimately sterile if students are unfamiliar with America's actions in the global arena. Knowledge of past patterns of behavior also provides students with a foundation for understanding the many foreign policy dilemmas currently facing the United States. Although the time frame of this edition is extended, the central themes that informed previous editions remain intact. If anything, the most recent developments reinforce our earlier impressions and provide further evidence of historical continuity in American foreign policy before, during, and after the Cold War.

THE FOCUS OF THIS STUDY

This book covers the period since World War II. A close look at America's conduct over this time span reveals important lessons about the nation's style of foreign policy and how America's behavior has been influenced by long-standing cultural values, by the perceptions of its leaders and their definitions of friends and enemies, and by the inescapable demands posed by the international system. In short, a careful examination of this period reveals how the United States behaves as a superpower.

In informing students about American foreign policy, this book advances a distinctive point of view. As we will argue, the United States has approached the international system with a very peculiar national style, a product of its geographic position, abundant natural resources, and revolutionary origins at the height of the Enlightenment. Any nation's foreign policy is in large measure an expression of its national style, which affects its relationship with its citizens, its creation of political institutions, and, most important for our purposes, its approach and response to the outside world.

Underlying American foreign policy is the tension between the anarchic and conflict-prone international system and the normative values widely held by Americans on individual liberty, representative government, free markets, and national self-determination. This tension first produced a foreign policy of detachment from the great powers of Europe, whose "entanglements" were viewed as threatening to America's fragile political system, its economic well-being, and its secure position in the Western Hemisphere. As the United States emerged as a regional and then global power, such splendid isolation was no longer possible. In the popular imagination, the nation then had an obligation, and increasingly the means, to project its liberal ideals worldwide. American foreign policy thus became a moral crusade aimed not simply at protecting the nation's interests but also at redeeming the international system from itself. Indeed, the two goals were commonly regarded as inseparable.

For all of their idealistic rhetoric, the aspirations of American leaders for a more democratic world were deeply rooted in their own self-interests. The cataclysmic wars among the European powers were fueled by autocratic governments and abetted by the passive civil societies of the feudal era. A more democratic world, it was assumed, would be more peaceful, and only in such a world would the United States be truly secure. These attitudes prevailed as American military forces overcame the challenges of fascist Germany, Italy, and Japan in World War II; they were further reinforced as the United States resisted Soviet and Chinese communism during the Cold War. In the 1990s the equation of democracy overseas with American security at home prompted the Clinton administration to identify the "enlargement" of democratic rule as a pillar of its security strategy.[3]

This missionary impulse compelled an activist, often interventionist foreign policy once the United States attained the status of a great power. The worldwide struggle against communism was seen as vital to preserve the newly established democratic orders in Western Europe and Japan and to consolidate self-rule in the post-colonial states of Africa and southern Asia. Yet the American government's conduct of the Cold War often contradicted its proclaimed values. Economic and military support for authoritarian regimes in Iran, the Philippines, Chile, and Nicaragua offended the sensibilities of many Americans who feared that the United States, like the great powers of the past, had itself been corrupted. Most of all, the country's tragic involvement in Vietnam recalled Pascal's phrase, "Who would be an angel becomes a beast."

This book further considers the extent to which today's international problems are legacies of the Cold War. American foreign policy in the twenty-first century continues to bear the Cold War's imprint in many important respects, including the structure and global deployment of U.S. armed forces, the composition of bilateral and multilateral alliances, ongoing tensions in many former theaters of the superpower conflict, and unresolved disputes between the executive and legislative branches over war powers. Strong anti-American sentiment lingers in much of the developing world, where intervention by both superpowers foiled efforts to create viable, autonomous governments and improve living standards.

Despite its domestic apprehensions, and in the absence of a formidable challenger to American hegemony, the United States retains its pos-

3. *A National Security Strategy of Engagement and Enlargement* (Washington, D.C.: U.S. Government Printing Office, 1994).

ture as the "stabilizer of last resort." Thus the nation will continue to play a crucial if not determinant role in preserving stability at the global level and in suppressing regional conflicts. The extent to which the United States maintains this stature will likely depend as much on the outcome of domestic struggles as on the worldwide balance of power. Readers have much to gain, therefore, by exploring America's love-hate relationship with the outside world and by assessing the consequences of its often schizophrenic national style, which remains torn between a "persisting desire to remain the premier global power and an ever deepening aversion to bear the costs of this position." [4]

Several steps have been taken to make this edition of *American Foreign Policy Since World War II* more instructive. The early chapters provide more focused coverage of Cold War developments. The final four chapters are exclusively devoted to the post–Cold War period. The first of these chapters reviews the policy debates and shifts that immediately followed the collapse of the Soviet Union; the second and third chapters consider America's response to problems in the developing world and in Europe, respectively; and the final chapter examines the most pressing dilemmas facing the United States today. New maps have been added to this edition, and those retained from past editions have been redrawn to highlight the most essential details. A new feature entitled "Impact and Influence" highlights the key figures at home and abroad who most strongly influenced American foreign policy during this period. This feature allows students to visualize and hear the stories of these notable men and women. Finally, we have expanded our Web site directory, list of suggested readings, and chronological summary of the postwar era.

We hope these refinements make this book more readable and useful for students of American foreign policy. We do not expect, nor do we desire, this most recent account to silence our critics. Indeed, our goal is to contribute to the ongoing debate and, along with our students and colleagues, to seek a better grasp of American foreign policy since World War II.

ACKNOWLEDGMENTS

We wish to express our gratitude to a far-flung group whose combined efforts greatly strengthened this volume. Three external reviewers—John H. Gilbert of North Carolina State University, Jay Goodman of Wheaton College, and Louis Hayes of the University of Montana—provided invaluable guidance. The comments of John Gargan and Richard Robyn also were very helpful, as was the research assistance of

4. Robert W. Tucker, "The Future of a Contradiction," *National Interest* (spring 1996): 20.

Jeremy Lesh and Guang Zhang. We received strong editorial and production support from Charisse Kiino, Sabra Bissette Ledent, and Jon Preimesberger of CQ Press, whose consistent enthusiasm for this project has sustained our own. Most of all, this edition has been well served by the informed critiques of our past readers, students and instructors alike, who have freely pointed out deficiencies in our analysis. We can only hope the readers of this edition will be similarly unrestrained.

American troops and others from the North Atlantic Treaty Organization (NATO) greet Kosovar refugees after NATO's liberation of the Yugoslav territory in June 1999. The U.S.-led NATO mission in Kosovo was one of many that tested American foreign policy in the turbulent post–Cold War decade.

CHAPTER ONE

The American Approach to Foreign Policy

The United States entered the twenty-first century as the world's preeminent power. American military forces maintained an unmatched global presence, the nation's economic output far exceeded that of any other country, and the American political system, for all its highly publicized faults, served as a model for many other governments. Taken together, all these factors gave the United States "unprecedented freedom of action in international affairs." [1]

Yet despite this good fortune, many Americans felt unsure about the country's role in the world. Old questions were raised anew about what obligations, if any, the United States should assume beyond its borders. This sense of detachment, common in times of peace and prosperity, took on a sharper edge during the 1990s as several regional crises shat-

1. David A. Lake, *Entangling Relations: American Foreign Policy in Its Century* (Princeton: Princeton University Press, 1999), 198.

tered the "new world order" that had been widely anticipated after the Cold War. The Berlin Wall had barely come down in 1989 before Iraq invaded neighboring Kuwait and threatened the Persian Gulf's oil supplies. Soon afterward, Yugoslavia broke apart as the dominant Serbs unleashed a campaign of "ethnic cleansing" against Muslims that was reminiscent of Nazi Germany. In Africa renewed tribal warfare produced casualties on a gruesome scale. And in East Asia a prolonged economic boom suddenly went bust, provoking political chaos, military unrest, and economic shocks in other regions.

A string of foreign interventions by the United States merely fueled citizens' doubts about the nation's global responsibilities. American troops took the lead in expelling Iraq's Saddam Hussein from Kuwait, but the Bush administration's unwillingness to oust the Iraqi dictator led to endless postwar sanctions, punitive air strikes, and growing opposition to these moves by other countries. Armed forces were again deployed to "restore hope" in the African nation of Somalia, but they withdrew hastily after coming under fire from rival militias. And after the United States brought the Balkan rivals together to create a new government in Bosnia, the leader of Yugoslavia simply set his sights on a new target: the province of Kosovo and its population of ethnic Albanians. The American-led North Atlantic Treaty Organization (NATO) tried to rescue the Kosovars by bombing the Yugoslav heartland, but that strategy triggered the very outcome NATO tried to prevent—mass murders and expulsions, systematic rape and torture, and the plundering of Kosovo.

Meanwhile, foreign leaders were dismayed by America's internal squabbles over foreign policy, by the mixed signals coming from Washington, and by the seemingly arrogant attitude of American leaders on a variety of global issues. The United States was openly condemned for failing to pay its more than $1 billion in back dues to the United Nations; for cornering the global arms market at a time of heightened concern over weapons proliferation; for opposing global bans on chemical weapons, land mines, and nuclear testing; and for maintaining ineffective economic sanctions against several "rogue states." In addition, America's commitment to "sustainable development" was questioned as Congress slashed foreign aid budgets and opposed measures to curb global population growth. In short, as one analyst put it, the United States was widely perceived abroad as "intrusive, interventionist, exploitative, unilateralist, hegemonic, [and] hypocritical . . . with a foreign policy driven overwhelmingly by domestic politics." [2]

Much of this hostility toward the United States was a carryover from the Cold War, when the goal of "containing" communism shaped every

2. Samuel Huntington, "The Lonely Superpower," *Foreign Affairs* (March–April 1999): 43.

aspect of American foreign policy and led the United States into numerous foreign interventions. Yet despite its flaws, the containment strategy had given some clarity to America's world role. In the 1990s such clarity was not to be found. Reflecting the nation's detachment from foreign affairs and preference for addressing domestic issues—crime, education, and health care—the American people had turned for leadership in 1992 and again in 1996 to Democrat Bill Clinton, a former governor with no experience in foreign policy. In keeping with the national mood, President Clinton converted foreign policy into an extension of his domestic agenda, based primarily on promoting the nation's economy. As the world scene grew more chaotic, Clinton called on the United States to "remain the indispensable nation." But his appeal, which seemed half-hearted, was met with public skepticism. When congressional leaders sought a more modest American role in world politics, one based primarily on the country's self-interests rather than global concerns, Clinton, whose priorities and energies were directed elsewhere, did not put up a fight.

Lacking a coherent strategy and strong direction by the president, American foreign policy fell prey to competing interests—both within and outside the federal government.[3] The crippling political stalemate between Clinton and the Republican-led Congress, which led to the president's impeachment in 1998 over a sex scandal, further diminished the prospects for a united front in foreign policy. Unfortunately, the general public offered no guidance to policy makers. When asked to identify the biggest foreign policy problem facing the United States in 1999, respondents in a prominent national survey most often replied, "Don't know." [4] Although the survey registered strong *general* support for an active American role in world politics, most respondents favored a cautious and limited response to problems overseas that did not directly affect the United States.

In this void, the central questions about American foreign policy remain unresolved today: What is the appropriate role of the United States in world politics? Should Americans be concerned only about matters close to home, or should they also be concerned about global problems such as population growth, environmental decay, terrorism, and the spread of nuclear weapons? How deeply should the American government be immersed in the world economy, and on whose behalf?

3. For elaborations on the domestic politics of this period, see James M. Scott, ed., *After the End: Making U.S. Foreign Policy in the Post–Cold War World* (Durham, N.C.: Duke University Press, 1998); and Randall B. Ripley and James M. Lindsay, eds., *U.S. Foreign Policy after the Cold War* (Pittsburgh: University of Pittsburgh Press, 1997).

4. John E. Rielly, ed., *American Public Opinion and U.S. Foreign Policy 1999* (Chicago: Chicago Council on Foreign Relations, 1999), 11.

Under what conditions and for what purposes should the United States intervene in conflicts overseas? How strongly should the United States press other governments to create democratic institutions and respect human rights? Finally, what ties should the United States maintain with its potential adversaries in Russia and China, which remained formidable powers long after the Cold War?

LEARNING FROM EXPERIENCE

One way to address these questions is to examine how past leaders defined American interests and how well they succeeded in achieving their goals. Furthermore, because foreign policy not only adjusts to new circumstances but also demonstrates continuities over time, historical experience can usefully inform and guide both those who study foreign policy and those who practice it.

The post–World War II era witnessed the longest and most active involvement of the United States in world affairs in its history. This book examines how the United States defined its national interests during that turbulent period and how U.S. leaders pursued these interests. The chapters that follow also consider how American actions reflected the nation's proclaimed moral principles and to what extent the country's behavior contradicted these principles. They describe as well how the ambivalent attitude of many Americans suggested a return to historic patterns established long before the United States became a global superpower. By understanding American foreign policy since World War II, readers can more fully grasp the dilemmas currently facing America's leaders. They also can understand more easily why the post–Cold War world, which was expected to usher in new era of peace, has in fact been so troublesome.

This study begins at the end of World War II and the outbreak of the Cold War. Anyone who doubts the continuing relevance of the Cold War—why it erupted and how it was fought—need only consider the events that followed it. If the Cold War were still on, there likely would not have been a war in the Persian Gulf, nor would there have been an exchange of recognition in 1993 between the Israeli government and the Palestinian Liberation Organization, two longtime bitter enemies. And certainly it is doubtful whether Czechoslovakia would have fragmented into two separate republics, or whether Yugoslavia would have dissolved into a vicious and bloody civil war. Nor is it likely that the United States would have intervened in Somalia to feed its people or in Haiti to restore its elected leader who had been overthrown by a military junta. Finally, it is worth considering that India and Pakistan waited until after the Cold War to cross the nuclear threshold.

Coming to terms with the problems confronting the United States since World War II begins with the proposition that the American people, like those in other countries, have a distinctive perspective on world politics. How nation-states act in the international arena depends in large measure on their geography, resources, and historical backgrounds, as well as the environment in which they coexist with other states. These "national styles" vary considerably, but all states bring them to bear as they adapt to the rules of the power game and do what they must to ensure their survival and achieve a measure of security.[5]

Because for most of its existence the United States detached itself politically and militarily from the European powers, its national style was molded far more than that of other Western powers by its domestic experiences and cultural traditions. Not schooled by continuous immersion in international politics, Americans approached foreign policy in a way that was peculiarly their own. The contrast in approaches to foreign policy was particularly strong between the United States and the Soviet Union, which emerged after World War II as America's chief adversary. Perhaps one reason for their different approaches was that the United States felt secure in the Western Hemisphere, but czarist Russia (later the Soviet Union) could never feel secure because of its proximity to many other great powers which, over the centuries, had their own problems and ambitions. Thus the United States confronted a formidable rival, one that combined this historic insecurity with strong, often repressive centralized control, abundant natural resources, and a revolutionary ideology based on the inevitable global expansion of its political and economic system.

This book, then, explores how America's political culture, or national style, has influenced the conduct of its foreign policy and how these cultural factors have led American leaders to perceive allies and adversaries in a certain way. More directly, it questions whether America's approach to foreign affairs contributed to its victory over the Soviet Union, or whether that approach might instead have prolonged the struggle. Indeed, in the post–Cold War period many observers have expressed doubts about whether America's policy of "containment" really was a prerequisite for the Soviet defeat.[6] Finally, this book considers how America's style of foreign policy has helped or hindered the nation's ability to adapt to the more complex, and in many ways more unstable, international system of the post–Cold War era.

5. Robert Dallek, *The American Style of Foreign Policy: Cultural Politics and Foreign Affairs* (New York: Oxford University Press, 1989).

6. See, for example, Richard Ned Lebow and Thomas Risse-Kappen, eds., *International Relations Theory and the End of the Cold War* (New York: Columbia University Press, 1995).

Chapter One

THE VOLATILE STATE SYSTEM

American foreign policy since World War II is largely the story of the tension between the nation-state system, created long before the United States was founded, and the American style of dealing with other countries. Both the monumental achievements of the United States and its failures can be attributed to this uneasy relationship.

In the nation-state system, each member—especially the great powers, its principal actors—is prone to a high degree of insecurity. In the absence of a world government able to safeguard it, each state ultimately must depend on itself for its preservation and safety. Understandably, then, national leaders tend to regard their counterparts as potential adversaries, threats to their nation's territorial integrity and political independence. Indeed, the very nature of the state system breeds such feelings of insecurity, distrust, suspicion, and fear.

But neither the flaws in human nature nor the desires of political leaders to acquire ever-greater power account for what is popularly called *power politics.* Rather, power politics stems from each state's essential concern for its security, the essential prerequisite for citizens' enjoyment of their way of life. Because states often view the external environment as a threat to their security, they are prone to enhance their power relative to that of other states. In such an environment it does not take much for one state to arouse another's suspicions and to stimulate reciprocal images of hostility that each finds easy to substantiate by its opponent's behavior. Indeed, in most instances this enmity is maintained despite contradictory evidence and even avowedly friendly acts. Conciliatory behavior is often seen as a sign of weakness and may invite exploitation. Or it may be regarded as a trick to persuade a state to relax its guard. In view of this "security dilemma," and in the absence of a world government, a balance of power among the strongest states is required to keep this volatile system from breaking down. As the balance of power among nation-states shifts at both the regional and global levels, it alters the strategic environment, defines the options available to states, and informs their policy choices.

THE SHIFTING BALANCE OF POWER

During the nineteenth century the United States was able to enjoy an unprecedented degree of security because a balance of power, created at the Congress of Vienna in 1815, existed on the European continent and was effectively maintained by Great Britain together with France, Austria, and Russia. The Concert of Europe imposed a rare degree of stability on Europe. Furthermore, it allowed the United States to fulfill President George Washington's pledge, made as he left office in 1796, to "steer clear of permanent alliances with any portion of the foreign world."

Some seventy-five years later, Germany's unification in 1870 and the demise of several European-based empires shattered the balance and forced the United States to play a pivotal role as a great power. The growing strength of Germany coincided with and hastened the decline of Great Britain's power. Indeed, the early years of World War I showed clearly that even when British power was thrown in on the side of France and Russia, the three allies could barely contain Germany. With the collapse of czarist Russia in 1915 and the transfer of almost two million German soldiers from the Russian to the western front, a German victory became a distinct possibility. The United States would then have faced a Germany astride an entire continent, dominating European Russia and, in alliance with Austria-Hungary and perhaps the Ottoman Empire, extending German influence into the Balkans and the Middle East. It was at that point that Germany's unrestricted submarine warfare, which included attacks on American shipping, led to a U.S. declaration of war. With America's entry into the conflict, the Allies were able to contain Germany's spring 1918 offensive, leading to its defeat.

After its victory the United States retreated into its hemispheric shell, but only after a failed attempt by President Woodrow Wilson to make the world "safe for democracy." In his famous "Fourteen Points" speech delivered in January 1918, Wilson called for all countries to reduce arms, end colonialism, refrain from secret diplomacy, respect freedom of the seas, and take other steps to establish trust and goodwill. In addition, Wilson proposed that a "League of Nations" be established to prevent future wars through a system of "collective security." Under this system, member countries would agree to defend any nation that had been invaded. Given such a deterrent, foreign aggression would presumably never be contemplated. The son of a Presbyterian minister, Wilson was so convinced of the righteousness of his cause that he personally represented the United States at the Paris Peace Conference, which lasted six months. Almost single-handedly, Wilson persuaded European leaders to sign the Treaty of Versailles, which ended the war, and join the League of Nations, which was established by the treaty. Upon returning from France, Wilson proclaimed victory and declared that "America is the hope of the world."

In seeking to transform world politics, however, Wilson forgot about American politics, particularly the role of Congress in ratifying treaties. Senate leaders felt snubbed by Wilson, who excluded them from the peace conference. More important, they questioned whether the League would undermine the nation's sovereignty by forcing the United States to deploy troops overseas even when its own vital interests were not

IMPACT AND INFLUENCE

WOODROW WILSON

The American style of foreign policy was personified nearly a century ago by President Woodrow Wilson (center). Wilson, the son of a Presbyterian minister, often described world politics as a struggle between good and evil. The United States, he believed, had a moral responsibility not merely to promote its own self-interests, but also to free the interstate system from its anarchic structure and warlike tendencies.

Wilson led the United States and its allies to victory in World War I, and then chaired the U.S. commission (pictured) at the Paris Peace Conference in 1919. He proposed "Fourteen Points" to reform world politics, including global disarmament, decolonization, freedom of the seas, and the abolition of secret diplomacy. Wilson also called for an "association of nations" to maintain order through a system of collective security. More than sixty foreign governments approved his plan and created the League of Nations. But Wilson, who won the Nobel Peace Prize for his efforts, could not persuade leading members of the Senate to ratify the Treaty of Versailles.

threatened. The Senate therefore rejected the treaty, and the United States never joined the League of Nations.

Although the postwar U.S. economy rivaled that of all Europe and the United States exercised great economic influence, the government refused to define for the nation a political and military role consistent with its economic power. U.S. military power had been decisive in Germany's defeat, but the United States wanted nothing to do with great-power politics. To the contrary, the United States sought again to abolish war, this time through the 1928 Kellogg-Briand Pact, in which sixty-two countries renounced war "as an instrument of national policy." Then, as Adolf Hitler consolidated his power in Germany in the 1930s and as Benito Mussolini, the Italian dictator, moved into Africa, the U.S. Congress passed two Neutrality Acts that prevented an assertive American response. At the same time, a congressional committee held hearings to probe allegations that U.S. involvement in World War I had been inspired by international banks, arms manufacturers, and other "merchants of death."

The United States began to play a political role again only when the balance of power in Europe was upset once more by the eruption of World War II in 1939 and the defeat of France in 1940. With America facing the possibility of Britain's defeat and the control of Eurasia by Germany and its allies, President Franklin Roosevelt undertook several measures to help Britain withstand any Nazi assault. He sent fifty old destroyers to defend the English Channel and established a "lend-lease" program to provide munitions, food, and other material support. This commitment to Britain was necessary even though Roosevelt's actions increased the risk of war with Germany. In fact, by the time Japan bombed Pearl Harbor in December 1941, the United States was engaged in an undeclared naval war with Germany in the Atlantic. Full-scale war was merely a matter of time.

THE AMERICAN CONCEPT OF SECURITY

In any assessment of U.S. actions leading up to World War II, two points deserve emphasis. First, the defense of the United States always has involved more than physical security. The German threat during World War I was not one of an immediate invasion, nor was an invasion the main threat even after the defeat of France early in World War II. Then why did the United States twice forsake its "splendid isolation" from foreign entanglements? Surely the width of the Atlantic and Pacific Oceans would protect the United States.

American security was threatened for one reason: any state—especially an antidemocratic state—that controlled all the resources of Eurasia, the Middle East, and Africa, and then converted those resources into military power, might someday be able to attack North America. This would be particularly true if Great Britain were defeated and the British navy no longer guarded the sea highway to the Western Hemisphere. Even if Britain sank its navy rather than see it joined with the fleets of Germany and its allies, the German navy might come to dominate the Atlantic approaches to the Western Hemisphere. Such circumstances would require the United States to mobilize its resources fully and be on constant alert for attack by an opponent with superior resources. Moreover, to match this dominant Eurasian power, the United States would probably have to transform itself into a "garrison state"—a disciplined, militarized society that, in the name of security, would have to sacrifice democracy and individual liberty in the name of self-defense.

The broader rationale for U.S. intervention was that the security of a democratic America was inextricably interwoven with the survival of other democracies, especially France and Britain. After France collapsed in 1940, Roosevelt explained to the American public why the United States had to assist Britain: America could not survive as a lone democratic island surrounded by totalitarian seas—that is, democracy in America could not flourish unless democratic values prospered in other societies. There might be no physical threat to the nation, but the aim of American foreign policy had never been just the security of the United States as a piece of real estate. It had always sought to defend the security of a democratic America, which required that democratic values flourish internationally.

The second point deserving emphasis is that despite the U.S. concern with security in Europe, the timing of the interventions in 1917 and 1941 was not in each case a rational decision made in Washington. It was Berlin's decision in 1917 to launch unrestricted submarine warfare against all shipping to England that brought the United States into the war, and it was Tokyo's decision in December 1941 to attack the U.S. fleet at anchor in Hawaii that led to the American declaration of war against Japan. Without Hitler's reckless 1941 declaration of war against the United States—a country he held in great contempt—U.S. power would have been directed only against Japan, and Germany, the far stronger power, would have faced only Britain and Russia, both already reeling from German blows. Therefore, but for German and Japanese mistakes, the United States might *not* have entered the two world wars, even though the balances of power in Europe and Asia were transformed. The United States, in this respect, was saved from itself by its enemies.

Great powers usually do not leave decisions about their security to their adversaries. The strategy of the major states in the state system is—or should be—to oppose any state that seeks predominance because such predominance would constitute a grave threat to their own security. The failure of the United States twice to act according to the logic dictated by the balance of power largely stemmed from its own particular national style.

THE AMERICAN NATIONAL STYLE

The style reflected in the American response to war in Europe and later to the Cold War was the product of domestic experience. By giving priority to internal political and economic tasks—a characteristic of the

United States since its founding—the nation had successfully remained aloof politically and militarily from European power politics. With nonthreatening neighbors to the north and south and open seas to the east and west, the United States could take its security for granted. Free from external threats, it could focus on its own economic and political development.

THE AMERICAN SENSE OF DESTINY

The ability of the United States to maintain its detachment from great-power politics for such a long time cannot be attributed *only* to the nation's distance from Europe, or to Europe's preoccupation with industrialization and class conflict at home and colonialism abroad, or to the strength of the Royal Navy. The nature of democracy has to be considered as well. The United States saw itself as more than just the world's first "new nation"; it also was the world's first constitutional democracy and, as such, the first country in history whose government was self-consciously designed to make its leaders politically accountable to the public at large. The "more perfect union" was to be an egalitarian society. European concepts of social hierarchy, nobility and titles, and bitter class struggles were not to be planted in America's democratic soil.

From the very beginning of their national life, Americans professed a strong belief in what they considered to be their destiny—to spread, *by example,* freedom and social justice and to lead humankind away from its wicked ways to the New Jerusalem on earth. Early settlers declared America to be "a city on a hill" and considered it their providential mission to inspire other societies to follow their lead. The massive immigration of the late nineteenth century served to reinforce this sense of destiny. "Repudiation of Europe," novelist John Dos Passos once said, "is, after all, America's main excuse for being." In the popular mind, Europe stood for war, poverty, and exploitation; America, for peace, opportunity, and democracy. But the United States was not merely to be a beacon of a superior democratic domestic way of life. It also was to be an exemplar of a morally superior pattern of international behavior. The United States, then, would voluntarily reject power politics as unfit for its foreign policy.

Democratic theory posits that people are potentially rational and moral, which means that they can settle their differences by reasoned deliberation and moral exhortation. Since people are endowed with reason and a moral sense, what quarrels could not be settled given the necessary goodwill? Peace—the result of harmony among people—was considered the natural or normal condition. Conflict, on the other hand, was considered a deviation caused primarily by wicked leaders whose morality and reason had been corrupted by their exercise of unconstrained authority. Power politics was an instrument of selfish and autocratic rulers—that is, leaders unrestrained by democratic public opinion—who enjoyed wielding it for personal advantage. To them, war was a grand game. They could remain in their palatial homes, continuing to eat well and to enjoy the luxuries of life, and suffer none of the hardships of war. These fell upon the ordinary people who had to leave their families to fight, endure the higher taxes to pay for the war, and possibly see their homes and families destroyed. The conclusion was clear: undemocratic states were inherently warlike and evil; democratic nations, in which the people controlled and regularly changed their leaders, were peaceful and moral.

The American experience seemed to support this conclusion: the United States was a democracy, its economy was growing steadily, and it generally was at peace with foreign powers. Furthermore, peace seemed to be the normal state of affairs. It was logical, then, that democracy and peaceful behavior and intentions should be thought of as synonymous. Americans rarely asked themselves whether democracy was responsible for the peace they enjoyed, or whether peace was the product of other forces. The frequent wars in Europe appeared to provide the answer: European politics was power politics, reflecting the feudal origins of European regimes. Americans had cut themselves off from Europe and its class conflicts and power politics after the Revolutionary War; America had to protect its democratic principles and abstain from any involvement in the affairs of Europe lest it be soiled and corrupted. Hemispheric detachment, therefore, was the morally correct policy, for it allowed the United States to quarantine itself from Europe's hierarchical social structures and violent conflicts.

It was the Monroe Doctrine, proclaimed in 1823, that first stressed, officially and explicitly, this ideological difference between the New World and the Old World. President James Monroe declared that the American political system was "essentially different" from that of Europe, whose nations engaged frequently in warfare. The implication was very clear: democratic government equals peace, and aristocratic government—which was identified with despotism—means war. In this spirit Monroe warned, "We should consider any attempt on [Europe's] part to extend their system to any portion of this hemisphere as dangerous to our peace and safety." [7]

This view also allowed the United States to behave hypocritically by acting like other nations in its continental expansion but disguising its

7. Quoted in Armin Rappaport, ed., *Sources in American Diplomacy* (New York: Macmillan, 1966), 53. For a recent assessment, see Gaddis Smith, *The Last Years of the Monroe Doctrine, 1945–1993* (New York: Hill and Wang, 1994).

motives in the noblest of terms. In advocating U.S. military expansion into Mexico in 1845, for example, journalist John O'Sullivan argued that it was

> the right of our manifest destiny to overspread and to possess the whole of the continent which Providence has given us for the development of the great experiment of Liberty and federated self-government entrusted to us. Its floor shall be a hemisphere—its roof the firmament of the star-studded heavens, and its congregation a Union of many Republics, compromising hundreds of happy millions . . . governed by God's natural and moral law of equality.[8]

By drawing the distinction between the New and Old Worlds, and by warning the Europeans to keep their hands off the Western Hemisphere, Americans were in effect opening the way for the establishment of U.S. preeminence and dominance. It would not be the last time the United States would invoke such a double standard, proclaiming a moral position loftier than that of other great powers—then behaving in much the same way.

THE DEPRECIATION OF POWER IN INTERNATIONAL POLITICS

The American perception of an international harmony of interests contrasted sharply with the state system's emphasis on the inevitability of conflict and differences of interests among states. Americans traditionally regarded conflict as an abnormal condition; the rest of the state system perceived harmony to be an illusion. The United States, long isolated from Europe and therefore not socialized by the state system, did not accept the reality and permanence of conflicts among its members. Indeed, differences between nation-states were considered unnatural. But when they did occur, such differences should not be deep or long-lasting. Rather, they were attributed to wicked leaders (who could be eliminated), authoritarian political systems (which could be reformed), or misunderstandings (which could be straightened out if the adversaries approached each other with sincerity and empathy). Once these obstacles were removed, peace, harmony, and goodwill would reign supreme.

Because the United States considered itself a morally and politically superior society, its attitude toward the use of power internationally was dominated by the belief that any struggle could be avoided either by refraining from intervention in great-power conflicts or by crusading against those countries indulging in power politics. Moralism in foreign policy proscribed the use of power in peacetime; power should be

8. Quoted in Howard Jones, *The Course of American Diplomacy: From the Revolution to the Present,* 2d ed. (Chicago: Dorsey Press, 1988), 143.

employed only in confrontations with unambiguous aggression, transformed then into an obligation to fight on behalf of righteous causes. In short, only the use of power for democratic purposes was legitimate. The perception of power as simply the raw material of international politics—its use as an instrument of compromise, conciliation, and moderation in interstate politics, its discriminating application toward achievement of specific and less-than-total objectives—was clearly antithetical to the American understanding of power. The term *power politics* was itself an anathema, a reminder of a way of doing things that the New World hoped it had left behind.

The association of peace with democracy was not the only reason for the American depreciation of power politics in the eighteenth and nineteenth centuries. Another was that the United States was largely a one-class society, in which most citizens shared a belief in a common set of middle-class, capitalistic, and democratic values. America was unique among nations in this respect. The European countries were, by contrast, three-class societies. In addition to the middle class, they contained in their bodies politic an aristocratic class, whose energies were devoted either to keeping itself in power or to recapturing power and returning to the glorious days of a feudal past. Moreover, European urbanization and industrialization during the nineteenth century had given birth to a proletariat which, because it felt it did not receive a fair share of the national income, became a revolutionary class. The nations of the Old World were a composite of these three elements: a reactionary aristocracy, a small but democratic middle class, and a revolutionary proletariat. These nations had, in an intellectual as well as a political sense, a right, a center, and a left.

The United States had only a center, both intellectually and politically. It had never experienced a feudal past and therefore possessed no large, powerful aristocratic class on the right. Because it was by and large an egalitarian society, it also lacked a genuine left-wing movement of protest, such as socialism and communism. America was, as French political observer Alexis de Tocqueville observed in 1835, "born free" as a middle-class, individualist, capitalistic, democratic society. "As a result one finds a vast multitude of people with roughly the same ideas about religion, history, science, political economy, legislation, and government." [9]

This widespread agreement on the fundamental values of American society and Europe's intense class struggles reinforced the American misunderstanding of the nature and functions of power on the international scene. Dissatisfied groups never developed a revolutionary ideol-

9. Alexis de Tocqueville, *Democracy in America* (New York: Harper and Row, 1966), 56.

ogy because the growing prosperity spread to them before they could translate their grievances against the capitalist system into political action. African Americans were an important exception because they never shared this wealth or political power; in fact, the "peculiar institution" of slavery so defied America's democratic principles that it thrust the country into a calamitous civil war. Otherwise, the United States was politically secure, socially cohesive, and economically prosperous. It was able to resolve most of its differences peacefully, and its people could believe in an evolutionary, democratic, economically prosperous historical process. Revolution and radicalism were condemned from this perspective. In sharp contrast, because of their internal class struggles and external conflicts among themselves, the nations of Europe fully appreciated that social conflict was natural and that power played a crucial role in resolving conflict.

In the past, in fact, Americans have been so in accord on basic values that whenever the nation has been threatened externally it also has become fearful of internal disloyalty. It is one of the great ironies of American society that, while Americans possess this unity of shared beliefs to a greater degree than most other people, their apprehension of external danger has repeatedly led them, first, to insist on a general and somewhat dogmatic reaffirmation of loyalty to the "American way of life," and, second, to hunt for internal groups that might betray this way of life. Disagreement often has become equated with disloyalty; people have been accused of "un-American" thinking and behavior and labeled "security risks." Perhaps only a society so committed to one set of values could be so sensitive to internal subversion and so fearful of internal betrayal. By contrast, perhaps only a society in which two or more ideologies have long since learned to live together can genuinely tolerate diverse opinions: after all, who has ever heard of "un-British" or "un-French" activities? The United States often has been called a "melting pot" because of its many different nationality groups, but, before each generation of immigrants has been fully accepted into American society, it has had to be "Americanized." Indeed, few Americans have ever accepted diversity as a value. American society, in fact, has taken great pride in destroying diversity through assimilation.

Politics did not, in any event, seem very important to Americans during the nineteenth century when, in an era of rapid economic growth, the basic assumption was that people were motivated by their own material welfare. Self-interest governed economic behavior. Manufacturers and providers of services, seeking to maximize their profits, produced what consumers wanted. The laws of supply and demand and the free market therefore transformed each person's economic selfishness into socially beneficial results—"the greatest good for the greatest number." Politics mattered little in this utilitarian system based on entrepreneurs whose combined efforts improved the general welfare. The best government, as Thomas Jefferson declared, was the government that governed least. Arbitrary political interference with the economic laws of the market only upset the results these laws were intended to produce. Private property, profit, and the free market were the keys to ensuring the happiness of people by providing them with abundance. Capitalism, in short, reflected the materialism of the age of industrialization.

When distilled, these views came down to one simple statement: economics was good and politics was bad. The United States would not isolate itself from the outside world in a commercial sense. Far from it. Economic expansion based on foreign trade was a central element of early American foreign policy. The key was assuring that no political strings would be attached. As George Washington proclaimed in his Farewell Address, "The great rule of conduct for us, in regard to foreign Nations is, in extending our commercial relations, to have with them as little Political connection as possible."

This simple dichotomy between economics and politics came naturally to the capitalist middle class. For them, the benefits of economic freedom were as "self-evident" as the truths stated in the Declaration of Independence. Many asked: had not this economic freedom been gained only through the long and bitter struggle of Europe's middle class to cut down the authority of the powerful monarchical state and, in France, to overthrow it by revolution? As this middle class grew more prosperous and numerous, it became increasingly resentful of having to pay the taxes from which the aristocracy usually was exempt, of the restrictions placed on trade and industry, of the class barriers to the social status that came with careers in the army and the bureaucracy, and of the general lack of freedom of thought and expression.

Because the middle class identified the power of the state with its own lack of freedom, it struggled to restrict this power. Only by placing restraints on the authority of the state could it gain the individual liberty as well as the right to private enterprise it sought. Democratic philosophy stated these claims in terms of the individual's "natural rights." The exercise of political authority was equated with the abuse of that authority and the suppression of personal freedoms. The power of the state had to be kept to a minimum to ensure the individual citizen's political and economic liberties.

It was with this purpose in mind that the drafters of the U.S. Constitution divided authority between the states and the federal government, and, within the latter, among the executive, legislative, and judicial branches. The principles of federalism and separation of powers were deliberately designed to keep all governments—and especially the national government—weak. Domestic conflicts would be resolved not by the state's political actions, but by the individual citizen's own economic actions in society in peacetime.

The American experience reflected this philosophy; millions of people came to the United States from other lands to seek a better way of life. America's territory was so vast that seemingly everyone could earn a respectable living and pursue happiness in his or her own way. Abundant natural resources, innovative technologies, individual enterprise, and supportive government policies enabled the American people to become the "people of plenty."[10] A good income was sought for two reasons: economically, to attain a comfortable standard of living and, psychologically, to gain social status and earn the respect of one's fellow citizens.

It was hardly surprising that in these circumstances the solution to international problems in America's first century was considered a matter of economics—not politics. Economics was identified with social harmony and the welfare of all peoples; politics was equated with conflict, war, and death. Just as the "good society" was to be the product of free competition, so the peaceful international society would be created by free trade. Trade depended on mutual prosperity; by contrast, war impoverished and destroyed and created ill will among nations. Commerce, which benefited all the participating states, created a vested interest in peace; war was economically unprofitable and therefore obsolete. Free trade and peace, in short, were one and the same cause.[11]

THE PENCHANT FOR CRUSADING

As noted earlier, America's leaders in the eighteenth and nineteenth centuries drew a clear-cut distinction between war and peace in their approach to foreign policy. Peace was characterized by a state of harmony among nations; conflict was considered abnormal and war a crime. In peacetime one needed to pay little or no attention to foreign problems; indeed, to do so would divert people from their individual concerns and professional aspirations. The effect of this attitude was clear: Americans turned their attention toward the outside world with reluctance and usually only when provoked—that is, when a foreign menace had become so forbidding that it could no longer be ignored. In other words, the United States rarely initiated foreign policy; the stimulus that dictated America's response generally came from beyond its borders.

But once Americans were provoked and the United States had to resort to force, the employment of force was justified in terms of the moral principles with which the United States, as a democratic country,

10. David M. Potter, *People of Plenty: Economic Abundance and the American Character* (Chicago: University of Chicago Press, 1954).

11. These ideas were most thoroughly developed at the time by Scottish economist Adam Smith in his 1776 book *The Wealth of Nations* (New York: Oxford University Press, 1976).

identified. War could be justified only by presuming noble purposes and completely destroying the immoral enemy who threatened the integrity, if not the existence, of these principles. American power, then, had to be "righteous" power; only by exercising it fully could Americans ensure salvation or the absolution of sin. Moreover, the national aversion to violence became transformed on occasion into a national glorification of violence, and wars became ideological crusades to destroy the enemy state and then send its people to democratic reform school. Making the world "safe for democracy"—Woodrow Wilson's stated objective during World War I—was to be achieved by democratizing the populace of the offending nation—in this case, Germany—making its new rulers responsible to the people they governed, and thereby converting the menacing regime into a peaceful democratic state and banishing power politics for all time. Once that aim had been achieved, the United States could again withdraw into itself, secure in the knowledge that American works had again proved to be "good works."

This has been the historic pattern of American foreign policy: a pendulum-like swing "back and forth between the extremes of an indiscriminate isolationism and an equally indiscriminate internationalism or globalism." [12] According to Harvard professor Stanley Hoffmann, "both extremes have in common the intention to avoid the contamination of unhealthy foreign troubles." [13] As a self-proclaimed morally and politically superior country, the United States could remain pure only by abstaining from involvement in a corrupt world or, if the world would not leave it alone, by destroying the source of evil through the application of maximum force and total war. In short, both the isolationist and the crusading impulses sprang from the same source. These swings tended, moreover, to be accompanied by radical shifts of mood: from one of optimism, which sprang from the belief that America was going to reform the world, to one of disillusionment as the grandiose objectives the United States had set for itself proved beyond its capacity to reach. Feeling too good for this world, which clearly did not want to be reformed but preferred its old, corrupt habits, the nation retreated in order to perfect and protect its way of life. Having expected too much from the use of its power, Americans then also tended to feel guilty and ashamed about having used their power at all.

For similar reasons, American leaders consistently divorced force from diplomacy. In peacetime, diplomacy unsupported by force was supposed to preserve the harmony among states. But in time of war

12. Hans J. Morgenthau, *A New Foreign Policy for the United States* (New York: Praeger, 1969), 15.

13. Stanley Hoffmann, *Gulliver's Troubles, or the Setting of American Foreign Policy* (New York: McGraw-Hill, 1968), 98.

political considerations were subordinated to force. Once the diplomats had failed to keep the peace with appeals to morality and reason, military considerations became primary, and the soldier was placed in charge. The United States, then, rejected the concept of war as a political instrument and Carl von Clausewitz's definition of war as the continuation of politics by other means.[14] Instead, Americans regarded war as a politically neutral operation that should be guided by its own professional rules and imperatives. Military officers conducted their campaigns in a strictly apolitical, technically efficient manner. Politics and strategy were unrelated; strategy began where politics ended.

Thus for Americans, war was a means employed to abolish power politics. This same moralistic attitude also militated against the use of diplomacy in its classical sense: to bring contending states to the bargaining table to conciliate their differences, and to moderate and isolate conflicts. Although Americans regarded diplomacy as a rational process for straightening out misunderstandings between nations, they also were extremely suspicious of it. For this reason, the U.S. government refused to create a large, permanent diplomatic corps until long after the nation's arrival as a great power.

If the United States was by definition moral, it obviously could not compromise, for a nation endowed with a moral mission could hardly violate its own principles. That constituted appeasement and national humiliation. The nation's principles would be transgressed, the nation's interests improperly defended, the national honor stained. Moreover, to reach a settlement with enemies rather than wiping them out in order to safeguard American principles would be to condone moral compromise. This attitude toward diplomacy—which, in effect, made its use as an instrument of compromise difficult—reinforced the American predilection for violence as a means of settling international problems. War allowed the nation to destroy its evil opponent but permitted it to keep its moral mission intact and unsullied by compromise.

SELF-DOUBTS AND REVISIONIST HISTORIES

One of the most telling characteristics of America's national style in conducting foreign policy has been the scrutiny and criticism applied during and after every major war to the reasons for the country's participation in the struggle. Antiwar activists organize demonstrations

14. This phrase sums up the essence of Clausewitz's famous book, *On War.* First published in 1832, it remains the most outstanding effort in Western history to understand war's internal dynamics and its relationship to political policy and goals. The best modern translation and editing are by Michael Howard and Peter Paret, *On War* (Princeton: Princeton University Press, 1976).

and encourage resistance; former government officials challenge the country's behavior on the op-ed pages of national newspapers; and scholars "revise" the historical record to rebut the conventional wisdom.

Over the years the revisionist histories have featured two common themes. First, the conflicts in which the United States became entangled did not in fact threaten its security interests. Second, the United States became involved because its leaders were seduced by propagandists who aroused and manipulated public opinion, by military officials with bureaucratic motives, and, above all else, by bankers and industrialists—the "merchants of death" of the 1930s, the "military-industrial complex" of the 1960s—whose economic interests benefited from the struggle. In the early stages of World War I, the prospect of German hegemony across Europe was downplayed by many, as was Hitler's juggernaut in World War II. As the Cold War settled in, critics of American activism doubted that Joseph Stalin, the Soviet ruler, was really as committed to a hostile relationship with the West as he claimed to be in his public statements. America's entry in the two world wars of this century, as in the Cold War, was therefore a mistake; it was really unnecessary or immoral, if not both. The enemy identified as the aggressor and *provocateur* actually did not represent a direct threat to American security at all; to the contrary, the threat came from within.

A central critique among revisionists was that a "power elite," including a small group of government and business leaders, propelled the United States into war.[15] Writing in the late 1950s, William Appleman Williams, the foremost proponent of this view, contended that the United States was driven to global expansion and foreign conflicts by the threat of economic stagnation and the fear of social upheaval at home.[16] Similarly, Joyce Kolko and Gabriel Kolko argued that American foreign policy after World War II was driven "not by the containment of communism, but rather more directly the extension and expansion of American capitalism."[17] Writing at the end of the Cold War, Michael Parenti observed that the "primary task" of the American government during the struggle was "to protect capitalism as a system."[18] And in the aftermath of the Cold War, Thomas McCormick argued that "short-term

15. C. Wright Mills, *The Power Elite* (New York: Oxford University Press, 1956).

16. William Appleman Williams, *The Tragedy of American Diplomacy* (New York: Harper and Row, 1959). For a related critique of early American foreign policy, see Walter LaFeber, *The New Empire: An Interpretation of American Expansion, 1860–1898* (Ithaca: Cornell University Press, 1963).

17. Joyce Kolko and Gabriel Kolko, *The Limits of Power: The World and United States Foreign Policy, 1945–1954* (New York: Harper and Row, 1972), 480.

18. Michael Parenti, *The Sword and the Dollar: Imperialism, Revolution, and the Arms Race* (New York: St. Martin's Press, 1989), 198.

concerns over the American and global economies" led the United States to war in the Persian Gulf.[19]

These critics challenged the traditional view that the pursuit of economic gain served as an acceptable objective for the United States and its citizens because it reduced rather than increased the nation's appetite for war. Economic expansion, they argued, far from serving as a worthy objective, risked corrupting America's very soul because it diverted attention and resources from reform at home to military preparation and war. This viewpoint, originally maintained by a small group of critics, became widespread as the United States intervened repeatedly in regional conflicts during the Cold War, particularly in Vietnam. Not surprisingly, skepticism about American motives persisted into the 1990s as American leaders embraced global economic integration as a primary foreign policy goal.

Inspired by the revisionist historians of the Cold War, a new generation of political scientists argued in the 1990s that concepts such as sovereignty, anarchy, and "Third World" (see Chapter 4) were "socially constructed" by government leaders and were therefore not a legitimate basis for diplomatic relations.[20] In their view, American leaders dominated the "discourse" of foreign policy during the Cold War. Their public speeches routinely glorified the nation's values, vilified the communist countries, and frequently exaggerated overseas threats in order to preserve America's dominant position in the world. The news media—primarily television networks and large, corporate-owned newspapers—served as an accomplice in this effort by the U.S. government to manipulate public opinion. "The Cold War, then, was both a struggle which exceeded the military threat of the Soviet Union, and a struggle into which any number of potential candidates—regardless of their strategic capacity to be a threat—were slotted as a threat." [21]

Such critical interpretations brought needed attention to the cultural foundations of foreign policy. Cultural values are intimately linked to political institutions and, in turn, to the domestic and foreign policies of all states. Indeed, the considerable impact of American cultural values—and of such commonly used expressions as "manifest destiny"—is a central assumption of this book. But any comprehensive understanding of American foreign policy also demands recognition of a broader context—of the global setting that surrounds the state; of the prevailing

19. Thomas McCormick, *America's Half-Century: United States Foreign Policy in the Cold War and After,* 2d ed. (Baltimore: Johns Hopkins University Press, 1995), 248.

20. See Alexander Wendt, "Anarchy Is What States Make of It: The Social Construction of Power Politics," *International Organization* 46 (spring 1992): 395–424.

21. David Campbell, *Writing Security: United States Foreign Policy and the Politics of Identity* (Minneapolis: University of Minnesota Press, 1992), 34.

norms of interstate relations; and of the national characters, historic inclinations, and ongoing practices of other states. In this respect, the process of "social construction" does not occur in a vacuum, but in a complex global environment in which other states and societies exist with very different cultural traditions, national styles, and global ambitions. These external forces, often reflecting inescapable conflicts of interest, create their own pressures on foreign policy.

External pressures clearly were brought to bear on American leaders during and after World War II. The Japanese empire, which by 1941 included most of China and East Asia, threatened the United States in the most direct fashion by attacking U.S. forces at Pearl Harbor. This aerial assault was immediately followed by Hitler's declaration of war against the United States, whose government had stubbornly refused to intervene during the previous two years despite passionate appeals for assistance by the occupied European powers. After the war the United States faced a formidable challenge from the Soviet Union and its leader Joseph Stalin. His prolonged assault on his own people in the 1930s led to the deaths of more than 10 million Soviet citizens, even before another 25 million were killed in World War II.[22] American leaders who knew and worked with Stalin during World War II were deeply concerned in the postwar period: Would the aging Soviet dictator, strengthened by nuclear weapons and the extension of his empire into central Europe, commit even more unspeakable acts against other nations, including the United States? The answer to this question was unclear. But in Stalin's internal policies prior to World War II, his public statements, and his actions immediately after the war, American leaders and their allies found nothing to reassure them.

Indeed, America's Cold War adversaries proved to be the true masters of social construction. The writings of Karl Marx, Vladimir Lenin, Stalin, and Mao Zedong formed the basis of primary education and established a rigid government line that was transmitted daily by a state-controlled press and was immune from public debate or criticism. When political opponents or religious leaders challenged these regimes, they were imprisoned or executed en masse. In the Soviet Union social engineering was imposed with little regard for the diversity and spiritual aspirations of its people. In China Mao's attempts to impose a new social order reached ghastly proportions during the Great Leap Forward, initiated in 1958, and the Cultural Revolution of the mid-1960s. The Great

22. When the Soviet archives were opened in the late 1990s, the depths of Stalin's internal repression both before and during the Cold War become better known. See John Lewis Gaddis, *We Now Know: Rethinking Cold War History* (New York: Oxford University Press, 1998); and R. C. Raack, *Stalin's Drive to the West, 1938–1945: The Origins of the Cold War* (Stanford: Stanford University Press, 1995).

Leap Forward, designed to accelerate agricultural and industrial development, instead produced an economic calamity that required decades to overcome. During the Cultural Revolution, Mao's Red Guards violently cracked down on teachers, workers, and peasants who allegedly defied his revolutionary vision.

These events were not lost on the United States, explicitly identified as the primary adversary of both regimes and by many revolutionary movements in the developing world. The American strategy of "containment," described in Chapter 2, recognized this challenge and called for a sustained response on a global scale. To critics of this strategy, the Soviet Union was a "satisfied" power that did not seek expansion. Thus the assertive American response was unjustified. But this was hardly the signal sent by Stalin in the postwar years as he broke his promises to Iran and Poland, staged a coup in Czechoslovakia, blockaded West Berlin, and approved North Korea's invasion of South Korea.

The bitter domestic debates over America's intentions and conduct in the three global conflicts of the twentieth century were revealing, particularly given the favorable outcome of all three conflicts for the United States. And these divisions have persisted long after the Cold War. Disagreements about America's global responsibilities have been further sharpened by the absence of any single challenger to U.S. military and economic preeminence. In any case, the domestic quarrels are much more than academic exercises. Unresolved questions about foreign policy dampen the prospects for concerted action between Congress and the White House. Meanwhile, America's allies have difficulty conducting their own foreign policies when the United States fails to provide coherent leadership. Potential adversaries are then tempted to exploit the lack of American resolve.

In sum, in the new millennium the United States faces the world with attitudes and behavior patterns formed by its long and ambivalent relationship with foreign powers. The Soviet-American rivalry dominated world politics for nearly half a century, with profound implications for the domestic and foreign policies of nearly every country in the world, and the legacy of the U.S. role in that rivalry continues to be felt in the twenty-first century, at home and abroad. The country's erratic behavior since the Cold War has equally profound consequences for the new century. The chapters that follow will explore both the Cold War experience and the subsequent conduct of the United States in the context of this enduring style of foreign policy.

President Franklin Roosevelt (center) confers with Soviet leader Joseph Stalin and British prime minister Winston Churchill in Tehran in November 1943. The three leaders, who had joined forces to defeat Germany, would meet again in Yalta in February 1945 to discuss military strategy and the structure of the postwar world.

CHAPTER TWO

From World War to Cold War

The European landmass from France to Russia lay in ruin after World War II. In the East, Japan and its short-lived East Asian empire were devastated; China was immersed in civil war. The United States, however, remained strong after the war and emboldened by its victory over fascism in Europe and Asia. For the second time in three decades the United States had been drawn into world war and had triumphed. It had attained a "preponderance of power" after seeing its influence expand steadily from continental to regional to global scale.[1] For those who were convinced that America was bound to achieve its "manifest destiny," the moment of truth seemed to have arrived.

1. See Melvyn P. Leffler, *A Preponderance of Power: National Security, the Truman Administration, and the Cold War* (Stanford: Stanford University Press, 1992), 203–206.

But even before the embers of World War II had cooled, the sparks of a new conflict illuminated the future of American foreign policy, and the elation over military victory quickly was overtaken by new problems, responsibilities, and challenges to regional and global stability. Americans would face the equally daunting task of winning the peace.

Signs of the coming schism were largely ignored as the final battles of World War II were waged in central Europe and East Asia. Before one of the wartime conferences between Prime Minister Winston Churchill and President Franklin Roosevelt, a U.S. War Department memorandum forecasting the Soviet Union's postwar position concluded that it would be the dominant power in Eurasia for the foreseeable future:

> With Germany crushed, there is no power in Europe to oppose her [the Soviet Union's] tremendous military forces. . . . The conclusions from the foregoing are obvious. Since Russia is the decisive factor in the war, she must be given every assistance, and every effort must be made to obtain her friendship. Likewise, since without question she will dominate Europe on the defeat of the Axis, it is even more essential to develop and maintain the most friendly relations with Russia.[2]

The importance of this assessment lies less in its prediction of the Soviet Union's postwar position, which was fairly obvious, than in its statement of American expectations about future Soviet-American relations. Military leaders apparently accepted without any major misgivings the prospect of the Soviet Union as the new dominant power in Europe; they did not imagine that it might replace Nazi Germany as a grave threat to the European and global balance of power. Although twice in the twentieth century the United States had been propelled into Europe's wars at exactly those moments when Germany became so powerful that it almost destroyed this balance, the lessons of history—specifically, the impact on American security of any nation's domination of Europe—had not yet been absorbed. Roosevelt and the American government did not attempt to reestablish a balance of power in Europe to safeguard the United States; they expected this security to stem from mutual Soviet-American goodwill, unsupported by considerations of power. This reliance on goodwill and mutual esteem was to prove foolish at best—and at worst potentially fatal.

AMERICAN WARTIME ILLUSIONS

Postwar expectations of an "era of good feelings" between the Soviet Union and the United States epitomized the quixotic style of American foreign policy, which perceived war as a disruption of the normal har-

2. Quoted in Robert E. Sherwood, *Roosevelt and Hopkins, An Intimate History,* vol. 2 (New York: Bantam Books, 1950), 363–364.

mony among nations, military force as an instrument to be used only to punish the aggressors or war criminals, and by those who cooperated in its ideological crusade as equally moral and peace-loving. Once the war was finished, this thinking presumed, natural harmony would be restored and the struggle for power would end.

The implication was clear: the United States need take no precautionary steps against its wartime allies in anticipation of a possible disintegration of the alliance and potential hostility among its partners. Instead, it was hoped that the friendly relations and mutual respect that American leaders believed had matured during the war would preserve the common outlook and goals and guarantee an enduring peace. This rosy scenario pertained especially to the Soviet Union itself, despite its alien ideology and the tyrannical conduct of its leader, Joseph Stalin.

In Washington, government leaders generally reflected this idealism. They hailed the globalization of America's moral vision and its rejection of old-style power politics. As World War II wound down, Secretary of State Cordell Hull anticipated the day in which "there will no longer be need for spheres of influence, for alliances, for balance of power, or any other of the special arrangements through which, in the unhappy past, the nations strove to safeguard their security or to promote their interests." [3]

These optimistic expectations of future U.S.-Soviet relations made it necessary to explain away continuing signs of Soviet distrust. This was particularly true during World War II when the West delayed opening up a second front against Germany. When the front was postponed from 1942 to 1943 to 1944, Stalin became bitter. He brusquely rejected Allied explanations that they were not yet properly equipped for such an enormous undertaking, and he especially denounced Churchill for declaring that there would be no invasion until the Germans were so weakened that Allied forces would not have to suffer forbiddingly high losses. To Stalin, this was a weak explanation because the Soviets accepted massive casualties as a matter of course. "When we come to a mine field," Marshal G. K. Zhukov explained to Gen. Dwight Eisenhower after the war, "our infantry attacks exactly as if it were not there. The losses we get from personnel mines we consider only equal to those we would have gotten from machine guns and artillery if the Germans had chosen to defend that particular area with strong bodies of troops instead of with mine fields." [4]

It was no wonder, then, that the Soviets dismissed Allied explanations and fastened instead on what was for them a more reasonable interpre-

3. Quoted in Herbert Feis, *Churchill, Roosevelt, Stalin: The War They Waged and the Peace They Sought* (Princeton: Princeton University Press, 1957), 238.

4. Quoted in Dwight D. Eisenhower, *Crusade in Europe* (Garden City, N.Y.: Doubleday, 1948), 514.

tation of American and British behavior. From the Marxist viewpoint, the Allies were doing exactly what they should be doing, postponing the second front until the Soviet Union and Germany, the two parties to the Molotov-Ribbentrop Pact, had exhausted each other. Then the United States and Britain could land in France, march into Germany without heavy losses, and dictate the peace to Germany and the Soviet Union. The Western delay was seen as a deliberate attempt by the world's leading capitalist powers to destroy their two major ideological opponents at one and the same time. Throughout the war the Russians displayed this fear of hostile Western intentions.

American leaders found a ready explanation for this perceived Soviet suspicion. They thought of Soviet foreign policy not in terms of the internal dynamics of the regime and its ideological enmity toward all noncommunist nations, but solely in terms of Soviet reactions to Western policies. New to great-power politics, they had little knowledge of Russian history and therefore of Russia's historical goals under czarist and Soviet rule. The few experts in the State Department were ignored; in fact, Roosevelt never took the secretary of state along to any of his wartime conferences with Churchill and Stalin.

Soviet distrust of the West was viewed by the president against the pattern of the West's previous anti-Sovietism: the Allied intervention in Russia at the end of World War I aimed at overthrowing the Soviet regime and, after the failure of that attempt, the establishment of a *cordon sanitaire* in eastern Europe to keep Soviet influence from spreading; the West's rejection of Soviet offers in the mid- to late 1930s to build an alliance against Nazi leader Adolf Hitler; and, especially, the effects of the Munich agreement of 1938, when Britain and France stood by while the Nazi dictator destroyed Czechoslovakia, opening his gateway to the East. These efforts by the West to weaken and ultimately destroy the Soviet Union, as well as its attempts to turn Hitler's threat away from Western Europe and toward Russia, were considered the primary reasons for Soviet hostility.

To overcome this attitude, American leaders thought they had only to demonstrate good intentions. The question was not *whether* Soviet cooperation could be won for the postwar world, but *how* it would be gained. And if these efforts bore fruit and created goodwill, what conflicts of interest could not be settled peacefully in the future? Various Soviet policies and acts during the war—the disbanding of the Comintern (the vehicle for international communism), the toning down of communist ideology and the new emphasis on Soviet nationalism, the relaxation of restrictions on the church, and, above all, the statement of Soviet war aims in the same language of peace, democracy, and freedom used by the West—seemed to prove that if the Western powers demonstrated their bona fides (good faith) they could convert the Soviets into allies.

Roosevelt's efforts to gain this cooperation focused on Stalin. In that respect Roosevelt's instincts were correct: if he could gain Stalin's trust, postwar Soviet-American cooperation would be possible. But in another respect his instincts were poor. Roosevelt's political experience was in the domestic arena. He had dealt successfully with all sorts of politicians and had managed to resolve differences by finding compromise solutions. As a result, he had great confidence in his ability to win Stalin's favor. He would talk to Stalin as "one politician to another." In short, Roosevelt saw Stalin as a Russian version of himself, who, as a fellow politician, could be won over by a mixture of concessions and goodwill. It did not occur to Roosevelt that all of his considerable skills and charm might not suffice. At home, these qualities were enough because he and his opponents agreed on ultimate goals; differences were largely over the means to achieve them. But between the United States and the Soviet Union the differences were over the ends, the kind of world each expected to see when the war was over.

In February 1945 at the Yalta Conference of the Big Three—Roosevelt, Stalin, and Churchill—Roosevelt and his advisers believed they had firmly established amicable and lasting relations with the Soviet Union. Stalin had made concessions on a number of vital issues and had promised cooperation in the future. He had accepted the establishment of the United Nations on the basis of the American formula that the veto in the Security Council would be applied only to enforcement action, not to peaceful attempts at the settlement of disputes. Moreover, in the Declaration of Liberated Europe he had promised to support self-government and allow free elections in Eastern Europe. He also had responded to the wishes of the American military and promised to enter the war against Japan after Hitler was finally subdued. And Stalin, to whom Roosevelt often referred in congenial terms, had repeatedly expressed his hope for fifty years of peace and great-power cooperation.

The new era of goodwill was to be embodied in the United Nations, where the peoples of the world would exercise vigilance over their national leaders. The United Nations was regarded as democracy working on an international scale. Just as citizens within democratic states were able to watch their representatives and prevent them from effecting compromises injurious to their interests, so the people of all countries would now be able to keep an eye on their national leaders, making it impossible for them to strike secret deals that would betray the people's interests and threaten the peace of the world. International public opinion, expressing its pacific ideals across national boundaries, would maintain vigilance over the diplomats and hold them accountable. Power politics would be replaced by reliance on sound universal principles and good faith. Upon his return from Yalta, Roosevelt told Congress and the American people that his recent conference with Stalin and Churchill "ought to spell the end of the system of unilateral action, the exclusive alliances, the spheres of influence, the balances of power, and all the other expedients that have been tried for centuries—and have always failed." Instead: "We propose to substitute for all these, a universal organization in which all peace-loving nations will fully have a chance to join." [5]

The State Department had been even more emphatic about the subordination of power politics to universal moral principles. Its Subcommittee on Territorial Problems stated that "the vital interests of the United States lay in following a 'diplomacy of principle'—of moral disinterestedness instead of power politics." No comment could have summed up more aptly the American habit of viewing international politics in terms of abstract moral principles rather than in terms clashes of interest and power. Moreover, no institution could have embodied more fully the immediate postwar hope for a return to "normalcy," the desire for minimal international involvement, and the expectation that the wartime cooperation with the Soviet Union would continue, than the United Nations. It was seen essentially as a *substitute* for a vigorous, self-reliant foreign policy.

THE RUSSO-SOVIET APPROACH TO FOREIGN POLICY

In Chapter 1 it was argued that before World War II American foreign policy was to a large degree driven by a cultural tradition that reflected the nation's detachment from Europe and its pursuit of a democratic way of life in the New World. Such cultural influences affect the foreign policies of every nation-state. It is thus useful to contrast the American tradition with that of its Cold War rival, the Soviet Union, whose leaders also inherited a distinct cultural style of foreign policy, the product of centuries of fractious coexistence with a diverse and often-menacing external environment. These leaders then integrated the lessons of Russian history with the maxims of Marxist-Leninist ideology to fashion an aggressive approach to postwar foreign affairs. But how were these historic Russian roots rendered compatible with communist ideology under the banner of the Soviet Union?

5. Quoted in James MacGregor Burns, *Roosevelt, The Soldier of Freedom* (New York: Harcourt Brace Jovanovich, 1970), 582.

THE RUSSIAN BACKGROUND

As in the American case, understanding the source of the Russo-Soviet "style" of foreign policy begins simply by analyzing a globe. Unlike the United States and other maritime powers, Russia was not blessed by geography. Unprotected by natural barriers such as oceans or mountains, its people were vulnerable to invasions from several directions. And the enormous size of its territory rendered internal cohesion, communication, and transportation very difficult, especially given the diverse ethnic backgrounds of the Russian people.

During the thirteenth and fourteenth centuries, Russia was ruled by the Mongols from the East. By the 1460s Mongol domination had been repelled and Muscovy had emerged as the capital of a Russian superstate. In more modern times, Napoleon Bonaparte's armies invaded and captured Moscow in 1812; British and French armies landed in the Crimea in 1854–1856; and Japan attacked and claimed territories in eastern Russia in 1904–1905. Germany invaded Russia twice during the twentieth century, its first attack prompting the final collapse of the Russian monarchy, civil war, and the rise of the Bolsheviks to power.

Historically, then, Russia could not take its security for granted or give priority to domestic affairs. In these circumstances, political power became centralized in the state which, under both the czars and communist leaders, firmly held the far-flung regions together. Such efforts, however, required large standing military forces, and much of the Russian population was mobilized in their service. Indeed, the Russian armed forces were consistently larger than those of the other European great powers, a fact not lost on leaders in Warsaw, Budapest, Paris, and London.

This militarization of Russian society, purportedly for defensive purposes, also carried with it the potential for outward aggression. To the historian Richard Pipes, Russia no more became the world's largest territorial state by repelling repeated invasions than a man becomes rich by being robbed.[6] The same lack of natural frontiers that failed to protect Russia from invasion also allowed its power to extend outward from its frontiers. Indeed, sustained territorial expansion has been called the "Russian way." According to President Jimmy Carter's national security adviser, Zbigniew Brzezinski, any list of aggressions against Russia in the last two centuries would be dwarfed by Russian expansionist moves against its neighbors.[7]

6. Richard Pipes, as quoted by Zbigniew Brzezinski, *Game Plan: A Geostrategic Framework for the Conduct of the U.S.-Soviet Contest* (Boston: Atlantic Monthly Press, 1986), 19–20.

7. Zbigniew Brzezinski, "The Soviet Union: The Aims, Problems, and Challenges to the West," in *The Conduct of East-West Relations in the 1980s*, Adelphi Paper No. 189, Part I (London: International Institute for Strategic Studies, 1984).

Whether Russian motives were defensive or offensive, the result was a pattern of expansion. To the degree that Russian rulers feared attacks, they pushed outward to keep the enemy as far away as possible. Territorial extension became a partial substitute for the lack of wide rivers or mountains that might have afforded a degree of natural protection. Individual rulers' ambitions, such as Peter the Great's determination to have access to the sea, also resulted in territorial conquest and defeat of the power blocking that aim (in this case, Sweden). Even before the Bolsheviks seized power, authoritarianism, militarism, and expansionism characterized the Russian state; being a good neighbor was an alien concept. The basic "rules" of power politics—the emphasis on national interests, distrust of other states, expectation of conflict, self-reliance, and the possession of sufficient power, especially military power—were deeply ingrained in Russia's leaders.

THE SOVIET INGREDIENT

These attitudes were modified and strengthened by the outlook of the new regime after 1917. Russian political culture was fused with Marxist ideology, as adapted to Russian circumstances by Vladimir Lenin, to create an all-encompassing *weltanschauung* (worldview). The new leaders' ideological outlook did not dictate action in specific situations, but it did provide them with a broad framework for perceiving and understanding the world.

To these new leaders, history centered around the class struggle between, on the one hand, the rich and privileged who owned the means of production and, on the other hand, the greater numbers of propertyless citizens who worked for them. Why were most human beings poor, illiterate, and unhealthy? Why did states fight wars? The answer was that a small minority of capitalists, monopolizing the industrialized world's wealth and power, exploited the men and women who worked in their factories to maximize profits. To keep wages down, they kept food prices low so that agricultural labor also lived in destitution. Domestically as well as internationally, wars were one result of the ongoing search by these capitalists for profits.

Another result was the conflict waged over dividing up the non-European colonial world. For Lenin, global imperialism represented the "highest stage of capitalism." He viewed World War I as a climactic showdown among capitalist empires, a fight for the spoils of the developing world now that their own frontiers were closed. If human beings were ever to live in freedom and enjoy a decent standard of living in peace and fraternity with other countries, capitalism would have to be replaced by communism.

As Lenin was aware, the application of Marxism to Russia suffered from one glaring deficiency. In Karl Marx's dialectic view, communism stemmed directly from the failures of capitalism. Thus a communist society must first experience industrialization, urbanization, and the enlistment of its working classes into an organized "proletariat." This, of course, did not pertain to the largely agrarian Russia whose population was only then emerging from its feudal traditions. So Lenin attempted to resolve this problem by centralizing power in a "vanguard" of enlightened Marxists, who would bring communism to the Russian people without first exposing them to the contradictions and inequalities of capitalism. Once firmly in place within the Kremlin, this vanguard would then disseminate Lenin's ideological vision through a pervasive propaganda campaign.

Ideology was more than a way of viewing the world; it also gave Soviet leaders a mission. For them, capitalism was the chief obstacle to humanity's liberation. Thus Soviet leaders considered the American and West European governments to be enemies because of what they were—capitalist. Moreover, unlike the traditional thinking of the great powers, who had no "permanent" friends or enemies and who shifted allegiances as the distribution of power changed, Soviet ideology clearly discriminated friend from foe on a permanent basis. Because the Soviet Union defined capitalist states as foes, and because the Soviet mission was to export its revolution and create a new postcapitalist international order, the relationship between it and the capitalist states would be marked by conflict until the victory of Soviet ideology. Its leaders, moreover, took it for granted that the capitalist states were equally hostile and determined to eliminate communism and the Soviet Union, if only to avoid their own demise.

The effect of this pattern was to perpetuate historic Russian suspicions of foreigners and feelings of insecurity. Soviet leaders believed the state system, increasingly composed of capitalist states with close economic ties, was a very hostile environment. They rejected the latter's professions of goodwill and peaceful intentions and committed their country to the "inevitable and irreconcilable struggle" against these states. They fostered a strong emphasis on self-reliance and an equally intense concern with Soviet power. Tactically, they were convinced that when an enemy made concessions in negotiations or became more accommodating, it was not because the enemy wanted a friendlier relationship but because it was *compelled* to do so by the Soviet Union's growing strength, a viewpoint that led to a self-sustaining rationale for ever more military power.

Russian history stood as a warning to Soviet leaders that peace was but a preparation for the next war. Their ideological perceptions strengthened the view that peace was but the continuation of the last war by other means. The Soviet worldview, in short, reinforced the historically repetitious cycles that had resulted in further expansion of Soviet power. Even if insecurity, rather than any historical mission, drove this expansion, the result for neighboring states remained the same—they were vulnerable. They were perceived as inherent threats to Soviet interests and they represented possible additions to the Soviet Union's own frontiers. Such a drive to achieve absolute security in a system in which no state could achieve that aim short of total domination left other states insecure and contributed to the volatility of the international system throughout the Cold War.

The contrast between American culture and national style, which emphasized peace as normal and conflict as abnormal, and that of the Soviet Union, which stressed the pervasiveness of war, could not have been more striking. Both societies felt a sense of historical mission, yet their principles, goals, and tactics were worlds apart. These clashing approaches to foreign policy were to confront one another as the Soviet and Western armies, led by the United States, advanced from the opposite sides of Europe.

SOVIET EXPANSION AFTER WORLD WAR II

The American dream of postwar peace and Big Three cooperation was shattered when the Red Army, having finally halted the Nazi armies and decisively defeated the Germans at Stalingrad in late 1942, slowly began to drive the enemy out of the Soviet Union and then pursue the retreating Germans to Berlin. The Soviet Union, which in 1940 had annexed the three Baltic states (Latvia, Lithuania, and Estonia) after signing the Nazi-Soviet pact, thus expanded into eastern and central Europe and began to impose its control on Poland, Hungary, Bulgaria, Romania, and Albania even before the end of the war. (Yugoslavia was by then under the communist control of Marshal Josip Tito, the Yugoslav partisan leader who had fought bravely against the German occupation, and Czechoslovakia was under the threat of the Red Army.)

In each of the nations of Eastern Europe occupied by their troops, the Soviets unilaterally established pro-Soviet coalition governments. The key posts in these regimes—the ministry of the interior, which usually controlled the police, and the ministry of defense, which controlled the army—were in the hands of the communists. With these decisive levers of power in their grasp, the Soviets found it an easy matter to extend their domination and subvert the independence of these countries. As the war drew to a close, it became clear that the words of the Yalta Declaration, in which the Soviets had committed themselves to free elections and democratic governments in Eastern Europe, meant quite different things to the Soviets and to the Americans. For the Soviet Union, control of Eastern Europe, and especially Poland, was essential because this area was a vital link in its security belt. After suffering two German invasions in less than thirty years, it was perhaps inevitable that the Soviet Union would try to establish "friendly" governments throughout the area. To the Soviets, democratic governments meant communist regimes, and free elections meant elections from which parties not favorable to the communists were barred. The peace treaties with the former German satellite states (Hungary, Bulgaria, Romania), which were painfully negotiated by the victors in a series of foreign ministers' conferences during 1945 and 1946, could not loosen the tightening Soviet grip on what were by now Soviet satellite states.

In terms of the state system, the Soviet behavior was understandable. Each state had to act as its own guardian against potential adversaries in a system characterized by conflict among states and a sense of insecurity and fear on the part of its members. As the alliance against the common enemy came to an end, the Soviet Union predictably would strengthen itself against the power most likely to be its new opponent. As czarist Russia, with a long history of invasions from the East and West, it had learned the basic rules of the international game through bitter experience. As *Soviet* Russia, its sense of peril and mistrust had been intensified by an ideology that posited capitalist states as implacable enemies. In the war it had suffered over twenty million casualties, soldiers and civilians. Thus the establishment of noncommunist regimes in Eastern Europe was unacceptable. The American insistence on free elections was seen as an attempt to push the Soviet Union out of Europe. The assumption was that a noncommunist government would be an anticommunist one.

U.S.-SOVIET DIFFERENCES

No issue could have reflected more accurately the differences between the United States and Soviet Union. Roosevelt acted precisely on the assumption that noncommunist did not have to mean anti-Soviet. During the war, he had been all too aware of the consequences of a possible Soviet-American clash in the wake of Germany's defeat. He therefore single-mindedly pursued a policy of friendship toward the Soviet Union. Roosevelt, however, did not view free elections in Eastern Europe in terms of the creation of a new anti-Soviet belt. For him, free elections, noncommunist coalition governments in which communists might participate if they gained a sizable vote, and a friendly attitude between East and West were quite compatible.

The model he had in mind was Czechoslovakia. As the only democracy in that area, Czechoslovakia had maintained close ties with the West since its birth after World War I. But because France and Britain had failed to defend Czechoslovakia at Munich in 1938 and betrayed it by appeasing Hitler, it also had become friendly with the Soviet Union. After 1945 Czechoslovakia, like the other East European states, knew that it lay in the Soviet sphere of influence and that its security depended on getting along with, not irritating, its powerful neighbor. Thus Czech leaders expressed only amicable feelings for the Soviet Union and signed a security treaty with Moscow. And in one of the rare free elections the Soviets allowed in Eastern Europe, the Communist Party received the largest vote of any party and therefore the key posts in the government. To share power in a coalition government, however, was to share power with class enemies. A "friendly" state, to Soviet leaders, was one totally controlled by the Communist Party. Soviet security therefore required ideological homogeneity in Eastern Europe and Soviet domination. By contrast, a "friendly" state in Roosevelt's eyes was one sensitive to Soviet security interests but possessive of its domestic autonomy. A Communist Party monopoly of power was not a prerequisite for the states of Eastern Europe to adopt a pro-Soviet foreign policy. Great powers historically have created spheres of influence on their borders, and the neighboring states usually have accommodated this notion because they have recognized the wisdom of doing so.

During World War II, the heroic Soviet war effort and sacrifices had created an enormous reservoir of goodwill in the West. Had the Soviets acted with greater restraint after the war and accepted states that, regardless of their governments' composition, would have adjusted to their Soviet neighbor, Stalin could have had the security he was seeking. But Stalin did not trust Roosevelt. No matter how personable the president was, no matter how sincere his statements of goodwill and postwar friendship, Stalin saw him as the leader of a capitalist nation. As a "tool of Wall Street," Roosevelt could not be sincere in his peaceful professions. To Stalin, Roosevelt was an American version of himself, a man who was fully aware of the impending postwar Soviet-American struggle and equally determined to weaken his adversary and gain the advantage for his nation. In Eastern Europe, Soviet bayonets enforced Stalin's will. The Soviet style ensured that the wartime alliance would break up and that eventually the Western allies would return Stalin's hostility, proving to him that he had been right all along about Western enmity!

Churchill, concerned about Stalin's behavior in Eastern Europe, urged the United States to send forces to capture the symbolically important German capital of Berlin (instead of rounding up the remnants of Germany's defeated army) and to advance U.S. troops as far east as possible, including farther into Czechoslovakia. He also suggested that, until Stalin observed his agreements in Eastern Europe, U.S. forces not pull back to their agreed-upon occupation zones in Germany and the United States not shift the bulk of its military power from Europe to the Far East for the final offensive against Japan. Roosevelt rejected all of these suggestions. He had assured Stalin that all American troops would be withdrawn within two years after the war. Why then should Stalin worry about American opposition to his efforts to control Eastern Europe? The Soviet leader exercised caution when he encountered opposition, but he ignored diplomatic notes of protest. Carefully waiting to see what the United States would do, Stalin allowed free elections in Czechoslovakia and Hungary, the two states closest to American power. But continued U.S. and British verbal warnings, unsupported by action, did not impress the Soviet leader.

Consequently, Hungary's freedom was soon squashed by the Soviets.[8] Then in 1948 even the Czech government, in which the Communist Party had the largest plurality, was overthrown by the Soviets in a coup d'état. Contrary to Roosevelt's expectations, not even a communist-controlled coalition government was acceptable to Stalin. Indeed, as the Soviet satellization of Eastern Europe was to show, the failure of the United States was not the failure of efforts to accommodate Soviet interests in Eastern Europe; it was the failure to resist Stalin earlier. Because Stalin apparently saw no limits to Soviet expansion and his conception of Soviet security left little, if any, security for his neighbors. Those limits had to be defined by the two Western powers, of which the United States was by far the stronger at the end of the war.

THE SOVIET PUSH TO THE SOUTH

Just as in the two world wars when Britain had led the effort to contain Germany, London—not Washington—took the first step toward opposing the Soviet Union after 1945. Indeed, the United States at first tried to play the role of mediator between the Soviet Union and Britain. Only when British power proved to be insufficient did the United States take over the task of balancing Soviet power. America's initiative evolved gradually over 1946–1947 and was precipitated by Stalin's attempt to consolidate his power beyond Eastern Europe. The United States had finally accepted Soviet control of Eastern Europe, especially Poland, the corridor through which Germany had attacked Russia twice in a quarter-century. Moscow's security interests in this region were understandable, and Washington, despite its disappointment over the Soviet failure to fulfill its Yalta obligations in Poland, quickly recognized the new Polish government as well as the other Soviet-installed regimes in Eastern Europe.

8. For elaboration, see Charles Gati, *Hungary and the Soviet Bloc* (Durham, N.C.: Duke University Press, 1986).

While these events were unfolding, however, the Soviets began moving toward the Mediterranean and the Persian Gulf. Turkey, Greece, and Iran were the first to feel pressure. If Soviet behavior in Eastern Europe could be explained in defensive terms, this was less true for the area south of the Soviet Union, the line that runs from Turkey to India. Long before Stalin, the czars had sought access to the Mediterranean via the Dardanelles Straits. Simultaneously they had tried to expand southward to establish a warm-water port and to bring Soviet power closer to the Middle East and the Persian Gulf.

The Soviet Union first sought to gain influence in Turkey. Indeed, the Soviets had begun to do this as early as June 1945 when they made several demands: the cession of several Turkish districts lying on the Turkish-Soviet frontier, a revision of the Montreux Convention governing the Dardanelles Straits in favor of a joint Soviet-Turkish administration, the severance of Turkey's ties with Britain and the conclusion of a treaty with the Soviet Union similar to those the Soviet Union had concluded with its Balkan satellites, and finally, an opportunity to lease bases in the Dardanelles for Soviet naval and land forces to be used for "joint defense." The United States sent a naval task force into the Mediterranean immediately after the Soviets issued these demands. Twelve days later, the United States formally replied to the Soviets by rejecting their demand to share responsibility for the defense of the straits with Turkey. Britain sent a similar reply.

In Greece, communist pressure was exerted on the government through widespread guerrilla warfare, which began in the fall of 1946. Civil war in Greece was nothing new. During World War II communist and anticommunist guerrillas had spent much of their energy battling each other instead of the Germans. When the British landed in Greece and the Germans withdrew, the communists attempted to take over Athens. Only after several weeks of bitter street fighting and the landing of British reinforcements was the communist control of Athens dislodged; a truce was signed in January 1945. Just over a year later the Greeks held a general election in which right-wing forces captured the majority of votes. In August 1946 the communist forces renewed the war in the north, where the Soviet satellites in Eastern Europe could keep the guerrillas well supplied.

Meanwhile, the Soviet Union intensified pressure on Iran by refusing to withdraw its troops from that country. The troops had been there since late 1941, when the Soviet Union and Britain had invaded Iran to forestall increased Nazi influence and to use Iran as a corridor through which the West could ship military aid to the Soviet Union. The Soviets had occupied northern Iran, the British the central and southern sections. When the British withdrew, the Soviets sought to convert Iran into a Soviet satellite. The Iranian prime minister's offer of oil concessions to get the Soviets to withdraw was rebuffed. Moscow's goal was nothing less than detaching the northern area of Azerbaijan and then by various means pressuring Iran into servile status. The American government was once more confronted with the need to support Great Britain. After the United States and Britain delivered firm statements that they would use force to defend Iran, Stalin finally relented.

Although U.S. efforts in these areas were largely effective, actions taken by President Harry Truman, Roosevelt's successor, were merely swift reactions to immediate crises; they were not the product of an overall American strategy. Such a coherent strategy came only after a reassessment of Soviet foreign policy that placed the Soviet Union's actions in Eastern Europe and beyond in historic perspective.

TOWARD THE STRATEGY OF CONTAINMENT

Eighteen months passed before the United States undertook that review—from the surrender of Japan on September 2, 1945, until the announcement of the Truman Doctrine on March 12, 1947. Perhaps such a reevaluation could not have been made any more quickly. Public opinion in a democratic country does not normally shift drastically overnight. It would have been too much to expect Americans to suddenly abandon their friendly attitude toward the Soviet Union, inspired largely by the images of Soviet wartime bravery and endurance and by hopes for peaceful postwar cooperation. Moreover, war-weary citizens of the United States wished to be left alone to occupy themselves once more with domestic affairs.

In May 1945, at the end of the war with Germany, the United States had an army of 3.5 million organized into 68 divisions in Europe, supported by 149 air groups. By March 1946 only 400,000 troops remained. Overall, the army had been reduced from 8 million to 1 million, the navy from 3.5 million to 1 million, and the air force from more than 200 combat groups to fewer than 50. Thus the "most rapid demobilization in the history of the world" had largely been completed.[9]

This reduction in military strength, a symptom of America's psychological demobilization, no doubt encouraged the Soviet Union's intransigence in Europe and its attempts to extend its influence elsewhere. American diplomacy and force retained their traditional separation. America's large and powerful armed forces and its enormous industrial strength, which could have provided the basis for serious negotiations

9. Stephen E. Ambrose, *Rise to Globalism: American Foreign Policy since 1938,* 5th rev. ed. (New York: Penguin, 1988), 79.

SOVIET EXPANSION IN EUROPE, 1939–1948

about Eastern Europe, were dismantled and converted back to the production of consumer goods. American policy, unsupported by sufficient conventional military power, was impotent. And "atomic diplomacy," despite what revisionists have written, was not used extensively in the immediate postwar period. If it was used at all, it certainly did not frighten Stalin or deter him from strengthening his grip on Eastern Europe and trying to expand Soviet power into new areas.

When Soviet expansion finally led to a reevaluation of American policy, three strategic positions became clear. At one extreme stood that old realist Winston Churchill, who had long counseled against the withdrawal of American troops from Europe. He insisted that the presence of British and American troops would force the Soviet Union to live up to its Yalta obligations to allow free elections in Eastern Europe and to withdraw the Red Army from eastern Germany. After the United States rejected his plea, Churchill took his case directly to the American public in a March 1946 speech at Fulton, Missouri:

> From Stettin in the Baltic to Trieste in the Adriatic, an iron curtain has descended across the continent. Behind that line lie all the capitals of the ancient states of Central and Eastern Europe. Warsaw, Berlin, Prague, Vienna, Budapest, Belgrade, Bucharest, and Sofia, all the famous cities and populations around them lie in the Soviet sphere and all are subject in one form or another, not only to Soviet influence but to a very high and increasing measure of control from Moscow.[10]

Churchill did not believe that the Soviets wanted war: "What they desire is the fruits of war and the indefinite expansion of their power and doctrines." And the only thing lying between the Soviets and their desires was the opposing power of the British Commonwealth and the United States. In short, Churchill was saying bluntly that the Cold War had begun, and that Americans must recognize this fact and give up their dreams of Big Three unity in the United Nations.

At the other extreme stood Secretary of Commerce Henry Wallace, who felt it was precisely the kind of aggressive attitude expressed by Churchill that was to blame for Soviet hostility. The United States and Britain, he said, had no more business in Eastern Europe than the Soviet Union had in Latin America; for each, the respective area was vital for national security. Western interference in nations bordering the Soviet Union was bound to arouse Soviet suspicion. "We may not like what Russia does in Eastern Europe," said Wallace. "Her type of land reform, industrial expropriation, and suspension of basic liberties offend the great majority of the people of the United States. But whether we like it or not, the Russians will try to socialize their sphere of influence just as we try to democratize our sphere of influence." The tough attitude

10. The entire speech can be found in Thomas G. Paterson, ed., *The Origins of the Cold War*, 2d ed. (Lexington, Mass.: D. C. Heath, 1974), 11–17.

demanded by Churchill and other "reactionaries" at home and abroad was precisely the wrong policy; it would only increase international tension. "The tougher we get, the tougher the Russians will get," Wallace pointed out.[11] Only mutual trust would allow the United States and the Soviet Union to live together peacefully, and such trust could not be created by an unfriendly American attitude and policy.

The American government and public wavered between these two positions and tentatively adopted a third strategy. The administration recognized that Big Three cooperation had ended. The U.S. government, then, would make no further concessions to lend the appearance of cooperation with the Soviet Union. It had tried to gain Soviet amity through cooperation and unilateral defense cutbacks; now it was up to Soviet leaders to demonstrate a constructive approach toward the United States as well. Paper agreements, written in such general terms that they hid divergent purposes, were regarded as having little value. Something more was needed: Soviet words would have to be matched by deeds. Thus the United States would seek neither to roll back communism nor to maintain cordial relations with Moscow.

The American secretary of state, James Byrnes, called this third strategy the "policy of firmness and patience." American steadfastness presumably would wear the Soviets down and moderate their conduct. But there was no suggestion in this call for a tactical shift in how to negotiate with Moscow that the United States needed to organize international opposition to the Soviet Union. The new American position, as one political analysis concluded, "meant to most of its exponents that the Soviet Union had to be induced by firmness to play the game in the American way. There was no consistent official suggestion that the United States should begin to play a different game." [12] The prerequisite for such a suggestion was that American policy makers recognize that the Soviet Union was no longer just a difficult ally but an enemy.

GEORGE KENNAN AND THE NEW AMERICAN POLICY

George Kennan, the U.S. State Department's foremost expert on the Soviet Union, presented in 1946 the basis of what was to be a new American policy that recognized the hostile character of the Soviet regime. In a detailed telegram sent from the U.S. embassy in Moscow, Kennan analyzed the communist outlook on world affairs.[13] In the minds of the

11. Henry Wallace, "The Way to Peace," *Vital Speeches,* October 1, 1946, 738–741.

12. William Reitzel, Morton A. Kaplan, and Constance G. Coblenz, *United States Foreign Policy, 1945–1955* (Washington, D.C.: Brookings, 1956), 89.

13. This "long telegram" was later reprinted in the famous "X article," entitled "The Sources of Soviet Conduct," which appeared in the July 1947 issue of *Foreign Affairs.* Also reproduced in George F. Kennan, *American Diplomacy, 1900–1950* (Chicago: University of Chicago Press, 1951), 107–128.

IMPACT AND INFLUENCE

GEORGE KENNAN

The euphoria surrounding the end of World War II quickly gave way in the United States to concerns about the emerging Cold War. The U.S. government turned to George Kennan, a State Department officer based in the Soviet Union during and after World War II, to devise an appropriate response to the Soviet challenge in central Europe. U.S. presidents would follow Kennan's "containment" strategy, described in this chapter, until the collapse of the Soviet Union in 1991.

Although Kennan profoundly influenced American foreign policy after World War II, he spent most of the postwar era out of government. In 1950, he joined Princeton University's Institute for Advanced Study, from where he continued to inform the foreign policy debate, often deflecting criticism that his containment policy had led directly to U.S. interventions in Korea, Vietnam, and Latin America. Defending his record, Kennan charged that American leaders had strayed from the strategy he proposed. More generally, he criticized the "legalistic-moralistic" approach to American foreign policy and claimed it had prevented the nation from focusing on its national interests in the late twentieth century. In this respect, Kennan is considered one of the key post-

Soviet leaders, he said, the Soviet Union had no community of interest with the capitalist states; to the contrary, they saw their relationship with the Western powers as one of innate antagonism. Moreover, communist ideology had taught them that it was their duty to overthrow eventually the political forces in the outside hostile world, and in this feeling they were sustained by "the powerful hands of Russian history and tradition." After some time, observed Kennan, "their own aggressive intransigence with respect to the outside world began to find its own reaction. . . . It is an undeniable privilege for every man to prove himself right in the thesis that the world is his enemy; for if he reiterates it frequently enough and makes it the background for his conduct, he is bound to be right." [14]

According to Kennan, this Soviet hostility would continue until the capitalist world had been destroyed. From this antagonism flowed many of the elements the West found "disturbing in the Kremlin's conduct of foreign policy: the secretiveness, the lack of frankness, the duplicity, the war suspiciousness, and the basic unfriendliness of purpose." He explained that "these characteristics of the Soviet policy, like the postulates from which they flow, are basic to the *internal* nature of Soviet power, and will be with us . . . until the nature of Soviet power is changed." [15] Until that moment, he said, Soviet strategy and objectives would remain the same.

The Soviet-American struggle would thus be a long one, but Kennan stressed that Soviet hostility did not mean the Soviets would embark on a do-or-die program to overthrow capitalism by a fixed date. Given their sense of historic inevitability, they had no timetable for conquest. In a brilliant passage, Kennan outlined the Soviet concept of the struggle:

> The Kremlin is under no ideological compulsion to accomplish its purposes in a hurry. Like the Church, it is dealing in ideological concepts which are of a long-term validity, and it can afford to be patient. It has no right to risk the existing achievements of the revolution for the sake of vain baubles of the future. The very teachings of Lenin himself require great caution and flexibility in the pursuit of communist purposes. Again, these precepts are fortified by the lessons of Russian history: of centuries of obscure battles between nomadic forces over the stretches of a vast unfortified plain. Here caution, circumspection, flexibility, and deception are the valuable qualities; and their value finds natural appreciation in the Russian, or the Oriental mind. Thus the Kremlin has no compunction about retreating in the face of superior force. And being under the compulsion of no timetable, it does not get panicky under the necessity of such a retreat. Its political action is a fluid stream which moves constantly, wherever it is permitted to move, toward a given goal. . . . The main thing is that there should always be pressure, increasing constant pressure, toward the desired goal. There is no trace of any feeling in Soviet psychology that the goal must be reached at any given time.[16]

14. Kennan, *American Diplomacy,* 111–112.
15. Ibid., 115. Italics added.
16. Ibid., 118.

How could the United States counter such a policy? Kennan's answer was that American policy would have to be one of "long-term, patient, but firm and vigilant containment." He viewed containment as a test of American democracy to conduct an intelligent, long-range foreign policy *and* simultaneously contribute to changes within the Soviet Union that ultimately would bring about a moderation of its revolutionary aims. The United States, he emphasized in a passage that was to take on great meaning four decades later,

> has it in its power to increase enormously the strains under which Soviet policy must operate, to force upon the Kremlin a far greater degree of moderation and circumspection than it has had to observe in recent years, and in this way to promote tendencies which must eventually find their outlet in either the breakup or the gradual mellowing of Soviet power. For no mystical, messianic movement—and particularly not that of the Kremlin—can face frustration indefinitely without eventually adjusting itself in one way or another to the logic of that state of affairs.[17]

And why was the United States so favorably positioned for a long-term struggle with the Soviet Union? The reason, Kennan argued, was that industry was the key ingredient of power and the United States controlled most of the centers of industry. There were five such centers in the world: the United States, Britain, West Germany, Japan, and the Soviet Union. The United States and its future allies constituted four of these centers, the Soviet Union just one. Containment meant confining the Soviet Union to that one. The question, Kennan said, was not whether the United States had sufficient power to contain the Soviet Union, but whether it had the patience and wisdom to do so.

ALTERNATIVES TO CONTAINMENT

Kennan's containment strategy was generally well received in Washington, whose leaders then embarked on the complex task of translating its generalities into specific initiatives. These would entail new strategies for the military services, a greater emphasis on economic statecraft and foreign assistance, and an ongoing effort to enlist foreign countries into bilateral and multilateral alliance networks (see Chapter 3). But in adopting containment, the Truman administration implicitly rejected two other courses of action that had substantial support.

The first was a retreat into the traditional pattern of U.S. isolation from European diplomacy. This alternative was rejected when, on the afternoon of February 21, 1947, the first secretary of the British embassy in Washington visited the State Department and handed American officials two notes from His Majesty's government. One concerned Greece,

17. Ibid., 127–128.

the other Turkey, but in effect they said the same thing: Britain could no longer meet its traditional responsibilities to those two countries. Because both countries were on the verge of collapse, the meaning of the British notes was clear: a Soviet breakthrough could be prevented only by an American commitment to stopping it.

February 21, then, was a turning point for the West. Great Britain, the only remaining power in Western Europe, was acknowledging its exhaustion. It had fought Philip II of Spain, Louis XIV and Napoleon Bonaparte of France, Kaiser Wilhelm II and Adolf Hitler of Germany. It had long preserved the balance of power that had protected the United States, but its ability to protect that balance had declined steadily in the twentieth century and twice it had needed American help. Each time, however, Britain had fought the longer battle; the United States had entered the wars only when it was clear that Germany and its allies were too strong for Great Britain and that America would have to help safeguard its own security.

The second course rejected in adopting the strategy of containment was a preventive war. The United States had an atomic monopoly until late 1949. In 1950 the United States had fifty bombs plus the means to deliver them, while the Soviet Union had only tested an atomic device. For a short time, then, the United States possessed the opportunity to establish a *Pax Americana,* or world empire. But exploitation of this atomic monopoly was never seriously considered. Quite apart from the relatively small size of the stockpile, the launch of an atomic Pearl Harbor on the Soviet Union was contrary to American tradition and universal standards of morality. Indeed, after Hiroshima the conviction grew that atomic weapons were too horrible to use and that in a future war there would be no winners. By the mid-1950s, after both superpowers had tested nuclear devices and had confronted one another in a number of crises, and after the range of destruction had taken a quantum leap from kilotons (thousands of tons of TNT) to megatons (millions of tons of TNT), this conviction grew to absolute certainty.

The bomb, then, signaled a significant change: historically the principal task of the military had been to win wars; from now on its main purpose would be to *deter* them. Atomic weapons could have no other rationale. Conflicts between great powers—between Athens and Sparta for the control of ancient Greece, between Rome and Carthage for control of the Mediterranean, or, in more modern times, between Germany and England for control of Europe—had been settled on the battlefield. Such a solution, however, was no longer feasible; the United States now had to conduct a *protracted conflict* alien to its style. The term frequently given to this conflict—Cold War—was apt indeed. *War* signified that the U.S.-Soviet rivalry was serious; *Cold* referred to the fact that nuclear weapons were so utterly destructive that war, even with conventional weapons, could not be waged.

While communist containment was adopted as the linchpin of U.S. strategy, it continued to attract widespread criticism. Some felt it did not go far enough, that it failed to exploit U.S. military and economic supremacy and provided the Soviets with the initiative to set the time and place of superpower confrontations. Others felt it went too far. By codifying the Soviet-American conflict, it cemented a pervasive U.S. role in Europe and beyond and ensured a prolonged and dangerous global competition. Located as it was between the two extremes, however, the containment alternative attracted support among moderates both in the United States and abroad. While future leaders would modify the strategy, they adhered to its broader objectives with unusual consistency. It thus heralded an auspicious new era in U.S. foreign policy, perhaps best reflected in the title of Secretary of State Dean Acheson's memoir, *Present at the Creation.* To Acheson, the late 1940s

> saw the entry of our nation, already one of the superpowers, into the near chaos of a war-torn and disintegrating world society. To the responsibilities and needs of that time the nation summoned an imaginative effort unique in history and even greater than that made in the preceding years of fighting. All who served in those years had an opportunity to give more than a sample of their best.[18]

The Cold War that followed was characterized by long-term hostility and by a mutual determination to avoid a cataclysmic military showdown. As it took over Britain's role as the keeper of the balance of power, the United States had to learn power politics. But in protecting itself, it also had to learn how to manage a protracted conflict in peacetime, a new experience and one at odds with its historic ways of dealing with foreign enemies and the international system.

THE CHANGING OF THE GUARD: SEA POWER VERSUS LAND POWER

The United States was to play a role in the Cold War similar to that played traditionally by Britain: primarily a naval power, the United States was to contain the outward thrust of a land power from the Eurasian "heartland." After World War I a British geographer, Halford Mackinder, interested in the relationship of geographic position to international politics (referred to as *geopolitics*), stated the axiom "Who rules East Europe commands the Heartland [Eurasia]; Who rules the Heartland commands the World-Island [Eurasia and Africa, which, on the map, look like a centrally located island]; Who rules the World-Island commands the

18. Dean Acheson, *Present at the Creation: My Years in the State Department* (New York: Norton, 1969), 725.

World." [19] A generation later an American geopolitician, Nicholas Spykman, coined a reply to Mackinder: "Who controls the Rimland [the peripheral areas around Eurasia] controls Eurasia; who rules Eurasia controls the destinies of the world." [20] Although these axioms may be considered too simplistic—and there is some danger in accepting geography as too deterministic a factor in explaining the behavior of states—they explain rather well the essence of the British-German and the U.S.-Soviet conflicts.

Indeed, before World War I, before the German threat received Britain's primary attention, *czarist* Russia—then incorporating Finland, the three Baltic states, and Poland—had been London's concern. Russian power was spreading east to the Pacific, southeast toward the frontier of British India (today's Afghanistan and Pakistan), southeast from Siberia into Manchuria and into northern China, and southwest from the Caucasus to Turkey and Iran. British power along the rim running from Turkey to India guarded the perimeter around Russia. When Russia pushed into Korea toward Japan, Japan attacked and defeated Russia, thereby also limiting the spread of Russian influence in northern China. After that, Russia focused on the Balkans, where it came into conflict with Austria-Hungary, the ally of Germany, which had become the European continent's most powerful country. Germany became the great threat to British interests, and Britain twice went to war with Germany, which, in each conflict, invaded Russia. A victorious Germany would have controlled the heartland—indeed, in World War II victory would have conceivably given Germany control from the Atlantic to the Pacific—as well as the Middle East, the area linking Europe, Asia, and Africa.

After Germany's second defeat in 1945 the Russian threat reemerged. Already the heartland power, Soviet Russia extended its arm into the center of Europe, reclaimed its dominant position in northern China, and sought to exploit weaknesses along its southern border from Turkey to Pakistan. Thus one reason for the postwar conflict was *geopolitical:* Russian land power expanded but was halted by the countervailing power exerted by a maritime nation, the United States. These clashes occurred along the perimeter from Turkey to Iran and then in Western Europe.

It is important to understand the location of the initial conflicts because revisionists argued that whatever the Soviet Union's intentions were, its lack of a large fleet and intercontinental air power meant that it

19. Sir Halford J. Mackinder, *Democratic Ideals and Reality: A Study in the Politics of Reconstruction* (New York: Henry Holt, 1919), 150.

20. Nicholas Spykman, *The Geography of the Peace* (New York: Harcourt, Brace, 1944).

represented no threat to the United States. Moreover, they pointed out that the United States held an atomic monopoly. Thus the demobilization of U.S. conventional forces counted for little. They asserted, in fact, that the United States was a hegemon—that is, it was the dominant power in the system and there really was no serious Soviet threat.

Only one part of this argument was correct, however: the Soviet Union did not represent a direct threat to the security of the United States in the Western Hemisphere. But the Soviet army, even after substantial demobilization, remained a formidable force of 175 divisions and certainly one able to pressure Soviet neighbors to the south and in Europe and hold America's friends and potential allies hostage. That is why the governments of Iran, Turkey, Greece, and Western Europe feared a revival of American isolationism and sought U.S. countervailing support. To be sure, the small U.S. atomic arsenal could have wreaked great damage on Russian cities, but it could not have stopped the Soviet army from overrunning Western Europe.

In the balance that emerged after World War II, the United States greatly benefited from its productive economy, which had not been damaged by the war; from its atomic monopoly, although the number of bombs and bombers available to deliver them remained small in the first years after the war; and from the appeal of its democratic political system. The Soviet Union had the advantages of its powerful conventional forces; its geographical position at the center of Eurasia; and, at a time when democracy was still widely identified with the failed capitalism of the 1930s and the Soviet Union with its heroic resistance to the Nazis, its communist ideology. That ideology appealed to the working classes in nations such as France and Italy, as well as to the political movements that were seeking power in countries such as China. Thus American political leaders after 1945 did not conclude that the United States was a hegemonic power. To the contrary, they were anxious about a balance of power that appeared to them to be very precarious.

DECLARING COLD WAR: THE TRUMAN DOCTRINE

On March 12, 1947, President Harry Truman went before a joint session of Congress to deliver one of the most important speeches in American history. After outlining the situation in Greece, he spelled out what was to become known as the Truman Doctrine. The United States, he said, could survive only in a world in which freedom flourished. And it would not realize this objective unless it was

> willing to help free peoples to maintain their institutions and their national integrity against aggressive movements that seek to impose upon them totalitarian regimes. *This is no more than a frank recognition that totalitarian regimes*

imposed on free peoples, by direct or indirect aggression, undermine the foundations of international peace and hence the security of the United States. . . .

At the present moment in world history nearly every nation must choose between alternative ways of life. The choice is often not a free one. . . .

I believe that we must assist free peoples to work out their own destinies in their own way.[21]

The president asked Congress to appropriate $400 million for economic aid and military supplies for Greece and Turkey and to authorize the dispatch of American personnel to assist with reconstruction and to provide their armies with appropriate instruction and training. And he implicitly offered U.S. assistance to other states with his open-ended appeal to "free peoples." One of his most critical tactical victories in winning approval for these measures was that over Michigan senator Arthur Vandenberg, a prominent Republican isolationist and chairman of the Senate Foreign Relations Committee. With Vandenberg's endorsement, the spirit and financial requirements of the Truman Doctrine were embraced by Congress.

The United States thus initiated the policy of containment. The emerging clash between the postwar superpowers, anticipated by the Truman administration in the late 1940s, was evident in the hostile actions being taken on both sides. To many, the defining moment occurred on July 2, 1947, when the Russian delegation walked out of a meeting in Paris of Americans and other Western leaders to discuss the distribution of Marshall Plan aid (see Chapter 3). From then on, the two antagonists would not even put forward the appearance of great-power cooperation or *rapprochement.*

In this volatile atmosphere, Soviet behavior left the United States with little choice but to adopt a countervailing policy. During World War II, the United States had sought to overcome the Kremlin's suspicions of the West, to be sensitive to Soviet security concerns in Eastern Europe, and to lay the foundation for postwar cooperation. At the end of the war the principal concern of American policy makers was not to eliminate the self-proclaimed bastion of world revolution and enemy of Western capitalism, or to push the Soviet Union out of Eastern Europe. American policy was not the product of a virulent and preexisting anticommunist ideology. Rather, it was activated by its desire to prevent a major nation from achieving dominance in Europe, an occurrence that twice in the twentieth century had led the United States into war. Thus American policy after 1945 was consistent with U.S. behavior in 1917 and 1940–1941 when the nation had gone to war to prevent such an outcome. It was not fundamentally an ideological issue. In the two world

21. Italics added. The drama of this period and Truman's speech to Congress are still best captured in Joseph M. Jones, *The Fifteen Weeks* (New York: Viking Press, 1955), 17–23.

wars the enemy was Germany. In the first engagement Germany was led by a conservative monarchy, in the second by an extreme right-wing fascist regime. In the Cold War the adversary was the Soviet Union, a radical left-wing regime. American action, however, remained the same regardless of the ideological nature of the opponent.

The contrasting nature of American and Soviet conduct after World War II was a factor as well. The Soviet Union, which already had annexed the Baltic states, imposed communist regimes on its neighbors and stationed Soviet forces there to ensure the loyalty of these states. None of these governments could have survived without the presence of Soviet troops. By contrast, Iran, Turkey, and Greece invited American assistance because they feared Soviet pressure and intimidation. Soviet expansion meant their loss of independence; American assistance was designed to preserve it. If ever there was a defensively motivated expansion, it was the U.S. commitment in the eastern Mediterranean, which was followed by an even larger commitment to first revive and then defend the nations of Western Europe. All shared the U.S. perception of the Soviet Union as a threat to their political independence and territorial integrity and urged Washington to redress the post-1945 imbalance. Their concern was not U.S. expansion but a return to U.S. isolation.

The role of containment in American foreign policy was essentially to mobilize congressional and public support for the policy once it had been decided on. A nation that historically had condemned power politics as immoral needed a moral basis for its new use of power. For a people who were weary after four years of war, who identified the termination of war with the end of power politics, and who were historically accustomed to isolation from Europe's internal affairs in peacetime, the containment strategy served as a call to arms. The strategy fit neatly into the traditional American dichotomy of seeing the world as either good or evil, thereby arousing the nation for yet another foreign policy mission. President Truman was conscious of Americans' desire to retreat into isolationism after a war, and he was unsure they were ready to commit themselves to a potential conflict. The pressure for demobilization and a return to "normalcy"—isolationism—was strong in Congress. Thus Truman recognized the need to "sell" the public on the need for an activist foreign policy.

The Truman Doctrine in its immediate application was intended to be specific and limited, not global. American policy makers were well aware that the United States, although a great power, was not omnipotent; national priorities had to be decided carefully and power applied discriminately. American responses, then, would depend both on where the external challenges occurred and on how Washington defined the relation of such challenges to the nation's security. Containment was to be implemented only where the Soviet state appeared to be expanding its power. The priority given to balance of power considerations was evident from the very beginning.

Despite the democratic values expressed in the Truman Doctrine, it was first applied to Greece and Turkey, neither of which was democratic. Their strategic locations were considered more important than the character of their governments. In Western Europe, however, America's strategic and power considerations were compatible with its democratic values; containment of the Soviet Union could be equated with the defense of democracy. The United States thus confronted a classic dilemma: protecting strategically located but undemocratic nations, such as Iran, Turkey, and Greece, might make the containment of Soviet power possible, but it also risked America's reputation and weakened the credibility of its policy. Yet alignment only with democratic states, of which there were all too few, might make U.S. implementation of its containment policy impossible. The purity of the cause might be preserved, but the security of democracy would be weakened. This dilemma was to plague U.S. policy throughout the Cold War.

In summary, the emerging bipolar state system and the character and behavior of the Soviet Union were fundamental factors precipitating the Cold War. What, if any, was America's contribution to the onset of the Cold War? Perhaps at the time the United States could not have done more than simply protest the Soviet satellization of Eastern Europe. It was true that the American people, like the British, admired the heroic efforts of the Red Army in stopping and driving back the Nazi forces. Moreover, the staggering Soviet losses, compared with the relatively light losses of the Allies, were recognized in the West. In these circumstances, the hope for good postwar relations with the Soviet Union was understandable.

These optimistic projections, however, were quickly dispelled by events in Eastern Europe. As the United States proceeded with its withdrawal and military demobilization, Soviet leaders made it clear that their control over the region would be firm and anything but temporary. Thus the threatened states bordering the Soviet bloc, which were greatly weakened by the war, looked to Washington to exert countervailing power. The United States finally took the necessary measures to oppose Stalin and draw the lines beyond which Soviet expansion would not be tolerated. Stalin, incapable of defining the limits of his ambitions, now found that the United States would do it for him.

Members of the U.S. Army's Second Infantry Division search for communist-held positions during the Korean War. The conflict, which erupted in 1950, represented a direct challenge to the containment doctrine adopted by the United States in the late 1940s.

CHAPTER THREE

Containment: From Theory to Practice

Twenty-one years separated the two world wars, providing their combatants with time to recover from their losses, restore some semblance of domestic order, redefine their national interests, and prepare for future challenges. But that was not the case after World War II, which led directly to the Cold War. Even before the war was over, both the Soviet Union and the Western allies were posturing for spheres of influence in central Europe. And it was only six months after the Japanese surrender that Winston Churchill gloomily proclaimed that an "iron curtain" had descended across central Europe, defining the battle lines of the next global confrontation. If there was an "interwar" period in this case, it was hardly perceptible.

Fortunately for the United States the late 1940s were among the most imaginative years in U.S. diplomatic history. With the guidance of an unusually cohesive team of advisers, President Harry Truman transformed the nation's foreign policy so the United States could compete indefinitely as a political, economic, and military superpower. The "wise men" of the Truman administration established the basis of the Western strategy that ultimately prevailed in the Cold War.[1]

America's political leaders generally agreed that George Kennan's containment strategy was the most sensible response to Soviet expansionism in the aftermath of World War II (see Chapter 2). A retreat into isolation was not possible, particularly because U.S. withdrawal in the 1920s only provided encouragement to German and Japanese expansionists. Nor was it feasible to attempt to destroy the Soviet Union through a preemptive military strike. Representing a middle ground, the goal of containment seemed most consistent with the country's means.

The global scope of the challenge guaranteed that implementing containment would be a monumental task. The obstacles were especially great given the traditional American penchant for withdrawal and isolation from great-power politics in peacetime. Further hampering the United States was the lack of an institutional basis for dealing with a worldwide threat that was not likely to disappear or be defeated militarily within a few years. The U.S. government had maintained a permanent Foreign Service only since the end of World War I, and a standing army always had been viewed with great apprehension. But as this chapter describes, America's leaders overcame these obstacles and created a web of national security structures, bilateral ties, and multilateral regimes that transformed Kennan's theory of communist containment into practice.

In its first step, the Truman administration sought to revive its war-ravaged allies in Western Europe, which, from Washington's point of view, urgently needed to form a united front against the Soviet Union. Such a task would be impossible, however, if the historic internal rivalries among the European states were allowed to persist. The United States thus encouraged close cooperation among the European governments in rebuilding their economies, settling their political disputes, and protecting the region from external aggression.

But the United States could not stop with Europe. To contain communism it also would have to become actively engaged elsewhere. In the late 1940s and early 1950s, the Asian perimeter of the Soviet Union and China became a second target of U.S. containment. In contrast to Western Europe, many Asian states had only recently emerged from colonial-

1. Walter Isaacson and Evan Thomas, *The Wise Men: Six Friends and the World They Made* (New York: Simon and Schuster, 1986).

ism and their nationalistic and anti-Western feelings were very strong. The collapse of Nationalist China and establishment of a communist Chinese government on the mainland in 1949 particularly weakened the U.S. position in Asia. The United States, then, no longer confronted only the Soviet Union; instead it faced the combined strength of two large, heavily populated, militarily powerful communist states. And, whereas pressure on Europe united the Western powers, pressure on Asia divided them by producing a split over the character and nature of the new Chinese regime and the degree to which it threatened Western interests. In Washington, developments in Asia inspired a prolonged and heated debate between "Asia firsters" and those seeking to limit U.S. containment efforts to Western Europe. Events would propel the United States into action on both fronts.

NEW ECONOMIC AND MILITARY STRUCTURES

Unlike the situation confronting other great powers, U.S. military strength was greater *after* World War II than before the conflict, accentuated by the country's undiminished industrial capacity, its monopoly on nuclear weapons, and its global deployment of troops. Moreover, the U.S. economy had been strengthened by the war on an absolute basis and relative to those of its competitors, which were devastated physically and faced years of reconstruction. The United States accounted for nearly half of global output in the immediate postwar years, giving it unprecedented economic clout to match its military muscle.

An essential first step for the United States, then, was to convert its vast resources into the brick and mortar of government institutions. A globalist foreign policy required more than a grand strategy, no matter how widely supported the strategy was. American officials focused on two areas. First, they created an international economic system to support commerce among the capitalist states. Second, they rebuilt the country's military structures and created an elaborate web of alliances. Taken together, these reforms established the institutional blueprint that remained in place throughout the Cold War and endured in its aftermath.

THE BRETTON WOODS SYSTEM

Long before World War II ended, Western governments agreed that a new framework was needed to manage global economic relations. They recognized that trade restrictions, subsidies for national industries, and other forms of mercantilism had contributed to the Great Depression of the 1930s, which in turn had aroused nationalist passions and led to the birth of Nazi Germany. It was widely believed that a "liberal international economic order," based on open markets and economic cooperation and leading to the recuperation of the European industrial states, could prevent a recurrence of this pattern.[2] The market-based economic order also would reduce the appeal of communism by creating prosperous capitalist societies. But the latter goal was secondary to the former. Even before the Cold War, America's leaders had agreed that the country's economic prosperity, and global stability in general, depended on an integrated global economy that encouraged trade and investments across national borders.[3]

American officials welcomed the opportunity to replicate the U.S. economic model on an international scale. Along with European leaders, they devised a plan for international economic, fiscal, and monetary cooperation to be underwritten by the vast economic resources of the United States. In 1944 representatives of forty-four countries met at Bretton Woods, New Hampshire, to approve this plan, which already had been devised by American and British officials. The Bretton Woods system played a critical role in hastening the recovery of the industrialized states. Along the way, the new system strengthened the market economies against their communist rivals.

The Bretton Woods accords created three institutions to promote economic growth among the market economies. First, the International Bank for Reconstruction and Development (IBRD), or World Bank, would lend the funds needed by member states to rebuild their industries. The United States provided much of the World Bank's funding in the institution's early days, which it lent to member states on generous terms. As the recipients of World Bank funding recovered, which they did with surprising speed in the late 1940s and 1950s, they in turn contributed to World Bank programs designed to speed economic growth in developing countries, many of which were becoming free of colonial rule. Second, the International Monetary Fund (IMF) would govern currency exchanges and provide credits for member states facing short-term currency crises. To receive these credits, recipients were required to enact IMF provisions for government taxing and spending and for adopting "responsible" monetary policies. Members were thus prevented from simply printing more money to cover their deficits, a practice that had led to rampant inflation and the collapse of central banks in many countries during the 1930s. And third, the General Agreement on

2. An influential argument at the time was made by theorist Nicholas John Spykman in *America's Strategy in the World* (New York: Harcourt, Brace, 1942).

3. See Robert L. Pollard, *Economic Security and the Origins of the Cold War, 1945–1950* (New York: Columbia University Press, 1985).

Tariffs and Trade (GATT) would establish rules to promote open markets and greater commerce across state borders.[4]

The Bretton Woods system laid the foundation for a more integrated world economy. The stability of the market economies was maintained by a system of fixed currency exchange rates based on the U.S. dollar, which itself was based on the value of U.S. gold reserves at $35 an ounce.[5] The dollar thus became a world currency that provided reassurance to financial markets and a simple framework for trade and foreign investment. Once they had benefited from the Bretton Woods reforms, the Marshall Plan (described later in this chapter), and other assistance programs from Washington, U.S. allies in Western Europe and Japan were able to rebound quickly from World War II and enjoy unprecedented economic growth. Meanwhile, the Soviet Union continued to isolate itself from the market-based global economy, a move that had ominous implications for the outcome of the Cold War.

THE NATIONAL SECURITY ACT

As the Cold War set in, President Truman received strong congressional support to reshape the nation's military structures so they would be able to meet the demands of containing communism. Under the National Security Act of 1947, the formerly separate Departments of the Army and Navy were brought together in the new Department of Defense (DOD), a successor to the Department of War. Now the United States would have a *permanent* military establishment based on the general principle of national defense rather than war fighting. As part of the reorganization, the air force, a third branch of the military formerly controlled by the army, became an independent service. It soon overshadowed the two older services because its principal task was to organize the growing U.S. nuclear arsenal.

In addition, the act created the Central Intelligence Agency (CIA), an offspring of the Office of Strategic Services (OSS) which had gathered foreign intelligence and conducted secret spy operations during World War II. The OSS, widely considered a "rogue" operation that undertook secret missions around the world with little oversight, was disbanded immediately after the war. A larger intelligence operation than OSS, the CIA quickly became an essential, and controversial, part of America's containment effort. The agency was essential because it collected and

4. For a comprehensive historical review, see Harold James, *International Monetary Cooperation since Bretton Woods* (New York: Oxford University Press, 1996). For a more focused study of the creation of the Bretton Woods system, see Richard N. Gardner, *Sterling-Dollar Diplomacy in Current Perspective: The Origins and the Prospects of Our International Economic Order* (New York: Columbia University Press, 1980).

5. The United States held about 75 percent of the world's gold reserves at the time, amounting to about $25 billion.

analyzed information that became the basis of American foreign policy. It was controversial because it, in the tradition of the OSS, often carried out "dirty tricks" overseas and sought to subvert governments believed hostile to the United States.

Finally, the act established the National Security Council (NSC) to help the president coordinate foreign policy. Located in the White House, the NSC was composed of the president (its chair), the vice president, and the secretaries of state and defense. The head of the Joint Chiefs of Staff and the CIA director also often attended NSC meetings, along with other government officials whose advice the president sought. A small NSC staff was created to provide information to these leaders, and the national security adviser, a new position, was to serve as a "gatekeeper" and close confidant of the president. Through the NSC, the president gained greater control over U.S. foreign policy, in part by reining in departments such as State and Defense, whose leaders were widely suspected of being captives to their respective bureaucracies. And, no less important, the NSC became the primary crisis management agency for the president, a function that took on increasing urgency in the nuclear age.[6]

The concentration of foreign policy powers within the executive branch and the creation of a large, permanent military force ran counter to the nation's traditional style of foreign policy. Indeed, the Founders had deliberately constrained presidential powers and avoided standing armies in order to prevent the United States from behaving recklessly in foreign affairs. Their concerns were quickly overridden in the early days of the Cold War. Given the transformed role of the United States, such a fundamental shift was widely accepted as the price of world power.

REVIVING THE WESTERN EUROPEAN ALLIES

Europe's collapse after World War II raised anew a fundamental question that had bedeviled U.S. leaders since the nation's founding: Was European stability vital to U.S. security? America's interventions in the two world wars suggested the answer was obvious. But both times the United States had been drawn into the conflicts only after prolonged periods of hesitation and by threats of German domination of the continent. At the end of each conflict the United States had tried to regain its detachment from Europe, the almost pathological instinct of Americans dating back more than two centuries. After the Second World War, however, the United States was forced, for the first time, to establish an

6. See John Prados, *Keeper of the Keys: A History of the National Security Council from Truman to Bush* (New York: Morrow, 1991).

ongoing, multifaceted relationship with Western Europe because, in the precarious postwar order, America alone had the resources to take the initiative.

Europe's vital importance became especially clear in the emerging bipolar world. The region ranked second only to the United States in its collective economic power—in industry, productivity, and skilled workers, scientists, and engineers. Moreover, trading networks and cultural ties between the United States and Western Europe were long-standing and strong. And, not least, Western Europe critically represented a "buffer zone" between the two superpowers and thus occupied a crucial strategic position in the emerging Cold War. Given Western Europe's enormous potential and its geographic position, its stability was inseparable from U.S. security.

The war in Europe had devastated the economies of all its countries, winners and losers alike. Great Britain's state of postwar exhaustion, largely economic in nature, was symptomatic of the situation throughout Europe. An island nation, Britain traditionally depended on international trade for its livelihood. But the war had crippled its merchant marine industry and destroyed many of its factories. With the means of financing its imports all but gone, Britain had to increase its exports; indeed, just to maintain the 1939 standard of living it had to raise its exports by 75 percent. By December 1946 Britain had reached only its prewar level of production. Meanwhile, postwar conditions in Germany also were dreadful. The war had been carried into its heart, and few cities or towns had escaped Allied bombing, street fighting, or willful destruction by the Nazis as they retreated. Millions of people had no food or shelter. Three-quarters of the factories still standing in the American and British zones of occupation were closed. By January 1947 production had fallen to 31 percent of the 1936 level.

The Allies' postwar policy was not designed to alleviate Germany's economic woes. They were engaged primarily in disarming Germany and eliminating all industries whose output could be used for military production. In fact, the United States and Britain were not particularly eager to rebuild Germany's industrial power; after all, it had taken the combined efforts of three world powers to bring the Nazi war machine to a halt. Nor were the Allies especially concerned with the lot of the German people in the immediate postwar period. After six years of brutal warfare, such concern hardly could have been expected. The record of Nazi atrocities and crimes, wanton destruction, and slaughter of millions of innocent people in concentration camps was too appalling to be dismissed or forgiven.

The French, more than all others, were not in the mood to rebuild their huge, troublesome neighbor. The French economy had been damaged badly during the war; its iron and steel production had reached only half the prewar total by 1947. Unable to import coal from the other European states, French manufacturing industries were unable to produce sufficient goods to meet demand. Meanwhile, the urban population was short of food, and the government had to spend scarce resources to buy food from abroad. The harsh winter of 1946–1947 only intensified these problems.

This situation was made to order for the large, well-organized French Communist Party. One-quarter of France's electorate—practically the entire working class—voted for the communists just after the war. In Italy one-third of the electorate cast their lot with the party. The reason was simple: French and Italian capitalism had alienated the voters. The workers were, in effect, internal émigrés who voted communist to protest a system they felt had long mistreated them. Unlike workers in Britain and the United States, they had suffered all the hardships of capitalism while enjoying few of its benefits, such as good wages and social opportunities. As a result, the communist parties in France and Italy enjoyed a powerful position in regional politics and trade unions.

These difficult conditions forced American officials to respond immediately. It was obvious they could not limit their actions to a single area such as economic development, military defense, or political reform. Their response must be comprehensive, including all these areas, and dedicated to preserving Western Europe as the front-line of Cold War defense.

THE MARSHALL PLAN

With Western Europe on the verge of not only economic ruin but also political and social upheaval, everything seemed to force it into dependence on the United States. Most of the items needed for reconstruction and economic vitality—wheat, cotton, sulphur, sugar, machinery, trucks, and coal—could be obtained in sufficient quantities only from the United States. But short of food and fuel, with its cities and factories destroyed, Europe could not earn the dollars to pay for these products. Moreover, the United States was so well supplied with everything that it did not have to buy much from abroad. The result was an ominous *dollar gap*, a term that frightened Europeans; it denoted their dependence on the United States for recovery.

Because the United States could not permit the Soviet Union to extend its influence beyond the iron curtain, U.S. policy makers had to find a way to help Western Europe recover. The prescribed cure was a massive injection of dollars. Secretary of State George Marshall, stressing the economic cooperation required by the United States, called on the European states to devise a plan for their *common* needs and *com-*

mon recovery. The United States would furnish the funds through the European Recovery Program (later known as the Marshall Plan), but the Europeans had to assume the initiative and do the planning. The result was the Organization for European Economic Cooperation (OEEC), which estimated the cost of Europe's recovery over a four-year period to be $33 billion. President Truman asked Congress for $17 billion, but lawmakers cut the sum to $13 billion. The amount actually spent between 1948 and the end of 1951, when the program ended, was just over $12 billion. Britain, France, and West Germany received more than half of this amount.

The original offer by the United States was deliberately extended to *all* European countries, including the Soviet Union and the nations of Eastern Europe. If the United States had invited only the nations of Western Europe, it would have placed itself in a politically disadvantageous position in which it would have been blamed for the division of Europe and the intensification of the Cold War. Actually, had the Soviets participated, Congress probably would not have supported the Marshall Plan for two reasons: first, the costs would have risen astronomically because of the very heavy damage suffered by the Soviet Union during the war, and, second, hostility toward Moscow was growing stronger each day. The risk had to be accepted, however. It had to be the Soviets who, by their rejection of Marshall Plan aid, would be responsible for the division of Europe. Fortunately, Stalin failed to call the Americans' bluff. He refused the offer of assistance and ordered his clients in Eastern Europe to do likewise.[7]

Was the Marshall Plan a success? The results tell their own story. By 1950 Europe already was exceeding its prewar production by 25 percent; two years later this figure was 200 percent higher. British exports were doing well, French inflation was slowing, and German production had reached its 1936 peak. The dollar gap had been reduced from $12 billion to $2 billion. Europe's cities were being rebuilt and its factories were busy, its stores restocked, and its farmers productive. The Marshall Plan was a huge success, and at a cost that represented only a tiny fraction of the U.S. national income over the same four-year period. The Europeans themselves, of course, were primarily responsible for their achievements, but such a rapid turnaround would not have been possible without the Marshall Plan, which Winston Churchill called "the most unsordid act in history."

7. In place of the Marshall Plan the Soviet Union created the Council for Mutual Economic Assistance (CMEA) to provide economic assistance to the Eastern European governments. The actual aid extended by Moscow, however, was modest compared with that of the Marshall Plan.

ROOTS OF THE EUROPEAN UNION

In making American aid to Western Europe conditional on economic cooperation among the European states, the United States clearly was holding itself up as a model. The Economic Cooperation Act of 1948 called specifically for the creation of an integrated European market—much like the fifty American states were organized economically. America, it stated, was "mindful of the advantage which the United States has enjoyed through the existence of a large-scale domestic market with no internal trade barriers and [believed] that similar advantages can accrue to the countries of Europe." In official American opinion, economic integration was essential for Europe's recovery and for long-range prosperity.

Renewed fears of Germany's rising strength further stimulated efforts toward European integration. The specter of a fully revived Germany struck fear into most of its neighbors. The French, with their memories of the Franco-Prussian War (1870–1871) and both world wars, were particularly alarmed by the prospect. Germany's recovery, stimulated by America's response to the Cold War, posed a serious problem for Germany's partners: How could they hold Germany in check when it was potentially the strongest nation in Europe outside of the Soviet Union?

After Germany's unification in 1871, France had dealt with the greater strength of its aggressive and militaristic neighbor by forming alliances that could balance Germany's power. Because Britain usually preferred to retain a free hand, and because British interests were at times opposed to those of France, the French had relied primarily on continental allies. Before World War I they had discovered such an ally in Russia, and between the two wars they had found partners in Poland, Czechoslovakia, Romania, and Yugoslavia. None of these alliances had saved France, however. In both world wars British and American power (aided by the Soviets in World War II) had been the decisive factor in defeating Germany. After the Second World War and despite the extension of Soviet power into the heart of Europe, France still saw Germany as the enemy. Growing Cold War tensions, however, forced French leaders to distance themselves from the Kremlin and made it necessary to add Germany's power to that of the West.

The failure of the traditional balance of power strategy, in which a weaker power seeks to balance against a stronger one, led France to seek a new way to exert some control over Germany's growing power. French leaders found an imaginative means in European integration. Through the creation of a *supranational* community, to which Germany and other European states would transfer certain sovereign rights, German power could be controlled. Instead of serving national purposes, Germany's strength would serve Europe's collective purposes while its government regained some measure of regional credibility.

France made a bold move in the direction of a united Europe in May 1950, when Foreign Minister Robert Schuman proposed the formation of the European Coal and Steel Community (ECSC) composed of "Little Europe" (France, West Germany, Italy, and the "Benelux" countries of Belgium, the Netherlands, and Luxembourg). The aim of the Schuman Plan was to interweave German and French heavy industry to such an extent that it would be impossible to separate them. Germany never again would be able to use its coal and steel industries for nationalistic and militaristic purposes. War between Germany and France would become not only unthinkable but also impossible. The combination of the French and German coal industries would strengthen French heavy industry and create a Franco-German equilibrium within the ECSC. Economic integration would allow France to overcome its inferior industrial strength, caused primarily by its lack of energy sources.

In addition, French leaders eagerly anticipated a united Europe that would be independent of American pressure. Acting alone, France was too weak to pursue an active role in a world dominated by the two superpowers. Even in the Western coalition, the most influential European nation was not France but Great Britain. With Germany's recovery, its role in regional affairs would likely expand. By itself, France would remain dependent on its American protector, powerless to affect major Western policy decisions. A united Europe, with Franco-German unity at its core, was France's alternative to remaining subservient to the United States.

As the benefits of pooling heavy industry became clear, European leaders expected that other sectors of the economy would follow suit, possibly leading to political integration and the creation of a "United States of Europe." [8] They took a momentous step in this direction in 1957 when the six governments of "Little Europe" established the European Economic Community (EEC), more commonly known as the Common Market. Its objective was to join the countries together in an economic union. Members of the EEC agreed to eliminate the tariffs and quota systems that hampered trade among them and to abolish restrictions on the regional movement of goods, services, labor, and capital. In addition, they created a variety of governing bodies, including a European Parliament, to pave the way toward political unification.

Not surprisingly, the Soviet Union voiced strong opposition to the Common Market. A thriving Western Europe, economically prosperous

8. For an early elaboration of this "functionalist" approach to regional integration, see David Mitrany, *A Working Peace System* (Chicago: Quadrangle Books, 1966). Also see Ernst Haas, *The Uniting of Europe: Political, Social, and Economic Forces, 1950–1957* (Stanford: Stanford University Press, 1958).

and politically stable, not only would prove a powerful barrier to Soviet expansion, but also might threaten the status quo in Eastern Europe. The Western European societies were a magnetic attraction for the Soviet clients, especially when the gaps in living standards between the two blocs became evident. After Stalin's protests fell on deaf ears in the West, the Soviet leader redoubled his efforts to isolate Eastern Europeans and subject them entirely to Moscow's control.

MILITARY REARMAMENT AND THE NATO ALLIANCE

Soon after the Marshall Plan was launched it became clear that economic measures alone would not adequately counter Soviet expansion. In February 1948 the Soviets engineered a coup d'état in Prague, and—ten years after the Munich agreement and Adolf Hitler's subsequent seizure of that betrayed nation—Czechoslovakia disappeared behind the iron curtain. A few months later, in June, the Soviets challenged the postwar division of Germany that had left West Germany occupied by the Western powers, East Germany in Soviet hands, and the city of Berlin similarly divided. The challenge took the form of a Soviet blockade of West Berlin in an effort to dislodge the occupying Allied powers. It is not surprising that Western Europeans were alarmed by these overt acts of Soviet hostility. It suddenly became clear that a second prerequisite for Europe's continued economic recovery, along with regional integration, was military security.

The Europeans already had taken modest steps in this direction. In March 1947 France and Britain had signed the Treaty of Dunkirk to provide for their mutual defense against a threat to their security. A year later, Great Britain, France, the Netherlands, Belgium, and Luxembourg signed the Brussels Pact for their collective self-defense. Its members expected the system of collective defense, officially proclaimed the Western European Union, to attract American military support. They were not disappointed. In April 1949 these countries—along with the United States, Canada, Denmark, Iceland, Italy, Norway, and Portugal—created the North Atlantic Treaty Organization (NATO). The NATO treaty called for "continuous and effective self-help and mutual aid" among its signatories; an invasion of one "shall be considered an attack against them all." Former isolationist Arthur Vandenberg, chairman of the Senate Foreign Relations Committee, hailed the agreement as "the most important step in American foreign policy since the promulgation of the Monroe Doctrine."

The creation of NATO set a precedent for the United States. Long wary of "entangling alliances," especially with the European powers, the United States committed itself to an alliance in peacetime. It would not allow another gap in the balance of power, nor would it allow itself to become drawn into a war after it had begun. It would committ itself indefinitely to preserving the European balance. From Washington's perspective, NATO would serve two vital functions. First, in countering the Soviet threat the alliance would enhance the *collective defense* of its members against Soviet provocations. Second, by subordinating their military forces to the U.S.-led alliance, the Western European governments would defuse their internal rivalries, which had sparked both world wars. This function of regional *collective security,* though rarely emphasized by European and American leaders, played a vital role in their calculations.[9] When West Germany joined NATO in May 1955, the alliance's role in dampening internal tensions became even greater.

Like the Marshall Plan, the birth of NATO provoked the Soviet Union to respond in kind. Just after Germany's entry into NATO, the Soviets established the Warsaw Treaty Organization, comprising the Soviet Union and its seven satellite states in Eastern Europe (see Chapter 2). The Warsaw Pact, as it became known, was modeled on NATO, although the Soviet satellites played a relatively minor role in managing the alliance. Indeed, Eastern Europeans had little choice in the matter given that their governments were controlled by Moscow.

The creation and expansion of NATO were closely linked to the future of Germany, which bordered on the Soviet bloc. Germany had held the key to the European balance of power since at least 1870 when Prussia defeated France, Europe's preeminent land power, and established a united Germany. And Germany continued in that role even after its defeat in 1945. Given this crucial role, it was inevitable that the Soviet Union and the United States would clash over the future of Germany. As noted, Soviet troops occupied the eastern part of Germany, and the Allies controlled the western region. Late in the war, the leaders of the Soviet Union, Great Britain, France, and the United States had established a four-power Allied Control Commission to administer postwar Germany as a single unit. The occupying powers would, under the plan, control separate zones until a reformed German state could be created. But in practice this task proved impossible; the Allied and Soviet powers pursued very different goals in the occupied zones.

This stalemate produced the division of Germany along Cold War lines. The Allies, which had merged their territories, sought to create an independent, democratic, and economically viable West Germany based in Bonn. Meanwhile, the Soviet Union consolidated its hold over East Germany and installed a pro-Soviet government that would become part of the communist bloc in Eastern Europe. The Allies,

9. This dual purpose helps to explain NATO's persistence today, long after the collapse of its proclaimed adversary. See Steven W. Hook and Richard Robyn, "Regional Collective Security in Europe: Past Patterns and Future Prospects," *European Security* 8 (autumn 1999): 82–100.

which had decided to assist rather than punish their former enemy, benefited most from this arrangement. West Germany contained the great majority of Germany's population and the heart of its industrial power. East Germany possessed far fewer resources, and what little of value it retained after World War II was hauled away in boxcars to the Soviet Union.

RECURRING CONFLICTS OVER BERLIN

The Soviets reacted to the creation of a potentially strong West Germany by blockading West Berlin in 1948. Berlin, like Germany, was supposed to be administered by the four occupying powers, but the growing Cold War had divided the city just as it had Germany. Lying deep in East German territory, surrounded by Soviet divisions, the western half of the city was a vulnerable spot in which the Soviets could apply pressure on the Western powers. But the issue at stake was more than the Western presence in Berlin: it was Germany itself. Berlin, as the old capital of Germany, was the symbol of the ongoing conflict between the Soviet Union and Germany. Furthermore, if the Allies could be forced out of Berlin, German confidence in the United States would be undermined. The Germans would not attach themselves to a friend too weak or too fearful to protect them. Indeed, if American willpower crumbled under Soviet pressure, France and Britain also would lose confidence in the United States. Thus had it not been met, the Berlin crisis would have destroyed the evolving U.S. commitment in Europe and nullified U.S. efforts to create a transatlantic military alliance such as NATO.

The Soviet attempt to drive the United States out of Western Europe left Washington with little choice but to defend its position in West Berlin. To that end, Truman launched a continuous airlift of supplies to Berlin instead of attempting to puncture the blockade on the ground, which might have sparked armed conflict between the superpowers. The Soviets waited to see if the Western powers could take care of West Berlin's 2.5 million citizens indefinitely. It would require a minimum of 4,000 tons of food and fuel daily—an enormous amount of tonnage to ship in by air. But after 324 days the Soviets were convinced that the Americans and British were more than equal to the task. Although the total supplies did not immediately reach the 4,000-ton target, Western planes, landing at three-minute intervals, eventually flew in as much as 13,000 tons daily, or 60 percent more than the 8,000 tons previously sent in each day by ground transport. Faced with this colossal Allied achievement, the Soviets called off the blockade in May 1949.

The U.S. determination to hold Western Europe and not allow further Soviet expansion had been demonstrated. The West Germans saw clearly that they could count on America to protect them. The United

States had laid the basis for Germany's economic recovery through Marshall Plan funds. In NATO, West Germany would be given the sense of military security required for its economic reconstruction and political rehabilitation. Thus West Germany after May 1955 served as the base for the alliance's "forward strategy" in central Europe.

Later attempts by the Soviet Union to evict the Western allies from Berlin only strengthened West Germany's resolve and its stature within NATO. West Berlin hampered Soviet control of East Germany because in the 1950s thousands of young, skilled professionals left East Germany through West Berlin. Indeed, the real issue was the very survival of East Germany, whose repressive political system and unproductive communist economy had demoralized its population and provoked occasional unrest. If East Germany were to collapse, would Poland's restive population and other Eastern European states seize the opportunity to join the Western alliance? This certainly seemed possible, particularly after Hungary's attempt in 1956 to leave the Warsaw Pact was met with a violent crackdown by Soviet troops. Stalin's successor, Nikita Khrushchev, was left with an almost impossible task. His attempted reforms, designed to soften the hard edges of Stalinism, only encouraged dissent and threats to Soviet control over Eastern Europe. If the existence of West Berlin and West Germany made Khrushchev feel insecure about the status quo, the notion of a Europe united against the Kremlin made his apprehensions far greater.

From Khrushchev's vantage point, the stability of the Soviet position depended basically on destroying the freedom of West Berlin. To achieve this objective Khrushchev announced in November 1958 that in six months he would end the four-power occupation of the city. This ultimatum—the first Moscow had ever given the West—was clearly aimed at forcing the Allies to withdraw from West Berlin, thereby turning it into a "free city." In effect, though, the Soviets intended to incorporate West Berlin into East Germany. Moreover, if the Soviets could drive the Western powers out of Berlin, they would be able to shatter the NATO alliance and cut off the development of the Common Market before it gathered too much momentum.

In an effort to defuse the crisis, President Dwight Eisenhower invited Khrushchev to visit the United States in September 1959. His acceptance represented a tactical victory for the Soviets because Khrushchev knew that the summit meeting could raise fears among the NATO allies that the United States and Soviet Union would negotiate a separate agreement at their expense. This being said, Khrushchev's visit to the United States did have one positive result: the Soviets withdrew their threat to take unilateral action in Berlin in return for American willingness to negotiate at a four-power conference scheduled for May 1960 in Paris.

Shortly before the Paris summit, however, an event took place that shattered the conference after only one session and further postponed negotiations on Berlin. More than a thousand miles into Soviet territory, the Soviets downed an American U-2 spy plane loaded with photographic equipment for gathering intelligence data. American officials responded with considerable diplomatic ineptitude—first by lying about the U-2's mission and then, when the Soviets exposed the lie, by admitting that the American pilot had been taking aerial photographs of the Soviet Union. For the Soviet leader to let this pass would be like surrendering to the United States the right to violate Soviet territory. He therefore struck a belligerent pose in Paris, launching a blistering personal attack on Eisenhower and telling the president that he would not be welcome to visit the Soviet Union in June, as the two had previously arranged.

It was inevitable that the Berlin problem would continue after Eisenhower left office in January 1961. Khrushchev, who had earlier vowed to "bury" the West, remained confident that his country was powerful enough to acquire West Berlin. The new president, John Kennedy, met the Soviet leader in Vienna to convey to him America's determination to defend West Berlin. The Western presence in the city and the freedom of West Berlin were not negotiable. Kennedy said, "We cannot negotiate with those who say: 'What's mine is mine, and what's yours is negotiable.' " More specifically, he asked, if the West refused to meet its clear-cut commitments in Berlin, where would it meet them?

In the summer of 1961, Khrushchev, faced with America's hard-line position, ordered the construction of a wall through Berlin to separate the eastern and western parts of the city and eliminate the escape hatch for East Germans. More than 100,000 already had escaped to the West in 1961 alone. They added to the 2.5 million East Germans who had already migrated westward—20 percent of the country's population. The wall, which ended West Berlin's usefulness as a "showplace for Western capitalism," was allowed to stand by the United States and its allies. But Kennedy's refusal to withdraw remained firm, and the walled city of Berlin became the most vivid symbol of the protracted Cold War in Europe.

Overall, America's postwar strategy in Western Europe during the early phases of the Cold War accomplished its many objectives. The Truman Doctrine discouraged Soviet meddling in the domestic politics of America's allies. The Bretton Woods accords and Marshall Plan set Western Europe on the path to economic recovery, democracy, and social stability. Through NATO, the United States established a formidable military presence that further enhanced European security. Most of all, by drawing a clear line between the American and Soviet spheres of influence, the United States demonstrated that it was in Europe to stay.

CONFRONTING REVOLUTION IN EAST ASIA

Europe held strategic priority in the U.S. defense strategy of the early Cold War years; Asia was of secondary interest, as it always had been. In fact, the United States found Western Europe so vital to American security that it vowed that any Soviet move into the region would provoke an all-out clash with the United States and NATO. Moreover, it explicitly delivered this promise to Soviet leaders throughout this period. By contrast, no single area in Asia was thought to be worth the cost of total war. The region was too distant, its economies too peripheral to Western interests, and its political and social systems too distinct from those in the West. Yet as the United States undertook efforts to revive Western Europe, it also began to recognize that, to contain communism, it would have to channel its economic resources and combat forces to other parts of the world, including the Asian perimeter of the Soviet Union and China.

The collapse in 1949 of Nationalist China, on whom the United States was counting in the emerging Cold War, led to the establishment of the People's Republic of China (PRC) under the leadership of communist Mao Zedong. The communists' victory was quickly followed by China's annexation of neighboring Tibet, a treaty of friendship between China and the Soviet Union, and the invasion of South Korea by communist North Korea. The logic of George Kennan's containment strategy would be put to the test far from the iron curtain, as would the leadership of the United States in the emerging anticommunist coalition. American resolve required more than words. Concrete action was essential to sustain containment on a global scale.

THE CHINESE REVOLUTION

During World War II the United States had two goals in the Pacific: to defeat Japan and to help sustain the government of Nationalist China so it could play a leading role in protecting the postwar peace in East Asia.[10] At a meeting in Cairo in 1943 President Roosevelt and Prime Minister Churchill promised Chinese premier Chiang Kai-shek that all Chinese territories conquered by Japan would be returned to China after the war. In subsequent meetings, Western leaders awarded China one of the five permanent seats on the United Nations Security Council, along with the France, Great Britain, the Soviet Union, and the United States.

In typically American fashion, President Roosevelt and his advisers thought that the mere pronouncement of China as a great power could

10. See Herbert Feis, *The China Tangle: The American Effort in China from Pearl Harbor to the Marshall Mission* (New York: Atheneum, 1967).

actually convert it into one: one need only believe strongly enough in the desirability of an event for it to happen. Perhaps American policy makers also hoped that if China were considered a great power, it would behave like one. But American faith without a viable Chinese government was not enough to accomplish the task. In their desire to create stability in East Asia based on a Sino-American alliance, the Roosevelt and Truman administrations ignored the depth of hostilities between the Chinese Nationalists and communists, who at the time were engaged in a protracted civil war.

Already in control of large segments of northwest China before World War II, the communists had extended their sphere during the war by expanding into north-central China. Meanwhile, the pro-American Nationalist regime was losing popular support and disintegrating. The government had to fight for its very survival against the Japanese forces that occupied large areas of the country during World War II and the communists. Faced with both external and internal dangers, Nationalist leader Chiang Kai-shek had neither the time nor the resources to formulate and implement the political, social, and economic reforms China needed. His principal concerns were military: to stem the Japanese advance and maintain himself in power. The modernization of China—above all, the problem of meeting peasant aspirations—was strictly secondary.

Chiang's failure to appease the peasants, the vast majority of China's population, as well as the unchecked inflation and rampant corruption among government officials, proved fatal to his efforts to gain control of the country. A government whose principal social and economic support came from the landlords was unlikely to carry out reforms the peasants sought. These same peasants provided most of the conscripts for the army, whereas the eligible sons of the rich avoided military service because their families were able to bribe corrupt officials. In the same way, the rich avoided paying taxes. Thus Chiang's government, far from attracting the peasants, did its best to alienate them. As the government continued to lose popularity, it turned to repressive measures to hold its position. The resulting police and military crackdowns further alienated the people, ensuring a communist victory in the civil war.

Ultimately, it was the military struggle in China that played the key role in determining the outcome of the civil war and the communist victory. Gen. David Barr, head of the American military mission in China, summed up the situation succinctly: "No battle has been lost since my arrival due to lack of ammunition or equipment. Their [the Nationalists'] military debacle, in my opinion, can all be attributed to the world's worst leadership and many other morale-destroying factors that led to a complete loss of the will to fight."[11] Recognizing his defeat, Chiang withdrew to Taiwan (then called Formosa), an island lying one hundred miles off China's coast. In the fall of 1949 the leader of the insurrectional communist forces, Mao Zedong, proclaimed their victory and established the People's Republic of China.

In Washington, pundits and policy makers debated the question of whether the United States could have prevented the PRC's victory. The answer was "perhaps"—*if* American officers had taken over the command of the Nationalist armies; *if* the United States had been willing to commit large-scale land, air, and sea forces; and *if* the United States had been willing to commit even more financial aid than the approximately $2 billion it had contributed since its victory over Japan. But these conditions could not have been met. America's rapid demobilization had left it with too few forces either to supply the officers needed to direct the Nationalist forces or to intervene in China. The United States had only a modest standing army at home, even after the signing of the National Security Act. Nor were the American people in any mood to rearm and remobilize in the late 1940s. There was little enough sentiment in favor of "rescuing" Eastern Europe from Soviet hegemony—far less for fighting a war in China.

Nor could more economic aid have saved Chiang, whose corrupt and incompetent government was unwilling and unable to carry out the meaningful reforms China needed. By contrast, U.S. economic aid to Europe, the area considered most vital to American security, had a good chance of achieving its objectives. It would have been unwise under these circumstances to divert a large slice of the U.S. budget toward attempting to salvage a government that had lost the confidence of its own people. The power and wealth of the United States were, after all, not infinite; they had to be applied selectively. Areas of vital interest were to be the prime focus.

Looking beyond the communist victory in China, American officials were optimistic. Secretary of State Dean Acheson expressed his belief that, despite the common ideological points of view of the Chinese and Soviet regimes, they eventually would clash. Acheson predicted that Russia's traditional appetite for a sphere of influence in Manchuria and northern China would arouse Chinese nationalism. Thus Acheson warned the Truman administration and Congress that the United States "should not deflect from the Russians to ourselves the righteous anger and hatred of the Chinese people."[12]

11. U.S. Department of State, *United States Relations with China, with Special Reference to the Period 1944–1949* (Washington, D.C.: Government Printing Office, 1949), 358.

12. Dean Acheson, *Present at the Creation: My Years in the State Department* (New York: Norton, 1969), 356.

The implications of Acheson's point of view were clear. If the Chinese communists were genuinely concerned with the preservation of China's national interest, they would resist Soviet advances. Mao might become an independent communist leader like Yugoslavia's Marshal Josip Tito, who refused to join the Soviet bloc in Eastern Europe. If Mao proved subservient to the Soviet Union, however, he would lose the support of the Chinese people. His regime would be identified with foreign rule because he would appear to serve the interests of another power, not of China. The United States could only gain from the contradictions between communism and Chinese nationalism.

In short, Truman and Acheson sought in 1950 to do what the Nixon administration finally did in 1972—reconcile its ideological differences with the PRC, then drive a wedge between the two communist powers. The divide-and-conquer strategy seemed especially promising given the simmering tensions between Stalin and Mao, two strong leaders who distrusted one another despite their ideological affinities. Even as the two leaders signed a treaty of friendship in 1950, their mutual antagonism was apparent. But before the U.S. strategy could be tested, war broke out in another part of East Asia. The conflict on the Korean peninsula created a bitter gulf between the United States and the PRC that lasted for a generation.

HOT WAR IN KOREA

Mounting concerns within the Truman administration led to the release in April 1950 of the report known as NSC-68, a dire warning by the National Security Council about communist expansion beyond Europe. "The issues that face us are momentous, involving the fulfillment or destruction not only of this Republic but of civilization itself," wrote Paul Nitze, the primary author of the government report.[13] The report was designed to gain congressional approval for a major increase in U.S. defense spending. More important, the authors of NSC-68 sought to alarm the general public, whose support would be required for the escalation of the Cold War advocated in the report.

Events in East Asia quickly affirmed NSC-68's call to arms. The invasion of South Korea by North Korea in June 1950 provoked a military response by the United States, under the aegis of the United Nations, and represented the first test of George Kennan's containment strategy. More broadly, the Korean War demonstrated that the Cold War would occasionally become "hot," thrusting the superpowers into active hostilities all along the containment frontier.

13. Quoted from the report in Ernest R. May, ed., *American Cold War Strategy: Interpreting NSC-68* (New York: Bedford, 1993), 26.

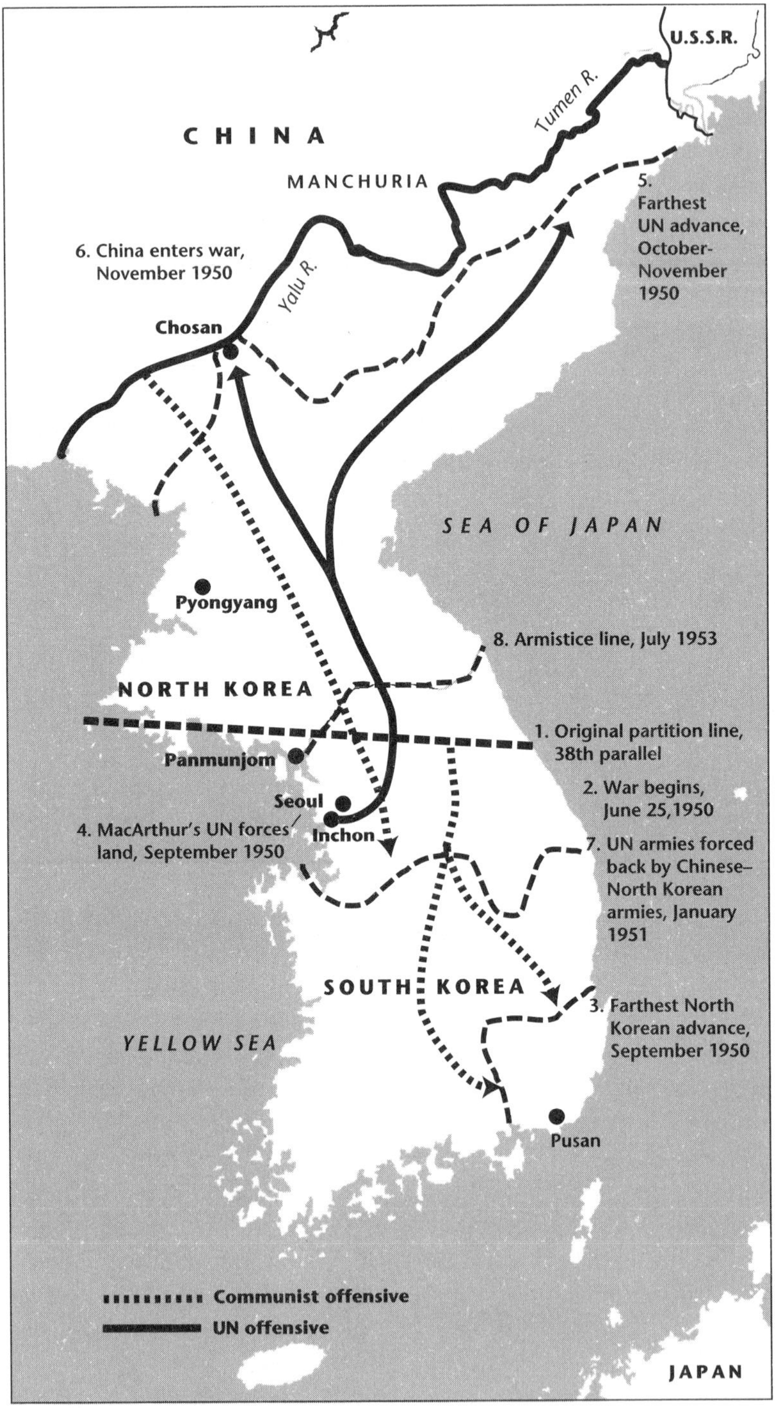
U.S.S.R.
Tumen R.
CHINA
MANCHURIA
5. Farthest UN advance, October-November 1950
6. China enters war, November 1950
Yalu R.
Chosan
SEA OF JAPAN
Pyongyang
8. Armistice line, July 1953
NORTH KOREA
1. Original partition line, 38th parallel
Panmunjom
2. War begins, June 25,1950
Seoul
4. MacArthur's UN forces land, September 1950
Inchon
7. UN armies forced back by Chinese–North Korean armies, January 1951
SOUTH KOREA
3. Farthest North Korean advance, September 1950
YELLOW SEA
Pusan
Communist offensive
UN offensive
JAPAN

THE KOREAN WAR, 1950–1953

Korea had been a divided country since the end of World War II. Under the terms of the postwar settlement, the Soviets would disarm the Japanese above the thirty-eighth parallel and the United States would take on the task below, thereby dividing the country until a new government could be established. With the beginning of the Cold War, however, this division became permanent. All American attempts to negotiate an end to the division and establish a united Korea failed.[14] The United States had taken the problem to the United Nations in 1947, calling on it to sponsor free elections throughout the Korean peninsula. The Soviets, however, refused to allow elections in North Korea, which had been transformed into a dictatorship, and thus only the South Koreans cast ballots. After the elections the United States recognized South Korea as the official republic and the government of Syngman Rhee as its legitimate representative. The Truman administration also extended economic, technical, and military aid to bolster his government. Although South Korea was not formally an ally of the United States, there could be little doubt that it was America's protégé.

Both the South and North Korean governments regarded themselves as the legitimate representatives of the Korean people, and each was dedicated to the reunification of the peninsula under its control. In that sense, the war that broke out when North Korea attacked South Korea on June 25, 1950, was a civil war between two regimes determined to eliminate each other. But it also was an international war because events in Korea after 1945 served as a microcosm of the Cold War rivalry. North Korea's invasion could not have occurred without Stalin's approval, which, according to evidence revealed later, was given in March 1949.[15] For reasons that have puzzled analysts ever since, South Korea was excluded from the American Pacific defense perimeter, which, as Acheson explained in congressional testimony, ran from the Aleutian Islands off the Alaskan coast to Japan, through the Ryukyu Islands (Okinawa) to the Philippines. Thus the absence of a clear American commitment, represented in Europe by NATO, turned South Korea into a vacuum for communist expansion. Not expecting the United States to intervene in these circumstances, Stalin assented to the North Korean invasion and offered Soviet assistance in the event of war.

The survival of South Korea became immediately identified with the security interests of the United States. North Korea's aggression altered the basis on which Korea's strategic significance had been originally cal-

14. See William W. Stueck, *The Korean War: An International History* (Princeton: Princeton University Press, 1995). Also see Bruce Cumings, *The Origins of the Korean War* (Princeton: Princeton University Press, 1981).

15. See Kathryn Weathersby, "The Soviet Role in the Early Phase of the Korean War: New Documentary Evidence," *Journal of American–East Asian Relations* 2 (winter 1993): 425–458.

culated. If the principal purpose of containment was to prevent further Soviet expansion, American inaction in the face of such an overt provocation would only encourage future aggressive acts. And if the United States stood by while South Korea fell, it would demonstrate to the world that the United States was either afraid of Soviet power or unconcerned with the safety of its allies. American guarantees to help preserve other nations' political independence would be regarded as valueless, leaving them with no alternative but to turn to neutralism for protection and to seek some form of accommodation with the Soviet Union.

At first, the United States tried to stem the North Korean advance using air and sea forces alone. But after a few days, Gen. Douglas MacArthur, the military commander in the Far East, reported that Korea would be lost unless ground forces were deployed to halt the advancing enemy army. In response, Washington ordered its occupation troops from Japan to Korea to participate officially in a multinational United Nations peacekeeping force. The UN's involvement in the conflict suited the United States because one of the aims of American foreign policy was to associate its Cold War policies with the humanitarian values and peacemaking functions of the United Nations.[16] Although countries traditionally had justified their policies in moral terms, the United States had shown a marked propensity for doing so. American power had to be "righteous" power, used not for purposes of power politics and selfish national advantage but for the peace and welfare of all people. All this being said, the war in its execution was an American effort, not one controlled by the world body.

After initial setbacks the war went well for the U.S.-led UN forces. On September 15 in a daring operation, MacArthur, now UN supreme commander, landed an army at the west coast port of Inchon, 150 miles behind the North Korean lines. These forces then drove northward, trapping more than half the enemy army. The rest of the shattered communist army was in flight. On September 30 the UN forces reached the thirty-eighth parallel. The question confronting the United States was whether to cross it. The political aims of the war were compatible with the restoration of South Korea; they did not require a total war and the elimination of the North Korean government or the unconditional surrender of its troops. But the military situation favored the fulfillment of an American goal of several years' standing: the unification of the Korean peninsula. Thus the U.S. government shifted its emphasis from containing the expansion of Soviet power to the forceful elimination of a

16. The Soviet Union was boycotting the Security Council at the time to protest the exclusion of the PRC on the council, a move that backfired by allowing the UN resolution to pass unanimously.

communist state. The result—North Korean retrenchment, Chinese intervention, and ultimate stalemate—was to teach the United States the foolishness of changing limited political goals in the middle of a war in response to battlefield successes.

The new objective of a militarily united Korea was sanctioned by a UN resolution on October 7. The Chinese viewed the resulting march to their border as threatening, just as Washington had felt threatened by North Korea's march southward toward Japan. So Beijing sent its armies into North Korea under the guise of "volunteers" and in late November launched a major offensive that drove the UN forces south of the thirty-eighth parallel. Throughout December 1950 and early January 1951 it was far from clear that UN troops could hold the peninsula, but they rallied and turned back the Chinese offensive. By March they had once more advanced to the thirty-eighth parallel. The United States was again faced with the decision of whether to seek a militarily unified Korea or accept the status quo, a divided Korea.[17]

There was no doubt about what MacArthur, articulating the traditional American approach to war, wanted to do. War, he said, indicated that "you have exhausted all other potentialities of bringing the disagreements to an end," and, once engaged, "there is no alternative than to apply every available means to bring it to a swift end. War's very objective is victory—not prolonged indecision. In war there is no substitute for victory." [18] MacArthur recommended a naval blockade of the Chinese coast; air bombardment of China's industrial complex, communications network, supply depots, and troop assembly points; reinforcement of his forces with Chinese Nationalist troops; and "diversionary action possibly leading to counter-invasion" by Chiang Kai-shek against the mainland.

The Truman administration rejected MacArthur's proposals as too risky. It feared that bombing China and defeating the Soviet Union's principal ally would lead to another global war. The Sino-Soviet treaty bound the Soviet Union to come to the aid of China if it were attacked by Japan "or any other state which should unite with Japan" (an obvious reference to the United States). Soviet self-interest in the Far East and the need to maintain Soviet prestige in the communist sphere would make it difficult for the Soviet Union to ignore a direct attack on the Chinese mainland.

Inherent in the administration's rejection of MacArthur's recommendations—and his dismissal from his post when he continued to

17. See Rosemary Foot, *A Substitute for Victory: The Politics of Peacemaking at the Korean Armistice Talks* (Ithaca: Cornell University Press, 1990).

18. Quoted in John Spanier, *The Truman-MacArthur Controversy and the Korean War* (Cambridge, Mass.: Belknap Press, 1959), 222.

push them—was the abandonment of the total-war objective of a unified Korea and the elimination of its government. Instead, the original limited aim of the war, the defense of South Korea, was reasserted. This goal also was compatible with the other principal political reasons for which the United States had gone to war: the defense of Japan and the preservation of the NATO alliance. Indeed, by the time the war ended in 1953, Japan had reclaimed its political independence as a U.S. ally, and NATO had been not only preserved but also strengthened by its own rearmament and the stationing of four American divisions in Europe. The wisest course therefore was to end the war where it had begun.

The truce talks that had begun in the summer of 1951 had produced nothing but a deadlock. The war was a drain on the United States and had to be ended. When Eisenhower took office in January 1953, he decided that if his efforts to gain an armistice failed, the United States would bomb Chinese bases and supply sources, blockade the mainland coast, and possibly use atomic weapons. It is doubtful, however, that the administration's threats were primarily responsible for the Chinese government's willingness to conclude the war in July. Other factors appeared more critical. Chief among these was Stalin's death in March. His successors called for "peaceful coexistence" with the West and tried to convince the noncommunist world that they wanted to relax international tensions. Agreement on an armistice would provide evidence of their goodwill. More important, the Soviets could not afford to risk an enlarged war at a time when they were engaged in a struggle among themselves to succeed Stalin.

The Korean War thus ended just where it had begun—at the thirty-eighth parallel—and on basically the same terms the Truman administration had been unable to reach. As a result, the Korean partition became part of the global dividing line between the communist and noncommunist blocs. In August 1953 the United States signed a mutual security pact with South Korea designed to deter another attack from the north, a pact that remained in place throughout—and beyond—the Cold War.

CONFLICT IN THE TAIWAN STRAITS

The line of containment also was drawn in the Taiwan Straits, where Sino-American relations had turned increasingly bitter and confrontational after the United States intervened in the Chinese civil war and China intervened in Korea. Soon after the Korean War ended, the PRC sought to eliminate its rival, the Nationalist Chinese government on Taiwan. In taking one step toward that goal, during the summer of 1954 it ordered its military to shell the Nationalist-held offshore islands of Que-

IMPACT AND INFLUENCE

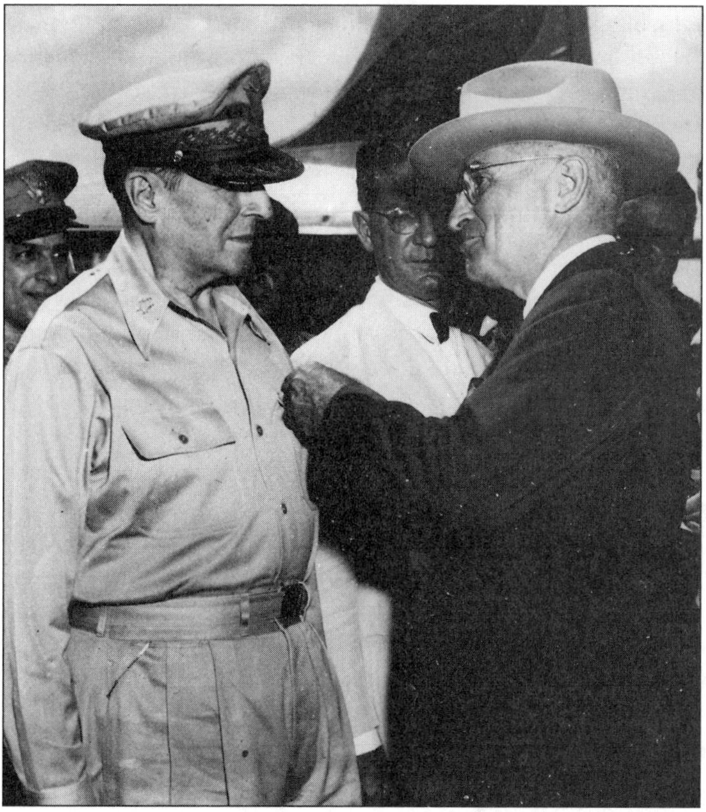

HARRY TRUMAN AND DOUGLAS MACARTHUR

The Korean War, which dragged on for more than three years, proved the undoing of many American leaders, including President Harry Truman (right) and Gen. Douglas MacArthur (left), commander of the United Nations forces. Prior to the war in Korea, Truman had effectively put George Kennan's containment policy into practice, but he was unable to overcome the domestic pressures produced by the war and Sen. Joseph McCarthy's crusade against suspected communists in the U.S. government. Thus Truman retired after his first full term ended in January 1953.

MacArthur, who had led U.S. forces in the Pacific region during World War II and oversaw the U.S. occupation of Japan, also was brought down by the Korean conflict. The strong-willed general clashed frequently with Truman and his advisers and was relieved of his duties in April 1951. Conservative Republicans urged MacArthur to run for president in 1952, as they had in 1944 and 1948. His refusal to do so opened the door for another war hero, Dwight Eisenhower. MacArthur spent the rest of his professional life in seclusion.

moy and Matsu, allegedly in response to Nationalist assaults against the mainland.

The United States and the Nationalists had signed a treaty of mutual defense in 1953 under which the United States guaranteed the security of Taiwan. In turn, the Nationalists pledged not to attack the mainland or to reinforce their offshore garrisons without the consent of the United States. While the offshore islands were not specifically included under the terms of the treaty, Washington viewed the PRC's escalating military campaign as another communist challenge to the U.S. position in East Asia. As a result, Eisenhower requested and received from Congress in January 1955 the authority to deploy American armed forces to protect Taiwan and "such related positions and territories" as the president judged necessary. Although the congressional mandate did not specify that the United States would defend the islands of Quemoy and Matsu, the communists certainly thought the United States might, and they abstained from any invasion attempts of these islands, which were within artillery range of the mainland. When in August 1958 the communists resumed shelling the offshore islands, the United States again supported the Nationalists and threatened to retaliate, with nuclear weapons if necessary. Once again, Mao halted the attacks.

As in Korea, the United States had established its commitment to defend a line of containment in East Asia, this time a few miles off the PRC's coast. Secretary of State John Foster Dulles later reaffirmed this line when he firmly rejected Chiang's calls to take back the mainland. American policy in the straits was committed to the preservation of the status quo. Each side should keep what it had and refrain from attacking the other. The Eisenhower administration thus recognized what neither it nor its predecessor had been willing to admit publicly before: that the Nationalists' expectation of recapturing the mainland was a fantasy. In so doing, the United States tacitly acknowledged the PRC as mainland China's de facto government.

In the Taiwan crisis the United States was able to support its position with air and sea power. Yet the possible use of nuclear weapons was mentioned—if it became necessary to defend the status quo. The nuclear threat, which also was invoked to end the Korean War, was, however, a bluff. For all of his talk of American readiness to use nuclear weapons in defense, Eisenhower had no intention of using them against China. As a military man he knew there were no appropriate targets, and as president he knew the use of nuclear weapons was not politically feasible. To drop a bomb once again on Asians would lead to condemnation from the whole world, including America's NATO allies. Thus while nuclear weapons made for dramatic threats, their military utility was limited.

DOMESTIC PRESSURES FOR A GLOBAL CRUSADE

The Chinese revolution and the Korean War dramatically altered American foreign policy in less than a decade after its conception in the wake of World War II. Whereas U.S. policy had been limited to containing Soviet power in Western Europe and the Mediterranean, it now spilled over into a broader anticommunist crusade.

The alleged "loss" of China initiated this change. Americans had regarded China as their special ward since just before the turn of the century. Their original interest in China had been not political but economic—China was a potentially huge market for American products. To that end, the United States had long regarded itself as the protector of China from foreign exploitation and invasion. This role had begun with the 1899 Open Door policy, aimed at preventing Great Britain, France, Russia, Germany, and Japan from shutting American commerce out of China. But, because the American people had never been prepared to fight for the objective of the policy, the United States failed to protect China from external pressures and invasions. The Russians had established a sphere of influence in Manchuria by 1900, and the Japanese replaced them after the Russo-Japanese War. During and after World War I, Japan expanded its influence and control over China and in 1931 began another war to further its ambitions. The Open Door policy was thus empty in practice. The result was the illusion that the United States had long been China's friend, extending to the Chinese people the benefits of Western power and coming to their rescue during World War II.

Americans were therefore shocked by the collapse in 1949 of Nationalist China and the establishment of communist control in the PRC, and they were unprepared for, and deeply resentful of, the propaganda emanating from Beijing accusing the United States of being "the Chinese people's implacable enemy . . . a corrupt imperialistic nation, the world center of reaction and decadence . . . a paper tiger and entirely vulnerable to defeat." They had expected that a "loyal" China, grateful to America for protection and help, would emerge from World War II as a strong friend and a powerful, reliable ally. The failure of these expectations came as a blow. Suddenly the security achieved by the containment policies in Europe—the Truman Doctrine, the Marshall Plan, the Berlin airlift, and NATO—seemed to have disintegrated. It appeared that the United States had stemmed the communist menace in Europe only to allow it to achieve a breakthrough in Asia.

The resulting insecurity and anxiety were further heightened by other developments. The first was the explosion in 1949 of the Soviet Union's first atomic bomb, which shattered the American monopoly on the weapon widely regarded as the principal deterrent against a Soviet attack. The second was the successful prosecution in early 1950 of Alger Hiss, a high-ranking U.S. government official during World War II, for perjury in connection with charges he had delivered classified U.S. documents to the Soviet government in the 1930s. The Hiss case was followed shortly by the confession of British scientist Klaus Fuchs that he had passed atomic secrets to the Soviets, apparently pointing to Soviet espionage in high places. The outbreak of the Korean War and communist China's subsequent intervention compounded America's sense of betrayal and anxiety.

At home, bipartisan support for U.S. policy in Asia was eroding. The conservative wing of the Republican Party had long been restless. In the past, these Republicans recognized, whenever the United States had been drawn into the international arena its actions had met with quick success. American forces had defeated the British, Mexicans, Spanish, Germans, and Japanese. And, unlike most other nations, the United States had never been invaded, defeated, or occupied. The nation's leaders had made many mistakes, but with their considerable resources and geographic advantages they had been able to rectify their missteps. America's history had witnessed only victories; the unbroken string of successes seemed to provide clear evidence of national omnipotence and "manifest destiny."

This unquestioned assumption suggested to Republicans the reason for America's failures: treason within its own government. If America was all-powerful, its setbacks must have been the result of its own policies. Ostensibly the reason China fell was that the "pro-communist" administrations of Franklin Roosevelt and Harry Truman had either deliberately or unwittingly "sold China down the river." This conspiracy charge, articulated by Republican senator Joseph McCarthy and supported by fellow Republicans Robert Taft and Richard Nixon (who became Eisenhower's vice president), was simplicity itself. America's China policy had ended in communist control of the mainland; the administration leaders and the State Department were responsible for the formulation and execution of foreign policy; therefore, the government must be filled with communists and communist sympathizers who "tailored" American policy to advance the global aims of the Soviet Union. Low morale among the Chinese Nationalists, the government's corruption and military ineptitude, and Chiang's repressive policies which had alienated the population had nothing to do with it. Nor did the communists' superior organization, direction, morale, and ability to identify with popular aspirations.

The State Department bore the brunt of this rhetorical onslaught; the attacks on its Foreign Service officers and regional directors and on Secretary of State Acheson himself were incessant. But the accusations, usually carried in the press, were not directed only toward the State Department or government officials. Academics and others also were charged as being security risks or were accused of being "un-American." Many of the accused were fired, and others—especially stage actors and Hollywood figures—were blacklisted. The political atmosphere during the 1950s bordered on national hysteria.

The most significant result was the transformation of U.S. foreign policy from a limited anti-Soviet orientation to a broader anticommunist crusade. To be sure, actions by the United States in the eastern Mediterranean and in Western Europe had been carried out in the name of anticommunism, but operationally those actions had been limited to countering Soviet moves. Washington had not hesitated to support communist Yugoslavia after its break with Moscow, and for a brief moment it had even predicted the likelihood of conflict between communist China and the Soviet Union. But for Republicans that was not enough. They accused Democrats of appeasement, of being soft on communism, of losing China, and of treason. In doing so, they paved the way for the election of one of their own to the presidency—Dwight Eisenhower.

The aim of U.S. policy now became to prevent any expansion by any member of the Sino-Soviet bloc. All communist states were considered enemies, regardless of size, location, or status—that is, tied to Moscow as satellites or existing as nationalist communist states (Yugoslavia and communist China) pursuing their own interests, even in conflict with the Soviet Union. Distinctions between America's vital and secondary interests, the importance of concentrating on the main adversary and not getting bogged down and wasting resources on conflicts with secondary threats, and the ability to distinguish communist regimes that represented a threat to American interests from those that did not—all were lost in the crusading spirit.

The United States paid a heavy price for the breakdown of bipartisanship, for McCarthy's charges of treason, and for the global anticommunist crusade that Nationalist China's collapse and the Korean War unleashed. But the even greater folly was that U.S. policy makers, now applying containment to the Sino-Soviet bloc, no longer seriously considered the possibility that Mao Zedong might become an independent communist leader, like Tito in Yugoslavia. Nor, therefore, did Washington any longer entertain the possibility that communist China might be used to contain Soviet power. Instead, for more than two decades the United States and China were bitter enemies because the United States felt compelled to contain both Soviet and Chinese power.

NUCLEAR STRATEGY AND THE 'BALANCE OF TERROR'

Nuclear weapons played a key role in the globalized struggle against communism. The fear of nuclear annihilation by the United States was expected to discourage the Soviets and Chinese from crossing the line. In the early 1950s Moscow had a very limited capability to reach the United States with nuclear weapons; Beijing had none. By contrast, the bomber forces controlled by the U.S. Strategic Air Command (SAC) were growing rapidly and could strike both communist powers from a variety of overseas bases.

In short, nuclear weapons were not so much designed to be used, but to serve the vital function of *deterrence* against communist attacks on the United States and its key allies.[19] A U.S. promise to respond to communist expansion with "massive retaliation" against population centers as well as military installations would presumably make Soviet and Chinese leaders think twice. Nuclear weapons also made possible a reduction in overall military expenditures. In addition to his credentials as a war hero, President Eisenhower was a fiscal conservative, and he was impressed by the ability of nuclear weapons to give the United States "more bang for the buck." For this and other reasons, Eisenhower assigned nuclear weapons a prominent role in his restructuring of U.S. security policy, labeled the "New Look." In the future, U.S. military forces would rely less on conventional forces—which cost a great deal to train, equip, and maintain—and more on nuclear firepower.

Above all, massive retaliation was consistent with America's style of foreign policy, a style that traditionally was based on a worldview of mutually exclusive conditions: war or peace, force or diplomacy, aggressors or peace-loving states. Peace was normal; war was abnormal. Force was not necessary in the absence of conflict and hostilities; it was to be used only in wartime to destroy the source of war itself. Massive retaliation, then, fit this American approach completely. It was an all-or-nothing strategy that could not be used short of a Soviet attack on the United States or Western Europe. At the same time, American presidents consistently rejected preventive war, both at the time of the nation's atomic monopoly and later, during the 1950s and 1960s, the period of gradually declining strategic superiority. Deterrence was the American goal; nuclear weapons would be used only after the opponent had struck

19. See Alexander George and Richard Smoke, *Deterrence in American Foreign Policy: Theory and Practice* (New York: Columbia University Press, 1974). For a recent critique, see Joseph S. Nye, *Understanding International Conflicts: An Introduction to Theory and History* (New York: Longman, 2000), 136–138.

first. If the United States were attacked, however, it would punish and destroy the enemy in ways not conceivable until 1945.[20]

In one sense, then, atomic weapons, and the more destructive hydrogen weapons that soon followed, enabled the United States to pursue an old American dream in a new and perverse way. By making nuclear war too destructive to fight, by making the distinction between victor and vanquished in such a conflict meaningless, the deterrent strategy aimed at eliminating war itself. The old American dream had been sought in vain through Woodrow Wilson's crusade to see that World War I would be the "war to end all wars," through international organizations, and through free trade and economic interdependence among nations. That dream could now be realized because war had become unthinkable: a balance of power would be punctuated by a "balance of terror."

For all his talk about giving American foreign policy a "new look," Eisenhower adopted a policy that was in effect not really that different from Truman's. Eisenhower sought not merely to contain communism but to extend containment beyond Europe by drawing a frontier around the Sino-Soviet periphery and supporting that frontier with nuclear weapons. Yet in one essential aspect the Eisenhower administration's policy was quite different—and this difference was critical. Truman had relied on nuclear power to deter an attack on either the United States or America's "first line of defense" in Europe, but he had met the challenge of limited communist aggression in Asia with ground troops. The Eisenhower administration also expected to deter an all-out war with the threat of massive retaliation, but it declared it would not fight local ground wars. Presumably this meant it planned to deter any future limited attacks by threatening to retaliate against the Soviet Union or China.

This basic policy decision reflected Secretary of State Dulles's strong conviction that the only effective means of stopping an invasion was to give fair warning of what constituted aggression and to make clear that the punishment for an attack would far outweigh any possible military gains. Dulles believed the communists would not have invaded South Korea had they known their attack would be met with retaliatory air strikes on Moscow. It was the absence of such a warning that had led North Korea to act. The Eisenhower administration did not intend to repeat this mistake. It meant to draw the line so clearly that the enemy would have no doubt about the consequences of crossing the line. The

20. See Lawrence Freedman, *The Evolution of Nuclear Strategy* (New York: St. Martin's Press, 1989), 83–88. Also see John Lewis Gaddis, *Strategies of Containment: A Critical Appraisal of Postwar American National Security Policy* (New York: Oxford University Press, 1982), chap. 5.

expectation was that by going to the "brink of war," the United States would be able to deter future Koreas.[21]

In the recurring crises of the early Cold War period, American leaders learned several lessons that were essential to preserving the line around what was then still viewed as a cohesive Sino-Soviet bloc. The first lesson was that the advent of nuclear weapons left no alternative to peace. However destructive, a conventional war distinguished winners from losers and, with time, both recovered from the human losses and the destruction of their cities and industries. But a nuclear war was likely to be suicidal; all participants would lose and no recovery would be possible. Total war, in short, had become irrational because the cost of war was disproportionate to any conceivable gains.

The United States, the Soviet Union, and the PRC were all very aware of this historic change in the nature of warfare. The world wars had been extremely costly; warfare now had become prohibitive. For that reason, policy makers in all major capitals, while on occasion talking tough and even threatening to go to war and use nuclear weapons, were extremely careful in the conduct of policy to ensure that confrontations were resolved diplomatically, even if they involved public retreat and humiliation. Such an outcome was better than military escalation that might lead to a nuclear holocaust. Thus despite massive retaliation and the talk of "brinkmanship," the United States did not credibly invoke the threat of nuclear war. The Soviet Union also remained extremely cautious even while its words were reckless.

A second lesson of the nuclear arms race was that mutual deterrence was not automatic. Indeed, advancing technology might upset the stability of the deterrent balance. Simply possessing the bomb was insufficient; the key to a *stable* deterrent balance was an invulnerable retaliatory force. If country A's forces were vulnerable to attack by country B, A might be tempted to strike B preemptively rather than have its forces caught on the ground. In the late 1950s and early 1960s the Soviets claimed they were mass-producing missiles that made American bombers vulnerable. If true, this would have meant that the credibility of U.S. deterrence had declined. Such developments affected the calculations of policy makers in Moscow and Washington whose adherence to the principle of "mutual assured destruction" (MAD) was essential to preventing a nuclear cataclysm.

In this environment the survival of U.S. nuclear forces became central not only to the nation's security, but also to that of its allies, which were protected by the "extended" deterrent of U.S. and NATO nuclear

21. See Richard H. Immermann, *John Foster Dulles and the Diplomacy of the Cold War* (Princeton: Princeton University Press, 1990).

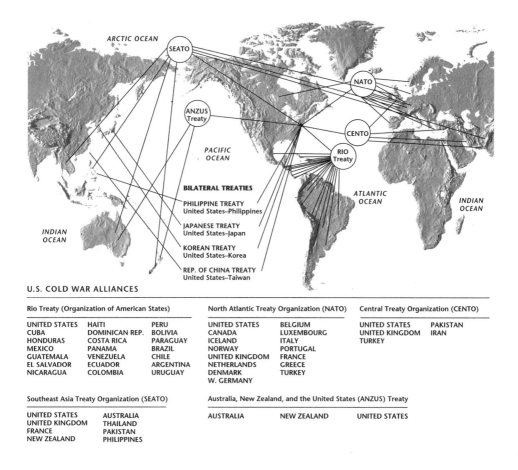

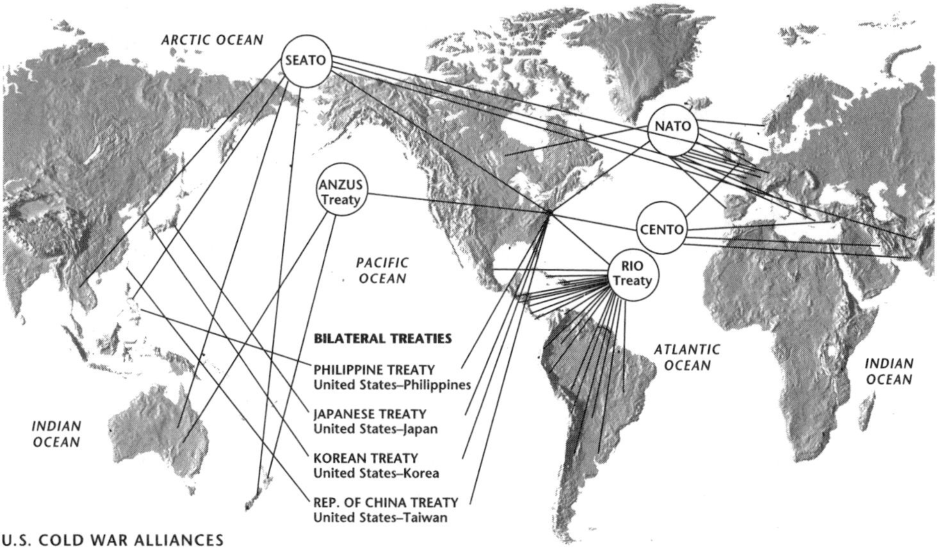

U.S. COLD WAR ALLIANCES

Rio Treaty (Organization of American States)

UNITED STATES	HAITI	PERU
CUBA	DOMINICAN REP.	BOLIVIA
HONDURAS	COSTA RICA	PARAGUAY
MEXICO	PANAMA	BRAZIL
GUATEMALA	VENEZUELA	CHILE
EL SALVADOR	ECUADOR	ARGENTINA
NICARAGUA	COLOMBIA	URUGUAY

North Atlantic Treaty Organization (NATO)

UNITED STATES	BELGIUM
CANADA	LUXEMBOURG
ICELAND	ITALY
NORWAY	PORTUGAL
UNITED KINGDOM	FRANCE
NETHERLANDS	GREECE
DENMARK	TURKEY
W. GERMANY	

Central Treaty Organization (CENTO)

UNITED STATES	PAKISTAN
UNITED KINGDOM	IRAN
TURKEY	

Southeast Asia Treaty Organization (SEATO)

UNITED STATES	AUSTRALIA
UNITED KINGDOM	THAILAND
FRANCE	PAKISTAN
NEW ZEALAND	PHILIPPINES

Australia, New Zealand, and the United States (ANZUS) Treaty

AUSTRALIA	NEW ZEALAND	UNITED STATES

forces. In recognition of this situation, the Eisenhower administration sought to disperse the nation's nuclear forces in a "triad"—ground-based launchers, aircraft, and submarines—so that the weapons were less vulnerable to a surprise attack. The goal of protecting nuclear forces thus became as crucial as their production. Preserving deterrence was a continuing, never-ending task, not simply because some change in the balance might precipitate war, but because shifting strategic balances might affect the risks each side was willing to take.

Given the vital importance of leaders' perceptions of the nuclear balance of power, the nuclear rivalry assumed a psychological as well as strategic dimension. This became especially clear as the Soviet Union accelerated its nuclear programs and reached parity with the United States in a number of key categories. The Soviet Union tested the world's first intercontinental ballistic missile (ICBM) in August 1957, then launched the first man-made satellite, *Sputnik,* two months later. This development, in particular, shocked the United States and its allies; they had long taken their technical superiority for granted. Although the United States maintained its technological edge in the production, deployment, and accuracy of nuclear weapons, the Soviet Union caught up in terms of the sheer destructive capacity (or throw-weight) of its nuclear forces.

The growing symmetry of nuclear forces led to an alteration of the strategic calculus. Whereas the United States had previously sought to exploit its nuclear advantage over the Soviet Union by threatening massive retaliation, the prospect of a devastating Soviet counterstrike made such threats less credible. As a result, the nuclear arms race reached the point of mutual assured destruction, a strategic stalemate that shifted the Cold War in new and unexpected directions. To many, the acronym MAD perfectly expressed the superpower arms race.

Finally, the early Cold War crises further revealed the extent to which military power, nuclear and conventional, would be used to protect "frontiers" across the globe. These frontiers were clear: along the inter-German border and through the middle of Berlin; at the thirty-eighth parallel in Korea; along the coast of China; and along the southern tier of Asian states from Turkey to Iran and Pakistan. Any attempt by communist forces to cross these frontiers, either openly by direct attack or covertly by guerrilla warfare, risked Western retaliation.[22] Conversely, the United States could not seriously entertain hopes of "rolling back" communist gains in Eastern Europe and elsewhere, despite the pledges frequently made by American leaders to do so.

Because the lines of containment drawn outside of Europe were extremely tenuous, revealed by North Korea's attack on South Korea, the U.S. government sought to clarify matters by creating a network of bilateral and multilateral alliances that would more explicitly define the containment belt. In doing so, American leaders departed even further from the nation's traditional aversion to "entangling alliances." In addition to NATO, the United States pledged in 1947 to defend the countries of the Western Hemisphere through the Inter-American Treaty of Reciprocal Assistance. The Rio Treaty, as it became known, was followed a year later by the creation of the Organization of American States, in which twenty-one countries in the region extended their cooperation beyond collective security. In 1951 the United States joined with Australia and New Zealand in creating the ANZUS alliance in the Pacific. Individual security guarantees also were extended to Japan, the Philippines, Taiwan, and

22. American leaders secretly deployed nuclear weapons along much of this frontier during the peak of the Cold War, transporting the missiles far beyond Western Europe to such front-line Asian states as South Korea, Taiwan, and the Philippines. See Robert S. Norris et al., "Where They Were," *Bulletin of the Atomic Scientists* 55 (November–December 1999): 26–35.

South Korean as "pactomania" took hold among American military planners.

This process of alliance building, however, proved more difficult than originally expected. The Southeast Asia Treaty Organization (SEATO)—established in 1954 by the United States, Britain, France, Australia, New Zealand, the Philippines, Pakistan, and Thailand—and the Central Treaty Organization (CENTO)—established in 1959 by the United States, Britain, Iran, Pakistan, and Turkey—were alliances in areas where nationalist forces opposed them. As a result, the alliances had little popular support in those regions, even within member states. When these states sought to maintain the containment walls, they were often unable, despite American help, to mobilize popular support.

Indeed, the United States may have been better off had it not created what turned out to be poor replicas of NATO, which existed in a region where its people supported containment against clearly perceived potential external aggression. The less-successful alliances were organized in developing regions where containment was widely perceived as an attempt to preserve Western influence and prop up authoritarian regimes. America's containment strategy thus encountered greater difficulties as its geographic scope widened, a pattern that became painfully evident in the developing world during the 1960s and 1970s.

Congolese refugees seek aid from UN peacekeepers during the African country's civil war in 1961. The conflict became enmeshed in the Cold War as the United States and Soviet Union intervened in behalf of rival armies in the former Belgian colony.

CHAPTER FOUR

Developing Countries in the Crossfire

The globalization of the Cold War in the early 1950s elevated four areas of the world to major power centers: the United States, Soviet Union, Western Europe, and People's Republic of China. "In all four," one scholar observed at the time,

> productivity is on the increase, and the political system performs relatively well its integrating and decision-making functions. Despite major differences among them . . . these four areas are likely to be in a position to play major roles in political, economic, and cultural international affairs in the coming decade. In contrast, the Middle East, Southeast Asia, tropical Africa, and Latin America are apt to

remain power vacuums during this period, owing to their lack of unity, political instability, economic stagnation, and cultural heterogeneity. It seems highly improbable that ten years from now any of the areas mentioned above will cease to be, respectively, a power center or a power vacuum.[1]

During the 1950s and 1960s, which witnessed the liberation of many European colonies in Africa and southern Asia, U.S. leaders became increasingly anxious about the unstable political and economic conditions that accompanied the birth of the new nation-states in the emerging "Third World." [2] The evolving membership of the United Nations confirmed the importance of these countries. In 1946 the United Nations had 55 members; in 1955, 76 members; in 1970, 127 members; and in 1980, 160 members. By 2000 UN membership exceeded 185. The vast majority of these member states (and most of the world's population) were in developing regions. In the UN General Assembly, with its principle of one country–one vote, these member-states could—and would—dominate the agenda.

In the bipolar context of the Cold War the developing countries did not represent an independent center of power but rather an object of competition for the two superpowers, each seeking the support, if not the allegiance, of Third World leaders. During their early years of independence, however, most former colonies refused to align themselves politically and militarily with either superpower. Among their first collective efforts was the establishment of a "nonaligned movement" and the assertion of their independence from Washington and Moscow, an effort that in most cases proved futile.

Communist leaders saw decolonization as proof that the international capitalist order was disintegrating. The colonial powers such as Great Britain and France had maintained capitalist economies that, according to Marxist-Leninist theory, depended on captive overseas territories for raw materials and export markets. This theory found it equally significant that World War I and the Great Depression occurred only after capitalist states had exhausted their opportunities for colonial expansion.[3] Given this perception of history, Soviet and Chinese leaders saw an opportunity to embrace and support the new states. Their overtures were frequently well received and appealed to the understandable hostility within many developing countries toward their former colonial rulers.

1. Guy J. Pauker, "Southeast Asia as a Problem Area in the Next Decade," *World Politics* (April 1959): 325.

2. Although the term *Third World* obscures the regional diversity among developing countries, for political leaders and most scholars of the period the term served to differentiate these largely impoverished states from northern capitalist countries—the *First World*—and communist countries—the *Second World*.

3. This argument was made by the first leader of the Soviet Union, Vladimir Lenin, in *Imperialism: The Highest Stage of Capitalism* (New York: International Publishers, 1939).

From Washington's very different perspective, the challenge of Soviet and Chinese communism in the developing areas stemmed not from conspiracy or military control but from the repressive model of development that communism offered the developing countries. The Soviet Union held itself up as a model of a primitive feudal society that had been transformed into a modern industrial state in one generation. Overlooked, however, were the force, massive terror, and staggering human costs associated with that accomplishment. Joseph Stalin's forced collectivization of Soviet agriculture resulted in the death of more than ten million peasants (*kulaks*), either through the purges and mass murders of Stalin's opponents or through the crushing famine of the early 1930s.[4] The Soviet leader waged an undeclared war throughout the period against non-Russian minorities in the Soviet Union, particularly Muslims, and his security forces brutally suppressed leaders of the once-flourishing Christian churches. The inefficiencies, corruption, and social exhaustion produced by the central planners further pulled the Soviet Union into a political and economic spiral from which it never returned.

An even greater number of Chinese peasants died under Mao Zedong's reform efforts, particularly the "Great Leap Forward" initiated in 1958. In the years that followed, the Chinese leader forced the huge population of peasants into huge agricultural collectives and then ordered them to produce steel and manufactured goods as well as commodities. In the end, though, his bizarre experiment produced mainly chaos and a massive famine, bringing China's agricultural and industrial production to a crashing halt.[5] Then, in the mid-1960s, Mao launched a "Cultural Revolution" against his enemies and dispatched thousands of Red Guards to harass, torture, and kill those who strayed from his "mass line." Teachers, artisans, and intellectuals were the primary targets, but the crackdown included anyone who was suspected of having sympathy for, or any contact with, Western values. The social upheaval that resulted further isolated China from most foreign countries and produced a sullen, resentful population that persisted long after Mao's death in 1976.

Despite these disastrous attempts by the Soviet Union and China at social engineering, U.S. leaders worried that the heads of poor countries might decide that the potential benefits of communism outweighed its social costs. Compounding their anxiety, the atrocities being committed

4. See Robert Conquest, *The Great Terror: A Reassessment* (New York: Oxford University Press, 1990).

5. See Frederick C. Teiwes, *China's Road to Disaster: Mao, Central Politicians, and Provincial Leaders in the Unfolding of the Great Leap Forward, 1955–1959* (Armonk, N.Y.: M. E. Sharpe, 1999).

under Stalin and Mao were generally unknown outside those closed societies; all that was conveyed publicly was the promise of mass liberation. In this context U.S. policy makers believed that the economic model the developing countries chose to adopt was critical to U.S. security and, more broadly, to an international environment safe for open societies and democratic values. Thus American offers to help the new countries establish a basis for economic growth stemmed not just from a humanitarian concern for the countries' long-suffering populations, but also from recognition that their progress toward prosperity and political stability would lessen the appeal of communism and prevent the global balance of power from shifting against the United States and its allies.

OBSTACLES TO POLITICAL AND ECONOMIC DEVELOPMENT

The Western powers, including the United States in the Philippines, had justified their imperial domination in terms of bringing the "backward" peoples of the earth the benefits of Western democracy, medical science, and technology. It was the "white man's burden," or duty, to educate the people so that one day they could govern themselves. The colonial powers apparently had taught their lesson well, but in a perverse way; they had ruled their colonies autocratically while proclaiming the virtues of democracy. The nationalist movements later used the same democratic ideals to challenge their rulers and ask them to practice what they preached. Indeed, many leaders of these movements, who often were educated in Europe or the United States, fought the colonial rulers by using the principles of democracy and national freedom they had learned. For them, these principles were incompatible with imperialism and a rationale for wars of "national liberation."

Once these countries became independent, they confronted a legacy of poverty, illiteracy, and disease. In the 1950s, for example, the annual per capita income of these states rarely reached $100, and life expectancies seldom exceeded fifty years. To remedy their distress, and to narrow the enormous gap between poor and rich nations, many new countries sought to transform their traditional agrarian societies into modern industrial states. This transformation also had great political significance, for it demanded that citizens transfer their allegiance from their local communities and the ethnic and religious groups that had held their loyalty to their new nations. The fact that the concept of national loyalty was largely unfamiliar to the citizens of the newly independent countries intensified the need to satisfy the popular "revolution of rising expectations." The fledgling states had to prove they could offer their people something not otherwise attainable. By achieving improved standards of living, their leaders would demonstrate that they deserved the popular support and allegiance they needed to survive and grow.

THE POPULATION EXPLOSION IN DEVELOPING COUNTRIES

In considering their prospects for economic development, leaders of the new countries realized their success depended on whether their economic growth would advance faster than their population growth. In 1830 the world population was one billion; by 1930 it had doubled to two billion, and by 1975—just forty-five years later—it had doubled again to four billion. In October 1999 the global population surpassed 6 billion. According to the best estimates, the world's population will continue to grow, to almost seven billion by 2010 and to more than eight billion by 2020. Just as developing countries represented a majority of nation-states by 1970, their share of the world's population also grew dramatically so that in 1995 nearly 80 percent of the world's population lived in the developing world.[6]

The concern among leaders of rich and poor countries alike in the 1950s and 1960s was that, despite the expected slowing of population growth rates sometime in the twenty-first century, developing countries would face the dilemma described by the Reverend Thomas Malthus two centuries ago. Simply put, Malthus predicted that growing poverty and human misery would result in countries where population growth exceeded economic growth. To Malthus, who also was an economist, this fate would be inevitable unless population growth was limited either by "positive checks" such as wars or epidemics, which result in high death rates, or by "preventive checks" such as family planning, which produce low birthrates.

In the West, birthrates did decline after 1850; with industrialization and the growth of cities came the spread of literacy and birth-control techniques. Indeed, the fate Malthus anticipated for the West did not materialize because preventive checks were adopted, with many industrialized states achieving zero population growth by the late twentieth century and some facing the prospect of *declining* populations. But developing states, in which improvements in health care raised life expectancies, did not reach a comparable level of economic development. Meanwhile, family-planning programs confronted an array of obstacles and spread more slowly than had been expected. The poorer

6. Population Reference Bureau, *1995 World Population Data Sheet* (Washington, D.C.: Population Reference Bureau, 1995).

the populations were in developing countries, the higher were their rates of population growth.[7]

In contrast to the developing countries, the West had made impressive economic progress after the Industrial Revolution of the late eighteenth century, despite a population increase. Improved harvesting techniques provided plentiful food, and industrial advances raised living standards to heights never before attained. The conditions facing developing countries, however, were quite unlike those found in Western countries. One chief difference was that the Western countries had far smaller populations when they began industrializing, and their population growth did not outpace economic growth. But India, for example, began its modernization with a population of 350 million, a number that exceeded 1 billion by the end of 1999. China, with a population of 547 million in 1950, was home to 1.3 billion people when the twenty-first century began.

As for feeding populations, the European states also reaped the benefits of the industrial age and of their colonial empires, which provided them with outlets to relieve their population pressures. Indeed, about 60 million Europeans emigrated during the nineteenth and early twentieth centuries. By the 1950s about 400 million people of European descent were living outside Europe. The United States and Canada, rich in resources and fertile land, easily absorbed millions of immigrants and still increased their living standards. Australia, New Zealand, and South Africa also expanded their populations and economies, though on a smaller scale. By absorbing a population that might otherwise have led to overcrowding in Europe, the colonies added materially to the European nations' wealth. Upon their independence, however, the developing countries were not able to find such empty, rich spaces to absorb their burgeoning populations.

New farming technologies increased food production in the industrialized countries, whose temperate climates were often more favorable to agriculture than the harsh climates prevalent in many developing countries. The former colonies often had few resources with which to adopt modern means of agricultural production. Even so, some developing countries experimented with intensive farming techniques. Using high-yielding crop varieties, improved but costly chemical fertilizers, and more effective pesticides, the so-called Green Revolution increased

7. Whereas the population growth rates of industrialized countries averaged 0.2 percent in 1995, the growth rates of developing countries averaged nearly 2 percent, with many of the world's poorest countries in sub-Saharan Africa recording growth rates well over 3 percent. For an elaboration of this trend, see Richard J. Tobin, "Environment, Population, and the Developing World," in *Environmental Policy in the 1990s: Reform or Reaction?* ed. Norman J. Vig and Michael E. Kraft (Washington, D.C.: CQ Press, 1997), 321–344.

food production enough in these countries to keep up with their population growth. By the 1990s, a handful even exported food. Still, many could not feed themselves. As a result, life expectancies fell between 1980 and 2000 in many poor countries, particularly those in sub-Saharan Africa.

FINANCIAL OBSTACLES TO DEVELOPMENT

With the exception of a few newly industrialized countries such as Taiwan and South Korea, most developing countries during the Cold War decades of the 1950s and 1960s failed to match economic development to their fast-rising rates of population growth, much less surpass them. To make matters worse, people tended to cluster in large urban centers that were unable to provide critical public services such as medical care, education, law enforcement, electrical utilities, and sanitation. Under these conditions, mass frustration often led to social unrest and political upheaval, which only further diminished the prospects for economic growth.

Many of these countries were burdened not only with too many people but also with inadequate capital. Sufficient internal savings could not be squeezed out of people living at a subsistence level—at least not without authoritarian controls. As for earning capital through trade—particularly exports of primary products or raw materials—the developing countries discovered that such exports often limited their earning capacity. Because their economies remained tied to their former colonial rulers and other industrialized states, their exports rose or declined with every fluctuation in Western prosperity. If a major Western recession reduced the demand for certain commodities, exporting states suffered a crippling economic blow. Furthermore, markets often became glutted with certain commodities. A state trying to raise its national income by increasing production found its competitors doing the same, which lowered world prices further. Another problem was that the Western industrial states, whose demand for raw materials was supposed to furnish the capital for economic development, no longer needed the developing countries to the degree anticipated because of the emergence of synthetic substitutes and changing consumer habits. The lack of stable commodity prices combined with technological innovations to limit the prospects of financing industrialization through the export of raw materials.

Foreign investment was another possible source of funding for economic development. In the first years after independence, however, private capital was in short supply for the kind of long-range investment needed by the developing countries. Private American investments outside the United States consisted largely of those made by a small group of oil companies to build refineries and to develop oil fields in the Middle East and Latin America. Most investment capital stayed home because of the boom the American economy experienced for most of the Cold War period. This situation also characterized European investment, which was concentrated on rebuilding, modernizing, and expanding the continent's industrial base. Moreover, any American capital that did go abroad, other than that earmarked for the oil industry, went primarily to the Western European countries, where it returned sizable profits.

Because the leaders of developing countries often associated capitalism with colonialism, they refused foreign investment and greater involvement in global trade and capital markets. Even so, economic growth was the principal task of these countries. Their leaders soon realized, however, that this was not just an economic undertaking; it was a political, social, and cultural undertaking as well. Indeed, economic development was a revolutionary process frequently marked by political instability and violence rather than by evolutionary, peaceful change.

TENSIONS BETWEEN NATIONALISM AND STATE BUILDING

One reason for this instability was that, as noted earlier, most of the new states lacked administrative and political cohesion. Their populations often had no common culture or language; ethnic and regional conflicts abounded. Citizens also had no natural loyalty to their newly created states, whose boundaries were frequently drawn crudely along colonial frontiers, and no tradition of cooperation was in place except on the one overriding issue of eliminating the colonial ruler. Once the struggle for independence ended, power tended to fragment. India, for example, split violently into Hindu and Islamic regions after independence, and the latter dissolved further into Pakistan and Bangladesh. The Belgian Congo fell apart when the Belgians withdrew (a situation described later in this chapter), and Biafra broke away from Nigeria, only to lose the subsequent civil war. Cyprus divided into Turkish and Greek factions, which resulted in partition and an endless United Nations peacekeeping presence.

Even where actual disintegration did not occur, religious, linguistic, and racial differences tended to tear apart the fabric of those states that lacked any history of unity. In 1972, for example, the Tutsi tribe in the African nation of Burundi slaughtered more than 100,000 Hutus, initiating a cycle of violence that reached a more horrifying scale in 1994, when half a million Tutsis were slain in Burundi and neighboring Rwanda. Sri Lanka, a large island lying just off the southeastern coast of India, was immersed in almost constant bloodshed between the Hindu Tamils

AFRICA IN 1945

and Buddhist Sinhalese. On the thousands of islands that formed the newly independent country of Indonesia, the government's first order of business was conquering and pacifying the Timorese and other ethnic minorities that were trapped within Indonesia's vast political boundaries. Despite these crackdowns, the fragmented peoples of these regions remained more loyal to their national identities than to the countries that ruled them.

The absence of a strong sense of state identity was soon reflected in the way many of the leaders of the new countries built themselves up as symbols of nationhood. They did not find this essential task difficult because, as leaders of the movements for independence, their prestige was usually high. Indeed, just as Louis XIV had proclaimed, "*L'état, c'est*

AFRICA TODAY

moi," they too *were* the state. Without their presence as its symbol, the nation would not hold together as a unit. One-party rule or military governments existed almost everywhere in the developing world. For example, in Africa, the world's last continent to be freed from colonialism, three-fourths of its 345 million people lived under single-party or military rule by 1970, ten years after independence.

Such regimes were highly undemocratic, but political leaders believed them to be justified and necessary. Most people in the new states felt less loyalty to the government than to their ancestors, families, villages, churches, or ethnic groups. Under these circumstances, an American-style democracy would have led not just to a change of government but to the disintegration of the state. Thus the alternatives facing the leaders of these countries often were not democracy or dictatorship but statehood or disintegration. The dual pressures of consolidating power at home and resisting foreign domination "helped ensure that leaderships willing and able to build up centralized coercive and administrative organizations would come to the fore." [8]

The political and revolutionary context of development also was revealed in the nature of nationalist revolutions, which directed their wrath not only against colonial rulers but also against traditional governing elites if they remained in power after independence. Many developing countries were split into three main groups when they gained independence. The first was the ruling minority, usually composed of landowners or merchants, whose vested interest lay in preservation of the status quo. Their wealth and power derived from continuing to export their natural resources rather than striving to become economically independent. The second group included peasants, villagers, small artisans, and shopkeepers—the vast majority of inhabitants, whose energies were spent largely on the day-to-day struggle for survival. This group, which had for centuries borne its hardships silently, arose and demanded a better life. The third group, the urban intelligentsia, educated in Western ideas and committed to nationalism and development, voiced its resentments against the old way of life and sought to transform the existing societies. Without such social change—that is, the overthrow of the old ruling elites—development was inhibited.

Domestic debates in these countries quickly moved beyond "reform" to revolution because of the crucial and competing interests at stake. Yet the fundamental question remained: Who could, or should, control the emerging nation-states? The ruling elites committed to the preservation of the traditional order, or those who sought its abolition? Only one thing was certain: few leaders who possess the instruments of power yield their dominant position without a struggle.

THE REVOLUTION OF RISING EXPECTATIONS

Social unrest occurred even where economic development was under way, where national bonds had not disintegrated, and where a reform-minded elite was in control. This instability stemmed from a standard of living that, while improving, did not improve rapidly enough to create a satisfied population.[9] Historically, capital for investment was sought in many poorer countries by keeping wages low, which, in turn, allowed the reinvestment of the capital saved into further economic expansion. In

8. Theda Skocpol, *States and Social Revolutions: A Comparative Analysis of France, Russia, and China* (Cambridge: Cambridge University Press, 1979), 286.

9. See Ted Robert Gurr, *Why Men Rebel* (Princeton: Princeton University Press, 1970).

the newly independent countries higher wages and mass consumption were postponed in favor of "capital formation" and economic expansion. Thus although living conditions may have improved slowly over time, they could not overcome rising expectations.

Once the populations of developing countries realized they no longer had to live in the poverty of the past, that change was possible, and that people could create a better life through their own efforts, their dissatisfaction grew. This gap between their expectations and achievements was particularly aggravating when the rulers lived in luxury. Those living less comfortably became frustrated, and their frustration spawned social discontent and an increasingly hostile and radical mood. In many cases, their wrath was directed not only toward their governments, but also toward the United States and other industrialized countries that supported their leaders.

Social instability and turmoil were further propelled by the intellectual and cultural changes that accompanied the transformation of a traditional, static, rural society into a modern, dynamic, urban-industrial state. Many of the old customary and religious values that had provided some measure of social stability simply collapsed. People became disoriented, torn from their age-old moorings for which they had not yet found a substitute. Their precolonial traditions had provided cultural meaning for their lives; robbed of this, they became isolated and insecure in a rapidly changing environment that they neither made nor comprehended. In short, people had to forget many of their old ways and adapt to new conditions. In the best of circumstances these changes were difficult and agonizing. In other cases they produced social revolutions that often brought new regimes to power—and turned back development efforts.

The Iranian people, for example, experienced this kind of upheaval in late 1978 and early 1979: their religious leaders opposed the American-backed shah, leading to his overthrow and the establishment of an Islamic theocracy.[10] Precisely because economic development was associated with secular values, few in the West took seriously the possibility of the Ayatollah Ruhollah Khomeini's succession. The idea of a religious icon coming to power was so at odds with contemporary ideas of modernization that the likelihood of such an outcome was dismissed as preposterous. But for the poor and the powerless in a rapidly changing society where tradition and customs were being eroded, often by forces alien to the indigenous population, religion retained a strong attraction and comfort.

10. See Said Amir Arjomand, *The Turban for the Crown: The Islamic Revolution in Iran* (New York: Oxford University Press, 1988).

Confronting an amalgam of political, social, and cultural changes, developing countries in the 1960s were uncertain they could climb what the economist Robert Heilbroner termed the "great ascent."[11] In this context, the Soviet Union and China were willing to present themselves as models of development. To people suffering from chronic hunger and poverty, it may not have mattered that the Soviet Union had advanced economically by brutally squeezing the necessary sacrifices out of the people, or that Maoist China had modernized its system of agriculture at the cost of tens of millions of lives. "Command" economics would at least provide the organization and efficiency to extract the sacrifices from the masses and the discipline to hold the nations together, to speed up the pace of their cultural revolutions while controlling social tensions produced by the early stages of development, and to depose ruthlessly the traditional ruling classes blocking progress.

To many in the developing countries, communism offered a disciplined means of bringing about rapid political, social, economic, and cultural changes. The beneficiaries of this system supposedly were not the rulers, to whom communism offered a means of seizing power and legitimizing dictatorial rule, but the mass populations who had labored for centuries without receiving a significant share of the wealth they produced. Communism, either in the Soviet (Leninist) or Chinese (Maoist) forms, thus promised an egalitarian form of economic growth with the benefits of development redistributed fairly among all segments of the population. The emphasis was to be on internal development and the detachment of the developing countries from a global market that, according to neo-Marxist thought, benefited the "core" Western capitalist states and perpetuated the dependency of "peripheral" developing countries.[12]

These arguments appealed to the leaders of many developing countries, who sought to create a "new international economic order" that would be less dependent on the wealthy industrialized states. In the United Nations, the developing countries formed the Group of 77 to serve as a catalyst for promoting their economic interests. Given their

11. Robert L. Heilbroner, *The Great Ascent: The Struggle for Economic Development in Our Time* (New York: Harper Torchbook, 1963).

12. Influential works during the period included Immanuel Wallerstein, *The Modern World-System: Capitalist Agriculture and the Origins of the European World-Economy in the Sixteenth Century* (New York: Academic Press, 1974); Gunner Myrdal, *Economic Theory and Underdeveloped Regions* (New York: Harper and Row, 1971); and Andre Gunder Frank, *Capitalism and Underdevelopment in Latin America: Historical Studies of Chile and Brazil* (New York: Monthly Review Press, 1969). For a more recent assessment, see Immanuel Wallerstein, "The Inter-State Structure of the Modern World-System," in *International Theory: Positivism and Beyond*, ed. Steve Smith et al. (Cambridge: Cambridge University Press, 1996), 87–107.

numerical superiority in the UN General Assembly, the developing countries expected to control the UN's agenda, dictate the structure and goals of UN agencies, and, through their strength in numbers, force the industrialized states to meet their demands.

But this would not be so easy. Many Western scholars and political leaders insisted that the economic development of developing countries would stem from their integration in, not their isolation from, the market-based economic order established by the Bretton Woods system. Although authoritarian rule might be necessary in the short term to ensure stability, economic growth would pave the way for political reform.[13] For these analysts, global markets were the engine for economic growth, and they rejected the claims of neo-Marxist critics that the governments of capitalist states were merely the puppets of business interests. To the contrary, they optimistically predicted that, with the assistance of industrialized states, the developing countries would evolve through predictable "stages of growth" into modern, industrial, democratic societies.[14]

To make this happen, the industrialized countries agreed to contribute a fixed share of their gross national product (GNP) for development aid. In 1969 the World Bank's Pearson Commission endorsed a minimum contribution of 1 percent of GNP, a figure that was lowered to 0.7 percent by the United Nations and widely accepted by the governments of industrialized states. Western aid was intended to close the gap between rich and poor states, modernize the new nations, satisfy their rising expectations, and create socially stable societies. This process, in turn, was expected to establish democratic governments and a more peaceful world by giving developing countries the means for sustained economic growth.

But in practice these aid flows benefited the donors as much as the recipients. After the eruption of the Korean War, most U.S. economic aid was, in fact, military aid, especially since "economic" aid could free up funds for military spending. Moreover, after Western Europe's recovery, most U.S. aid was channeled to pro-U.S. regimes that were not among the world's poorest. These recipients included Turkey, Pakistan, South Vietnam, South Korea, and, in the 1980s and 1990s, Israel and Egypt. Meanwhile, Britain and France disbursed foreign aid primarily to their former colonies, prompting charges of "neocolonialism," while Japan offered large-scale aid only to its neighbors in East Asia so they could

13. See Samuel Huntington, *Political Order in Changing Societies* (New Haven: Yale University Press, 1968). For a critique, see D. Michael Shafer, *Deadly Paradigms: The Failure of U.S. Counterinsurgency Policy* (Princeton: Princeton University Press, 1988), chap. 3.

14. See W. W. Rostow, *Politics and the Stages of Growth* (New York: Cambridge University Press, 1971).

pay for Japanese exports. Wealthy countries that actually offered aid to countries based on objective measures of human need were few and far between. Sweden and Denmark, for example, became respected "aid citizens," but they provided far less development aid than the larger industrialized countries.[15]

The self-interests underlying the U.S. aid program were widely apparent in developing countries, and their leaders became increasingly cynical about the proclaimed U.S. effort to raise global living standards. American policy toward the developing countries suffered from three other liabilities as well. The first was that American dollars were all too often offered with the explicit or implicit assumption that the recipients would associate themselves with U.S. Cold War policies. Even if they did not formally ally themselves with the United States, the aid recipients should thank Washington for its generosity, praise it for the morality of its anticommunist stand, and certainly refrain from criticizing its actions. The United States was reluctant to give foreign aid to countries that would not join its anticommunist crusade. But in these developing countries, the basic aspiration was to concentrate on internal improvements, to raise the standard of living and strengthen independence, and to minimize any involvement in the Cold War. Most, therefore, sought to remain above the fray.[16]

In preferring a nonaligned position, the leaders of many developing countries believed they were following America's example. After all, after the United States had gained its independence, it too had avoided "entangling alliances" and occupied itself with internal developments. As a developing country, the United States had been aware that its newly realized independence meant little without economic and political strength. Moreover, the United States had just thrown off the shackles of colonialism; its citizens had no desire to be once more tied to European powers. But American policy makers, especially during the 1950s and 1960s, forgot that it was the United States that had set this example.

The second liability that hampered U.S. policy toward the developing countries during the early Cold War was its own racial discrimination. The persistent segregationist practices and exploitation of blacks flagrantly violated the democratic principles of freedom and human dignity so often proclaimed by the United States. Conditions in the United States began to change, however, during the 1960s. As African Americans heard the Reverend Martin Luther King Jr. articulate their aspira-

15. See Steven W. Hook, *National Interest and Foreign Aid* (Boulder: Lynne Rienner, 1995).

16. Although Soviet leaders vowed to provide large volumes of foreign aid to developing countries, they were prevented from doing so by their own economic problems. Chinese leaders also were preoccupied with improving living standards within their borders.

tions for a life of greater dignity and fuller participation in American society—and as the ghettos exploded after King's assassination—the U.S. government sought to curb racial discrimination. But racial problems continued to haunt the United States overseas. In Rhodesia (now Zimbabwe) and South Africa, minority white-controlled governments, determined to stay in power, used abhorrent methods to control and exploit the majority black populations. The United States, despite its oft-expressed disapproval of these policies, did not follow through with action. American firms imported Rhodesian chrome for years despite a UN embargo. And American companies in South Africa, given a green light by the U.S. government, continued to support that country's *apartheid* (strict racial segregation and discrimination) policy through their foreign investment. America, the world's first nation-state to proclaim that all men were created equal, ignored its own principle as a matter of course.

Third, and more fundamental, U.S. relations with many developing countries were hampered by America's poor understanding of class struggle and social politics. "Born free" as a bourgeois democratic society, America had managed to avoid the kinds of domestic conflicts over basic values that the countries of Europe had experienced and that plagued many developing countries. The United States had not experienced a genuine social revolution at its birth, one that seeks to destroy the institutions and social fabric of the old society and create a new society with new institutional and social class arrangements. Despite its self-proclaimed revolutionary character, the United States was, according to Sen. William Fulbright, chairman of the Senate Foreign Relations Committee from 1959 to 1974, a nonrevolutionary, conservative country.[17] America, then, was not particularly sympathetic to revolutions and tended to equate revolution with communism. Deviations from middle-class American values were likely to be condemned as "un-American" and sinful, to be rooted out so that the "American way of life" would remain pure and unadulterated.

Indeed, the principal challenges to these values had come not from within the system but from outside the U.S. borders, and the United States reacted to foreign threats in two ways. Internally the government hunted subversives, a procedure that violated civil liberties and endangered the security of traditional freedoms. Externally, government policy aggressively sought to achieve the destruction of the hostile regime so that American principles could survive untainted. Thus, as already noted, the real or imagined communist threat in the early 1950s led to

17. J. William Fulbright, *The Arrogance of Power* (New York: Vintage Books, 1967), 72–73.

McCarthyism, a search for heresy in which the goal of eliminating alleged un-American attitudes and behavior justified any means, including disregard for due process of law, the basic guarantee of all civil liberties. In foreign policy the reaction to the communist threat was to support almost any regime, no matter how repressive, if it claimed to be anticommunist. As a result, the United States often allied itself with governments whose days were numbered; Chiang Kai-shek in China, Bao Dai in Indochina, and Ferdinand Marcos in the Philippines were but three of many examples.

This attitude was typical of America's self-righteousness and its inability to understand the deeper social struggles of the Third World. In its attempt to contain communism—that is, to preserve the global status quo—the United States became committed to the domestic, social, and political status quo in these regions. In trying to preserve freedom, the United States was paradoxically supporting ramshackle anticommunist autocracies that were unrepresentative of their peoples' aspirations. But this internal contradiction within the U.S. alliance system eventually had to resolve itself. American support for "traditional" regimes only bottled up the social and political resentment and ferment even more, thereby adding to the explosive forces that would burst forth during the Cold War and in its aftermath.

REGIONAL CONFLICTS IN AFRICA AND THE MIDDLE EAST

During the 1960s and 1970s, the domestic transformation of the developing countries had repercussions beyond their borders. The upheavals tended to disturb an international system largely defined by the frontiers drawn between the two superpowers' spheres of influence. When the internal difficulties of the developing countries spilled over into neighboring states, or when they resulted in political disintegration and civil war, they attracted the Soviet Union or the United States, leading to confrontation and, often, military conflict.

The two superpowers were attracted to conflicts in developing nations because such friction could either bring to power a group one superpower liked and the other disliked or result in regional expansion and influence that could be perceived as benefiting one and hurting the other. If one superpower was unwilling to tolerate what it considered to be, in terms of the overall balance of power, a local or regional setback, it would intervene. Or, if it feared that if it did not intervene then its opponent might, the result might be preventive intervention. In both cases it risked a similar move by its opponent. Looking to the future, Guy Pauker observed in 1959: "Power vacuums are likely to disturb international relations increasingly. They are the natural targets for power centers wishing to extend their hegemony. They should be the object of anxious attention for those powers which want to strengthen the international balance."[18]

NATIONAL DISINTEGRATION AND CIVIL WAR IN THE CONGO

If a new nation-state disintegrates into two or more parts, those who seek to reunify their land or establish new splinter states may appeal for help to sympathetic states that, for reasons of their own, may wish to see either a nation preserve its unity or a splinter state establish its independence. Such appeals were addressed especially to the Soviet Union or the United States in the early years of the Cold War.

One of the more dramatic examples of the way the survival of a new state involved the superpowers occurred in 1960 when the Belgian Congo became independent. Almost immediately the Congo fell into disorder. First, the rich mining province of Katanga, which provided the copper and cobalt exports that were a major source of revenue for the Congo, split off into a separate state. Katanga's president had the support of the powerful Belgian mining interests, eager to protect their investments. Then the Congolese army began to revolt because it resented the continued presence of its Belgian officers and wanted them replaced with native leadership. In a wild spree, Congolese soldiers began to attack white women (including nuns) and children, causing the Belgian settlers to flee, as well as the experts the Belgians had expected to leave behind to help the Congolese in their early period of self-government. All public services then collapsed because the Congo lacked an educated native elite. The Belgians had never trained one.

When the Belgians flew in paratroopers to protect their nationals, Congolese premier Patrice Lumumba saw the move as a Belgian attempt to restore colonial rule, and he appealed to the United Nations to send forces to help him. It was at this point that the Cold War was injected into the Congo. The UN troops, with no forces from the great powers, did not compel the Belgians to evacuate their paratroopers because UN Secretary-General Dag Hammarskjöld had ordered UN forces not to become involved in internal conflicts or in the contending political factions seeking to gain power over their rivals. This order, however, had the effect of reinforcing the divisions of the Congo. Lumumba turned against the United Nations, bitterly attacked the secretary-general, and accused Belgium and the Western powers, especially the United States, of conspiring against him. Finally, he asked the Soviet Union for help

18. Pauker, "Southeast Asia," 325.

and received Soviet diplomatic backing, military supplies, and offers of troops, or "volunteers."

In early 1962, after all efforts to unify the Congo had failed, the United Nations reversed its original stand in order to preempt possible Soviet intervention. It finally adopted the policy of forcefully quashing the opposition. Although UN efforts took many months and cost lives, the country was "unified." Mobutu Sese Seko, who emerged as the Congo's leader for several decades and who renamed the country Zaire, was supported by the United States for his anticommunist policies. Mobutu received vast amounts of U.S. foreign aid, much of which he used to solidify his rule. Along the way, he managed to expropriate much of the aid and the country's mineral wealth for his own purposes, to the point that he became one of the world's richest men while his country slipped further into poverty and internal turmoil. His actions, and the case of Zaire in general, symbolized the disarray that resulted when Cold War politics collided with Third World development. The experience had profound implications for the post–Cold War era as well, a period that witnessed Mobutu's ejection from power and the creation of a fragile new government. The overthrow of Mobutu in 1997 demonstrated how vulnerable such tyrants were to popular backlash once deprived of their Cold War patrons.

REGIONAL RIVALRIES: THE ARAB-ISRAELI WARS

Beyond the impoverished states of Africa, no area better exemplified how regional disputes became intertwined with the Cold War than the Middle East, where three sets of rivalries intersected: Arab-Israeli tensions, intra-Arab rivalry, and the superpower competition. Each tended to reinforce the other. The Arabs, especially Egypt and Syria, received weapons and political support from the Soviet Union; Israel received similar support from the United States. With all this help, then, the Arabs and Israelis were able to fight repeated wars.

Arab antagonism toward Israel stemmed from the Balfour Declaration of 1917, in which Britain pledged the establishment of a "national home" for the Jewish people in Palestine while promising the Arabs that the rights of non-Jews would be protected. Zionists took this pledge as a promise to convert Palestine into a Jewish state; they considered Palestine, which became a British mandate after the disintegration of the Ottoman Empire during World War I, their ancient and traditional homeland. The Arabs, meanwhile, feared that a Jewish state would deprive them of what they also regarded to be their rightful homeland. In November 1947 the United Nations partitioned Palestine into two independent states, one Jewish and the other Arab, but the Arabs refused to accept this solution. On May 10, 1948, the armies of the Arab League

(Egypt, Jordan, Syria, Lebanon, and Saudi Arabia) invaded the new state. In the ensuing war the Israeli army defeated the larger Arab armies, and the state of Israel became a political fact of life.

The Arabs, however, still refused to recognize Israel. But Egypt, the leading Arab power, needed arms before reconfronting Israel. In September 1955 Egypt stunned the West by concluding an arms deal with Czechoslovakia, acting for the Soviet Union. Under this arrangement Egypt received a large quantity of arms, including MIG-15 fighter planes and tanks. Egypt's leader, Col. Gamal Abdel Nasser, thought he had the means to achieve a decisive military victory over Israel. In April 1956 Egypt tightened the ring around Israel by forming a joint command with Syria, Saudi Arabia, and Yemen. When the United States angered Nasser by retracting its offer to finance his pet project, the Aswan High Dam, Nasser vowed to nationalize the Suez Canal, which connected the Red Sea and the Mediterranean, and use the revenues collected from it to finance the dam. Arab nationalists were ecstatic, and Nasser's stature reached new heights.

In this overheated environment, Israel took the offensive and marched into Egypt, where it quickly defeated the Egyptian forces on the Sinai Peninsula. British and French forces, still seeking a presence in the region, intervened in Israel's behalf and sought to gain control of the canal. Far from receiving an American endorsement, however, their action infuriated President Dwight Eisenhower, who saw the invasion of Egypt as a golden opportunity to win Arab friendship. U.S. support of Britain, France, and Israel would leave the Soviet Union as the sole champion of Arab aspirations, but by saving Nasser, the United States could align itself with Arab nationalism. The favorable global contrast—Washington opposing foreign intervention in the Middle East at a time when the Soviets were intervening in Hungary to suppress its aspiration for national self-determination—provided further incentive for the United States to rebuff its allies.[19] In fact, in the end America's opposition to the invasion proved decisive. Given worldwide condemnation of the invasion, the British, French, and Israeli governments withdrew their forces.

Yet, unfortunately for Eisenhower, the Soviet Union reaped the benefits of the Suez crisis. After it had become clear that the United States would not support the British and French invasion, Soviet leaders threatened "to crush the aggressor." The Soviet Union risked nothing by

19. In 1956, amid growing anti-Soviet protests and a Hungarian declaration of independence, Soviet troops launched a brutal three-day assault on Budapest, killing 25,000 Hungarians and imposing even tighter control over the country. The Eisenhower administration allowed the Soviet crackdown to stand, despite its previous pledges to support the "liberation" of Eastern Europe.

delivering these threats to exterminate Israel and attack Britain and France, yet it received most of the credit from the Arabs for saving Nasser. Recognizing this Soviet public relations coup, Eisenhower urged Congress to support a new commitment to resisting communism in the Middle East—and it did. In 1957 Congress pass a joint resolution, known as the Eisenhower Doctrine, that declared the preservation of the Middle Eastern states vital to U.S. security. The United States was prepared to use armed force to assist any state requesting U.S. help to counter military threats "from any country controlled by international Communism."

Ten years later, in 1967, intra-Arab rivalries, combined with domestic economic failure, led Nasser to reassert his leadership of Arab nationalism. The result was another war. The Syrians, who had joined Egypt in a United Arab Republic only to quit it when Nasser moved to dominate the union, now sought to displace him as the leader of pan-Arabism. They openly and repeatedly called for Israel's destruction and stepped up their raids into that country. After the Israelis retaliated, the Syrians claimed in May 1967 that the Israelis were assembling their forces for a full-scale invasion of Syria. Nasser saw in that threat an opportunity to regain his leadership of Arab nationalism. The Egyptian leader was confident that, after eleven years of receiving Soviet training and arms, his forces could destroy Israel, which this time would be fighting by itself, without the aid of France and Britain.

In preparation for the confrontation, the Egyptian leader moved reinforcements into the Sinai Desert and then demanded and obtained the withdrawal of the UN peacekeeping forces. Egyptian and Israeli forces now confronted each other for the first time since 1956. In his most deliberate provocation of Israel, Nasser blockaded the Gulf of Aqaba, Israel's lifeline through which it received its oil and other goods. He then signed an alliance with Jordan. As a result of that bold move, Arab armies surrounded Israel: Syria to the north, Egypt to the south, and Jordan to the east. Their military strategy was designed to cut Israel in two at its narrow waist. All these actions were accompanied by increasingly shrill calls for a holy "war of liberation" and the extermination of all of Israel's inhabitants.

In these circumstances war was inevitable, unless Israel was willing to accept a major political defeat—an unlikely prospect. The preservation of peace, which could be achieved primarily by Nasser's removal of the blockade, depended on the United States and the Soviet Union. Washington was caught in a dilemma. On the one hand, the United States had recognized Israel's right to send ships through the gulf after compelling Israel to withdraw from that area after its 1956 victory. On the other hand, America was becoming deeply involved in Vietnam (see Chapter

5) and was therefore reluctant to take on a second conflict. Furthermore, a key question for American policy makers was whether such a test would precipitate a clash with the Soviet Union, which had with great fanfare sent warships into the eastern Mediterranean, fully supported the Arabs in their aims, and continually denounced Israel as an aggressive tool of American imperialism.

For Moscow, the Arab-Israeli conflict had global implications. If Western influence could be expelled from the Middle East and if the Soviet Union could establish itself as the dominant power over that oil-rich region, Europe would be weakened and perhaps even neutralized. If the Gulf of Aqaba blockade succeeded, the Soviet Union would earn the Arabs' everlasting gratitude as the primary force behind Egypt's political victory. Moreover, an effective blockade would demonstrate the Soviet Union's ability to inhibit the American navy and would jeopardize future American commitments to Israel. In short, the Soviet Union had an opportunity to replace the West as the region's leading power.

But Moscow's ambitions were quickly frustrated in the region. Because Washington was unable to arrange a diplomatic solution, the Israelis attacked to seize the initiative in what had become an unavoidable clash. Routing the air forces of their Arab opponents in a brilliantly coordinated set of air strikes during the first hours of hostilities, they defeated the Egyptian army and reached the Suez Canal in three days—two days ahead of the record they set in 1956. Israeli forces also routed the Jordanian army, then captured half of Jerusalem and the western bank of the river Jordan. Finally, they turned on the Syrian army and eliminated the bases on the Golan Heights from which Syria had been launching terrorist raids and shelling Israeli settlements. Nasser's dreams of an Arab empire, and the Soviet Union's hopes for regional hegemony, were quickly shattered. Meanwhile, the United States maintained its imposing presence throughout the Middle East.

U.S. POLICY TOWARD LATIN AMERICA

Events in Latin America further illustrate how American foreign policy, and the Cold War in general, were propelled by events in the developing world. As U.S. leaders saw it, mass-based revolutions in Latin America created a foothold for communism in the Western Hemisphere and thus constituted a threat to the United States. They responded to the growing unrest in their "backyard" by intervening throughout the region, indirectly in most cases, but directly when a communist victory was seen as imminent.

In the 1950s and 1960s Latin Americans shared two aspirations that were sweeping through the developing areas: a better life for their mass-

LATIN AMERICA

es and self-determination of their national destinies. Since the early 1800s the United States had dominated its hemispheric neighbors, usually through alliances with the wealthy, land-owning, governing class. Americans may have believed they were free of Europe's taint of colonialism, but Latin Americans disagreed. The Monroe Doctrine had turned the entire Western Hemisphere into a U.S. sphere of influence; the United States did not have to resort to direct colonial rule. Invested American capital spoke louder than guns, and the U.S. government did not have to give political orders when a nation was a "banana republic." In contrast to their rhetorical calls for democratic rule, U.S. leaders actively supported military rulers throughout Latin America and exercised their self-appointed "international police powers" to maintain stability in the region.[20]

The U.S. attitude toward Latin America took on a harder edge during the Cold War, when the perceived threat was no longer defined generally as internal unrest but very specifically as communist revolution. As in Africa and southern Asia, the vast majority of Latin Americans possessed little wealth and even less political power. Their plight strengthened the appeal of Marxist ideology, which not only sought to explain their difficulties but also promised the peasants a way out. Consequently, the long-standing U.S. interest in dominating Latin American affairs became even stronger. Through the Organization of American States (OAS), which was created in 1948, the United States effectively guaranteed the security of its neighbors throughout the hemisphere. In so doing, the U.S. government also guaranteed that communism would not take hold in the region without a fight.

No single event more epitomized this approach than the 1954 U.S. intervention in Guatemala, one of the poorest and most repressive states in Latin America. For decades the country's large and productive agricultural plantations had been controlled by a small elite that maintained closer contacts with U.S. banks and corporations than with the landless *campesinos* who made up more than 90 percent of Guatemala's population. Thus it should have come as no surprise when democratic reforms in the country produced opposition leaders who sought to abolish this system.

The United States, though preoccupied with fighting World War II, viewed warily the spreading protests against Guatemala's dictator, Gen. Jorge Ubico. Outrage against Ubico's repressive rule led to his downfall in 1944 and his replacement by Juan José Arévalo, a popular school-

20. This term was coined by President Theodore Roosevelt, whose 1905 "corollary" to the Monroe Doctrine legitimized the recurring series of U.S. interventions and occupations in Latin America. See Walter LaFeber, *Inevitable Revolutions: The United States in Central America,* 3d ed. (New York: Norton, 1993).

teacher and political activist who became the first democratically elected leader in Guatemala's history. Arévalo was successful at first in instituting reforms, but his supporters soon fragmented into several competing factions. As the Cold War settled in, the political climate in the country became more ideologically charged, and in the elections of 1950 a more radical leftist candidate, Jacobo Arbenz Guzmán, gained power and promised additional sweeping reforms.

Arbenz, who received support from a growing Communist Party in Guatemala, attempted to take over many of the plantations and give the land, including 225,000 acres owned by the U.S.-based United Fruit Company, to the peasants. Fearing that such drastic "land reform" would provoke further uprisings elsewhere in Central America and threaten U.S. control of the Panama Canal, the Eisenhower administration supported a plan to overthrow Arbenz. After Arbenz provided the pretext needed by the United States in 1954—the importation of weapons from Czechoslovakia—the Central Intelligence Agency (CIA) executed its military coup. Within days, Arbenz was removed from power, his reforms were abolished, the military regained control of the *campesinos*, and the United States reinforced its image as an enemy of revolution in Latin America.[21]

In the face of this widespread resentment, American leaders declared their intention to improve the living standards of Latin Americans with foreign assistance. Their stated goal was to help the Latin American economies foster a self-sustaining rate of economic growth and develop conditions in which private capital would be attracted to projects other than the extraction of raw materials or growth of single exportable crops. Given the projected rapid increase in Latin America's population, the efforts to achieve these goals became all the more urgent. To meet this challenge, President John Kennedy, soon after assuming office in 1961, established the Alliance for Progress. He pledged $20 billion of primarily public money over the next decade to Latin America, and, even more significant, he emphasized the need for social change. Through the Peace Corps and other innovations, Kennedy hoped to revitalize Franklin Roosevelt's aspiration to make the United States a "good neighbor" of Latin America. Kennedy realized that, in the absence of such an effort, the possibilities of economic development were slight and the prospects of additional communist insurgencies were strong.

Kennedy's Alliance for Progress, however, never lived up the president's stated objectives. The political atmosphere throughout Latin America had become so polarized that any attempt by the United States

21. For an elaboration, see Stephen Schlesinger and Stephen Kinzer, *Bitter Fruit: The Untold Story of the American Coup in Guatemala* (Garden City, N.Y.: Anchor Press, 1982).

to support moderates proved futile. And in the economic sphere, any discussion of reducing the disparity of wealth and creating a middle class was thwarted by the elites, who clung to their wealth and to their close ties to the military. On the home front, Kennedy was unable to gain support for his initiative because congressional leaders stubbornly identified reform with revolution, and revolution with communism. As a result, the president was forced to maintain the status quo in Latin America which, during the peak of the Cold War, meant a high level of economic distress, political repression, and social unrest.

SUPERPOWER CONFRONTATION IN CUBA

The intrusion of Cold War tensions into U.S. relations with Latin America was most sharply demonstrated in Cuba. Its revolutionary government dated from January 1, 1959, when armed rebels overthrew the U.S.-backed dictatorship of Fulgencio Batista. Among the rebels, Fidel Castro identified himself with democratic government and social and economic justice and gained widespread popularity among the Cuban people. This public support ensured the victory of his guerrilla army against the larger government forces. The Castro revolution was essentially a social revolution. Thus in its opening months, the new government moved to remedy the conditions of the people by instituting land reform and building low-cost housing, schools, and clinics. But some features of this social revolution were bound to clash with the interests of the United States.

Although the United States had been instrumental in freeing Cuba from Spain in the Spanish-American War at the turn of the century, members of Congress engineered in 1902 an amendment to the Cuban constitution, known as the Platt Amendment, which granted Americans the right to intervene at any time in Cuba to preserve Cuban independence, to protect life, property, and individual liberty, and to help discharge of Cuba's treaty obligations. By 1934, when the amendment was repealed, the United States had intervened militarily in Cuba once (1906–1909) and had established a naval base at Guantànamo Bay. American capital controlled 80 percent of Cuba's utilities, 90 percent of its mines and cattle ranches, nearly all of its oil, and 40 percent of its sugar production (approximately 25 percent of the American market was reserved for Cuban sugar). Despite this special commercial link, it was not surprising that the Cuban revolution directed its long pent-up nationalism and social resentment against the "Yankee imperialism" that dominated Cuba's economy. America's support of the Batista dictatorship until the moment of its collapse intensified anti-American sentiment. "Cuba, si! Yanqui, no!" became the Castro regime's rallying cry,

IMPACT AND INFLUENCE

FIDEL CASTRO

Both during and after the Cold War, no developing country leader played a more visible role in denouncing the United States than Fidel Castro. In 1959 the Cuban leader directed a successful revolution against the U.S.-backed regime of Gen. Fulgencia Batista. He then took control of Cuba's new communist government, the first of its kind in the Western Hemisphere, and became a close ally of the Soviet Union.

Castro, along with his brother Raul and Ernesto "Che" Guevara, hoped to make Cuba an inspiration for other revolutionary movements. An attorney before the revolution, Castro extended social services to all Cubans, including education and health care. His dictatorial rule, however, prompted many to flee the island for the United States, and the Cuban economy steadily deteriorated under communist control. But Castro remained popular as a symbol of defiance as the feud between the United States and Cuba continued into the twenty-first century.

the ceremonial burning of the American flag its ritual, and the confiscation of American property its reward.

This anti-American nationalistic feeling, deliberately fostered by Castro to increase the popularity of his regime, led his government to become increasingly identified with communism. If he was going to break with the United States, which, Castro assumed, would oppose his reforms, then he had to look to Moscow, its rival. By doing so, the Cuban leader betrayed the revolution's original democratic promises, and Cuba became a dictatorship. All political parties were abolished except for one—the Communist Party—and Castro became increasingly dependent on its organizational strength. He then quickly aligned Cuba with the Soviet Union, which supplied Cuba with vast amounts of arms and military advisers. Cuban airmen were sent to Czechoslovakia to learn how to fly Soviet fighters, and a large number of Cuban technicians were trained in communist countries. Cuba's armed services soon ranked second only to America's as the largest in the Western Hemisphere. On the diplomatic front, relations were established with all communist countries except East Germany, and economic agreements were signed with many of the same countries, including East Germany. Cuba's economy soon became integrated into that of the communist bloc; 75 percent of the island's trade was with countries behind the iron curtain.

In January 1961 the United States cut off diplomatic relations with Cuba after a series of alleged provocations. If Castro at that point had attempted to seize the Guantànamo base, there would have been an excuse for open American intervention. Castro, however, was too shrewd to risk a seizure, but he also ruled out an accommodation with the United States. Above all else, Castro wanted to play a major role on the world stage—a role he could not achieve as the leader of either a pro-American or a neutral developing country of ten million people. He could do so only as a revolutionary leader who took on his giant neighbor as an enemy. But to stand up against the United States he would need the support of the other giant, the Soviet Union. Thus Castro turned down friendly overtures from the United States after he took power: a new, sympathetic American ambassador was kept waiting for weeks before being allowed to present his credentials, and offers of foreign aid were rejected.[22]

THE BAY OF PIGS

As Cuban-Soviet relations tightened, American leaders began to plan secretly for Castro's overthrow. To this end, in April 1961 the new Kennedy administration launched an attempt by a small force of Cuban exiles—many of them former Castro associates who had become disillusioned by the dictator's increasingly tyrannical rule, communist sympathies, and alignment with the Soviet Union—to land in Cuba and attempt to overthrow Castro. The CIA, which had developed the plans

22. The changing U.S. views of Castro and his policies during his first two years in power are chronicled in Peter D. Eicher, ed., *Emperor Dead and Other Historic American Diplomatic Dispatches* (Washington, D.C.: CQ Press, 1997), 442–448.

for this operation and supervised their execution, assumed that once the exiles had gained a beachhead in the Bay of Pigs, some units of Castro's army and much of Cuba's population would welcome the invaders as liberators.

But the CIA predictions proved wrong, and the operation was a dramatic and appalling failure. The United States bungled it by basing a major foreign policy move involving American prestige on the glib assumption that a feeble beachhead operation would result in a mass uprising of Cubans against their government. Kennedy's refusal to provide air cover for the amphibious attack, on the grounds that such support would reveal U.S. complicity in the invasion, testified to his ambivalence while ensuring the military failure. Rumors and press reports conveyed the impression of a major invasion, making the Cuban victory appear even more spectacular.

American prestige, already damaged by the Guatemala coup and other U.S. interventions in the developing world, sank to a new low. In his pointed comment in the *New York Times,* columnist Cyrus Sulzberger observed, "We looked like fools to our friends, rascals to our enemies, and incompetents to the rest." The administration had fallen victim to its own half-heartedness. Worse, the United States had defied its own proclaimed standards regarding the sanctity of borders. As Sen. William Fulbright warned Kennedy days before the invasion, "To give this activity even covert support is of a piece with the hypocrisy and cynicism for which the United States is constantly denouncing the Soviet Union." [23] The results of the unsuccessful invasion were predictable: an increase in Castro's domestic support, a revival of Latin American hostility toward "Yankee imperialism," a blunting of Kennedy's initially successful attempts to identify the United States with anticolonialism, and a loss of confidence in America's leadership by its allies.

THE CUBAN MISSILE CRISIS

After the Bay of Pigs fiasco, Cuba was emboldened to act as a communist base from which the Soviet Union could threaten the United States and elicit support from other developing nations in the Western Hemisphere. With Castro's victory, the United States no longer held a monopoly of power in the Caribbean and Latin America, the stated intention of the Monroe Doctrine. The Bay of Pigs disaster also incited new Soviet provocations. In Moscow, where unfriendly regimes were not tolerated but crushed, Kennedy's prestige plummeted. In the view of Soviet leaders, if it had been in the interest of the United States to elim-

23. Quoted in Stephen E. Ambrose, *Rise to Globalism: American Foreign Policy since 1938,* 5th ed. rev. (New York: Penguin, 1988).

inate Castro, then U.S. military intervention should have followed the bungled attempt by the CIA. A "serious" power does not tolerate its enemies so near and does not act squeamishly. It does what it has to do, regardless of international opinion. Moreover, if Castro's elimination had not been important enough for the United States to risk criticism, then the intervention should not have been launched in the first place. But to do so and fail suggested weak nerves and a lack of foresight. Worse, it revealed fear of the Soviet Union. Why else would the United States not intervene with its own military forces in an area so close to it, as it had done many times in the past? Perhaps the Soviet Union should push a little further and see if Kennedy would tolerate a further extension of Soviet power.

And that is just what Soviet leaders did. Once the Soviets saw that the communist regime in Cuba was tolerated, they began to establish a missile base there. Washington had believed that the Soviet Union would not dare to do this in America's sphere of influence. But it did dare. In October 1962 a U-2 spy plane discovered, to the great surprise and consternation of American policy makers, that the Soviets were building launching sites for approximately seventy short- and intermediate-range ballistic missiles that could carry nuclear warheads. That Nikita Khrushchev, the Soviet leader, had dared to move his missiles so close to the United States, and that he apparently expected no reaction beyond diplomatic protests, were dangerous signs. But American vacillation at the Bay of Pigs and afterward had convinced Khrushchev that the United States would not fight to protect its vital interests. Besides, Khrushchev thought Kennedy too young and inexperienced. Kennedy, the Soviet leader said, was "too liberal to fight."

Khrushchev had a great deal to gain. A failure to respond to his move would prove to America's allies in the North Atlantic Treaty Organization (NATO) what they already feared: the United States had become vulnerable to attack and could no longer be relied upon to protect Europe. Moreover, inaction in the face of Soviet missiles so close to the American coast would validate Khrushchev's claim of a shift in the nuclear balance. The promised renewal of Soviet pressure on Berlin after the midterm U.S. congressional elections, together with the likelihood of an even more cautious American reaction than before, would reinforce this impression. Only this time the Soviets could deliver an ultimatum to get out of Berlin or else, and they were in an increasingly favorable position to exert their will.

The threat in Cuba therefore had profound consequences. For the first time a large part of the North American continent would be vulnerable to Soviet nuclear missiles. The early warning systems against bombers and missiles were in the north because a Soviet attack always had been expected to come in over the Arctic Circle. Moreover, American prestige was on the line, and not only in Europe. The sudden and unchallenged appearance of the opposing superpower in an area where the United States had long been paramount would erode America's authority and status and encourage the spread of Castroism throughout Latin America. All anti-Castro forces, including the indispensable and all too few genuinely democratic reformers, would be demoralized and perhaps paralyzed by Washington's inaction.

But for once Khrushchev overplayed his hand. He pressured the United States in the wrong place, and Washington could not resist the challenge. If the stakes were high for the Soviet Union, they were even higher for the United States, and Kennedy felt that under no circumstances could he afford to lose. Indeed, because he had warned the Soviet leader against placing offensive missiles in Cuba, Kennedy had to compel their withdrawal to preserve his credibility. From the outset, however, the young president realized that the central issue was Soviet and allied perceptions of the balance of power.

Khrushchev's confidence stemmed from a conviction that the United States no longer possessed the will to defend its interests. But for Americans such a notion was dangerous because, if left uncorrected, it would lead to a renewed and more determined challenge in Berlin—as Khrushchev already had announced. If the United States declared it would stand firm in Berlin but the Soviet leader did not believe it, a violent clash, possibly a nuclear war, might result. Characteristically, the Soviets had not committed themselves irrevocably in Cuba. They were willing to gamble for a big payoff, but they also were willing to suffer a serious setback to avoid a catastrophic clash. The Soviets, in effect, were testing the limits of U.S. influence in the Western Hemisphere.

In Washington, Kennedy met night and day with his political and military advisers. Some recommended a diplomatic compromise; others pushed for massive air strikes or even a full-scale invasion of Cuba. The first option was rejected for the reasons noted above, and Kennedy found the second and third options too dangerous. Thus the president chose a fourth option and ordered a blockade of Cuba to prevent any further missile shipments. Kennedy also demanded the removal of the missiles already in place. American firmness and determination left Moscow little choice. For once the Soviets had to decide whether to fire the first shot—to break the American blockade of their missile-carrying ships—and risk a possible escalation of the conflict. Much to everyone's relief, the Kremlin backed down, called back its ships, and ordered that the missile sites be deactivated. As Secretary of State Dean Rusk vividly described it, "We were eyeball to eyeball, and the other fellow just blinked."

Reasons for the Soviet capitulation have been debated ever since the Cuban missile crisis.[24] But it is clear that military considerations were central to Soviet calculations. Khrushchev recognized that the United States had enormous conventional, especially naval, superiority in the Caribbean, and that it could have mounted an overwhelming invasion. In the absence of sufficient conventional forces to support his ally so far away, Khrushchev was left with only one choice—risk nuclear war, which he was ultimately unwilling to do because he correctly recognized U.S. strategic superiority. His shipment of Soviet missiles to Cuba was part of an attempt to reduce the nuclear imbalance that resulted from Kennedy's rapid buildup, which in turn was stimulated by Khrushchev's own claims that he was mass-producing new Soviet intercontinental ballistic missiles. In any case, the strategic balance favoring the United States imposed a clear limit to the pressure the Soviets could exert. The crisis, therefore, quicky ended after America's determination to use its power was demonstrated.

The missile crisis was followed by years of relaxed tensions between the United States and Soviet Union. But there were other important outcomes as well. First, Kennedy declared publicly that the United States would not invade Cuba. Thus, although America had prevailed in the showdown, the Soviet Union retained its outpost in the Caribbean. Second, Khrushchev received assurances from Kennedy that the United States would dismantle the nuclear missiles it had recently installed in Turkey. While this concession was largely symbolic—the United States simply shifted its nuclear arsenal to submarines in the Mediterranean—it was viewed by Soviet leaders as a tactical gain. Third, Soviet leaders vowed they would never be humiliated again and pledged to increase their nuclear forces to U.S. levels, if not surpass them. In this sense the setback in Cuba only strengthened their resolve.

Finally, and most fundamentally, the Cuban missile crisis once again demonstrated the crucial role played by developing countries during the Cold War, mainly by serving as remote "theaters" of the struggle between the United States and the Soviet Union. In these areas, communism often proved appealing to impoverished peoples, many of whom were responsive to Soviet claims that the United States was primarily to blame for their troubles. Castro, who had unsuccessfully urged the Soviet Union to launch a direct attack against the United States during the crisis, nonetheless maintained his hold on power and became an even more

24. See Graham T. Allison and Philip D. Zelikow, *Essence of Decision: Explaining the Cuban Missile Crisis*, 2d ed. (New York: Longman, 1999); and Raymond L. Garthoff, *Reflections on the Cuban Missile Crisis*, rev. ed. (Washington, D.C.: Brookings, 1989).

dynamic symbol of anticapitalist defiance throughout the developing world.

Castro's influence in Latin America was aptly demonstrated by the U.S. intervention in the Dominican Republic. The impetus for this event was the overthrow in 1961 of Rafaél Trujillo, who had ruled as a dictator for thirty-one years. Following a brief period of political turmoil, Juan Bosch, a man of genuinely democratic convictions, was elected president. Seven months later, Bosch was overthrown by a military coup whose leaders announced they would reestablish a "rightist state." In April 1965 the pro-Bosch forces revolted against this right-wing military government. Communists were thought to be active in the movement against the junta, and Washington feared they would create a second Cuba in the hemisphere. But the rebels claimed their revolution was led by noncommunists who sought only a return to constitutional government. Before the evidence was clear that the revolution was in fact communist-run, President Lyndon Johnson ordered the U.S. military to intervene and restore order on American terms.

The Dominican crisis demonstrated how obsessed the architects of the floundering Alliance for Progress were with Castro, without whom there likely would have been no large-scale efforts to encourage economic and political reforms in Latin America.[25] The overt U.S. intervention—the first in fifty years in Latin America—therefore proved to be the death knell of the Alliance for Progress, which had sought to persuade the region's ruling elites to share their power and wealth if they wished to avoid revolutionary violence. Latin America's ruling classes could now relax because there was an alternative to reform: the United States would save them from the consequences of their folly in preserving unjust societies. Thus American policy south of the U.S. border, as in other areas of the world, continued to be dictated by the bipolar global struggle.

In Latin America, then, just as in Africa and the Middle East, the globalization of containment had profound consequences. As many critics of the policy feared, the United States gradually became immersed in civil wars and regional conflicts far from its shores, many of which were grounded less in communist subversion than in the masses' aspirations for the same political and economic freedoms enjoyed by most Americans. In escalating containment into a boundless anticommunist crusade, American leaders violated the democratic values they supposedly were promoting, and they turned their presumed beneficiaries—the mass populations of developing countries—

25. See Theodore Draper, *The Dominican Revolt: A Case Study in American Policy* (New York: Commentary, 1968).

against the United States. To make matters worse, interventions by the United States frequently backfired, leading to the establishment of new regimes that were openly hostile to Washington. But American leaders, bound by the logic of containment and fearful of losing ground to the communists anywhere on the planet, stayed loyal to the policy. Their strategy led to the calamitous U.S. intervention in Vietnam, where the faltering consensus in the United States favoring global containment was put to the ultimate test.

American F-105 Thunderchief bombers attack a North Vietnamese military target in June 1966. The bombing campaign, which escalated in the late 1960s and early 1970s, only hardened the resistance of North Vietnam during the war.

CHAPTER FIVE

Vietnam and the Cost of Containment

The wreckage of World War II yielded to an international order in the late 1940s and 1950s that was increasingly split between two rival blocs. Through their allies and proxies, the United States and Soviet Union confronted one another in every region of the world, and, in a series of actions and reactions, established "frontiers" between their spheres of influence. Even regions of otherwise marginal concern became arenas for the superpowers.

During the early Cold War period, which was shaped by a bipolar balance of power, each superpower was highly sensitive to the slightest shifts in power lest such shifts upset the equilibrium and give the enemy the upper hand. A gain for either side, in short, was perceived as an equivalent loss for the other. The opponent's moves, even if alleged to be defensive, were typically viewed as deliberate and offensive. Similarly, internal developments in distant countries received close scrutiny because the allegiance of their governments toward either superpower might tip the scales in the global competition. The early Cold War thus consisted of efforts by the United States and Soviet Union to guard their spheres of influence against encroachment, subversion, and defection.

The developing world, as we saw in Chapter 4, quickly emerged as a crucial battleground in this struggle. Decolonization produced a large number of new countries that, despite their best efforts to remain nonaligned, often fell into the U.S. or the Soviet blocs. In Korea both superpowers claimed vital interests to be at stake, leading to the country's partition and a protracted "hot war." Elsewhere, efforts by the developing countries to produce viable governments and improve living standards were hampered, if not prevented altogether, by the intrusion of the superpower rivalry.

One part of the developing world to take center stage in the Cold War was Southeast Asia, or Indochina, which had been a French colony since the 1860s. For nearly a century Indochina served as a key part of France's colonial empire and provided France with vast quantities of rice, rubber, oil, tungsten, and tin. As a result, French officials were reluctant to grant independence to Indochina after World War II, even though the French administration had earlier been displaced by Japanese forces during the conflict. As the United States prepared the Philippines for independence in July 1946, and as the British followed suit in India, Burma (now Myanmar), and Ceylon, French leaders insisted on reimposing colonial rule over Indochina. Their decision would prove disastrous not only for France but also for the United States, which could not resist the temptation to view the conflict in Indochina as a microcosm of the East-West struggle.[1]

EJECTION OF THE FRENCH FROM VIETNAM

Although they refused to leave Indochina, the French offered political concessions to one of its provinces, Vietnam, a heavily populated, resource-rich region located on the South China Sea. France recognized the Democratic Republic of Vietnam as a "free state" within the newly formed French Union, which also included Laos and Cambodia. Under the agreement, the French would be allowed to maintain garrisons in

1. For a detailed account of American misperceptions about Vietnam, see Jeffrey Record, *The Wrong War: Why We Lost Vietnam* (Annapolis: Naval Institute Press, 1998).

Vietnam for five years in return for allowing the Vietnamese to determine their future in a plebiscite. But in less than a year the Vietminh, as the Revolutionary League for the Independence of Vietnam was known, accused the French of violating the agreement, and open conflict erupted in 1946 between the two sides. The fighting soon escalated into the "first" Vietnam war, which lasted eight years.

Ho Chi Minh, who had organized the Vietminh (also called the Viet Cong) during World War II, sought to convert Vietnam from a colonial ward to a classless communist society.[2] Ho had embraced communism in the 1920s after his efforts to establish an independent and democratic state were rebuffed by Western leaders at the Paris Peace Conference that followed World War I. During the period of Japanese occupation, however, the popular leader had shifted the Vietminh's emphasis from communism to nationalism in order to gain independence for Vietnam. After the war, emboldened by Japan's defeat and inspired by the United Nations's pledge to end colonial rule, Ho had reason to believe his nation's time had finally come. For the second time in less than three decades, however, he was sorely disappointed by the lack of support among the Western powers. His decision to launch a full-scale rebellion quickly followed.

With Vietnam under siege, French leaders installed Emperor Bao Dai, who previously had ruled the coastal region on behalf of the French government, as Vietnam's new leader. The Vietminh then escalated their campaign for independence, declaring themselves to be the true representatives of the Vietnamese people. By contrast, Bao Dai, who spent much of his time on the French Riviera, was widely viewed as a French puppet who could not survive one day without French military aid. In the continuing civil war, Ho, like Mao Zedong in China, adopted a strategy of guerrilla warfare that depended on control of the countryside and support among the peasants. The French, who generally held the cities, were at a disadvantage from the beginning. In the absence of genuine independence, most Vietnamese identified themselves with the Vietminh and saw the French, quite accurately, as illegitimate rulers.

American public opinion was unsympathetic to France's attempt to reestablish its colonial control over Indochina. Three events, however, led to U.S. involvement in this conflict. The first was the defeat of Chiang Kai-shek in 1949 and the creation of the communist-led People's Republic of China (PRC). This development was a blow to France because the PRC could now provide assistance to the Vietminh. The second event was the outbreak of the Korean War, a direct challenge to the U.S. containment strategy. Finally, the third development was the shift in

2. See Stanley Karnow, *Vietnam, A History* (New York: Penguin, 1983), chap. 3.

American public opinion away from its narrow concern with European security and toward a much wider campaign of anticommunism. As a result, perceptions of the French role in Vietnam changed. Rather than colonialists trying to hold onto the vestiges of their decrepit colonial empire, they now were fighters in the global crusade against communism.

In 1950 the United States began to provide France with economic and military aid for use in the conflict; by 1954 American taxpayers were funding about 75 percent of the costs of the war. The French position continued to deteriorate, however, especially after the Korean armistice was signed. Despite American warnings against intervention, the PRC shifted its pressure from Korea to Indochina and increased its assistance to the Vietminh. As a result, Ho's position grew steadily stronger at the very time France was losing its already feeble grip on the countryside. On March 13, 1954, Vietminh forces launched an assault on the strategically vital French fortress at Dienbienphu. With the French position in northern Vietnam close to collapse, it became painfully clear that the French could not hold on without American intervention. What was the United States to do?

Dienbienphu was the moment of decision for the United States. Eisenhower had declared Indochina to be of strategic importance to American security and had cautioned China against direct or indirect intervention. But the Chinese had ignored these warnings, and the U.S. government had to "put up or shut up." When push came to shove, American leaders shut up; their threats turned out to be bluffs. The reason for U.S. inaction was clear: American public opinion might have been strongly anticommunist, but the nation was tired of war. For that reason Eisenhower had withdrawn from Korea, and now he was unwilling to involve the United States in another such war. Furthermore, the administration was cutting the size of the army as part of the "New Look" military reorganization, and the army chief of staff had counseled against intervention because of a lack of available troops.

With these factors in mind, the administration considered two courses of action. The first was to rescue the French by attacking the communist positions around Dienbienphu with air power, but this strategy was rejected because air strikes by themselves could not halt the Vietminh's ground advance. Air power had failed to stop the North Korean army during the opening days of that war, forcing the commitment of U.S. troops. The alternative course of action was to attack China with nuclear weapons. That would have been consistent with the administration's announced policy of massive retaliation. But the administration did not follow its own policy for one simple reason: it is one thing to deliver a threat of massive retaliation to an opponent and quite another to have the opponent believe it. The Soviets had not believed such threats in Korea, nor would the Chinese in Vietnam. Thus the possible use of nuclear weapons was discussed—and rejected—by the president and his advisers. Both communist powers correctly guessed that the United States would not risk a total war for anything less than an attack on the United States or Western Europe.

In the end, the French government decided to make the best of the situation by negotiating in Geneva, Switzerland, for an end to the war. The French people, who were mired in a second war in Algeria during this period, were as weary of Vietnam as the American public had been of Korea. Under the Geneva agreement, the war ended with the "temporary" division of Vietnam at the seventeenth parallel. Two separate and interim governments were to be established during this transition period: a communist regime in the north and a noncommunist regime in the south. Elections were scheduled for July 1956 to bring about Vietnam's "unity and territorial integrity."

THE 'DOMINO THEORY' AND U.S. INTERVENTION

Because the Geneva agreement called for a general election to be held in 1956, the Vietminh expected the unpopular regime in South Vietnam to collapse. Leaders in Hanoi, the North Vietnamese capital, assumed that most of the twelve million South Vietnamese would vote for Ho, who had led the nationalist struggle against the French. When those votes were added to the widespread support for Ho in the North, the country would likely be reunited under communist control.

But American leaders maintained a strong interest in preventing this outcome in Vietnam, which was now liberated from France. They believed the seventeenth parallel dividing North and South Vietnam represented one of many crucial boundaries between the "free world" and the communist bloc. Just as these leaders decided to defend South Korea when North Korea crossed the thirty-eighth parallel, so they now decided to rescue South Vietnam. The United States sought to prevent a communist takeover by supporting the new government of Ngo Dinh Diem, a staunch anticommunist. The Eisenhower administration provided Diem with massive economic and military aid to "stabilize" the situation in Vietnam, a strategy that guaranteed yet another armed struggle for the control of Vietnam. Like the war in Korea, the "second" Vietnam War would be fought at a great distance from the United States in a remote area that was little known to most Americans.

Distance, however, was only one of the problems the United States encountered. Vietnam was a divided society: North against South, Buddhists against Catholics, lowlanders against *montagnards,* and peasants against urban dwellers. Moreover, loyalties were primarily local, and hostility to the central government ran deep because, as in most developing countries, the government historically had been that of the colonial power, represented at the local level by the tax collector and recruiting sergeant. Further complicating the matter, transportation and communication networks were primitive and industrial development nonexistent. South Vietnam had no established political institutions and a precarious economy.

Ho's popularity compelled the United States and the new South Vietnamese government to oppose and ultimately prevent the 1956 elections promised in the Geneva agreement. The United States wanted the seventeenth parallel to be accepted as the new frontier, and Diem, a fervent Catholic and anticommunist, wanted to stay in power no matter what the Geneva agreement said about elections. In the face of such strong opposition, Hanoi saw its chances for a peaceful takeover fade, and so did its restraint. In 1959 the North Vietnamese began the armed struggle to unify the country, and the second Vietnam War commenced.

Despite the many similarities between the Korean and Vietnamese conflicts, U.S. involvement in Vietnam began quite differently. The Korean War had begun with a clear-cut, aggressive attack that had aroused the American public and united the principal Western allies against the common threat. Korea also had been a conventional war in which regular communist forces were checked by regular South Korean, American, and United Nations troops. By contrast, the French defeat at Dienbienphu in 1954 was a decisive moment in contemporary history because it demonstrated that guerrilla tactics could prevail against the larger and stronger army of a major power. An internal uprising of guerrillas was therefore a shrewder manner of "crossing" the seventeenth parallel. Diem's autocratic rule and his failure to enlist the support of his population—especially the peasantry—through political, social, and economic reforms helped to prepare the ground for a successful guerrilla campaign.

For the U.S. government, the Vietnam conflict represented a test of the nation's will, and the United States had to meet the test to maintain all frontiers. Until the noncommunist states in the region became more economically developed and possessed stable political systems and military defenses, the Asian balance seemed to depend on the United States. American leaders believed they could no more forgo the defense of the frontier in South Vietnam than in Korea. If either country fell, more communist victories would inevitably follow and the containment strategy would fail.

Given this logic, American leaders advanced a "domino theory" that sought to justify intervention in Vietnam. In their view, the political and

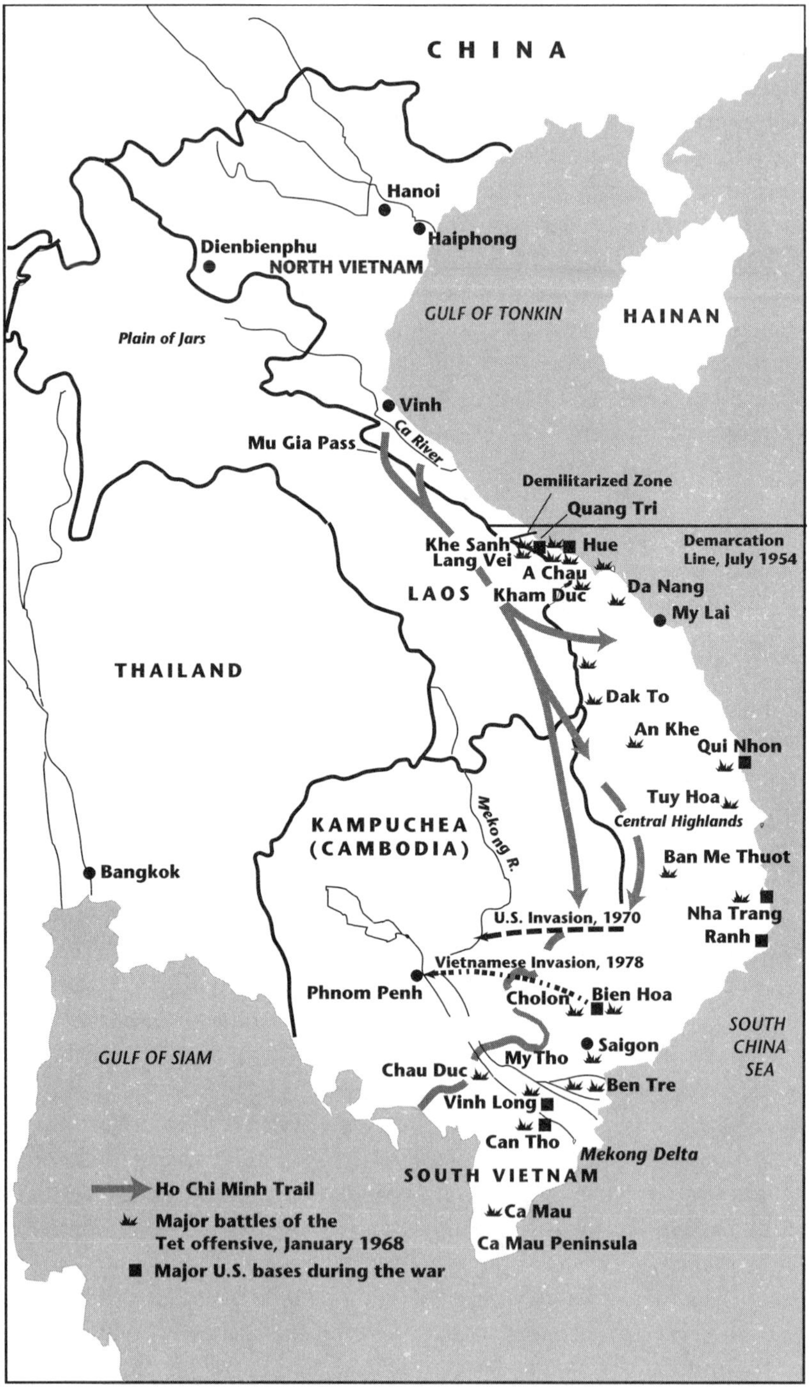

THE VIETNAM WAR

psychological impact of a U.S. pullout would have repercussions elsewhere and ultimately upset the global balance of power. Specifically, Vietnam's collapse would provoke communist challenges throughout Indochina, across Burma, and into the Indian subcontinent. The Middle East would then feel the pressure, followed by the newly independent states of Africa. As Eisenhower stated, "You have a row of dominoes set up, you knock over the first one and what will happen to the last one is the certainty that it will go ever so quickly. So you could have a beginning of a disintegration that would have the most profound influences." [3]

The assumption underlying this viewpoint was that the Sino-Soviet bloc was united, despite increasing evidence to the contrary. Signs of discord between the Soviet Union and China were generally explained as tactical differences about how the "communist world" should wage its "war" against the United States, not as fundamental conflicts of national interests between the two powers. But even if observers had recognized the fundamental conflicts, it probably would not have made much difference because the PRC, with its population approaching one billion and its revolutionary rhetoric denouncing "American imperialism," was, in Washington's opinion, far more militant and dangerous than Moscow. Ho Chi Minh and the Vietminh were, Washington believed, puppets of China, applying Mao Zedong's guerrilla warfare tactics to destroy a noncommunist government in a country within the American sphere of influence. If they succeeded, Vietnam would be added to the Sino-Soviet bloc's column in the global power balance. Vietnam also would serve as proof for other revolutionary movements in Asia and elsewhere that the United States, despite its nuclear weapons and vast economic resources, could be defeated. As for the nature of the warfare itself, Washington believed that the Vietminh's war against the South was similar to North Korea's aggression against South Korea, even if the Vietminh had not flagrantly crossed the dividing line. For U.S. military commanders, the struggle for Vietnam was just another variant of conventional warfare for which their soldiers and superior firepower were well prepared.

There was a double irony in this pattern of thinking. First, if the United States had sent diplomats to Beijing, they would have known that North Vietnam was not a puppet. Historically, China and Vietnam had been enemies, and in the early 1960s the last thing Mao wanted, with

3. Quoted in *New York Times*, April 8, 1954, 18. For a detailed critique, see Paul M. Kattenburg, *The Vietnam Trauma in American Foreign Policy: 1945–1975* (New Brunswick, N.J.: Transaction Books, 1980). For a recent defense of the theory and of the U.S. intervention more generally, see Michael Lind, *The Necessary War: A Reinterpretation of America's Most Disastrous Military Conflict* (New York: Free Press, 1999).

China in the midst of a domestic upheaval, was to risk a confrontation with the United States. Thus the United States, not aware of China's political situation or intentions—as was the case for China's earlier intervention in Korea—once again paid a high price for its refusal to recognize the PRC. Second, if the containment of China had been a key goal of the U.S. intervention, then the United States should have let South Vietnam fall. Ho was a nationalist, not just a communist, and a nationalistic Vietnam would have proven a stronger barrier to any possible Chinese ambitions of hegemony in Southeast Asia than a noncommunist South Vietnam governed by a despotic, despised regime.

In truth, then, far from ensuring containment, the Vietnam War undermined containment. The beneficiary of this U.S. engagement was the Soviet Union, which gained an enormous advantage in the quest for global public opinion. Indeed, the key domino that fell was not South Vietnam, but the consensus within the U.S. and allied governments that had favored the containment strategy.

THE PERILS OF INCREMENTALISM

The massive U.S. intervention in Vietnam by President Lyndon Johnson was by 1965 inevitable because, beginning with the administration of Harry Truman, every president had deepened the involvement in Vietnam. Although Truman at first opposed France's postwar efforts to restore its colonial rule, he changed his position to overcome French resistance to the American plan for the revival of Germany, especially its rearmament. After the Korean War erupted, the French war in Indochina became part of the global struggle against communism. At the time of France's defeat at Dienbienphu in 1954, Eisenhower, though deciding not to intervene militarily, backed the new government in South Vietnam, organized after France's defeat and withdrawal, with economic assistance and military training for its armed forces. But this training was in orthodox warfare, not in the unorthodox or guerrilla warfare that already had been observed in Vietnam. Besides, the Southeast Asia Treaty Organization (SEATO) was supposed to be the new state's security guarantee (see Chapter 4). President John Kennedy escalated the U.S. commitment in the early 1960s by sending in 16,500 military advisers to help the South Vietnamese army. Beginning in the spring of 1965, Johnson transformed this commitment—and the conflict in general—by sending in a steadily growing U.S. troop presence that ultimately included more than 500,000 soldiers.

Particularly significant during these years of piecemeal commitments was that at no point did policy makers in Washington resolve some basic questions about Vietnam: Was it vital to American security interests and, if so, how vital? If it had been vital earlier, was it still so in the early 1960s? Could the situation in South Vietnam be saved militarily given the nature of the government in Saigon (the South Vietnamese capital) and its seeming lack of popular support? If American forces were sent, then in what numbers? And how could they be used effectively in unorthodox warfare? What cost, if any, was South Vietnam "worth" to the United States?

Because incremental U.S. commitments were made whenever conditions in South Vietnam appeared ominous, these questions were never really debated at the highest levels of the government. And if the reasons for American involvement were not clear to leaders, they were lost entirely on millions of citizens. But past American commitments foreclosed any meaningful debate except over how much force was needed to "save" South Vietnam. Once committed, American forces could not be withdrawn without the failure of their mission being widely recognized.

During the Kennedy years, military advisers managed to prevent South Vietnam's total collapse, but by 1965 Johnson—who after Kennedy's assassination in November 1963 had concentrated on passing a major domestic reform program and getting elected in his own right—could no longer operate on this basis and avoid the central question of what the United States ought to do. South Vietnam was rapidly crumbling under the weight of its corrupt and incompetent government. In the face of this reality, Johnson sent in 200,000 troops in 1965, deepening the U.S. involvement and turning an incremental policy into a long-term commitment. After years of neglect and procrastination and with the situation growing worse daily, Washington had neither the time nor the inclination to make a carefully calculated decision; when the crucial decision was made, it was made by Johnson, a new president, on the advice of the Kennedy staff and cabinet he had inherited. Long-range policy had become a prisoner of the earlier short-range decisions made to tackle crises. Johnson's misfortune was that he could not procrastinate or make any more piecemeal moves. He was stuck with the decision of whether to escalate to prevent the defeat of the South Vietnamese army or to become, as he phrased it, the first president in U.S. history "to lose a war." Each president had done just enough to prevent this defeat. Johnson's escalation was the logical culmination of his predecessors' decisions.

But perhaps even more important than foreign policy considerations in this escalation was American domestic politics. Originally, in 1947, anticommunism often was used as a means of arousing the public and mobilizing popular support for Cold War policies while the nation in fact pursued more limited aims. But once an administration had justified its policy in terms of an anticommunist crusade and had aroused the public by promising to stop communism, it opened itself to attacks by the opposition party if setbacks were encountered, even if they occurred for reasons beyond America's ability to prevent them. The ousted party could then exploit such foreign policy issues by accusing the party in power of appeasement, of having "lost" this or that country, and of being "soft on communism." These kinds of accusations made it difficult to recognize the People's Republic of China, to build bridges to Eastern Europe, to negotiate with the Soviet Union or Cuba, and especially to discriminate between areas of vital and secondary importance to U.S. security.

Democratic administrations were more deeply affected by this political rhetoric than Republican administrations. The Democrats, who were in power when Nationalist China collapsed, were accused of "treason," of "selling out" China, and they lost the 1952 presidential election as a result. The desire to avoid accusations of being soft on communism was one key reason Truman advanced northward across the thirty-eighth parallel in Korea before the 1950 midterm elections, and one reason he found it impossible to negotiate any settlement of the war that left Korea divided. Kennedy, who had campaigned on a tough anti-Castro platform, found it impossible to reject the Eisenhower-initiated plan to invade Cuba, although the new president had serious doubts about it. Even Eisenhower, a conservative Republican president and victorious general who had led the Allies to victory over Germany, a man who hardly could be accused of disloyalty, had felt threatened enough by the right wing of the Republican Party that in 1954 he did not pull the United States out of Vietnam. Instead, he kept America in Vietnam by supporting the new South Vietnamese government. The fear of accusations of being soft on communism also led the Kennedy and Johnson administrations to make their piecemeal commitments in Vietnam, lest the Democrats be charged with the "loss" of Indochina as well as China, and it influenced Lyndon Johnson to bomb North Vietnam and to escalate the war by sending in the army.

Each president, then, thought each step in the growing involvement in Indochina to be less costly than doing nothing and disengaging from Vietnam. In the context of U.S. politics, defeat was believed to be unacceptable. The costs of nonintervention in terms of loss of public and congressional support were calculated to be much higher than the costs of intervention.

These examples illustrate the high price the United States consistently paid for its penchant to crusade and to moralize power politics. That price was overreaction, diplomatic rigidity, and unwise overt or covert interventions, with the attendant loss of lives and credibility of the policy and of the United States in general. National style was a principal cause of the long delay in recognizing China and the failure to exploit

Sino-Soviet differences. Worse, it was the main reason for misunderstanding Asian communism, including the war in Vietnam. It was certainly a key reason, if not *the* reason, for the protracted intervention. Because the domestic costs of losing a country to communism were so high, those in power felt compelled to intervene with the air force, navy, and army to avoid such losses. Presidents fervently wished to avoid accusations of appeasement, of betraying the nation's honor, and of weakening its security, especially just before elections, and there was always an election coming up.

THE MISCONDUCT OF GUERRILLA WARFARE

During its intervention in Southeast Asia, the United States virtually ignored the political structure of South Vietnam, and thereby imperiled its successful prosecution of the war. For years the United States had supported Ngo Dinh Diem, a devout Catholic whose authoritarian rule and aloofness alienated most of the mainly Buddhist population. By the time the military overthrew and murdered Diem in 1963, with Kennedy's knowledge and tacit blessing, the Vietminh already controlled much of South Vietnam; the social, political, and economic reforms needed to win the war had been neglected too long. That Diem's regime was so widely despised should have alerted future administrations; that Kennedy had said Diem had "gotten out of touch with the people" testified to the political bankruptcy in Saigon, as well as to the questionable wisdom of having the U.S. military intervention in the first place. Even with Diem gone, South Vietnam's governments were unable to rally popular support for a vigorous prosecution of the war against the Vietminh.

But Saigon's succession of corrupt, reactionary, and repressive regimes never reminded U.S. policy makers of Chiang Kai-shek and his Nationalist government in postwar China. At the time of China's fall, the Truman administration had decided the country could not be saved, except perhaps—and it was only *perhaps*—by incurring enormous military and economic costs, which it felt the American public would not be willing to pay. In addition, these costs would have diverted the nation's resources and efforts from its area of primary interest, Europe, where American security was at stake. According to Secretary of State Dean Acheson: "Nothing that this country did or could have done within the *reasonable* limits of its capabilities" could have changed the result in the conflict between Mao Zedong and Chiang Kai-shek.[4] Likewise, the attempt at containment in South Vietnam was risky in many respects.

4. U.S. Department of State, *United States Relations with Chin, with Special Reference to the Period 1944–1949* (Washington, D.C.: Government Printing Office, 1949), xvi. Italics added.

Truman's successors in Democratic administrations risked major domestic discontent. They also risked new questions about the fundamental assumptions of the foreign policy that had led to the war.

Certainly the possibility of achieving a quick victory over the Vietminh was remote, for guerrilla warfare is totally different from traditional warfare. The aim of a guerrilla war is to capture the government from within and do so by eroding the morale of the army and by undermining popular confidence in the government, thus isolating it. To achieve this objective, guerrilla forces do not have to inflict a complete defeat on the government's forces or compel them to surrender unconditionally. Indeed, guerrillas do not even meet these forces openly until the final stage of the war, and then they do so only to apply the coup de grâce. A guerrilla war is therefore a protracted conflict in which the guerrillas use hit-and-run tactics and engage only those smaller and weaker government forces they can defeat. The government's only defense against this strategy year is to deploy troops to guard every town, every village, and every bridge against possible attack. Unable to come to grips with the enemy and defeat it in battle, and suffering one small loss after another, the army becomes demoralized and its mood becomes defensive.

Although such tactics gradually weaken the military strength of the army, the guerrillas' main effort is directed at the civilian population. As the weaker side of the conflict, the guerrillas aim to wrest the allegiance of the population away from the government so that, without popular support, it simply collapses. The guerrillas do this in two ways. First, they gain control of the countryside where most of the people live, and, by winning battles with government forces, they demonstrate to the peasants that the government cannot protect them. The execution of village chiefs, who often are government representatives, is a common tactic to drive this point home. Second, and even more important, the guerrillas exploit any existing popular grievances. Communist guerrillas do not usually receive support because they are communists; the populace supports them because it believes they will oust the unpopular government and seek a new government that will meet the people's aspirations.

Indeed, according to Mao Zedong, guerrillas need the people "just as fish need water"; without popular support, guerrillas would not receive recruits, food, shelter, and information on the deployment of government forces. The guerrillas gain the support of the peasantry by successfully representing themselves as the liberators from colonialism or foreign rule, native despotic governments, economic deprivation, or social injustice. In this way they isolate the government in its own country. Thus, unlike conventional warfare in which each army seeks the destruction of the other's military forces, guerrilla warfare is based on a strategy of mobilizing popular support. A government that has the allegiance of its population does not provide fertile soil for guerrillas; where social dissatisfaction exists, however, guerrillas find an opening.

This is especially the case when the combatants in such conflicts oppose foreign troops whom they believe wrongly occupy their territory and must be expelled. European powers, including the French in Vietnam, were the targets of such uprisings during the colonial period, and the United States was widely perceived as carrying on France's imperial ambitions. In such cases, guerrillas are able to exploit the existing deep reservoir of hostility toward the foreign armies, along with the tactical advantage of fighting in their own familiar surroundings. Together, these factors place the occupying forces on the defensive and lead to a high level of confidence and *esprit de corps* among guerrilla fighters. As one scholar observed,

> The guerrilla's self image is not of a solitary fighter hiding among the people, but of a whole people mobilized for war, himself a loyal member, one among many. If you want to fight against us, the guerrillas say, you are going to have to fight civilians, for you are not at war with an army but with a nation. Therefore, you should not fight at all, and if you do, you are the barbarians, killing women and children.[5]

Guerrilla warfare is therefore not purely military; it also is political. Although the forces under attack must try to defeat the guerrillas in the field, their principal task is to tackle the political, social, and economic conditions that bred support for the guerrillas in the first place—that is, they must regain the "hearts and minds" of the populace. Counterguerrilla warfare, then, is an extremely difficult kind of war to wage—indeed, far more so than the traditional clash of armies—because the war cannot be won without extensive reforms. Yet these reforms have to be carried out in the midst of a war that is likely to last many years.

What all this means is that the United States, experienced only in conventional warfare, found guerrilla warfare hard to fight in Southeast Asia. Concerned primarily with social and political reforms, it ran counter to the traditional American military strategy, and the length of the war caused great frustration because the U.S. government, under intense public pressure, had promised repeatedly that the war would end soon, that its leaders saw "light at the end of the tunnel." When this very different kind of warfare did not yield swift and successful results, U.S. troops faced the choice of either pulling out or seeking some shortcut to victory through military escalation.

5. Michael Walzer, *Just and Unjust Wars: A Moral Argument with Historical Illustrations* (New York: Basic Books, 1977), 180.

THE MILITARY BATTLEFIELD: VIETNAM

During the war in Vietnam, American policy makers misplaced their confidence in U.S. military prowess and its ability to change the guerrillas' "rules of the game." In 1965 the illusion of American omnipotence had not yet died. After all, the United States had successfully confronted the Soviet Union in Cuba and compelled it to back down. Could there really be much doubt that its well-trained generals, in command of armies equipped with the newest and latest weapons from America's industry and under the leadership of that most efficient Pentagon manager, Secretary of Defense Robert McNamara, would be able to beat a few thousand "peasants in black pajamas"? With its sizable forces and its superior mobility and firepower, why should the United States have any problem finding the enemy's troops and destroying them, thereby compelling that enemy to desist from taking over South Vietnam? Characteristically, then, the emphasis was strictly military.

To win against guerrilla warfare, U.S. forces would have had to secure villages and to stay in them to root out the Vietminh and show the villagers that Saigon did care about them. Instead, the military carried out massive search-and-destroy operations. And the guerrillas, even if driven away from the villages, returned after the helicopters had left and continued to control the countryside. Because such large-scale operations could not be launched without preparation at the base camp and usually were preceded by air strikes and artillery bombardments of the area in which the troops would land, the Vietminh often disappeared and the whole operation ended in frustration.

American soldiers clearly did not understand the political nature of guerrilla warfare. They had been trained for conventional battle and to use maximum firepower to wear the enemy down in a war of attrition. The military was confident it could do this because its helicopters provided superior mobility and modern technology gave it the necessary firepower. The measure of success became the daily body count of communist dead.

When the war was extended by air to the North, the purpose of the bombing clearly was not military, although the United States claimed its goal was to stem the flow of men and supplies going south. The aim of the attacks was political—to persuade North Vietnam to stop the war. By gradually extending these attacks northward the United States was saying, in effect, that it would not withdraw, that the price Hanoi might have to pay for victory would be too high, and therefore that it had better desist.

But the bombing did not weaken Hanoi's will to prosecute the war, nor did it cut the flow of supplies sufficiently to hamper the fighting in

IMPACT AND INFLUENCE

ROBERT MCNAMARA

Robert McNamara, secretary of defense from 1961 to 1968, oversaw the American war effort in Vietnam. McNamara, a former president of the Ford Motor Company, joined other "whiz kids" who sought to introduce modern accounting methods and technical innovations to the armed forces. Among his other initiatives, McNamara led the effort to shift U.S. nuclear strategy from the "massive retaliation" of the Eisenhower years to a strategy based on a "flexible response."

The pressures of the war in Vietnam, however, gradually consumed McNamara's energies. An early advocate of U.S. military involvement, he began to question the war effort and called for a negotiated settlement. When this proved impossible, McNamara left the Johnson administration in February 1968 to become president of the World Bank. During his thirteen-year tenure at that institution, the World Bank greatly increased its assistance to developing countries.

McNamara's 1995 memoir, In Retrospect: The Tragedy and Lessons of Vietnam, *detailed the many mistaken assumptions, political problems, and tactical errors that led to the U.S. defeat in Southeast Asia.*

the South or greatly reduce troop infiltration.[6] Hanoi's persistence, in turn, led to increased calls by the military and Washington for more air strikes and new targets. Those who advocated intensifying the air war did not acknowledge that air power could not by itself win the war; instead, they insisted that it could if it were used with maximum effi-

6. Once again, important historical lessons were ignored. The sustained American attacks on Chinese supply lines in North Korea during the Korean War had shown that air power alone was unable to stop the flow of supplies to the fighting zone.

ciency. Air power, in short, came to be seen by some as an efficient, effective way of fighting the guerrillas, throttling their supply lines, breaking their morale, and finally compelling them to end the conflict at little cost in lives to the defender.[7]

This objective, however, remained unattainable. Moreover, the opposition was gaining strength. In South Vietnam, even the more stable military regime of Nguyen Van Thieu and Nguyen Cao Ky, which sought legitimation in the election of 1967, failed for years to implement a program of social and economic reform—that is, until 1970 when it adopted major land reform. It was particularly remiss in waiting so long to redistribute land from the usually absentee landlords to the peasants. Without such reforms, the Vietminh grew stronger. Militarily, every increase in American forces was met by the increased infiltration of both guerrillas and conventional troops from the North to the South. Nevertheless, the U.S. government issued optimistic battle reports and forecasts of victory on a regular basis.[8]

The 1968 Tet (Vietnamese New Year) offensive, launched on the last day of January, was the Johnson administration's Dienbienphu. Tet showed once and for all—and in full view of Americans, who could see it nightly on their television sets—that, despite the repeated optimistic predictions, the enemy had again been badly underestimated. It launched a major countrywide offensive and attacked Saigon, Hué, and every other provincial capital; a Vietminh squad even penetrated the U.S. embassy compound, thereby scoring a significant symbolic victory. The fighting that followed, however, was bloody and destructive of the Vietminh. In fact, because so many Vietminh were killed, the North Vietnamese army actually assumed the main burden of fighting the Americans. Nevertheless, the Vietminh had clearly demonstrated that neither an American army of a half million men nor the far larger South Vietnamese army could ensure the security of urban dwellers—and the communists presumably already controlled much of the countryside.

THE POLITICAL BATTLEFIELD: THE UNITED STATES

In Vietnam, then, American power and its effectiveness in unorthodox warfare proved to be greatly exaggerated. Tactically, American forces had seized and retained the offensive, claiming the destruction of large

7. Secretary McNamara and his top aides confidently defended this strategy and predicted victory based on advanced computer models and cost-benefit calculations, most of which were proven wrong in the context of guerrilla warfare. See David Halberstam, *The Best and the Brightest* (New York: Random House, 1972).

8. For an elaboration, see H. R. McMaster, *Dereliction of Duty: Lyndon Johnson, Robert McNamara, the Joint Chiefs of Staff, and the Lies that Led to Vietnam* (New York: HarperCollins, 1997).

numbers of enemy soldiers. But strategically the Vietminh had maintained the upper hand, and the Americans were on the defensive. For example, by using about 80 percent of their forces to find and destroy North Vietnamese troops in the relatively unpopulated central highlands and frontier regions, the Americans were unable to secure and protect the 90 percent of the South Vietnamese population living in the Mekong Delta and coastal plains. This strategy called into question not just America's protective capacity but also its wisdom. Having left the cities unprotected, except for elements of the South Vietnamese army, allied forces had to fight their way back into the urban areas and towns the Vietminh had infiltrated. Thus if after almost three years of American help South Vietnam was still that insecure and the enemy that strong, the wisdom of continuing the war, let alone sending further American reinforcements, was bound to be intensely debated.

As if this were not enough, a growing number of Americans believed the war to be morally ambiguous, if not downright immoral. There had never been a clear-cut transgression of the seventeenth parallel dividing North Vietnam and South Vietnam, which made the accusation that Hanoi was an aggressor less believable. The undemocratic Saigon government and its apparent lack of popularity gave credence to the view that the war was a rebellion against Saigon's repression and against the previous imposition of colonial rule.[9] The massive, sometimes indiscriminate use of American firepower, which led to the widespread destruction of civilian life; the creation of thousands of refugees; and, especially, the hostility of the peasants whose support was vital for military success—these things and more already had pricked the consciences of many Americans concerned about their nation's historic image as compassionate and humane. The tanks rumbling into cities after Tet, the divebombing of apartment houses, the civilian suffering, and the personal tragedies left television viewers—who saw only one side of the war and not, for example, the Vietminh's deliberate slaughter of thousands of professional people and bureaucrats in the city of Hué—asking themselves if there was any point in "destroying a country in order to save it."

Within the United States, the Tet offensive aroused antiwar feelings, which had been growing throughout 1967 as the war continued, seemingly without end. Johnson's initial support eroded on both the right and the left, with the right demanding an end to the war through escalation and the left seeking an end through de-escalation, if not with-

9. In 1950 the South Korean government had a similar autocratic reputation, but the attack across the thirty-eighth parallel focused attention on North Korean ambitions and justified the American intervention. No one in the United States raised questions about defending a "corrupt dictatorship."

drawal. The articulate opposition to the conflict expressed by a number of liberal and moderate Republican and Democratic senators, especially the chairman of the Senate Foreign Relations Committee, J. William Fulbright, lent respectability to the opposition also vocalized by many politicians, professors, students, journalists, editorial writers, and television commentators. Indeed after Tet, Fulbright and his committee became an alternative source of interpretation and policy recommendations for the president.

Thus, although the Vietminh suffered heavy losses during the Tet fighting, the United States suffered a political defeat. The guerrilla strategy of psychologically exhausting the opponent had succeeded; the American strategy of physical attrition had failed. The U.S. military won many battles but lost the war as the public grew tired of the struggle in Vietnam, which remained a mysterious and confusing place for the American public. Indeed, policy makers learned quickly that during such hostilities politics goes on as usual, with most domestic interest groups pursuing their specific sets of interests and preferences; butter is not automatically subordinated to guns. But, as the costs of a conflict rise in terms of lives, inflation, and taxes, public disaffection also grows. So do antiwar demonstrations and parades. In the 1960s some of these events spilled over into violent clashes with the police and supporters of the war.

The Vietnam War, then, involved two battlefields. The first, in Vietnam, was bloody but inconclusive militarily.[10] The second, in the United States, was not bloody, but it was decisive politically. As the war dragged on, the nation's will to continue it declined, unlike in the two world wars (total wars) when the United States sensed that its security, if not its survival, was at stake, and thus all issues were subordinated to the prosecution of the war. In a limited war important issues may be at stake, but the security threat to the United States may not be apparent. How could the loss of South Korea or South Vietnam have diminished U.S. security? Neither North Korea nor North Vietnam could invade the United States.

The guerrillas were well aware of the two battlefields and knew which one was more important. Gen. Vo Nguyen Giap, the North Vietnamese strategist who had overseen his country's victories against France and the United States, spoke of the impatience of democracies at war. He had surmised that a strategy in which the war never seemed to end, in which the minimum goal was simply not to lose, would eventually erode the opponents' will to continue. As the war dragged on and as the casualties

10. For a defense of U.S. military strategy after the Tet offensive, see Lewis Sorley, *A Better War: The Unexamined Victories and Final Tragedy of America's Last Years in Vietnam* (New York: Harcourt, Brace, 1999).

and costs mounted, the democracies would throw in the towel. It was their "home fronts" that were decisive, where the "real battle" would be won. For that reason, North Vietnam launched the Tet offensive just as the 1968 political primaries were about to begin in the United States against a background of widespread opposition to the war.[11]

Disagreement over the war led two senators from the president's party, Eugene McCarthy and Robert Kennedy, to contest Johnson's renomination as the Democratic standard-bearer. Running as "peace candidates," they provided a rallying point for the growing numbers of Americans disenchanted with the war. But then in March 1968, at the end of the speech that laid the basis for the Paris peace talks, the president announced he would not run for a second term. Lyndon Johnson's tragedy was that he had come into office seeking a "Great Society" in America; instead, the war destroyed him. The changing American mood was evident in the 1968 presidential campaign. Vice President Hubert Humphrey, nominated by the Democrats in Chicago after bloody clashes between police and antiwar protestors (many of them McCarthy supporters) and bitter disagreement among the delegates over Vietnam, was mercilessly heckled during most of the campaign. As a member of the administration, he found it difficult to disavow the war; when he took his own "risk for peace," it was very late in the campaign.

In these circumstances of Democratic disunity, former vice president Richard Nixon, a career anticommunist and the Republican nominee, found it inexpedient to charge the Democrats with a "no-win" policy; instead he softened his views on the war. Indeed, in his speeches the menace abroad suddenly ran a poor second to the "moral decay" at home. Generally both candidates fell over themselves in their eagerness to abandon both anticommunist slogans and the war, offering instead hopes for an "honorable" peace in Vietnam and for "law and order" at home. Halting communist aggression was abandoned as an issue; stopping further costly foreign adventures—"no more Vietnams"—became the new issue. In Vietnam the only question was when to get out and on what terms. By not losing, the North Vietnamese had won; by not winning, the United States had indeed lost.

DISENGAGEMENT FROM VIETNAM

Before the United States could reshape its relationship with the Soviet Union and China—the opposing superpowers which represented legitimate security concerns to Americans—it had to unburden itself of the Vietnam War. Vietnam was a drain on U.S. resources and a political

11. See Karnow, *Vietnam*, 558–566.

albatross for Nixon, who was reelected in 1972. But in their thinking about "acceptable" terms for withdrawal, Nixon and his national security adviser, Henry Kissinger, were heavily influenced by their perceptions of great-power relationships. One course open to Nixon, which would have brought him popular acclaim, was to pull all American forces immediately out of Vietnam on the grounds that the United States had fulfilled long enough its obligations to defend Saigon. But in the president's view the central issue was maintaining American credibility abroad. "Peace with honor" became his slogan.

The Nixon administration was determined that it would not simply withdraw or accept any settlement that was tantamount to a defeat—namely, a coalition government in Saigon controlled by the communists. Nixon believed that it would not be feasible to establish a relaxation of tensions (détente) with the Soviet Union and China if America's prestige—reputation for power—was tattered. Why should the Soviet Union, which was rapidly building up its strategic power, settle for parity and mutually acceptable peaceful coexistence if it sensed that America was weak and could be pushed around? Why should China tone down its revolutionary rhetoric and conduct a more traditional state-to-state diplomacy, and indeed move closer to the United States, if it could not count on American strength and determination to resist what it saw as Soviet attempts at hegemony in Asia? In short, Nixon calculated that the country had to "hang tough" in Vietnam to normalize relations with the Soviet Union and China.

Nixon and Kissinger therefore devised a twofold strategy. First, American ground troops would be withdrawn gradually to reduce the costs of the war and make further hostilities tolerable for the "silent majority" of Americans who, Nixon felt, were loyal, though fatigued, and would support him in an "honorable" ending of the war. He also hoped, however, that the continued involvement of some U.S. forces, especially in the air, would provide an incentive for Hanoi to negotiate an end to the war. This incentive would presumably be all the stronger if the president's strategy worked at home—that is, if it removed Vietnam as a principal issue in the 1972 presidential contest and facilitated Nixon's reelection. Hanoi, then confronted with the prospect that the war could last at least four more years, would have a reason to settle the war diplomatically.

The second part of the president's strategy was the "Vietnamization" of the war. While American troops were being withdrawn, the South Vietnamese forces would receive the training and modern arms they needed to take over the ground fighting. This would counter the criticism and pressure that had grown in Congress, on campuses, and elsewhere for faster U.S. troop withdrawals and for the abandonment of Saigon. But the danger inherent in the president's strategy was that the North Vietnamese would attack after American troops were withdrawn but before the South Vietnamese were ready to meet the enemy in battle.

In March 1970 Cambodia's Prince Norodom Sihanouk, who had long tolerated the communist troops and supply lines in his country, was overthrown by an anti-Vietnamese military regime that wanted communist troops out of Cambodia. When the communists moved toward the Cambodian capital to unseat the new government, Nixon decided to intervene and, without public knowledge, ordered air strikes deep into Cambodia. Once this became known, it reignited domestic dissension. After four students at Kent State University were shot to death on May 4 by Ohio National Guardsmen during an antiwar rally, campuses erupted nationwide and dozens of colleges and universities were completely shut down. Protesters once again turned out for peaceful mass demonstrations in Washington and in other cities. The reaction to U.S. policy in Cambodia made it clear that it would be foolhardy for the president to repeat such an action.

Unfortunately, South Vietnam's decrepit army remained the linchpin of the president's strategy. In the spring of 1972, after the withdrawal of the U.S. Army withdrawn from the battlefield, North Vietnam launched an unexpected, large-scale attack across the demilitarized zone between North Vietnam and South Vietnam. Again, the South Vietnamese army performed poorly. American air support staved off even worse losses, but the costs to Saigon were severe.

With Vietnamization in danger, Nixon "re-Americanized" the war by ordering extensive bombing of the North and a blockade of North Vietnam's ports with mines. The goal was to stop the flow of Soviet and Chinese supplies. Simultaneously Nixon offered Hanoi the complete withdrawal of all American forces from Vietnam within four months if all prisoners of war were returned and an internationally supervised ceasefire was established. The communists could keep their forces in the South—a significant concession previously offered only in secret talks. Equally important, the president did not insist on the survival of Nguyen Van Thieu's government. He instead expressed hope that the U.S. withdrawal "would allow negotiations and a political settlement between the Vietnamese themselves." This new set of proposals provided a concrete and serious basis for negotiations. But Hanoi rejected the offer. It appeared to want the president to do the one thing he refused to do: guarantee communist control in Saigon. His proposal, in fact, had seemed to suggest that the North Vietnamese should do this job for themselves, if they could.

The North Vietnamese also faced a dilemma. Despite the heavy U.S. bombing and blockade, the Soviet government was proceeding with direct negotiations with the U.S. government. And China no longer opposed a negotiated settlement of the war. Moscow and Beijing both gave priority to their relationships with Washington, leaving Hanoi isolated politically. Yet the North Vietnamese leaders had sought a unified Vietnam for so long, had paid such a high price for it, and had been so often cheated out of fulfillment of their dream by their adversaries that they were suspicious of Nixon's offer and resentful of the declining Soviet and Chinese support.

The situation, though, changed abruptly. A month before the 1972 U.S. presidential election, Hanoi, probably fearing that Nixon's reelection might make him less accommodating, signaled its willingness to accept something less than a total victory. By late October Hanoi had negotiated a tentative Indochina settlement. The terms included a supervised cease-fire that would halt all American bombing and mining and bring about withdrawal of all U.S. forces within two months; separate future cease-fires were expected in Laos and Cambodia. Prisoners of war would be exchanged by both sides. A series of mixed political commissions, composed of elements from the Vietminh, the Saigon government, and neutralists, would then be established to work out a new South Vietnamese political order leading to a new constitution and the election of a new government.

The Nixon administration felt it had achieved an "honorable peace." The North Vietnamese, after having declared for years that the Thieu government would have to go as a precondition for a cease-fire, now accepted Thieu as the leader of the government faction. He remained in control of a sizable army and large police forces that he used in administering most of the countryside and all the urban centers, leaving only minor areas and a small percentage of the population under the control of the Vietminh and the approximately 145,000 North Vietnamese troops. The Thieu faction therefore seemed to have a good chance to compete politically and militarily with the communists after the fighting ended.

But Thieu stalled in agreeing to the tentative October 1972 settlement because the United States had accepted the presence of North Vietnamese troops in areas of the South during the period of cease-fire. When Thieu stalled, so did the North Vietnamese; both sides appeared eager to strengthen their positions as the final stage of peace talks resumed in Paris. In response, Nixon ordered heavy bombing of the North, including civilian centers in Hanoi and Haiphong. The "Christmas bombings" of late 1972 continued for several days. But the president had to defend the bombardment against outcries from the public and the newly elected Democratic majority in Congress. He argued that it was necessary to demonstrate American resolve against North Vietnam in the crucial final days of conflict.

The end of the Vietnam War came in January 1973 when the North Vietnamese returned to the negotiating table and both sides signed a cease-fire agreement at the Hotel Majestic in Paris. Twelve nations, including the United States, the Soviet Union, and China, formally approved the treaty in March. In Washington, the Nixon administration could now focus on improving relations with China and the Soviet Union, and the United States would no longer have to pour its resources into a war that deeply divided the country.

Two years after the Paris conference, however, North Vietnamese troops launched a final offensive against the remnants of the South Vietnamese army. Although Thieu insisted that Nixon had pledged continued U.S. support in the event of such an offensive, Nixon had resigned under the cloud of the Watergate scandal and President Gerald Ford, under great pressure from Congress and public opinion, refused to recommit American resources to Vietnam.[12] Thieu resigned on April 21, 1975, and nine days later Saigon fell to the Vietminh as the last American officials in the city were hurriedly shuttled away by helicopter. South Vietnam then surrendered unconditionally. Twenty-one years after the failed Geneva agreement of 1954, Vietnam was again reunited, its long and painful quest for independence having finally borne fruit.

CONGRESS VERSUS THE 'IMPERIAL PRESIDENCY'

America's defeat in Vietnam revealed the limitations of its power and raised serious questions about its strategy of containing communism in all corners of the world. At home, the tragic events led lawmakers in Washington to curb presidential power in foreign policy, especially the power of the commander in chief to commit American forces to battle. Under the Constitution, the president is chiefly responsible for the routine conduct of foreign policy, but Congress also shares many of these responsibilities, including the power to declare war. In the 1950s congressional conservatives had wished to limit presidential authority because the president was, in their minds, not anticommunist enough, and he might, acting on the advice of the "pro-communists" in the State Department, sell the country down the river. Beginning in the late 1960s the liberals also sought to restrain the president's authority, but for a different reason: in their opinion, the president, the "military-industrial complex," and the CIA were *too* anticommunist and were intent on involving the country in too many costly adventures abroad.

12. This scandal involved illegal activities by the Nixon administration during its 1972 reelection campaign and the elaborate means devised by Nixon to cover up these activities.

Conservative or liberal, the remedy for the "imperial" presidency's alleged abuse of its authority and its virtually solo determination of foreign policy was the same: to reassert congressional control of the formulation of foreign policy and to restore the constitutional balance that presumably had been upset.[13] Presidents would be restrained so that they could no longer appease America's enemies, thereby pleasing conservatives, or act in an interventionist, warlike manner, thereby pleasing liberals. The abuse of power by Nixon, a conservative president whose anticommunist zeal dated back to the inception of the Cold War, reinforced the liberal sentiment to curb presidential powers and compel a more restrained and moderate policy.

Taking the political offensive, Congress passed in 1973 the War Powers Act to constrain the president and assert its own constitutional authority. Under the act, which was approved over President Nixon's veto, the president was obligated to consult Congress before committing troops overseas and to report to Congress immediately afterward about the need to continue the mission. The president was obligated to terminate the mission within sixty days unless Congress agreed to extend it, a provision designed to preclude the kind of "mission creep" that occurred in Vietnam. Although rejected by later presidents as unconstitutional and rarely invoked by Congress, the War Powers Act symbolized the national mood that blamed the war on excessive presidential power.[14]

Additional evidence of the new mood was the widespread belief that priority should be given to the nation's domestic problems. These problems became apparent in the 1960s when the "affluent society," as it was called in the 1950s, began to reveal its dark side, such as urban slums, suburban sprawl, air and water pollution, and deteriorating schools and hospitals. Critics of the war wanted to spend money to improve the quality of life for all American citizens. Instead of crusading for democracy abroad, they argued, the United States should start crusading to make *America* safe for democracy. Liberal critics of the war in Vietnam quoted Edmund Burke to the effect that "example is the school of mankind." The example should be one of a democratic society protecting the rights of its citizens as its paramount task.

But such freedom could not be fully enjoyed in a nation whose excessive preoccupation with foreign affairs drained its powers and resources,

13. See Arthur M. Schlesinger Jr., *The Imperial Presidency* (Boston: Houghton Mifflin, 1989).

14. "If events have suggested that the goal has not been reached," one scholar observed in 1990, "the [War Powers] resolution still remains as a serious legal attempt to solve an enduring dilemma." See Morris S. Ogul, "The War Powers Resolution: Congress versus the President," in *The Constitution and National Security: A Bicentennial View,* ed. Howard E. Shuman and Walter R. Thomas (Washington, D.C.: National Defense University Press, 1990), 314.

both human and material. An expansionist foreign policy, it was charged, was unlikely to bring with it any lasting greatness, prestige, and security. Rather, as the Founders of the United States were quick to emphasize centuries earlier, the constant expenditure of energy on adventures abroad would ruin the country's domestic base. The Cold War preoccupation was corrupting American society. An institutional imbalance was eroding constitutional processes, particularly when powerful and energetic presidents, in the name of national security, not only committed the nation to war but also sanctioned plots to assassinate foreign leaders such as Fidel Castro, lied to the American people and Congress about what they were doing or why they were doing it (intervention in Vietnam), acted covertly (bombing Laos and Cambodia, overthrowing elected regimes in Guatemala and Chile), and in various ways violated the constitutional rights of American citizens. Moreover, the large-scale diversion of the country's resources to its external commitments meant a corresponding neglect of domestic needs.

In short, extensive involvement in the world was tainting the American promise and vision, just as early American leaders had warned. This idea had been at the heart of the old isolationism: America could take care of its own needs, serve as an example for humankind, and remain pure in a morally wicked world only if it avoided or minimized political involvement in it. An active U.S. role internationally would endanger, not protect, American democracy.

Perhaps the most revealing evidence of America's reaction to Vietnam was the reassertion of the deep-seated attitude that the exercise of power internationally was immoral and corrupting. Once power politics could no longer be justified in moral terms of democracy versus dictatorship, as in the two world wars, the sense of guilt over using power returned. To many, the Vietnam War represented a moral turning point in American foreign policy; the United States was guilty of backing the more repressive and illegitimate side. Not surprisingly, sensitive people deeply committed to human values—and who watched history's first televised war—repented their former support of containment-through-power as if in giving that support they had been unwitting sinners. Fulbright, who had been a leading advocate of equating postwar foreign policy with moral mission, now attacked America's global role as evidence of an "arrogance of power." [15] He did not merely assert that the United States had overextended itself and needed to cut back on its commitments. He stated something far more fundamental: that all great powers seemed to need to demonstrate that they were bigger, better, and stronger than other nations and that this arrogance of power, from

15. J. William Fulbright, *The Arrogance of Power* (New York: Vintage Books, 1967).

which the United States then suffered, was the real cause of international conflict and war.

In brief, it was the exercise of power per se that, regardless of a nation's intentions, made it arrogant. Power itself was corrupting; even if justified in moral terms, its use was immoral except in clear, unambiguous cases of self-defense. No idea could have been more characteristically American. Power was evil and its exercise tantamount to the abuse of power; abstention from power politics, providing an example to the world of a truly just and democratic society, was a more moral policy. America should be loved for its principles and for practicing what it professed rather than feared for its might. Democracy and power politics were simply incompatible.

In the United States, the "Vietnam syndrome" lingered until the end of the Cold War in 1989. In terms of its influence on foreign policy, the country became far less willing to commit itself to military intervention abroad. Furthermore, the Vietnam syndrome entailed a growing skepticism and distrust toward the government and its military leadership. It did not help that Richard Nixon's administration was shamed during this period by the Watergate scandal. But even without Watergate, for the first time the United States was confronted with the prospect that its power in the world had peaked. For many Americans, disillusionment with Vietnam led them to believe that their country's reputation as the world's "beacon of democracy" had been tainted, and that during the war their leaders had been guilty of misjudgment, deception, and wanton destruction of human life. The United States, it seemed, had reduced itself to the status of an "ordinary" world power.

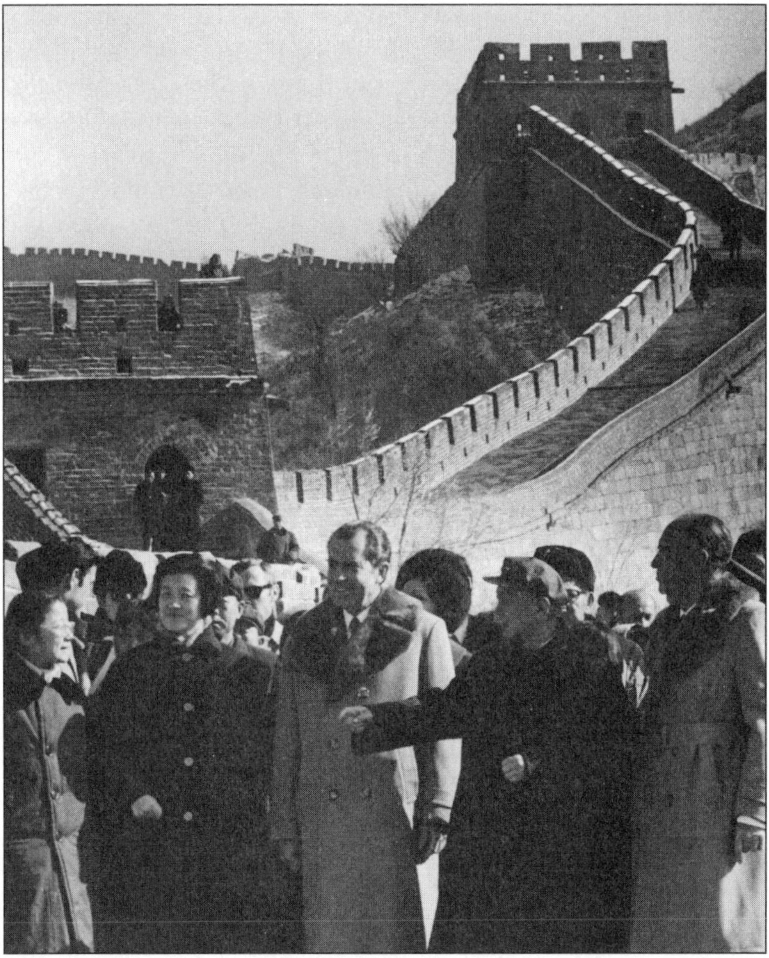

In 1972 Richard Nixon became the first U.S. president to visit the People's Republic of China.

CHAPTER SIX

The Era of Superpower Détente

The United States emerged from the Vietnam War with new doubts about its role in foreign affairs. Having assumed the status of a global superpower for only one generation, America found its traditional antipathy toward world politics quickly reasserting itself. The debacle in Vietnam confirmed many Americans' worst fears about how the United would behave once it joined the ranks of the great powers. The episode also raised serious doubts about using anticommunism as the basis for the country's foreign policy. Before Vietnam, the United States had readily asserted itself overseas to contain communism at every turn. After Vietnam, American leaders became much more cautious about intervening in regional conflicts.

The U.S. containment policy had been weakened by the increasing pluralism of the communist bloc. It was one thing to fight communism that appeared monolithic. But when the communist states became fragmented globally, and divided internally, the appropriate Western response became more difficult to define. Did the United States now have to distinguish among the communist states, determining which posed a true threat? What changes in the distribution of power could America safely allow? And where, if anywhere, and against whom did it still have to draw frontiers? These questions became troublesome in the 1970s because with each case policy makers would now face several policy options—and a situation fraught with intense controversy and bitter debate. In addition, anticommunism would no longer be as useful a means of eliciting popular support, not just because of the Vietnam debacle but also because the United States might well be supporting one communist state against another.

During this period the Nixon and Ford administrations pursued détente—a relaxation of tensions—because of changes in the United States and in the global balance of power. The United States had become, after Vietnam, a nation weary of its foreign policy burdens. As noted in Chapter 5, this mood was demonstrated by attacks on the "imperial presidency" and restraints imposed on the White House by a more assertive and watchful Congress.[1] In the pre-Vietnam era of containment, Congress rarely had questioned the president's authority to use the armed forces or the Central Intelligence Agency (CIA) to carry out U.S. policy. But after Vietnam, America's self-appointed role as "global policeman" was widely criticized and emphasis shifted to the nation's own shortcomings and to its limited power. Détente was a course to be pursued until the United States could once again play the leading role many felt was required to protect U.S. interests against Soviet expansion.

Fueling the drive for détente was a significant shift in the U.S.-Soviet balance of power. Simply put, in military strength the Soviet Union had caught up to the United States. Before 1970 the balance between the two superpowers had long been between the U.S. Strategic Air Command (SAC), increasingly bolstered by the navy's nuclear submarines, and the Red Army. American bombers and missiles deterred the Soviet Union by threatening to destroy its cities. The Soviets' achievement of an intercontinental capability and capacity to destroy the United States stemmed from their massive buildup beginning in 1964. From the 1950s

1. See Barbara Sinclair, "Congressional Party Leaders in the Foreign Policy and Defense Policy Arena," in *Congress Resurgent: Foreign and Defense Policy on Capitol Hill*, ed. Randall Ripley and James M. Lindsay (Ann Arbor: University of Michigan Press, 1993).

to the late 1960s, America's strategic power had been balanced not by Moscow's bomber and missile force, which had been relatively small, but by the Red Army. These powerful ground forces, it was believed, could overrun Western Europe and quickly defeat North Atlantic Treaty Organization (NATO) forces. Thus the balance of power had been asymmetric: the United States held strategic superiority and an intercontinental reach; the Soviet Union maintained conventional superiority and a regional reach. But by 1970 the Soviet Union's strategic power had achieved parity with that of the United States, and the Soviets could now hold America's population, as well as that of Western Europe, hostage. Moreover, the Soviet buildup showed no sign of slowing down, not even after a situation of mutual assured destruction (MAD) had been unarguably reached.

Even during the period of U.S. strategic superiority, Soviet leaders were willing to risk limited challenges, such as in Berlin and Cuba, but they remained cautious during confrontations. When there was resistance, the Kremlin retreated. American power, therefore, set limits as to how far the Soviets felt they could push. But because the strategic balance was now shifting, a continuation of the containment policy by means of nuclear deterrence was becoming riskier. Soviet leaders had gained a new sense of confidence in their power. Indeed, the Soviet Union now belonged to the most exclusive club in the world, and the implications of its membership were clarified when the Soviet foreign minister informed the world that, henceforth, no important issue anywhere could be resolved without the Soviet Union.

At the same time that it was strengthening its nuclear arsenal, the Soviet Union was engaging in a massive conventional buildup, particularly of a modern surface navy and airlift capability. Thus as the Soviet Union's ability to neutralize America's nuclear force grew, its capacity to project its conventional power beyond Eurasia also grew. The Soviet naval buildup, which by the late 1970s had produced a navy that exceeded that of the United States in numbers of combat ships, was not needed for defense. Would the Soviet Union, in these new circumstances, be content to expand its influence only on land and in nearby areas? Or would it, as a result of its new might, gain confidence and act more boldly? By contrast, would the United States, now that it had lost its strategic superiority, be more reluctant to react?

Henry Kissinger, Nixon's influential national security adviser, compared the Soviet Union's emergence as a world power to Germany's appearance on the world scene in the early twentieth century. In both cases the challengers were land powers. The symbols of their aspirations and determination to expand were the navies they built. Nothing could have carried greater symbolic weight for Great Britain and the United

States, the two greatest naval powers in their respective times. The United States recognized that Germany's emergence and desire to become a world power had resulted in World War I. In this respect, how could the Soviet Union's newly gained power and its determination to pursue a *weltpolitik* (global policy) be managed peacefully so as not to threaten American security interests? As a badge of its newly achieved equal status, Moscow, like Germany years earlier, sought overseas clients, revolutionary states that would become members of the Soviet bloc. Although these territories were usually of limited strategic and economic value, they were important as symbols of communism's global advance. Thus the Soviet Union's massive military buildup raised questions not just about the military balance and its stability but also about the Soviets' ultimate intentions.

Nations that have seen their power decline relative to that of other states normally adjust by reducing their commitments or by seeking new allies or greater contributions from current allies. They generally also seek to reduce threats to their interests through diplomacy. When it lost its strategic superiority, however, the United States did not curtail its obligations; instead, it sought to preserve them through détente. As a political means of managing the superpowers' adversarial relationship, this strategy was aimed at securing American interests at lower levels of tension and cost than those required by the policy of Cold War confrontation and crisis management. The U.S.-Soviet balance would still be bipolar, but it would be more complex and fluid than in the earlier Cold War era.[2]

MANAGING THE SUPERPOWER RIVALRY

One crucial question the decline of anticommunism posed for the future conduct of American foreign policy was whether, in the absence of anticommunism, the United States would dirty its hands by conducting diplomacy on the basis of traditional "power politics." When during the early Cold War *realpolitik,* based on power, was synonymous with *idealpolitik,* based on ideology, it had been easy for the United States to be a leader and to organize various coalitions against the ideological foe. The U.S. government could maintain the balance of power as long as it could disguise from its own people what it was doing and pretend it was engaged in a moral crusade. But could a nation that historically had condemned power politics adapt its outlook and style to a world in which

2. The post-Vietnam balance of power is best understood as *bipolycentric,* meaning that the two superpowers remained dominant but that other countries, particularly those in Western Europe and East Asia, became stronger and more assertive.

justifying foreign policy in terms of ideological crusades was outmoded? Or would America, no longer believing it had an ideological mission, lapse into its traditional withdrawal from great-power politics?

In 1968 the incoming Nixon administration confronted a novel postwar situation: how to conduct foreign policy in the absence of a domestic consensus. In response to this dilemma the administration turned to a foreign policy based on the traditional logic of the state system. This dramatic shift away from a style that stemmed from the nation's domestic values and experiences to a balance-of-power rationale was somewhat surprising because Nixon previously had been virulently anticommunist and possessed by an inflexible moralism that rejected having anything to do with communists. But as president, he and Henry Kissinger, a German-born Jewish immigrant and Harvard professor who also became secretary of state in Nixon's second term, rejected the traditional American justification for participating in foreign affairs.[3]

Indeed, the administrations of Nixon and his post-Watergate successor, Gerald Ford, might well be called the Kissinger era. Kissinger developed, articulated, and justified the new American grand strategy, which in many ways ran counter to the country's traditional style of foreign policy. He personally carried out much of its public as well as private diplomacy, and he provided an element of continuity amid the transfer of power in August 1974 from Nixon to Ford. Kissinger so dominated these eight years that one observer described him as the only national security adviser and secretary of state ever served by two presidents.

THE KISSINGER PHILOSOPHY

The philosophy underlying American foreign policy during the Kissinger years (1969–1977) began with the assumption that international politics was not a fight between the "good" side and the "bad" side. All states, communist or noncommunist, had the right to exist and possessed legitimate interests. A nation, therefore, did not launch crusades against an adversary on the assumption that differences of interests represented a conflict of virtue and evil. The better part of wisdom, Kissinger believed, was to learn to live with other states, to defend one's interests if encroached upon, but also to attempt to resolve differences and build on shared interests. International politics was not just conflict but cooperation as well. Differences, admittedly, would not be easily or quickly reconciled; views of national interests usually were deeply held and not easily relinquished. Summit meetings were an important part of

3. For a thorough review of Kissinger's life and career, see Walter Isaacson, *Kissinger: A Biography* (New York: Simon and Schuster, 1992). For a more critical appraisal, see Seymour H. Hersh, *The Price of Power: Kissinger in the Nixon White House* (New York: Summit Books, 1983).

the negotiating process, but one summit could not solve all problems, and to raise false hopes that it would was to produce the cynicism and disillusionment that would endanger diplomacy itself. Good personal relations among leaders might smooth this process, but they were not a substitute for hard bargaining, and accords basically reflected the ratio of power between the nations the leaders represented.[4]

How then should the United States deal with a communist dictatorship whose values and practices it abhorred? The most the United States could expect was to nudge the Soviet Union's international behavior in a responsible direction. American power was too limited to transform another superpower's domestic behavior. American demands would be resisted, which, in turn, would jeopardize accords on international issues that otherwise might have been resolvable. The United States, then, simply had to abandon its habit of crusading to democratize adversaries. Coexistence with a communist regime such as that of the Soviet Union was necessary if peace and security were to be preserved. The key, of course, was the balance of power, and the United States had to try to accommodate the legitimate needs of the principal challenger to that balance. Power neutralizes opposing power, and by satisfying the interests of other great powers the United States would be more likely to produce acceptance of the present international system than by perpetuating their hostility to a system in which they had little vested interest. No state could be completely satisfied, but a state could be relatively satisfied.

Kissinger's view, then, concentrated on the powerful actors in the state system. Although he brought the rhetoric and style of American foreign policy more in line with the operational norms of the international system, a fundamental continuity in policy remained in place. The Soviet-American balance remained the preoccupation; it was still the Soviet Union, as a great power, whose influence needed to be contained and its behavior moderated. This unity of rhetoric and action—the explanation of U.S. policy in terms of power, balances, spheres of influence, national interests, and the limits of American power, as well as the specific rejection of ideological justifications and crusades—represented the socialization of American foreign policy by the state system.

Kissinger, therefore, viewed détente not only as a strategy selected to secure American interests at a lower level of tensions and costs but also as a continuation of containment at a time when the United States had

4. For an instructive comparison of Kissinger's approach to that of other realists, see Michael Joseph Smith, *Realist Thought from Weber to Kissinger* (Baton Rouge: Louisiana State University Press, 1986). For an application of Kissinger's worldview to his actions as a policy maker, see Stephen G. Walker, "The Interface between Beliefs and Behavior: Henry Kissinger's Operational Code and the Vietnam War," *Journal of Conflict Resolution* (March 1977): 129–168.

IMPACT AND INFLUENCE

HENRY KISSINGER

For eight years during the height of the Cold War, Henry Kissinger (pictured above in 1976 Senate testimony) dominated the process of American foreign policy. A Jewish refugee from Nazi Germany, Kissinger served in the U.S. Army during World War II. He then joined the faculty of at Harvard University, where his studies of European power politics and nuclear strategy impressed Richard Nixon. As President Nixon's national security adviser, Kissinger took a lead role in seeking "peace with honor" in Vietnam, establishing superpower détente, and mediating peace talks between Israel and its Arab rivals.

Kissinger, like George Kennan, often criticized the U.S. government's moralistic approach to foreign policy. As a result, Kissinger often angered liberals and conservatives alike who considered the United States to be an exceptional world power that should rise above its own self-interests. Similarly, Kissinger's strategy in Vietnam drew condemnation from liberals, who demanded a prompt U.S. withdrawal from the war, and from conservatives, who charged him with depriving U.S. troops of the necessary means to defeat the communist forces.

lost its strategic superiority and when its own citizens were questioning its extensive role in world affairs. Détente was to achieve its purpose by exploiting the Sino-Soviet split, which resulted from insurmountable differences between the two communist powers, and by using American technology and food as nonmilitary "weapons." But this political-diplomatic strategy was not utopian; it did not assume that either communist regime had become benign or that the Cold War was over. Détente was intended to be a realistic strategy for a time when, because of neoisolationism at home and the shift in power internationally, the United States no longer was in a position to compete as vigorously with the Soviet Union as in the days before the Vietnam War. Détente was the continuation of containment by other means.

EXPLOITING THE SINO-SOVIET SPLIT

When the Nixon administration came into office in January 1969, the United States had no official relationship with the communist government in China. Leaders in Beijing opposed establishing relations with the United States as long as Washington officially recognized the Nationalist regime on Taiwan. But Nixon recognized the changing strategic circumstances and considered it vital to bring mainland China, still led by Mao Zedong, into the diplomatic constellation. By calling the regime by its chosen name, the People's Republic of China (PRC), ending regular patrols of the Taiwan Straits by the Seventh Fleet, and lifting trade and visitation restrictions against the PRC, Nixon opened the way for a personal visit to China in February 1972. For the American public and Congress, long hostile to dealing with Beijing, this visit symbolized a dramatic shift in American policy. By playing the "China card," Nixon and Kissinger began clearing away mutual hostilities and defining some of the more outstanding issues and problems impeding closer Sino-American relations.

Thus détente applied not just to the relationship between the United States and the Soviet Union but also to the relationship with China. Indeed, it may be argued that détente with China was the greater U.S. achievement because of the tremendous hostility that had existed between the two countries since 1949. At least with the Soviet Union the earlier period of high tension, confrontation, and recurring crises had been balanced by mutual recognition and increasing cooperation in several areas. In any event, détente with China was a prerequisite to détente with the Soviet Union. By bringing China into the superpower balance, Nixon and Kissinger increased the Soviet Union's incentive to improve relations with the United States if it wished to avoid even closer Sino-American relations.

In executing this strategy, Nixon was able to exploit the rivalry between the Soviet Union and China because relations between these two former allies had become deeply embittered. As the capital of the first communist-controlled state, Moscow had for too long, since the early 1920s, monopolized the international communist movement and dictated its policies. Moreover, after World War II it had established control over the states of Eastern Europe. Of these states, only Yugoslavia was controlled not by Moscow but by its indigenous Communist Party. When Yugoslavia resisted Joseph Stalin's efforts to impose absolute control, it was ejected from Stalin's empire. The birth of communist China—another state controlled by a home-grown, independent party—thus represented a serious problem for the Soviets. The Chinese leadership, while communist, was like that of Yugoslavia, highly nationalistic and therefore not likely to subordinate itself to the Kremlin. The potential for a schism, then, was built into the Sino-Soviet relationship.[5] That the leaders of these two huge communist states shared an ideological framework did not dampen their growing policy differences toward the United States—Moscow generally had a more accommodating attitude and Beijing a more belligerent one. A falling-out was therefore inevitable, despite the treaty of friendship signed by the two countries in 1950.

By the late 1960s both countries had allowed their treaty to lapse, leaving the Sino-Soviet split clearly visible to Western leaders. The epithets hurled between Beijing and Moscow reached a ferocity unknown since the early days of the Cold War. The Soviets compared Mao to Adolf Hitler and the Chinese to the Mongol hordes who overran Russia a millennium earlier. The Chinese, meanwhile, described the "Soviet revisionist clique" as a "dictatorship of the German fascist type" and quoted Karl Marx as saying that Russia's aim had been, and always would be, world hegemony.

As the struggle against the Soviet Union intensified, Mao and his followers were careful to avoid conflict with the United States. During the war in Vietnam, for example, China counseled Hanoi that revolutions had to be self-sufficient; it stated repeatedly that only an American attack on China would precipitate Beijing's intervention. In brief, North Vietnam should not and could not count on active Chinese assistance to help defeat American forces in South Vietnam. Rhetorically, Mao's policy was militantly anti-American, but in action it was restrained. Thus the incoming Nixon administration had a golden opportunity to exploit the Sino-Soviet tensions, to bring about closer Sino-American relations and potentially lucrative economic ties, and to end a hostile twenty-year relationship that had been strategically harmful, if not disastrous, for the United States.

But most important at the time, the Sino-Soviet split gave the United States more opportunities to bring pressure to bear on the Soviet

5. Historic distrust between the Russian and Chinese peoples, based largely on territorial claims, preceded the Cold War and further aggravated relations between the communist states.

Union. The clearly implied message to the Soviet leadership was that their obstinacy would compel Washington to align itself more closely with Beijing. To the Soviets, already fearful of China, such an alignment represented a worst-case scenario. It might encourage China to be more hostile, as well as renew tension on the Soviet Union's western front in Europe. Similarly, Beijing had for years complained about alleged American-Soviet collusion to isolate and contain China. But as the Soviet Union began to move huge numbers of troops eastward to defend its frontier with China, and on occasion let a rumor slip about the possibility of an attack on China, Beijing, apparently convinced that Nixon was pulling out of Vietnam, began to look toward detaching Washington from any possible cooperation with Moscow against China. Even more important, better relations with the United States would presumably restrain the Soviet Union from attacking China, for the Kremlin could not be sure that Washington would not support Beijing in such an event.

In the Shanghai communiqué released at the end of Nixon's historic visit to China in 1972, the United States and China declared their opposition to the hegemony of *any* power in Asia—but they clearly were referring to the Soviet Union. Thus Sino-American relations were established on a firm foundation of mutual self-interest. Moreover, the communist position had long been that Beijing would not establish any relationship with Washington before official U.S. ties with Taiwan were severed—such ties with the rival claimant to power being, Beijing claimed, interference in a domestic matter. The fact that, in these circumstances, the PRC would reverse itself and sign the Shanghai communiqué constituted evidence of its fear of the Soviet Union. As for the United States, the eagerness to attract China into an anti-Soviet coalition was reflected in America's declaration that it would gradually remove all its forces and installations from Taiwan and would not interfere in a "peaceful settlement" between the communists and Nationalists.

President Nixon's trip to Beijing in 1972 symbolized a dramatic change in Sino-American relations, ending once and for all the irrationality of a situation in which the United States for almost a quarter-century had ignored the existence of the world's most populous country, a nation with great potential power and an ideological rival of the Soviet Union. Just as Washington during the 1950s feared the Sino-Soviet coalition, and Beijing during the 1960s frequently pointed to alleged Soviet-American collusion to isolate China, so Moscow now became apprehensive of closer Sino-American relations. Such relations, Soviet leaders understood, gave the United States a persuasive lever—if used skillfully—in its negotiations with the Kremlin. The American shift of recognition from Taiwan to Beijing was long overdue. U.S.

domestic politics had too long blocked exploitation of the Sino-Soviet conflict—a conflict that saw tensions constantly shift in intensity, but one that was likely to continue despite leadership changes in both communist countries. Sino-Soviet quarrels reflected historic and entrenched differences of interest more profound than mere differences of personalities.

Indeed, the succession struggle in China and the change in the presidency in the United States did not stop progress toward full normalization. On January 1, 1979, the People's Republic of China and the United States exchanged diplomatic recognition and ambassadors. This was followed by an official visit to Washington by China's future leader, Deputy Premier Deng Xiaoping, who succeeded Mao as chairman of the Communist Party two years after Mao's death in September 1976. The timing of this last step toward normalization was driven by China, which, with increasingly obsolete weapons, confronted large modern Soviet forces along its 4,500-mile northern frontier. For the United States, the final shift from Taiwan to Beijing meant ending diplomatic recognition of Nationalist China and abrogating the Taiwan defense treaty, requiring the withdrawal of the last American military personnel stationed in Taiwan. In return, Beijing accepted the American position that the Taiwan problem be resolved peacefully. (The United States could, of course, at any time resort easily to force and defend Taiwan should Beijing some day violate the understanding about the peaceful resolution of this problem.)

With recognition of the mainland came new opportunities for trade. Although at first the United States did not sell arms to Beijing in order not to provoke Moscow, it was willing to let its European allies sell China arms, such as jet fighters and antiaircraft and antitank missiles.[6] But more important than arms sales, the opening to China paved the way for rapidly accelerating commercial ties between the two countries. China looked to the West to help it modernize everything from its hotel and steel industries to exploitation of its enormous oil reserves. By the 1990s China had emerged as one of the major trading partners of the United States; its importance to Washington was revealed annually when the U.S. government extended China most-favored-nation status despite the continuation of communist rule and political repression. For the United States, access to China's vast markets proved irresistible, a fact not lost on Chinese leaders who continued to reject American calls for political reforms and moderation.

6. The United States limited its own sales to dual-purpose equipment such as radar, trucks, and transport planes, which could be put to either civilian or military use. Later, Ronald Reagan's administration, in an effort to forge stronger links with China against the Soviet Union, offered to sell Beijing arms.

LINKING COOPERATION TO SOVIET RESTRAINT

The U.S. strategy for restraint, then, involved both communist powers. Beijing could be used to convince the Soviets to act with restraint and to show greater willingness to compromise if they wished to avoid closer Sino-American relations and collusion against the Soviet Union. Kissinger proposed to supplement the new relationship with a network of agreements and a set of rules of mutual restraint beneficial to both powers. Key to such an arrangement would be *linkage*, directed primarily toward Moscow. If a series of agreements and understandings on such matters as arms control and trade could be achieved, the Soviet Union would gain a vested interest in good relations with the United States. While the Soviet Union was to be faced, as before, with continued parity and a strong American military, this "stick" was to be supplemented with enough "carrots" to make a restrained foreign policy more rewarding. Indeed, military sanctions against the Soviet Union at a time of strategic parity were becoming riskier for the United States. Fortunately, the linkage strategy, which offered economic rewards for restraint, was thought to be particularly appealing to the Soviets.

Linkage also had another meaning: the various U.S.-Soviet issues would be linked together diplomatically. Progress on one front would be tied to progress on another; the Kremlin could not expect to make gains on one issue that interested it but refuse to meet American interests on others. If it did so, there presumably would be a penalty exacted through U.S. resistance on issues of interest to Soviet leaders or through the withholding of benefits Moscow was seeking.

The Soviet Union was particularly vulnerable in its inability to deal with one issue: the Soviet economy, which was in serious trouble by the time Nixon entered office. After its rapid expansion in the 1950s and early 1960s, the economy saw its 5 percent growth rate decrease to 2 percent by the early 1970s. The economic decline was particularly notable in those economic sectors associated with the "second" industrial revolution: computers, microelectronics, and telecommunications. In short, the Soviet Union was falling further behind the West in those industries that were most important for economic growth. Furthermore, the Soviet workplace was increasingly plagued by high absenteeism, drunkenness, corruption, and shoddy production. The implications of this decline could not be ignored; it damaged the Soviet Union's appeal as a socialist state, hampered its ability to compete with the United States, and threatened its future superpower status.

Even in agriculture the growth in Soviet production had fallen sharply below expectations and official plans. Workers on the land, like those in the factory, were far behind their American counterparts in per capita production. The Soviet Union's continued inability to provide a balanced diet—indeed, in some years to avoid widespread hunger—was not just the result of poor weather; it also stemmed from the ideologically determined organization of a command economy administered by a rigid bureaucracy. By contrast, the small private plots that some peasants were allowed to own produced much of the Soviet Union's poultry, grain, vegetables, and other foods.

The result of this dismal situation was that the Soviet Union was the only industrial society in which the peacetime life expectancy of males was declining and infant mortality was rising. Soviet leader Leonid Brezhnev, who replaced Nikita Khrushchev in 1964, was all too aware that his predecessor's failure to achieve a higher standard of living had played a large part in Khrushchev's fall from power. The Soviet leader had raised popular expectations and then failed to meet them. The same thing could happen to Brezhnev. In a system in which the leadership firmly maintained a monopoly on political power and control, it sought popular approval by providing jobs, as well as low-cost housing, health care, retirement benefits, and similar social services. The Soviet standard of living might not have been high by Western standards, but as long as it improved gradually the regime could claim to be fulfilling its aim of enhancing the lives of its citizens.

Conversely, a decline had ominous implications. The Kremlin had to look no further than Czechoslovakia and Poland for evidence of this. In 1968 a reform movement in Czechoslovakia led to calls for neutrality and withdrawal from the Warsaw Pact. Soviet troops poured into Prague, the capital, to squash the rebellion. In 1970 the decrepit state of the Polish economy and worker dissatisfaction led to riots in several cities and the collapse of the government, which, even in a communist-controlled state, had to be replaced. Similar unrest occurred in 1980–1981 and again in the late 1980s.

Soviet concerns about its ailing economy and lack of progress in the scientific-technological sector presented the Kremlin with two choices: to look toward the West for a "technological fix" to help stimulate the Soviet economy or to attempt a basic structural reform of the country's highly centralized and rigidly bureaucratic system. Not surprisingly, the Soviet leadership chose Western technology, machinery, and food—and the Western credit granted to buy them. Structural reform was rejected because it was not only antithetical to the regime's basic ideological beliefs about private property, the profit motive, and free markets, but also contrary to the deeply vested interests of the government bureaucrats who were committed to central planning, a command economy, and their own self-preservation. Decentralization of authority—shifting power to factory and farm managers and their workforces—was judged too risky because it might threaten the Communist Party's political control. Importing Western goods and food was considered safer than such a fundamental reform.

Trade with the United States, with its enormous mass-production capabilities, technological advances that the Soviets envied, and agricultural abundance, was especially desirable to Moscow since it also saw the benefits in broader collaboration. Because they had little to sell the United States, Soviet leaders offered to let Americans develop and exploit the huge Soviet deposits of raw materials, especially in Siberia. American capital to help finance this extraction would presumably be repaid in oil, natural gas, and other mineral resources in the future. The Soviets also looked to the United States for food in years of shortages, which occurred more and more frequently.

The Nixon-Ford administration believed these economic problems would give the United States leverage. Trade obviously was profitable for American industry and agriculture, but the main reason for permitting it was political. American productivity, it was hoped, would provide a powerful material reinforcement for a Soviet foreign policy of restraint and accommodation made necessary by the desire to prevent closer Sino-American "collusion," to achieve strategic arms agreements to stabilize mutual deterrence, and to gain American recognition of Soviet parity and equal status with the United States. According to Kissinger, economic relations could not be separated from the political context. The United States should not be asked to reward hostile conduct with economic benefits. In return for the expansion of trade, it was not unreasonable to require the Soviets to cooperate on key foreign policy issues. In effect, the linkage strategy would give Moscow the incentives to practice *self-containment.*

Kissinger's policy of using economic means to achieve political purposes suffered a significant setback, however, when the U.S. Senate approved offering the Soviets trade and credits only on the condition that Moscow allow more Soviet Jews to emigrate. Calling the provision, specified in an amendment by Sen. Henry Jackson and Rep. Charles Vanik, an intervention in its domestic affairs, the Soviet Union rejected the trade agreement. No great power—let alone the Soviet Union, which claimed to be a nation in which class distinctions and religious and other forms of prejudice no longer existed—would admit publicly that it mistreated part of its population and allow itself to be placed on probation by a foreign adversary in return for trade. As a result, the Soviet Union conducted its business mostly with Western Europe instead of the United States. To the extent, then, that the Soviets' primary motive for détente was economic, the lack of payoff reduced their incentives for maintaining a relaxation of tensions.

ARMS CONTROL AS THE CENTERPIECE OF DÉTENTE

Another area of potential U.S.-Soviet cooperation was in the area of strategic arms control, which over the years had assumed greater importance. The two powers had been rivals since the closing days of World War II; indeed, their rivalry reached into almost every region of the world. As a result, profound distrust and mutual fear, if not hatred, characterized their relationship. The arms race was an expression of their deep political differences. But the danger was, of course, that the arms race, fueled by continuing conflict, would at some point spill over into a nuclear war. To avoid such a cataclysmic outcome, each side built up its nuclear forces as a defense and negotiated agreements that reduced the chances of war breaking out. But as the basic conflict continued and as nuclear weapons were unlikely to be abolished, the next best tactic was to manage the nuclear balance by instituting arms control agreements and promoting mutual deterrence.[7]

During the 1960s arms control had dealt largely with issues such as the establishment of a hot line between the Kremlin and the White House for quick communication in a crisis and a limited ban on nuclear testing. Meanwhile, the United Nations had promoted a multilateral agreement on the nonproliferation of nuclear weapons. In the 1970s the focus of U.S.-Soviet arms control shifted to each side's nuclear forces, which by this time were more than adequate to deter a major challenge to the status quo.

The Strategic Arms Limitation Talks (SALT), one of Nixon's major achievements, stood at the center of détente. SALT, which involved high-level U.S. and Soviet officials, had four objectives. The first was to make the arms race more predictable by establishing, documenting, and reporting the number of strategic weapons possessed by each side. Such knowledge presumably would reduce the anxiety of the arms race; uncertainty and fear that the opponent might gain military superiority only fueled the competition.

The second objective of SALT was to ensure parity. The assumption was that if the two sides had approximately the same number of nuclear warheads (the explosives attached to ballistic missiles and bombs) neither side could launch a crippling strike against the other. More specifically, parity was a condition in which no matter who struck first, the attacked side would still have the capability to retaliate and destroy the

7. This effort was frequently at odds with the U.S. government's traditional approach to foreign affairs, as outlined elsewhere in this volume. See Colin S. Gray, *Nuclear Strategy and National Style* (Lanham, Md.: Hamilton Press, 1986).

aggressor. In the absence of nuclear superiority, the United States and the Soviet Union would each retain a sufficient second-strike capability to ensure "mutual assured destruction."

The third purpose of SALT was to reduce threats to each side's deterrent forces. By the early 1970s the balance was threatened not only by the continuing Soviet strategic growth but also by technological innovations that were widely believed in the United States to be undermining the stability of nuclear deterrence. One matter of concern was the development of a new defensive weapon. The Soviets had deployed antiballistic missiles (ABMs) around Moscow and were thought to be working on a second-generation ABM for possible nationwide deployment. If ABMs could shoot down enough incoming American intercontinental ballistic missiles (ICBMs) and reduce the destruction inflicted on the Soviet Union to an "acceptable" level of casualties, the ABMs would undermine U.S. deterrence, which depended on its capacity to impose "assured destruction." [8]

This defensive weapon stimulated the United States, in turn, to improve its offensive technology by developing the multiple independent reentry vehicle (MIRV)—a long-range missile with multiple warheads that separate in flight, change trajectory, and fly to assigned and dispersed targets. The advantage of MIRVs was that the large numbers of warheads would be able to overwhelm any ABM defense, enabling the United States to destroy Soviet society in a retaliatory blow. But MIRVs also threatened to destabilize the deterrent balance: multiplying the warheads and providing them with greater accuracy placed a premium on a preemptive attack. Destroying the launch platform of a "MIRVed" missile would be very tempting to both sides; thus "use them or lose them" could become their compelling logic. Furthermore, MIRVs were more difficult to "count" through satellite reconnaissance and other means of verification, a problem that would later plague arms control negotiations. Thus, as one analyst observed, "a world without MIRVs would be better and safer." [9]

The fourth reason for SALT was its importance for détente. On the one hand, the failure to arrive at an agreement or at least to continue the SALT dialogue was bound to have a debilitating effect on the overall U.S.-Soviet political relationship. On the other hand, only a relaxation of tensions could provide the diplomatic atmosphere that would enable the two nuclear giants to arrive at an arms agreement that would leave them feeling more secure, sanctify the strategic parity between them,

8. See Robert E. Osgood, *The Nuclear Dilemma in American Strategic Thought* (Boulder: Westview Press, 1988), 48–55.

9. Strobe Talbott, *Deadly Gambits* (New York: Knopf, 1984), 258.

and avoid new costly offensive and defensive arms races. SALT, in brief, became a symbol of détente.

The first set of agreements, known as SALT I, was signed by Nixon and Brezhnev in May 1972. SALT I had taken two and a half years to negotiate and incorporated two agreements. The first limited each country's ABMs to two hundred launchers, later to be reduced to one hundred each. For all practical purposes, by restricting ABMs the two powers acknowledged the dangers of strategic defense and shifted their focus to offensive weapons. Thus the second agreement froze offensive missile batteries at the number each side possessed at the time. Each side retained the right to improve its weapons within the overall quantitative agreement, thus preserving parity. Although no on-site inspection to check for violations was established, both sides pledged not to interfere with each other's reconnaissance or spy satellites, which would be the principal means of checking compliance with both accords.

The follow-up agreement, SALT II, was regarded as critical to a long-term effort to stabilize mutual deterrence. President Gerald Ford, after Nixon's resignation, arrived at the guidelines for SALT II at a 1974 meeting with Brezhnev in Vladivostok. This time each side would have an equal number of strategic weapons: 2,400 missiles and bombers; 1,320 of these delivery systems could have MIRVs. It was a complex series of agreements, carefully balancing the varying interests and different force structures of the two superpowers.

But after SALT II was signed by Brezhnev and President Jimmy Carter in 1979, the treaty became controversial in the United States. Proponents said it provided for real reductions of strategic launchers from the Vladivostok ceiling of 2,400 to 2,250. This change meant that the Soviets would have to reduce their force levels by about 150 older missiles, thereby setting a precedent for SALT III, whose main purpose was to bring about a major reduction in strategic forces. Critics noted, however, that the SALT II ceilings were so high that the agreement defied any reasonable interpretation of the words *arms control.* Other critics asserted that, despite the equal numbers provided for both sides, the treaty would give the Soviet Union strategic superiority because Soviet missiles were considerably larger, could carry more and bigger warheads, and were becoming more accurate (though less accurate than U.S. missiles). The Soviets, therefore, would presumably be capable of destroying up to 90 percent of America's ICBMs.[10]

The debate over SALT II became moot after the Soviet Union sent troops into Afghanistan in late 1979 to shore up a pro-Soviet military

10. For an elaboration of this debate, see Lawrence Freedman, *The Evolution of Nuclear Strategy,* 2d ed. (New York: St. Martin's Press, 1989), 344–395.

regime. Congress refused to ratify SALT II and, reversing his plans to reduce U.S. defenses, President Carter promised to counter the Soviet invasion with a U.S. military buildup. But despite heated rhetoric coming from both Washington and Moscow, the terms of SALT II were observed into the late 1980s, when efforts to reduce nuclear stockpiles accelerated again under President Ronald Reagan (see Chapter 8).

THE LIMITATIONS OF DÉTENTE

While the superpowers negotiated the size of their nuclear arsenals in the "spirit of détente," much of the outside world remained torn by internal unrest and regional conflict. Within the developing world, the ideological rivalry of the Cold War had infected many unstable governments, dividing their populations into hostile ideological camps, producing ever-greater forms of repression, and undermining their prospects for political stability and economic growth. The resulting calamity in Vietnam already has been reviewed at length. Among other flashpoints in the developing world, a military coup in Chile and the civil wars in Angola and Ethiopia clearly demonstrated the limitations of détente. Furthermore, the protracted Cold War struggle, merely codified by détente, led to strains within the network of military alliances the United States had created and dominated since World War II.

CHILE'S MILITARY TAKEOVER

After the declaration of the Monroe Doctrine in 1823, the United States regarded South America as within its sphere of influence. Although Washington gradually became more accommodating to the nationalism of its Latin neighbors, it feared the emergence of radical left-wing revolutions and regimes that might bring Soviet influence close to America's shores. When in 1970 Chilean citizens elected the Marxist Salvador Allende to the presidency, the Nixon administration sought first to prevent Allende from becoming president and then, when that failed, to make life difficult for him and ultimately to remove him from power through a military coup d'état engineered by the CIA. Ironically, the reasons for the Chilean coup, when it came in 1973, stemmed essentially from Allende's own actions and the domestic reactions they precipitated. Indeed, Chile provided a most persuasive example of why the United States should *not* have intervened; after all, the outcome was largely predetermined, and in the aftermath of the coup the U.S. role was widely criticized.[11]

11. For an elaboration, see Richard R. Fagan, "The United States and Cuba: Roots and Branches," *Foreign Policy* (January 1975): 297–313.

Allende came to power in 1970 with 36 percent of the vote, only two points ahead of his next competitor in a three-way race. In the runoff vote in the Chilean Congress, he received the support of the centrist Christian Democratic Party. At the outset of his rule the opposition supported much of his program, including land reform and the nationalization of U.S.-owned copper mines, banks, and major industries such as the International Telegraph and Telephone Company (ITT), whose senior officers pressured the Nixon administration to restore their holdings in Chile. Given his early popularity, it should have been possible for Allende to work within Chile's constitutional norms with a democratic consensus. But Allende deliberately pursued a policy of polarizing Chileans, a strategy that did more to consolidate the professional middle and lower-middle classes in opposition to him than to broaden his worker-peasant base of support. As a result, his vow to maintain constitutional rule fell by the wayside; he survived only by increasingly bypassing the Chilean Congress and the courts. When the Christian Democrats then joined the rightist opposition, the class polarization was at long last paralleled by the divisions between the executive and legislative branches.

The military during this period became more and more politicized. Asked by Allende at several points to participate in his cabinet to reassure those worried about law and order, the military at first served Allende, as it had his predecessors. Later, however, military commanders became alarmed by the rapid growth of paramilitary forces among Allende's followers, who called for armed confrontation against right-wing "reactionaries." These events, which apparently occurred with Allende's complicity, challenged the established order and raised tensions. The country was on the verge of civil war when the military rose against Allende. It did not need American urging.

After Chilean officials seized many U.S.-owned properties, often without compensation, President Nixon had cut off American credit for Chile and pressured international financial institutions such as the World Bank and International Monetary Fund to follow suit. But Allende had more than made up for his American losses with credits from communist states, other Latin American countries, and Western Europe. Chile also had rich copper mines. Had Allende imitated Egypt's Gamal Abdel Nasser, he likely would have survived U.S. pressure and hostility by arousing his people's nationalist ardor. But that was why Allende did not survive; he declared himself to be president of only some Chileans—against other Chileans. Had Nixon abstained from meddling, responsibility for the Chilean coup would properly have fallen on Allende. Instead, the United States was condemned for its covert intervention, and Chile became for many critics a symbol of American imperialism.

The overthrow and death of Allende in September 1973 were controlled by a four-man junta led by Gen. Augusto Pinochet, who assumed the office of president through force and intimidation. In the years to come, Pinochet emerged as a ruthless leader, but one loyal to the United States and determined to prevent Chile from enduring another socialist revolution. Despite charges that the United States was again "coddling" a foreign dictator in the name of containment, Washington actively supported the new Chilean government. In return for Washington's patronage, Chile served as a loyal U.S. client in South America through the end of the Cold War.[12]

REGIONAL CONFLICTS IN AFRICA

A second example of détente's limitations came in 1975 in Angola, a country rich in oil and mineral resources and one that geographically divided, white-ruled states of Africa—Rhodesia and South Africa—from black Africa. As a Portuguese colony, Angola had helped to protect the two racist states from black liberation movements. But as Portuguese colonialism came to an end, Angola's interim government, which was composed of three factions based on tribal allegiances, was consumed by a power struggle. This rivalry continued after Angola became independent, and the leftist Popular Movement for the Liberation of Angola attracted Soviet support and thousands of Cuban troops. Some claimed that the Cuban military intervention occurred after repeated South African military strikes into Angola, as well as intervention by Zaire. The Ford administration, however, believed the Soviets financed the deployment of Cuban military advisers and later provided massive numbers of jet fighters, mortars, rockets, armored cars, and ground-to-air missiles. The administration—including Secretary of State Kissinger—viewed the Cubans as Soviet proxies and their intervention in Angola as an outgrowth of Soviet expansionism.

The result was the introduction of the great-power rivalry into southern Africa. Rejecting U.S. military intervention (a direct result of the "Vietnam syndrome"), Washington provided covert arms to the faction opposing the Soviet-supported ones. But not only did this effort not match that of the Soviet Union, it also was cut off by the Senate, fearful of another Vietnam in an area that did not constitute a vital American interest. Rejecting the contention that Angola might become another Vietnam, Ford and Kissinger conceded that Angola was not a significant American interest. But they still believed that Soviet intervention could not be ignored. Angola might be far away, but, in their view, it was a test

12. Pinochet remained in power until 1990, when Chilean citizens voted to restore civilian rule.

case of the new superpower relationship. Soviet actions were simply incompatible with détente; the Kremlin was seeking unilateral advantage from the general relaxation of tensions. Indeed, Kissinger charged that Angola was far beyond any Soviet sphere of influence and that the Soviet action constituted a military intervention to impose a regime of Soviet choice. The Soviet Union defended its behavior by asserting that support of national liberation movements, including armed intervention, was not incompatible with détente—a view rejected by the United States. In this superpower stalemate, Angola endured a prolonged civil war that left nearly half a million dead and continued long after the Cold War.

Moscow's next move in Africa came in 1977 in Somalia, the Soviet Union's closest African ally and home to its naval base at Berbera. Using Soviet-supplied arms, Somalia was supporting the Western Somali Liberation Front in the Ogaden region of northern Ethiopia. Somali troops had invaded Ethiopia to support these rebels, who claimed that this area, populated by ethnic Somalis, should be part of Somalia. Ethiopia, already facing disintegration as it confronted other rebellions and secessionist movements, especially the attempt by Eritrea to establish an independent state on the Red Sea, rejected the claim. Like other new African states, it recognized the borders existing at the time of independence—that is, borders drawn by the colonial powers. Because Ethiopia was about ten times as large as Somalia and of greater strategic importance, the Soviet Union supplied Ethiopia with Soviet military advisers, twenty thousand Cuban advisers and troops, and an estimated $1 billion in military supplies to crush the Ogaden rebellion. Thus it was willing to risk alienating Somalia and losing its naval base and some air facilities facing the Indian Ocean because the stakes were even greater in Ethiopia than in Angola. The United States predictably seized the opportunity to aid Somalia after the Soviet reversal and to occupy the Berbera naval base, but even the influx of significant U.S. economic and military aid did not prevent Somalia from succumbing to its own internal collapse in the 1990s. There was irony in the Soviet rejection of its client in Somalia in favor of another Marxist regime, which the Ethiopian government had become after the overthrow in September 1974 of Emperor Haile Selassie.

As Soviet relations with Washington worsened, Moscow saw its opportunity to enhance its influence in the strategic Horn of Africa, which was just across the Gulf of Aden from Saudi Arabia. Washington feared that the Soviet Union would gain control of the southern entrance to the Red Sea, which led to the Suez Canal and Israel, and that it would pose a threat to the important oil routes from the Persian Gulf to the West. Thus both sides traded client states and inflamed the region with massive amounts of military hardware. In few other parts of the world was the spillover effect of the superpower rivalry so visible, and so disabling. Both Ethiopia and Somalia were decimated by the regional struggle and faced dire economic problems well after the conclusion of the Cold War.

THE EROSION OF U.S. ALLIANCES

The whole concept of détente was bound to pose several problems for the United States, especially in its relationships with its allies. Alliances normally are composed of countries drawn together by common perceptions of an overriding external threat. But what cements the bonds of such relationships when that threat is no longer seen as great by the principal members of the coalition? Is it not inevitable that the strands of such "entangling alliances" become untangled? In Europe, among America's most important allies, that appeared to be the situation in the 1970s and 1980s.

In the days when all members of NATO had perceived the Soviet threat as serious, the alliance had been a reasonably cohesive organization. To be sure, NATO had become strained because its European members, although still dependent on the United States for their security, had recovered from the war and wanted a greater voice in the alliance. But the common perception of external danger had been enough to keep the bonds of the alliance close. In the era of détente, however, several member states no longer were so willing to give priority to alliance interests. Washington now negotiated directly with the Kremlin on key issues, as relations with Moscow became in some respects more important than those with NATO members. Not surprisingly, the European states also went their own way; West Germany, for example, pursued a policy of *ostpolitik*, or accommodation toward its eastern neighbors.

Economic issues proved especially divisive among members of the Western allies. In the immediate postwar era economic policies such as the Marshall Plan had been consistent with and supported America's containment strategy. But now economic relations between the United States and Western Europe, which was rapidly forming a cohesive economic bloc, were complicating the other strands of NATO policy. As the 1970s began, Europe was no longer the weak, divided, and demoralized continent it had been after 1945. Indeed, the emerging Common Market had become an increasingly powerful economic competitor. During the Cold War the United States had been a leading proponent of European integration; a cohesive Western Europe could make a significant contribution to the U.S.-led struggle against the Soviet Union, and the competitiveness of an economically unified Europe was thought to be worth the risk. In a period of détente, however, and growing tensions between the United States and Europe, the united front that had long confronted the Soviet bloc threatened to fragment.[13]

The European-American relationship also was strained by the continued sense of vulnerability of the Europeans, fostered by their ongoing dependence on the United States for defense. To some extent, their concern reflected their fear of abandonment. As U.S. territory became more vulnerable to Soviet missile attack, many Europeans wondered if they could continue to rely on American protection. Without sufficiently large and credible nuclear forces of their own, their security was entirely in American hands. But, as Soviet intercontinental missile forces grew, what would happen if the Soviets made demands considered vital by the Europeans but not by Washington? Could the small British or French strategic force deter the Soviet Union? The U.S. management of the Berlin crises from 1958 to 1962 had not reassured the European countries—especially France and West Germany—of Washington's steadfastness as its risks and costs of defending the alliance rose. Europeans also feared entrapment. They had been deeply concerned about the diversion of U.S. resources and attention away from them during the Korean and Vietnam Wars. But while Europeans worried about U.S. recklessness, the United States resented their lack of political support for U.S. ventures outside of Europe. This feeling fueled U.S. resentment over the failure of the Europeans to play a far greater role in their own defense.

The alliance was further divided by the psychological fact that, while the United States had become a global power, the European states, having shed most of their empires, had largely relinquished their former extra-European role and had concentrated on their economic growth and regional integration. As former great powers, the European states naturally bemoaned their rapid postwar decline in prestige and status and their dependence on a vigorous, self-confident, and, in their eyes, often impetuous newcomer who might disregard their counsel—advice that, the Europeans felt, was based on their greater experience and wisdom. They became preoccupied with restraining the United States from doing anything that they perceived as rash and endangering détente, regardless of Soviet behavior.

While NATO unity weakened, the Southeast Asia Treaty Organization (SEATO) and the Central Treaty Organization (CENTO) collapsed. Indeed, the era of "pactomania" initiated under the Eisenhower administration came to an abrupt halt in the 1970s. SEATO was formally dissolved in 1975 after the fall of South Vietnam. Given that SEATO's pri-

13. For a review of Western Europe's progress toward "functional integration" during this period, see Martin Holland, *1* (London: Pinter, 1994), 22–59.

mary raison d'être was the conflict in Southeast Asia, the conflict's conclusion, even on terms contrary to SEATO members' desires, made the demise of the organization inevitable. The Central Treaty Organization died more slowly. First, with the splitting off in 1972 of Bangladesh from Pakistan, which also had been a SEATO member, India emerged as the dominant power on the subcontinent. Pakistan, which had joined both alliances primarily to receive U.S. arms for its adversarial relationship with India, no longer had much interest in either. In the meantime, it had moved close to China, a regional rival of India. Turkey, at the other end of the CENTO's geographic reach, was grappling with domestic conflicts and a U.S. arms embargo imposed after the escalation of fighting between Turkey and Greece over control of Cyprus. In between, Iran had become the only reliable U.S. ally in Southwest Asia. The fragility of this friendship, illustrated by the overthrow of the American-backed shah and the seizure of American hostages in 1979, was ample evidence of the weakness of CENTO in its final days.

DISILLUSIONMENT WITH DÉTENTE

In the context of America's national style, it was not surprising that views of détente swung from euphoria as the 1970s began to increasing disillusionment by 1975. Indeed, the United States had always wavered between such opposite and mutually exclusive categories: isolation or intervention, peace or war, diplomacy or force, idealism or realism, harmony or strife, optimism about America's destiny or cynicism about an evil world that resists reform.

The Nixon administration's overselling of détente and slogans such as "negotiation, not confrontation" reinforced the expectation that the Cold War was effectively over and that the superpowers had put their conflicts, crises, and the danger of war behind them. But raising people's hopes too high was bound to lead to disappointment when events did not live up to expectations. The problem was that each administration tended to package its foreign policy in slogans that emphasized how its policy differed from that of its predecessors. And, anticipating the next election, each administration wanted to make that policy look appealing and successful. Despite the high degree of continuity of American foreign policy, the United States had indulged itself by turns in the rhetoric of containment, "rollback," and détente. In addition, détente as a state of existence that combined both conflict *and* cooperation was more difficult to understand than the Cold War. It was easier to explain a relationship that was essentially one of confrontation *or* cooperation. The Cold War aroused people; détente relaxed them, as if it were the same thing as *entente*, meaning friendship. But détente meant a reduction of tensions, not an absence of tensions or superpower rivalry. Expectations that it represented a harbinger of harmony were bound to produce frustration.

Indeed, it is critical to remember that in its conception détente was intended to serve as another form of containment for a period of domestic retrenchment, superpower parity, and Sino-Soviet schism. The Cold War "stick" was to be supplemented by the "carrot" of détente, and issues were to be linked, explicitly or otherwise. The Soviet Union was to be constrained from undertaking foreign adventures by force, or the threat of force, along with the prospect that the United States could at any time withhold economic agreements desired by Moscow. The United States hoped that Moscow, enticed by Western goods, technology, and credits, would restrain itself to avoid the loss of such benefits. But whether or not the United States adopted détente as a diplomatic strategy because of the country's pervasive mood of withdrawal and its relative decline after the Vietnam War, these factors made containment of the Soviet Union at the moment it had become a global power very difficult. Détente was not a set of self-denying rules. If the Soviet Union faced favorable situations to exploit, should it shun those opportunities just because the United States was in no mood to resist? Self-restraint as a policy was asking a great deal of any major power, especially one that had just achieved strategic parity.

Within the United States, the Watergate scandal and Nixon's resignation in 1974 combined to weaken the presidency as an institution. As noted earlier, the passage of the War Powers Act in 1973 was symbolic of the shift of power from the executive to the legislative branch, and its purpose clearly was to restrain the U.S. role in international affairs. As the "Vietnam syndrome" took hold, Americans were increasingly reluctant to project the nation's power. To many, it was the exercise of *American* power, not the expansionist efforts of the Soviet Union, that was the main threat to stability. Restraint of the United States, not the containment of communism, emerged as the chief task if the world were to become a more peaceful place. The "limits of American power," the constant refrain after Vietnam, were widely proclaimed among critics of American foreign policy in the public and in Congress.

The built-in executive-legislative conflict resulting from the separation of powers always has complicated the formulation of U.S. foreign policy. World War I, America's first major experience in great-power politics after a century of great-power isolationism, ended in a peace treaty that the Senate defeated. Congressional assertiveness during the interwar period led President Franklin Roosevelt to rely on executive agreements in his conduct of foreign policy from 1939 to 1941. During the early stages of the Cold War, shared perceptions of great external threats and U.S. aims generally restrained the conflict between the two branches and increased the president's influence with Congress. But in the absence of a clear and present danger during the détente years, and amid intense disagreements about the use of American power in the wake of Vietnam, the White House and Congress pulled in different directions. Almost every policy became caught in a bitter dispute, often raising the most basic constitutional questions.

Meanwhile, the Soviet Union's conduct during this period was predictable. In the heyday of détente the United States continued to languish in Vietnam. And after renewed hostilities in the Middle East in 1973 (see Chapter 7), the United States promoted a Middle East peace settlement by making itself the arbiter between Israel and the Arabs and excluded the Soviet Union from playing a key role in the area. In this context, Moscow was especially likely to exploit America's paralysis of will and opportunities to enhance its own influence. Détente did not mean an end to the competition; it only meant competing at a lower level of tension so that the rivalry would not erupt in nuclear war. Soviet leaders had no intention of betraying their perceived historical mission to continue their revolution against Western capitalism.

Indeed, détente was a particularly favorable situation in which to promote this struggle. Détente was the product of a shift in the balance of power as a result of the new strategic parity in nuclear weapons. Note the cause and effect carefully: it was the growth of Soviet nuclear forces that induced the United States to behave with greater self-restraint. And consider the obvious corollary: the more military power the Soviet Union acquired, the more American compromises and concessions in negotiations would be offered. This perception of American behavior—and the breakdown of consensus in Washington—was nothing less than a rationale for continuing the struggle for preeminence. Strategic parity was the geopolitical status symbol of the Soviet Union's new standing in international politics. Thus the United States, despite its successful playing of the "China card" and its widening economic advantage over the Soviet Union, remained mired in the Cold War struggle that would far outlast the Kissinger era in American foreign policy.

Jimmy Carter grasps hands with Egyptian president Anwar Sadat (left) and Israeli prime minister Menachem Begin (right) at the signing of the Camp David accords. It would be one of Carter's final foreign policy achievements.

CHAPTER SEVEN

Jimmy Carter and World-Order Politics

In times of national self-doubt Americans often have turned to an outsider who appears untarnished by past government actions and who promises a fresh approach to domestic and foreign policy making. In the 1976 U.S. presidential campaign this role was filled by Democrat Jimmy Carter, a peanut farmer and former governor of Georgia.[1] Carter seemed to epitomize the moral virtues Americans found lacking in previous presidents. Drawing on his experience as a Sunday school teacher in his Baptist church, Carter eloquently described the country's need for moral rejuvenation and spiritual rebirth after the traumas of Vietnam and Watergate. His words struck a chord with the American people, who elected him as president over the seemingly lackluster Republican incumbent, Gerald Ford.

1. For a detailed account of Carter's rise to power, see Betty Glad, *Jimmy Carter: In Search of the Great White House* (New York: Norton, 1980).

President Carter's worldview differed profoundly from those of Richard Nixon and Henry Kissinger. Rather than emphasizing the Cold War and the East-West conflict, Carter paid more attention to global "interdependence" and the need for closer cooperation between the wealthier, more industrialized countries of the North and the poorer countries of the South. Carter's perspective incorporated several widely perceived trends in world politics, such as greater concern about the environment and global population growth and recognition of the growing importance of economic versus military power. In keeping with these views, he denounced U.S. military interventions abroad that caused death and destruction; like America's first generation of leaders, he believed such adventures threatened democracy at home and invited tyranny. Drawing on the idealism of President Woodrow Wilson, he placed the needs of the "world society" above selfish national interests and espoused universal standards of human rights as the appropriate basis of foreign policy. In equating American moral principles with these universal standards, Carter personified the American style of foreign policy.

The new president also offered a way out of what he called the "malaise" within the United States. The best course for the country, he argued, was to reject power politics, seek renewal and purification by concentrating on domestic affairs, and build a fully free and socially just society whose example would radiate throughout the world. Power politics would be replaced by social politics; America's foreign policy would be an extension of its domestic values. In the words of a former chairman of the Senate Foreign Relations Committee, America should "serve as an example of democracy to the world" and play its role in the world "not in its capacity as a *power*, but in its capacity as a *society*." [2] Virtue, not power, would be the hallmark of foreign policy; American influence in the world would be derived from the nation's moral standing as a good and just society. Other nations would be attracted to the United States by its principles, not its strength.

History has demonstrated that democratic states cannot effectively conduct foreign policy in the absence of a domestic consensus. For most of its history America had enjoyed such a consensus, which centered around the need for detachment from foreign affairs and the primacy of domestic economic and political development. In the absence of an external threat, the United States had wanted only to be left to its own devices. When provoked, however, its citizens had been easily mobilized and united for its foreign policy crusades. In the wake of Vietnam and in the midst of détente, however, no such provocation appeared on the horizon, and the American penchant for withdrawal returned to the surface.

2. J. William Fulbright, *The Arrogance of Power* (New York: Vintage Books, 1967), 256.

The task of re-creating consensus on foreign policy was embraced by Carter, who thought he could find it in America's self-proclaimed historical role as the defender of democracy and individual liberty. Human rights became the platform on which he expected to mobilize popular support. The liberal tradition, which Henry Kissinger had eschewed to the dismay of many in favor of his "amoral" geopolitics, was to be reunited with American foreign policy. Carter pledged to condition American relations with other countries, rich and poor alike, on their respect for human rights, but he largely directed his human rights campaign toward the developing world. That was where the majority of humanity lived, where living conditions were the worst, and where population growth was the most rapid. To pursue his vision of "world-order politics," Carter would focus on the relationship between the Western industrial democracies and the poorer developing world.[3] In its preoccupation with the ideological struggle of the Cold War—in Carter's words, the "inordinate fear of communism"—the United States had neglected these impoverished areas. Indeed, the superpowers, Carter felt, by extending their Cold War to many "frontiers" in developing countries, had encouraged military dictators on both sides of the ideological spectrum, undermined the prospects of the developing countries for democracy, and further retarded their economic development. In short, the Cold War had only made the already miserable conditions in the developing countries worse.

The United States thus once more stood for something, having reclaimed its democratic heritage and a moral basis for its foreign policy. American flirtations with the Machiavellian world of great-power diplomacy during the "high" Cold War had only confirmed the Founders' dire warnings. Indeed, the United States had learned its lesson; it would no longer search for "monsters to destroy." A new foreign policy more consistent with its traditional style would be adopted. Jimmy Carter, the born-again Christian, had become the redeemer of American ideals and moral principles.

RECOGNIZING GLOBAL INTERDEPENDENCE

By 1976 the nations of the world had become more interdependent, meaning that their fates were more closely connected than ever before. Shifts in economic production, the growth and movement of populations, environmental decay, and weapons proliferation did not respect national frontiers. Even in the area of national security, the continuing appeal of nuclear weapons meant that any large-scale war would affect

3. See Stanley Hoffmann, *Primacy or World Order: American Foreign Policy since the Cold War* (New York: McGraw-Hill, 1978).

all corners of the world—no nation was any longer "an island, entire of itself." The attraction of interdependence was its prospect of a more peaceful and harmonious world consistent with American values and an escape from the more troublesome world of power politics. Moreover, it was claimed, transnational economic and technological forces made this more cooperative world inevitable. The expansion of the global economy into a single marketplace, the perils of nuclear proliferation, and the effects of pollution and the population explosion collectively made interdependence not just an aspiration but a reality in world politics.

Four central assumptions underlay interdependence as a model for the future—and they continue to influence American foreign policy early in the twenty-first century.[4] First, it was asserted that, in an ironic paradox, nuclear weapons were assuring the peace. The superpowers' strategic nuclear arms were weapons of denial and deterrence, and their existence made the use of conventional arms less likely because of the danger of escalation of hostilities. Thus the likelihood of major war between the superpowers, even among their allies and friends, was minimal. When wars occurred, however, such as the one in Vietnam, the conflicts were likely to last a long time and to cost dearly in terms of lives lost, money, and increased social divisions—in short, the costs might be excessive in relation to the combatants' goals. Thus future Vietnams were unlikely, especially after the disastrous American experience.

The second and related assumption underlying interdependence was that economic or welfare issues (collectively referred to as low politics) had become at least as important to national security as military readiness (high politics). Believing their security more assured, the democratic societies of the West had become increasingly preoccupied with economic growth rates, consumerism, and ever-higher standards of living. The developing countries, too, were bent on modernizing and on satisfying their own people's expectations for a better life, an effort that Carter promised to support generously. The key issues were economic and social, in his view, and by their nature they fostered support for values such as social justice and human dignity rather than violence and destruction.

Third, under conditions of interdependence nations could not fulfill their socioeconomic goals by themselves. Western societies, for example, ran largely on oil imported from non-Western countries, which, in turn, sought Western capital, technology, and food. All countries, rich and poor alike, suffered from cyclical downturns in the world economy and

4. For a detailed examination and application of this concept, see Robert O. Keohane and Joseph S. Nye Jr., *Power and Interdependence,* 2d ed. (New York: HarperCollins, 1989).

prospered when these cycles reversed themselves. Thus nations no longer completely governed their own destinies, and no government by itself could meet the aspirations and needs of its people for a better life; only cooperation would enhance each nation's prosperity. More specifically, whereas in zero-sum military matters one nation's increase in power was seen by its adversary as a loss of power, on positive-sum economic issues each country's welfare was dependent on the existence of prosperity in other countries. Precisely because conditions in one nation were vulnerable to those in another, all nations needed to work out problems together. Such cooperation required a greater willingness to resolve disputes peacefully and to work together in international organizations, particularly the United Nations.

Fourth, and very important, great-power coercion was said to play a minimal role in resolving socioeconomic issues, again in strong contrast to the primary role such coverage might play in security issues. Even if coercive threats were effective once or twice, their frequent use would only alienate countries whose support was needed on other issues. Although many of the nations with which the United States had to deal were comparatively weak militarily, they were not helpless or without meaningful sources of influences beyond their shores. Their economic troubles would require commitments of foreign aid; their social problems would send thousands of refugees to neighboring countries. Furthermore, they possessed commodities that, if production were shut off, would hurt the consuming nations. And together they had considerable political influence, particularly in the United Nations and other international organizations. The traditional way of calculating power—by adding up human resources, industrial capacity, military strength, and other factors—did not reveal this.

It was not surprising that this vision of transnational interdependence strongly influenced the Carter administration's policy. Carter came to power just after the final collapse of South Vietnam, when the United States was sick and tired of the war and the power politics that presumably had been responsible for the country's involvement. Many of the administration's top officials, who as leaders or members of the bureaucracy under John Kennedy and Lyndon Johnson had participated in the decision making about the war, shared the widely felt sense of shame about that conflict. They felt guilty about the apparent abuse of American power, as well as about other misuses (such as covert political interventions). Thus they dismissed Kissinger's balance-of-power approach as obsolete; the world had moved beyond the days when this "European" approach seemed relevant. The incoming administration claimed it would be more sensitive to the "new" realities of a more complex world and no longer a prisoner of the old Cold War myth of superpower competition and confrontation, which had led to U.S. support for right-wing dictatorships in the name of freedom.

East-West matters, then, were no longer on the political front burner except in the sense of East and West working together for arms control to reduce the superpowers' nuclear arsenals, to prevent the outbreak of a catastrophic war, and to reduce the spread of nuclear weapons to nations that did not yet possess them. As for détente, it remained a prerequisite for doing "good works" in the developing areas of the world. This image of the post–Vietnam War world, with its distaste for national egotism and the use of power, represented more than the reassertion of an older and more "moral" American approach to foreign policy. To many, it signified the ultimate transformation of world politics.

A FOCUS ON NORTH-SOUTH RELATIONS

When social and economic strength supplemented military power as the foundation of national security in the 1970s, the instruments of foreign policy changed; many countries increasingly turned to the tools of "economic statecraft" in advancing their foreign policy goals.[5] For example, the United States often dangled the "carrots" of trade and technology (see Chapter 6) before Soviet leaders to induce their compliance in arms control negotiations. Other instruments included international organizations, particularly the United Nations, where developing countries had become numerically dominant and where their proposals for closer North-South collaboration would attract worldwide attention. Regional organizations such as the European Community, Organization of American States (OAS), and Organization for African Unity (OAU) brought their leaders together to devise common strategies for political stability and economic growth. Flows of foreign aid, both military and economic, increased dramatically during this period. These growing volumes of aid served the interests not only of the recipients but also of the donors themselves, who competed for political influence among developing countries. Finally, and perhaps most dramatically, the petroleum "weapon" was used by some small, weak (in traditional power terms) Middle Eastern states against the powerful Western industrialized countries whose economic prosperity was vulnerable to interruptions in the oil flow.

THE NEW INTERNATIONAL ECONOMIC ORDER

Before Carter's rise to power, Western leaders had often argued that the causes of the persistent poverty in so many of the developing coun-

5. For an elaboration, see David A. Baldwin, *Economic Statecraft* (Princeton: Princeton University Press, 1985).

tries were of those countries own making: the fragility of nationhood; inefficient farming techniques resulting in widespread hunger; high birthrates, which defeated the most valiant efforts aimed at economic growth; large defense budgets, often used to prop up dictators and repress citizens; and, all too often, widespread inefficiency and corruption. The developing countries rejected the argument, however, that they were responsible for their failure to modernize. They pointed to the external system—the international economy—in which they were the sources of raw materials for Western industry, as the culprit. When demand declined, which occurred frequently as Western industries found substitutes or synthetics, the prices of developing country exports fell. As prices declined, so too did the ability of the developing countries to earn foreign exchange with which to import manufactured goods. This situation in turn prevented these countries from building their own industries and urban centers, widely viewed as the catalysts of greater prosperity, and achieving higher levels of education and literacy and improved living conditions.

In short, the earnings of the world's poorest countries often declined while the cost of goods from industrialized societies steadily rose. Yet when these countries were able to develop some industry and export to the West, they often ran into protective tariff barriers. Thus even when the developing countries worked harder, it was of little use; the structure of the international economy was biased against them and kept them in a subordinate position as suppliers of cheap raw materials for the rich Western states and as consumers of their finished products. The developing world seemed condemned to poverty and to continuing political weakness.[6]

The leaders of the developing nations viewed their countries as dependencies. They may have gained political independence, but they remained chained economically to the Western industrialized economies, unable to grow in their own rights. Indeed, their status remained *neocolonial* because their economies were geared not to the needs of their own markets but to those of the developed countries' markets. The developing countries had been plundered during the colonial days, and this plunder continued as they sold their resources cheaply on the international market. In this context their demand for a "new international economic order" was a claim for a redress of past wrongs. The rich nations, having used their power unfairly to take from the poor countries what rightfully belonged to those countries, the argument

6. For a recent analysis, see John T. Passé Smith, "The Persistence of the Gap between Rich and Poor Countries: Taking Stock of World Economic Growth, 1960–1993," in *Development and Under-Development: The Political Economy of Global Inequality*, ed. Mitchell A. Seligson and John T. Passé Smith (Boulder: Lynne Reinner, 1998), 27–40.

went, were obligated to make restitution in the name of past abuses. The transfer of wealth from the West to the developing world was therefore seen as repayment of a moral debt, and as an overdue investment in the ravaged economies of the poorer nations.

Among the developing countries, the demands for a new international economic order included calls for the industrialized countries to stabilize commodity prices, link those prices to Western inflation rates, increase foreign aid, and establish preferential tariffs so that the developing nations could sell their products in Western markets. These countries felt they had the resources Western industry needed, and they vowed to press their demands through collective action. Toward that end, and recognizing their numerical superiority in the United Nations, the developing countries organized themselves into a cohesive bloc, the Group of 77 (G-77), as a vehicle to make their voices heard. As for their relations with the two superpowers, they reaffirmed their earlier adherence to "nonalignment" in the Cold War and to freedom from superpower interference.

While nonalignment was the geopolitical buzzword for much of the developing world, in reality the bias of many of these countries toward the Soviet Union was clearly visible. After all, the Soviets had charged all along that the poverty and misery of the non-Western world were the results of Western capitalism and imperialism. Still, it seemed odd to find Vietnam, Afghanistan, North Korea, and Cuba accepted as "nonaligned" nations and odder still that the 1979 conference of these countries was held in Havana. Furthermore, the support given by the developing countries to most Soviet positions in the UN General Assembly raised doubts about their independent status. There, these states routinely voted against the United States, and in the United Nations Conference on Trade and Development, which had been established in 1964 to promote greater cooperation between rich and poor countries, they opening criticized American actions.

In reality, though, this unofficial coalition between the Soviet Union and the nonaligned nations was largely cosmetic. The nonaligned countries were, above all, nationalistic; they had not fought for national independence only to lose it to Soviet hegemony. Yet it was a sign of the times that this coalition existed and that only a small number of developing country governments criticized the direction of the nonaligned movement and defended American policies.

THE FOREIGN AID 'REGIME'

While often critical of U.S. policy and supporting Soviet positions, the leaders of developing countries frequently criticized both superpowers for their Cold War preoccupations and their alleged neglect of the poorer nations of the world. Far from neglecting them, however, the United States, the Soviet Union, and other industrialized countries gave them attention and resources in the form of foreign aid wholly disproportionate to the developing world's power. The reason was the bipolar distribution of power, which conferred on these new nations, most of which were fragile both economically and politically, greater leverage than their strength and influence warranted. Confronted by two great powers competing for their allegiance and loyalty, the developing countries could lean first toward the communist states, thereby attracting Western economic and military aid and political support, and then toward the West, thereby attracting similar assistance from the Soviet Union or China.

The developing countries' exploitation of this foreign aid rivalry"continued throughout the Cold War. Even many wealthy states outside the superpower competition, particularly those in Scandinavia and later along the Pacific Rim, offered billions of dollars in aid to further their own designs for international development. As the era of "low politics" took hold, affluent states began to view foreign aid as an obligation. It was not a question of *whether* they would contribute foreign aid, but how much, to whom, for what purposes, and under what terms. As time went on, each wealthy state devised a program of foreign aid that promoted its own national interests as well as those of recipient states. Foreign aid, then, became an essential tool of foreign policy.

By the late 1970s, however, many industrialized states had become disappointed with the results of their assistance efforts. The passage of two decades revealed that the optimistic expectations of "instant development" underestimated the difficulties of modernization. Moreover, foreign aid had not even been successful in winning friends and gaining influence within developing countries. As a result, not only did American aid fall to its lowest point by 1980—less than half of 1 percent of the gross national product (GNP)—but the emphasis shifted from capital development to technical assistance and a bigger role for private enterprise, including multinational corporations.[7] In surveys, Americans consistently identified foreign aid as their least favorite government program.

Prospects for the developing countries grew worse as the Cold War dragged on. With few exceptions they were still impoverished. The optimism had faded that foreign aid would propel their modernization or, later, that "trade, not aid" would permit them largely to earn their own

7. In 1979 U.S. aid was only 0.2 percent of GNP, well behind the proportion of aid given by most other donors.

way and to finance their own development. Food shortages and famines in Africa and southern Asia were stark reminders of what could happen. Thus the expectation of the former colonial states that they would realize their dreams of better and more rewarding lives for their peoples was unfulfilled. Illiteracy, starvation, and disease continued to coexist with dreams of national dignity and material welfare. For a variety of complex reasons, the billions of dollars in annual support from the North had little or no impact in the Southern Hemisphere. Despite the creation of an elaborate development aid "regime," gaps between the world's richest and poorest populations only widened.[8]

OPEC'S ECONOMIC CHALLENGE

It was in the context of yet another Arab-Israeli war in 1973 (described in the next section) that the Organization of Petroleum Exporting Countries (OPEC) quadrupled oil prices, from $3 to $12 a barrel, and its Arab members embargoed shipments of oil to the United States and the Netherlands, both supporters of Israel. The oil companies, which were supposed to be such powerful multinational corporations that they dominated the countries in which they operated, were shown to be without much power.[9] Indeed, they were at the mercy of the governments of the countries in which they operated. The so-called imperialist states, whose governments were presumably controlled and directed by the capitalists, did not mobilize to quash the governments that were said to be their puppet regimes. Confronting a vital threat to their well-being and security from countries that had no military power to speak of, the industrial democracies did not even debate the issue of military intervention. After all, this was the era of "low politics," in which economic and social issues took precedence over security issues. The Western countries instead talked of accommodation and acquiesced. Had the OPEC countries flexed their collective muscle a few decades earlier, the West would not have hesitated to resort to force rather than face the possibility of being destroyed economically.

The OPEC cartel's action at the time was widely viewed in the developing world as symbolic of a general protest against the industrialized countries. In fact, the organization became a kind of vanguard for the world's poorest nations. They shared a mood of anger and resentment that was clearly directed against the North, particularly the United States. But ironically, the effects of the quadrupling of oil prices were felt most keenly by developing countries; it threatened their plans to indus-

8. See Robert E. Wood, *From Marshall Plan to Debt Crisis: Foreign Aid and Development Choices in the World Economy* (Berkeley: University of California Press, 1986).

9. See Daniel Yergin, *The Prize: The Epic Quest for Oil, Money, and Power* (New York: Simon and Schuster, 1991).

trialize and handicapped their efforts to grow more food using technologically intensive, petroleum-based agricultural techniques.

Despite the increased suffering brought on by the steep rise in oil prices, the developing countries did not form a coalition with the United States, Western Europe, and Japan to force lower oil prices. Their reasons were: their fear of irritating OPEC; their hope for promised but largely undelivered OPEC economic help (most went to fellow Muslim nations, where it was spent on arms); and their desire to imitate OPEC. More basically, though, the developing countries, as noted, identified emotionally with OPEC. The organization's action was widely perceived by these countries as "getting even" for past exploitation. It gave them a good feeling that for once the weak had turned the tables and made the strong suffer.[10]

The sharp rise in oil prices left no country untouched. In the United States and among its principal industrial allies, high oil prices slowed economic growth, brought on unemployment, created "stagflation" (simultaneous inflation and recession), lowered standards of living, created large Western imbalances of trade, and sharply lowered the value of the dollar. The energy crisis of the 1970s did not merely cause occasional inconveniences such as long lines to buy gas or higher prices at the gas pump; it profoundly upset entire economies and changed ways of life, as evidenced by smaller cars and lower speed limits in the United States. Moreover, the energy crisis raised the question of whether the Western states, which had paid for welfare programs by means of rapidly growing economies, could still afford such programs. Would they have to reduce defense expenditures in order to implement social policies? Or would they have to cut social expenditures to maintain strong defenses? Plenty of "guns" and "butter" no longer appeared affordable.

Mao Zedong, who once said that "power grows out of the barrel of a gun," would have been equally correct had he referred to a barrel of oil. Large-scale capital investments and many years are required to explore, find, and drill for oil, an irreplaceable commodity that cannot be recycled. Similarly, the development of new technologies to exploit solar energy or shale oil also require enormous investments of time and money. Other energy sources such as nuclear power are controversial or are, like coal, deemed environmentally undesirable. Thus no short-run substitute is readily available for economies that have long depended on relatively cheap oil and have neglected the development of alternative energy sources.

10. The German word *schadenfreude* says it best: pleasure received from seeing someone suffer who deserves it.

Is it any wonder, then, that the developing countries were delighted and held high hopes in the wake of the oil shocks of the 1970s? Indeed, OPEC's actions gave rise to three expectations: first, that OPEC would use its leverage to raise the prices of natural resources from the other developing countries; second, that the other commodity producers would follow OPEC's example by organizing their own cartels; and, third, that the OPEC "petrodollars" would flow to the developing world in the form of foreign aid. But to the chagrin of these countries, none of the three expectations materialized. OPEC fragmented as its members reverted within a decade to their previous patterns of undercutting the cartel oil prices.[11] And its example was not adopted by producers of other commodities, who remained consumed by their own competition for Western markets. Finally, OPEC profits were not shared with developing countries in the form of aid. After being deposited in New York banks, they were lent instead to many developing countries (particularly Mexico and Brazil) at market rates, which the borrowers could not repay, thus contributing to the debt crisis that afflicted much of the developing world in the 1980s.

CARTER'S MIDDLE EAST BREAKTHROUGH

Four years before Carter took office, in the waning days of the Nixon administration, tensions in the Middle East had erupted in warfare that threatened to draw in both superpowers. In 1973 Egypt and Syria attacked Israel on the highest of all Jewish holy days—Yom Kippur, or the Day of Atonement. Egypt, which was ruled by Anwar Sadat, the Egyptian nationalist who had succeeded Gamal Abdel Nasser, entered the conflict because it had become increasingly frustrated by Israel's refusal to relinquish the Egyptian territory (up to the East Bank of the Suez Canal) it had captured in the Six-day War in 1967. The Egyptians achieved initial success in crossing the Suez Canal and driving into the Sinai Desert. From the sidelines, fearing it would lose influence in the Arab world by remaining neutral, the Soviet Union delivered offensive arms to the Arab states. Then, when the Egyptian and Syrian armies proved successful in the opening round of fighting, the Soviets began a huge airlift of war materiel and opposed any cease-fire calls that were not linked to a pullback by Israel to the 1967 frontiers. Moscow also called on other Arab governments to join the war and approved the OPEC oil embargo.

The United States, under President Nixon, responded with its own massive airlift of military supplies in the face of enormous Israeli fight-

11. For an elaboration, see Fadhi J. Chalabi, "OPEC: An Obituary," *Foreign Affairs* (winter 1997–1998): 126–140.

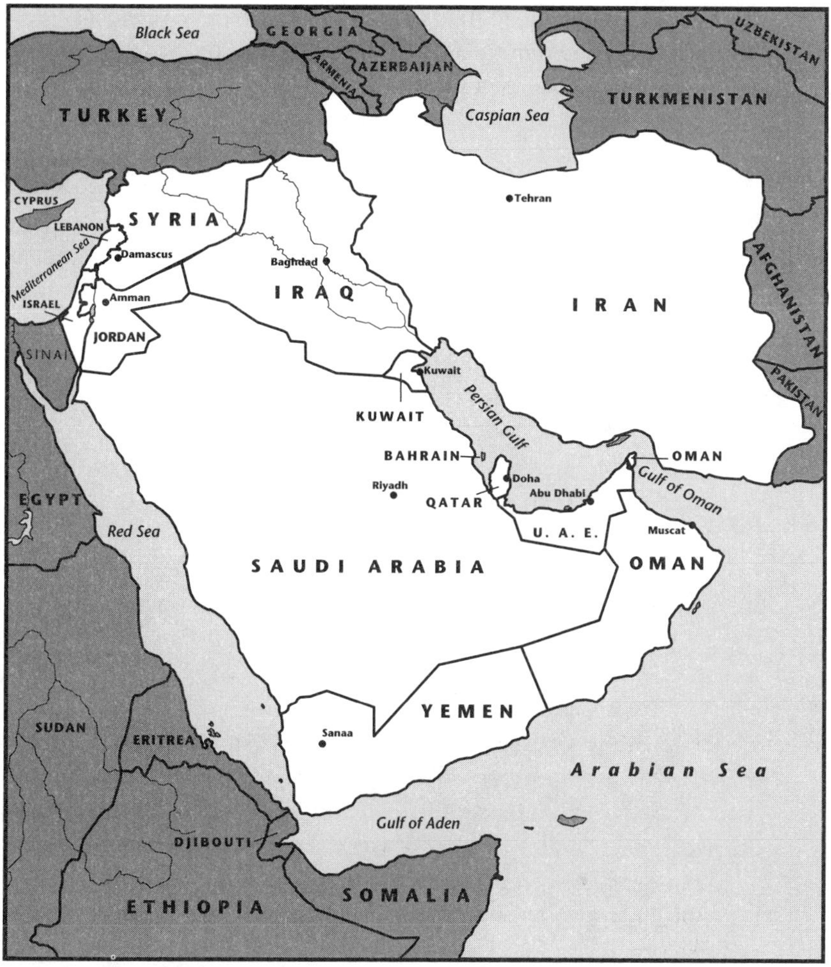

THE MIDDLE EAST

er plane and tank losses. Once Israel recovered from its shock and drove the Syrians back from the Golan Heights, its forces concentrated on Egypt, crossed the Suez Canal to the West Bank, and moved to cut off supplies to the Egyptian forces on the East Bank and to encircle them. At this point the United States and the Soviet Union agreed on a cease-fire resolution in the UN Security Council. But the shooting continued, and the Israelis drove to encircle and destroy the Egyptian army on the eastern side of the Suez Canal.

In response, the embattled Sadat asked the United States and the Soviet Union to use their own forces to impose their cease-fire resolution. The United States declined to intervene with its forces, but the Soviet Union threatened to do so unilaterally. Thus the two superpowers now confronted one another, and American military forces were placed on a worldwide nuclear alert. Moscow backed off, however, and the United States, also eager to avoid an escalation, pressured Israel to end its military advance. These moves assured the cease-fire.

For Henry Kissinger, the urgency of reaching a Middle East settlement was obvious, and the time seemed favorable. He campaigned actively for a settlement, engaging in "shuttle diplomacy" as he crisscrossed the Middle East mediating the dispute. Indeed, Sadat was the first Egyptian leader to declare his willingness to accept the existence of Israel and make peace with it on the basis of the 1967 frontiers. Moreover, an Arab-Israeli peace would prevent a U.S.-Soviet confrontation that could escalate into a superpower war. Each Arab-Israeli war had held the possibility of such a confrontation, and in 1973 that possibility had become almost real. Kissinger also was determined to avoid the past pattern of an Israeli military victory, which could not be translated into an acceptable political settlement, and an Arab defeat, which left the Arabs humiliated, resentful, and more determined than ever not to accept Israel's right to exist and use oil as a weapon against the West. When Ford left office, however, Kissinger's designs for a comprehensive peace settlement in the Middle East in effect left with him.

In 1976 the incoming Carter administration viewed the Middle East situation with alarm. Resentment from the Yom Kippur War remained sharp, with both sides acquiring new and more advanced weapons systems in its aftermath. Carter therefore proposed that all parties resume the negotiations that had begun at Geneva after the 1973 war.

In the final days of the Ford administration, Kissinger had fashioned his strategy to bring the Arabs and Israelis together step by step and exclude the Soviets; only at the final conference would the Soviet Union be invited for symbolic reasons. But Carter decided to approach the Soviets and enlist their cooperation in achieving a peace settlement. Moscow had influence with the more militant Syrians and within the Palestine Liberation Organization (PLO), which had formed to press the cause of renewed statehood for Palestine. The Soviets, therefore, could cause a lot of trouble and block negotiations. But if Moscow participated in the peace negotiations, it would retain a degree of influence in the Arab world if and when a peace treaty were signed, the possibility of a superpower clash would be reduced, and détente with the United States would be strengthened, a prerequisite for a U.S. focus on the developing countries.

The two superpowers reached agreement on resolution of the Middle East conflict late in 1977, but neither Jerusalem nor Cairo was happy with the Soviet-American accord. Israel did not want to face all its enemies again simultaneously, and Egypt already had broken with Moscow, which now favored Syria, Egypt's rival. Thus Israel and Egypt decided to bypass Moscow and Washington and negotiate directly. In a dramatic and internationally televised visit to Jerusalem in November 1977, during which he addressed the Israeli Knesset (parliament), Sadat extended recognition to the Arabs' archenemy. The mood afterward was euphoric; a comprehensive peace, a peace with all of Israel's Arab enemies, seemed near.

The mood did not last long, however. Sadat apparently believed peace was achievable easily and quickly because he had taken the significant psychological step of reassuring the Israelis that his peace offer was genuine, not a trick. Israel would withdraw to its 1967 frontiers from the Sinai, the West Bank, Syria's Golan Heights, and Jordan's East Jerusalem and would recognize the Palestinians' legitimate rights. In return for their land, the Arabs would sign a peace treaty and Israel would gain the legitimacy and peace with security it had sought since birth. The Israelis had always asserted that if the Arabs negotiated with them directly, implying recognition, they would be willing to return the territories taken in 1967. In fact, Israel had specifically disclaimed annexationist ambitions. After the 1967 war its Labor government had accepted UN Resolution 242 committing Israel to the withdrawal from the captured land (or, given some adjustments for security reasons, from almost all of these areas).

But Israel's new coalition government was led by Prime Minister Menachem Begin, leader of the principal opposition party, Likud. He proposed an Israeli withdrawal from the Sinai Desert, but offered the Palestinians on the West Bank and in the Gaza Strip only autonomy, or self-rule, not self-determination. Moreover, Begin referred to the West Bank by its ancient Hebrew names, Judea and Samaria, and claimed it was not occupied territory to be returned but liberated territory to be kept as part of the Greater Israel of which he had long dreamed. He left no doubt that he expected to establish Israeli sovereignty over both the West Bank and Gaza, each of which contained large Arab populations. In the meantime, the Israeli government announced that Jewish settlements in the Sinai and West Bank would remain, and it even encouraged the establishment of new ones.

When, to no one's great surprise, bilateral negotiations broke down, the United States reentered the negotiating process. Carter felt that Sadat was offering Israel the security and peace it had so long sought, and that if this opportunity was not seized the result would be politically disastrous for Israel and economically disastrous for the West. The president thought three conditions were necessary for a solution in the Middle East. First, Israel had to abide by UN Resolution 242 and return most of the Arab territory it had captured in 1967. Only minor adjustments for security reasons could be allowed. Second, because the key to peace was the Palestinian issue, the Palestinians had to participate in the peacemaking process. Carter himself declared that the Palestinians had a right to a "homeland," a deliberately vague term but one that nevertheless carried great symbolic weight. Third, in return for such Israeli concessions, the Arab states had to commit themselves not only to ending their state of hostilities with Israel but also to signing a peace treaty.

Begin was at odds with the first two conditions. He reinterpreted UN Resolution 242 to mean that Israel was not required to withdraw from the West Bank and Gaza. He also was opposed to a Palestinian state, which he—and indeed most Israelis—felt would endanger the existence of Israel. Moreover, he promoted his own plan for Israeli settlements in the occupied lands. Since 1967, however, the United States had consistently opposed these settlements as illegal. The Carter administration repeated this while it watched in disbelief as the Israeli government, in the middle of the peace process, actively encouraged new settlements on the land the Arabs claimed to be theirs. Washington was convinced that the Israelis were acting in bad faith in the midst of peace negotiations.

Repeated American efforts to halt this policy were in vain. By contrast, Sadat appeared reasonable and conciliatory. He had with great courage provided the psychological breakthrough with his trip to Jerusalem. He also had shown sensitivity to Israel's security needs and had been willing to accept Israel's demands for a peace treaty and the subsequent normalization of relations—not after twenty-five years, or even five years, but immediately. The stalemate continued.

In September 1978 Carter, aware that the three-year interim Sinai agreement would run out in October, gambled and invited Begin and Sadat to meet with him at Camp David, the presidential retreat in Maryland. The invitation was a gamble because had this summit meeting produced no results, the president's prestige, already low, would have been even more seriously impaired, American mediating attempts would have run their course, and Israeli-American relations would have been set back even further. But the president showed persistence and skill and after twelve days of patient negotiations emerged with a series of agreements, including a commitment by the two leaders to sign a peace treaty within three months.

Sadat made most of the concessions. He did not gain a commitment to an eventual Israeli withdrawal from the West Bank and Gaza Strip, or full Palestinian self-determination. The Israelis, however, promised to recognize "the legitimate rights of the Palestinians," to permit West Bank and Gaza Palestinians to participate in future negotiations on these areas and ratify or reject a final agreement, and to halt temporarily new Israeli settlements on the West Bank. In return, Israel gained a separate peace treaty with the strongest of its Arab neighbors; without Egypt the others could not by themselves take on Israel. Thus for a seemingly small investment Israel had gained the enormous dividend of a real sense of security.

Sadat hoped that a peace agreement would start momentum for further agreements with Israel. The first Arab reaction to the Camp David accords, however, was negative. Jordan, and even Saudi Arabia, joined Syria, Iraq, Libya, Algeria, and South Yemen in condemning Sadat, who became more isolated than ever. Under these circumstances, Carter's courageous personal intervention—including his visits to Egypt and Israel—produced the necessary diplomatic breakthroughs and brought peace between these two long-term enemies. Yet the treaty finally produced did not bring a stable peace to the area. Israel quickly resumed and accelerated its settlements policy in the West Bank; the Arab states, except Egypt, became more hostile to American "meddling" in the region; the key Palestinian issue remained unresolved; and all sides continued to import large volumes of military hardware in preparation for the next conflagration.

THE COLLAPSE OF CARTER'S FOREIGN POLICY

Jimmy Carter's embrace of world-order politics in the late 1970s coincided with the Soviet Union's achievement of nuclear parity and many Americans' "crisis of confidence" in their government, brought on by a series of domestic problems. Thus, while the new Carter administration was de-emphasizing the East-West conflict and focusing on North-South cooperation, the Soviet Union, perceiving the global balance of power to be shifting in its favor, saw opportunities to exploit and expand its influence militarily in the developing countries.

The East-West struggle was not just an old, bad memory. It was still very much alive, even if the United States preferred not to compete actively and even if it insisted that containment no longer seemed relevant in the face of the diffusion of power in the world, growing nationalism in the developing countries, and the shift in emphasis from power politics to world-order politics. As for the Soviets, they shared neither the belief that international politics had changed nor the view that military force had become an increasingly irrelevant instrument of policy. By 1979 the Soviet Union was thought to be heavily outspending the United States on military forces—by at least 25 percent, or perhaps by as much as 50 percent. Since the Soviet economic base was believed about half that of the United States, this disproportionate spending on "guns" at the cost of "butter" for the Soviet people suggested that these forces were intended for more than just defense. Abroad, the Soviet Union used its growing political-military involvement to exploit hostility among developing countries toward the North and to offer those countries, for emulation, its model of communism and centrally directed industrialization.

During the "high" Cold War, the United States had often erred by overemphasizing East-West relations. Indeed, some of its mistakes, particularly with regard to China, were costly. But experience also had shown that grave danger lay in ignoring or downplaying these relations. It was one thing to learn from the past and correct errors. It was quite another to dismiss the very nature of international politics, whose chief characteristic is its historic continuity. In the last half of Carter's presidency this lesson was painfully learned. His restraint in foreign affairs and appeals to universal moral standards were followed by the Soviet invasion of Afghanistan, the rise of a Marxist regime in Nicaragua, and the seizure of American diplomats as hostages in Iran. These three concurrent events, along with a second energy crisis, seemed to offer strong testimony to the limitations of world-order politics and raised the question of whether the Nixon and preceding administrations had been so wrong in giving priority to American-Soviet competition, in emphasizing military power, or in thinking that the East-West struggle could not be divorced from North-South relations.

THE SOVIET INVASION OF AFGHANISTAN

In the second half of Carter's term the divisions between the adherents of détente—among them, Secretary of State Cyrus Vance—and the hard-liners, epitomized by National Security Adviser Zbigniew Brzezinski—continued to fester. After Soviet troops and tanks poured into Afghanistan in late 1979, Vance's influence waned and Brzezinski's rose. The administration had overlooked the Soviet-inspired coup a year earlier in Afghanistan, but the 85,000 Soviet troops that entered the country during the last week of 1979 were hard to ignore. Fierce resistance by Muslim citizens to radical and antireligious reforms appeared to threaten the Soviet-supported regime.

Among their other concerns, the Soviets feared that the Islamic fundamentalism then sweeping Iran and Pakistan might engulf Afghanistan, which lay between these two countries, creating an insecure situation on the Soviet Union's southern border where approximately fifty million Soviet Muslims lived. In response to the situation, Moscow invoked the Brezhnev Doctrine, which asserted that once a nation had become socialist, it was not to be surrendered to counterrevolution (as the Soviets defined these terms). The march of history toward socialism was inevitable and irreversible. Earlier, this doctrine had been invoked only in Eastern Europe—in Hungary in 1956 and Czechoslovakia in 1968. Now the Red Army was to ensure history's progress outside of the Soviet sphere in a developing country.

The Soviets expected Americans to merely condemn the Soviet action as deplorable. In fact, believing their vital security interests to be at stake, the Soviets did not give much thought to American reactions and felt, in truth, they had little to lose. Carter, to gain ratification of the SALT II treaty in the Senate, had promised to increase defense spending and modernize American strategic forces. And the Soviet Union had received few of the trade, technology, and financial benefits it had expected from détente. Indeed, Moscow had been denied most-favored-nation commercial status, which China had received. Nevertheless, such a disregard for American reaction, implying contempt for American power, was rather new.

For Carter and Vance, who had pinned so much of their hopes for world-order politics on superpower cooperation, the Soviet invasion was a shock. Chagrined, Carter called the Afghanistan invasion the greatest threat to world peace since World War II and said, "[the Soviet action] made a more dramatic change in my opinion of what the Soviets' ultimate goals are than anything they've done in the previous time I've been in office." No president in the postwar era has testified more dramatically to his own naiveté.

The president, swinging with events, then became a hard-liner. He stepped up military spending, halted high-technology sales, embargoed grain shipments, and imposed a U.S. boycott on the Olympic Games scheduled for Moscow in the summer of 1980. The Senate, meanwhile, refused to ratify the SALT II treaty. Most important of all, Carter announced his own doctrine: the United States would henceforth consider any threat to the Persian Gulf to be a direct threat to its own vital interests. It would be one of many steps in Carter's anguished transition to a more aggressive, militaristic, and Cold War–oriented foreign policy.

Détente thus came to an end in 1980 as superpower relations disintegrated. Carter undoubtedly had been correct that not all regional conflicts were tests of superpower strength and credibility. In truth, however, few purely regional quarrels existed outside the context of global Cold War. Détente ultimately collapsed because of a series of regional conflicts that the administration had attempted to isolate from the Soviet-American rivalry—only to find that it could not do so. As Soviet activities in the developing world showed, the Soviet Union did not consider this rivalry over. Quite the opposite: it took advantage of America's post-Vietnam reluctance to act and its illusion that problems in developing countries could be separated from the superpower competition.

REVOLUTION AND COMMUNIST CONTROL IN NICARAGUA

History also was unkind to President Carter in Central America, where decades of economic distress, military dictatorship, and ideological polarization spawned a variety of revolutionary movements. These often were directed not only against the reigning rulers but also against the United States, whose support for dictators in the name of containing communism engendered widespread resentment throughout Latin America and the Caribbean. The United States, the self-proclaimed protector of the region under the Monroe Doctrine, was widely viewed by many as more of a menace than a supportive patron. Carter hoped to change this perception by reforming U.S. policy and establishing a new reputation as a truly "good neighbor."

In Nicaragua, Carter opposed the long-standing military dictatorship of Anastasio Somoza, whose family had ruthlessly controlled the country for nearly five decades (after the departure of U.S. Marines from the country). Carter's reversal of American policy was consistent with his overall effort to shift attention from Cold War concerns to internal social and economic problems in the poorer countries. Continued U.S. support for right-wing dictatorships, he felt, would certainly doom U.S. interests in the region and throughout the developing world. Popular resentment and anger would eventually lead to the overthrow of such dictatorships, and identification of America with the status quo would only alienate the new rulers. Unlike in Vietnam, the argument went, the United States had to place itself on the "right side of history." Thus the Carter administration favored social and political change and tried to identify U.S. policy with such change rather than oppose it.

The rebellion against Somoza accelerated in the late 1970s, despite the leader's increasingly brutal use of the Nicaraguan National Guard. The Organization of American States, which encouraged his overthrow, called for a democratic government and the holding of free elections as soon as possible. As a result of all these forces, Somoza's regime finally collapsed in 1979.[12] At first, Carter favored the coalition of anti-Somoza forces led by the Sandino Liberation Front (known as Sandinistas), which during Somoza's days supported on the domestic front by the Catholic Church, the educated middle class, and the business community. Thus in its first years under the coalition Nicaragua received allotments of $90 million in foreign aid from the United States and promis-

12. For a more thorough treatment, see Anthony Lake, *Somoza Falling* (Boston: Houghton Mifflin, 1989).

es for long-term support. "If you do not hold me responsible for everything that happened under my predecessors," Carter told Nicaragua's new leader, Daniel Ortega, "I will not hold you responsible for everything that happened under your predecessors."

The new regime in Nicaragua, however, did not live up to Carter's expectations. The broad-based anti-Somoza coalition rapidly dissolved as the Sandinistas centralized authority within a nine-member directorate. Free elections were delayed, the press was (again) censored, and other political restrictions were imposed by the junta, which turned increasingly to Marxist-Leninist models for building a self-sufficient communist state. In addition, the Sandinistas offered to assist their allies in El Salvador, where a similar civil war was erupting between its military dictatorship and left-wing guerrillas. The Salvadoran dictatorship responded by sending "death squads" into the impoverished countryside and murdering suspected insurgents. When their victims included three American nuns, the Carter administration rescinded U.S. aid to El Salvador and watched as the civil war became bloodier. Nicaragua and El Salvador remained battle zones into the mid-1980s and became a central preoccupation of Ronald Reagan's presidency.

More broadly, the unrest in Central America further demonstrated the limitations of Carter's efforts to redirect American foreign policy. To some degree he was held captive by the unstable conditions that had developed in the region before and during the Cold War. No immediate reversal of American policy, however well intentioned, was likely to counteract the bitterness and resentment that had developed for so long toward "*yanqui* imperialism." Far from engendering newfound trust between the United States and Central America, Carter's efforts instead provided an opening for anti-American forces to assume power and translate their resentment into revenge. As Carter attempted to purify American foreign policy, he discovered that the outside world was continuing to pursue the same *realpolitik* he had rejected. Ideological tensions only increased during his tenure, despite his best efforts to focus on areas of cooperation between the United States and its Latin American neighbors.

AMERICA 'HELD HOSTAGE' IN IRAN

The low level to which American credibility and power had fallen was symbolized in November 1979 by the storming of the American embassy in Tehran by a mob of protestors. In the melee, militant students seized fifty-two American embassy workers. This event came on the heels of the ouster of Iran's pro-American shah. Suffering from cancer, the shah was admitted to the United States for medical treatment.[13] The newly installed revolutionary authorities, hoping to create an Islamic theocracy in Iran, gave the unprecedented hostage-taking their blessing and support.

The seizure of American hostages paralyzed Carter, and his subsequent efforts to gain their safe release became high public drama. Nightly, U.S. television networks exposed the American public to pictures of Iranian crowds chanting, like well-rehearsed choruses, their hatred of America. The Ayatollah Ruhollah Khomeini, Iran's chief religious leader and *imam*, or leader, of all Shiite Muslims, called America the "Great Satan." "Death to America" was the battle cry as Carter was burned in effigy on the streets of Tehran.

Meanwhile, President Carter, who had stressed human rights in his election campaign and who had pointed to the shah, among others, as an example of his predecessors' amoral, if not immoral, policy, was as usual caught between conflicting views. The disagreements in Washington were such that the fall of the shah and Khomeini's triumph were greeted with relief. But, as had happened so often before, the Carter administration's understanding of Khomeini was superficial, consistent with its own hopes of what would happen. Yet perhaps Carter's confusion was understandable, for, after all, who in Washington or any other Western capital in that secular age would have given serious consideration to the strength of a religious movement and the possibility that it would transform Iran into a medieval theocracy? There was no precedent for such a reaction to efforts at modernization.

In the 444 days following the hostage-taking, the world watched as the Carter administration tried one means after another to gain the hostages' release. Among other things, the White House appealed to the United Nations and the International Court of Justice and applied a series of economic sanctions. But all was in vain. The holding of the hostages was a symbolic act of defiance and revenge for the shah, who was portrayed by the new regime as an American puppet who had cruelly exploited Iranians in behalf of U.S. interests. As the administration's patience wore thin, it attempted a rescue mission in the spring of 1980. The mission was called off, however, when three of the eight helicopters malfunctioned in a desert sandstorm. Even worse, one helicopter collided on the ground with the refueling aircraft for the flight out of Iran, killing eight servicemen and injuring five others. To a nation on edge, the failure of the mission dramatically symbolized the apparent helplessness of the United States, as well as the low level of readiness, com-

13. The shah died a few months later in Egypt. For a review of his long and intimate relationship with the United States, see Mrak Gasiorowski, *U.S. Foreign Policy and the Shah: Building a Client State in Iran* (Ithaca: Cornell University Press, 1991).

IMPACT AND INFLUENCE

AYATOLLAH RUHOLLAH KHOMEINI

Among foreign leaders who challenged American foreign policy during the Cold War, Iran's Ruhollah Khomeini assumed an unlikely but crucial role. The Islamic religious leader, or ayatollah, had long condemned the repressive rule of Shah Muhammed Reza Pahlevi, who had taken power in a CIA-backed coup in 1953. Khomeini was imprisoned by the shah and later exiled to Iraq and then France, where he continued to support protest movements against the shah. After the shah relinquished power in January 1979, Khomeini returned to the country as a hero and oversaw the creation of an Islamic republic.

In November 1979 a group of Islamic militants seized the U.S. embassy in Tehran and took fifty-two Americans hostages. Khomeini justified the seizure and prevented the hostages' release for more than a year. Long after Khomeini's death in 1989, Iran maintained its theocratic government and its intense hostility toward the United States and other Western powers.

petence, and reliability of its armed forces. Secretary of State Vance resigned in protest of the mission, revealing deepening divisions within the Carter administration over foreign policy.

Two events helped to gain the hostages' release on January 20, 1981, the day Carter left office. The first was the Iraqi attack on Iran in the fall of 1980. The war suddenly made the U.S. economic sanctions, especially the freeze on Iranian money in U.S. banks, painful for Iran because its military forces were largely American equipped. The need for spare parts and the cash to buy them and other goods grew as oil production in Iran fell to almost nothing. The second event was the November 1980 victory of Republican Ronald Reagan, the former governor of California, in the U.S. presidential elections. Because he had run on a tough foreign policy platform and had denounced the Iranians as "barbarians" and "kidnappers," the Iranians expected harsher measures from Reagan, including military action.

In these circumstances, diplomacy finally proved successful. The fifty-two hostages were released just after Reagan's inauguration in a gesture fraught with symbolism. A humiliating chapter in American history, coming so shortly after the Vietnam trauma, had ended. In the exuberance of the welcome that the ex-hostages received on their return to America, one could almost hear the refrain "never again," for, in a real sense, America itself and the U.S. government had been taken captive and held hostage. Combined with national frustrations over Afghanistan, Nicaragua, and the second oil crisis of the decade, which was precipitated by the turmoil in Iran, the Iranian debacle deepened the perception of an American "decline." Reagan vowed to reverse this trend upon his assumption of the presidency in January 1981.

LESSONS OF WORLD-ORDER POLITICS

As we have seen in this chapter, the Soviet invasion of Afghanistan, the Sandinista revolution in Nicaragua and its spin-off rebellion in El Salvador, and the hostage crisis in Iran collectively undermined President Jimmy Carter's attempt to promote world-order politics on the basis of global interdependence, universal standards of morality, and peaceful cooperation. Carter's efforts were frustrated for many reasons, some of which were beyond his control. The rise of mass movements in the 1970s, for example, fueled the anti-American campaigns in Nicaragua and Iran, along with populist assaults against dictatorial regimes elsewhere.

In any event, these events dispelled much of the post-Vietnam malaise and led to a demand for a more vigorous American foreign policy. In this respect, Leonid Brezhnev, Daniel Ortega, and the Ayatollah

Khomeini may have done the United States a favor, just as the German submarine attacks on U.S. ships in World War I, the Japanese attack on Pearl Harbor in World War II, and the Soviet seizure of power in Czechoslovakia early in the Cold War had served to mobilize the nation when the public mood was one of disengagement and relaxation. After America's years of withdrawal, the challenges of 1979 and 1980 may have been necessary to demonstrate that neglecting the unsavory realities of world politics, far from rendering such realities inconsequential, often encouraged their spread and provoked equally serious challenges to global stability.

Carter sensed this shift in mood as he assumed a harder stance toward the Soviets during his final year in office. For example, he increasingly followed the advice of White House hard-liner Zbigniew Brzezinski, his national security adviser.[14] And on Capitol Hill, Congress enthusiastically approved Carter's requests for a large increase in American defense spending. Thus began the process of national rearmament that Ronald Reagan would oversee and accelerate well into the 1980s. In all of these efforts, Carter was supported by the American public, which drew a connection between his previous condemnation of power politics and the calamities that befell his administration in its final two years.

Paradoxically, it was not the *recognition* of Carter's moralistic values but their *repudiation* that pulled the country out of its post-Vietnam "malaise." The widely perceived consequences of American introspection and self-doubt, which produced challenges to its interests on virtually every continent, mobilized public opinion and political consensus where appeals to universal moralism had fallen short in previous years. The American style of foreign policy, it appeared, seemed to require more than good intentions; support for democratic values and global progress could not be sustained at the cost of American national interests.

Carter was clearly anguished by the spreading challenges to his foreign policy. For weeks he confined himself to the White House while he considered ways to get the hostages home from Iran; in December 1979 he refused to light the White House Christmas tree while the hostages remained in captivity. Moreover, the downward spiral of events took a visible physical toll on the president, who was forced to reconcile his most basic spiritual beliefs with the unavoidable challenges of overseas competition. In response to these challenges and to the shift in American public opinion away from world-order politics, Carter abandoned many of his foreign policy beliefs and programs.

14. See Jeral A. Rosati, *The Carter Administration's Quest for Global Community* (Columbia: University of South Carolina Press, 1987), 142–149.

Reagan received the full benefit of this shift in mood. For decades he had taken a hard line toward the Soviet Union. Although inflation and the weak state of the U.S. economy may have been important factors in Reagan's election, the fact remained that because of OPEC and the overthrow of the shah, the domestic economic issue was inseparable from American foreign policy and the U.S. position in the world. Whereas Carter was forced to acknowledge that the events of 1979 and 1980 had undermined his idealistic worldview, Reagan was able to argue that they had confirmed his expectations. "Historical forces" were not moving in the direction of transnational cooperation, as Carter had claimed previously. They had never diverted from their consistent path, which was plagued by conflicting interests and tests of strength.

Ronald Reagan, often called the "great communicator," promoted hard-line policies toward communist countries during the early 1980s.

CHAPTER EIGHT

The Revival of Superpower Confrontation

Just as Jimmy Carter's rise to the presidency reflected the introspective American mood of the Vietnam-Watergate era, Ronald Reagan's leadership embodied the more assertive national spirit of the early 1980s. A former movie star and pitchman for General Electric, President Reagan was known neither for his intellect nor for his long hours spent in the Oval Office.[1] The contrast with his predecessor was widely apparent. Whereas Carter's worldview emphasized the complexities of interdependence, Reagan's was unabashedly one-dimensional. Whereas Carter pored over background reports and anguished over policy choices, Reagan literally dozed through high-level meetings. But he

1. For an informative biography, see Lou Cannon, *Reagan* (New York: Putnam, 1982). For a more recent and controversial treatment, see Edmund Morris, *Dutch: A Memoir of Ronald Reagan* (New York: Random House, 1999).

brought to the office two characteristics that were to help transform Soviet-American relations: strong anticommunist instincts and a powerful ability to mobilize public opinion. Both characteristics served him well.

Reagan attempted to restore the country's battered stature and the national pride of Americans by reviving the notion that an active U.S. role in international affairs was essential to world peace. Soviet leaders, he felt, had exploited détente, the Vietnam syndrome, and Carter's attempts to place human rights at the center of American foreign policy. As Reagan's supporters saw it, a clear line could be drawn from Carter's idealism to the Soviet invasion of Afghanistan, the Sandinista revolution in Nicaragua, and the seizure of American hostages in Iran. Believing the United States must match the Soviet nuclear and conventional military buildup of the 1970s, Reagan proposed a massive buildup of U.S. armed forces. A compliant Congress approved his proposals to double American defense spending in his first term and to match recent Soviet deployments of intermediate-range nuclear missiles in Europe with a new generation of North Atlantic Treaty Organization (NATO) missiles.

Reagan often boasted that he was blessed with the luck of the Irish. Indeed, he certainly had the good fortune to take office as the torch was being passed in Moscow from the old guard to a new generation of reformers ultimately led by Mikhail Gorbachev. The reduced tensions between the superpowers, so unexpected at the beginning of the decade, often have been attributed to Gorbachev, who took over the Kremlin in 1985, during Reagan's second term in office. The new Soviet leader was said to be the first enlightened ruler since the 1917 Revolution. His generation of Soviet elites hailed from urban rather than rural backgrounds and had some exposure to foreign countries. As a result, it was more aware of the failings of the Soviet system and critical of its internal defects. Had Brezhnev or his two immediate successors survived, Gorbachev's new domestic and foreign policies might not have seen the light of day. Nor is it likely the Cold War would have ended on terms that were as peaceful or as beneficial to the West.

To some, the collapse of the Warsaw Pact and the Soviet Union in 1991 was a fait accompli, a historical inevitability no matter who was the president of the United States in the 1980s. The ossified Soviet system was already in an advanced stage of decline, its internal problems were growing worse daily, and its hold on its clients in Eastern Europe and beyond was becoming more tenuous. Thus Gorbachev—or any leader of the country—had to implement drastic reforms in the Soviet Union's political and economic system; permit the restive populations in Warsaw, Prague, and East Berlin to express themselves; and adopt a more cooperative posture toward the United States. These measures would, according to those holding this view, only magnify the deficiencies of the Soviet system and hasten its self-destruction.

But this interpretation of events, which minimizes the roles of both Reagan and Gorbachev, does not tell the full story. It fails to recognize the crucial part Reagan played in raising the costs of the superpower competition and in forcing the Soviet Union to reform its system. The U.S. military buildup, which actually began in Carter's last year, required greater Soviet investments in arms at a time when the dwindling resources of the Soviet Union were needed for domestic priorities. Moreover, the new NATO missile deployments in Europe negated the strategic advantages of recent Soviet installations. The president's proposals for a Strategic Defense Initiative further worried the Soviets because, whether or not it succeeded in creating a missile-proof "shield" over the United States, the research might lead America to a quantum leap in technology at a time when the Soviet Union was struggling with growing economic problems at home. Finally, the Reagan Doctrine of supporting guerrillas against Soviet-backed Marxist regimes further increased the costs of Soviet expansion.

In short, the Brezhnev foreign policy, which at first had appeared so successful, had become counterproductive: it had provoked a strong American reaction, held NATO together, and left the Soviet Union surrounded by enemies (including Japan and China). For his part, Reagan had increased the strains on the Soviet Union so much that it could no longer muddle through. Moreover, Reagan eliminated any flexibility that Gorbachev might have had and forced him to retrench abroad, cut military spending, and subordinate foreign policy to domestic affairs. Initially thought to be reckless and widely condemned as a cowboy (especially in Europe) because he appeared trigger-happy, the president left office in January 1989 with the superpower relationship on the best terms it had been since 1945. Thus, despite some setbacks and a huge federal budget deficit that helped to make the United States, once the world's largest creditor nation, its greatest debtor, Reagan left office with a favorable conclusion to the Cold War within America's grasp.

REAGAN'S RHETORICAL OFFENSIVE

When Reagan came into office, the national disillusionment with détente was widespread and the term *Cold War II* was heard often. The president's longtime hostility toward communism in general and the Soviet Union specifically fit the new post-détente mood. He denounced Soviet communism as "the focus of evil in the modern world" and announced to Americans, "There is sin and evil in the world, and we're enjoined by Scripture and the Lord Jesus to oppose it with all our might."[2] Soviet leaders would "lie, steal, cheat, and do anything else to advance their goals," warned Reagan.[3] Opposition to the Soviet Union was, therefore, a religious as well as a political imperative. Reagan also spoke of the march of freedom and democracy that would leave "Marxism-Leninism on the ash heap of history." Of Eastern Europe he said, "Regimes planted by bayonets do not take root"—that is, the communist regimes had no legitimacy. The United States could not accept the "permanent subjugation of the people of Eastern Europe."[4] In making the point that democracy and freedom were the waves of the future, the president was not just giving the Soviets a dose of their own medicine, for the Soviets regularly denounced the United States and forecast the "inevitable end" of Western capitalism. More important, he was questioning the legitimacy and longevity of communism as a social and political system in Eastern Europe and the Soviet Union.

Many American critics dismissed Reagan's predictions about communism being swept aside by the tide of democracy as empty rhetoric. By the end of his second term, however, as many repressive noncommunist states were being transformed along democratic lines and communist regimes were being exposed to greater demands for liberties from within, Reagan's prediction looked less like right-wing rantings than accurate insights into historical development. While far from being a political theorist, he was a spirited polemicist whose expectation of communism's demise in Europe materialized on his watch.

Reagan's harsh denunciations of the Soviet Union were not mere statements of his personal ideology; they also served two tactical purposes. First, the war of words was intended to remobilize American public opinion after the years of détente. Reagan, to whom détente had all along been an illusion based on the unwarranted belief that the Soviets would change their character, sought to arouse American opinion for the longer term. Second, the president's public statements were intended to send the Soviet leaders a message, one that probably was heeded all the more because the Soviet leadership was in the throes of a geriatric crisis. Three Soviet leaders died in three years: Leonid Brezhnev in late 1982, Yuri Andropov in early 1984, and Konstantin Chernenko, in ill health when he took over, in 1985. Gorbachev, who had risen rapidly to the top of the Communist Party hierarchy, now became the Soviet Union's fourth leader since Reagan had assumed office. At

2. Remarks to the National Association of Evangelicals, March 8, 1983, in *The Russians and Reagan,* ed. Strobe Talbott (New York: Vintage Books, 1984), 113.

3. *New York Times,* January 30, 1981.

4. Address to members of the British Parliament, June 8, 1982, in Talbott, *Russians and Reagan,* 89–104.

age fifty-four, he was the youngest man to take charge of the Soviet Union since Stalin.

Reagan bluntly informed the new Soviet leaders that the Vietnam syndrome was a thing of the past. America's will to resist Soviet expansion was back. Reagan wanted to make sure the Soviet Union would not act, as it had during the 1970s, in the belief that America would not respond to its provocations. Minor U.S. military actions against Soviet proxies such as Libya and Grenada, which the United States could not lose and were not costly—were intended to drive this message home. In that sense, the tough words were essentially a substitute for riskier deeds.

The early Reagan years may have been characterized by rhetorical confrontations, but there were no direct encounters or crises. Despite his reputation for machismo, the president was operationally cautious. Indeed, to the extent the Soviets saw him as a leader spoiling for a fight, they were no doubt strengthened in their conviction that they needed to act with restraint. Reagan's foreign policy was basically a return to the containment policy of the immediate post–World War II years. The primary emphasis was on East-West relations, on the Soviet Union as a communist expansionist state, and on the need to contain that expansion—by force if necessary.

EXPANDING U.S. MILITARY FORCES

The late 1970s in the United States were rife with antimilitary sentiment, neoisolationist hopes, and cries for a renewed emphasis on domestic priorities and reductions in the defense budget. Indeed, those years witnessed "the most substantial reduction in American military capabilities relative to those of the Soviet Union in the entire postwar period." [5] American defense expenditures had fallen to the 1950 (pre–Korean War) low of 5 percent of the nation's gross national product (GNP) at a time when the Soviet Union, despite having an economy only half the size that of the United States, was spending substantially more than the United States on defense. By 1981 any president would have been concerned about Soviet intentions and capabilities. Carter's defense secretary, Harold Brown, already had noted that "as our defense budgets have risen, the Soviets have increased their defense budgets. As our defense budgets have gone down, their defense budgets have increased again." And Reagan had once asked, "What arms race? We stopped, they raced."

5. John Lewis Gaddis, *Strategies of Containment: A Critical Appraisal of Postwar American National Security Policy* (New York: Oxford University Press, 1982), 320–322.

After a decade and a half of Soviet efforts to exploit America's Vietnam-induced isolation and a weakened American presidency, the Soviet Union possessed the strategic and conventional forces needed to project its power beyond Eurasia. It was in the context of their perceptions of a changing "correlation of forces" that the Soviets had exploited unstable situations in the poorer countries to increase their influence. This task was undertaken by military advisers and arms, proxies such as the Vietnamese in Cambodia and the Cubans in Africa, and, of course, their own troops in Afghanistan.

The Reagan administration was especially worried about the state of U.S. nuclear forces. The vulnerable land-based Minuteman intercontinental ballistic missiles (ICBMs) and the aging B-52 bombers and Polaris submarines had been built in the 1950s and mid-1960s. As Reagan's military advisers saw it, these strategic forces had to be modernized quickly so they could continue to deter more direct Soviet challenge. At the center of this rearmament program and its political debate was the MX (missile experimental) missile with ten warheads. Highly controversial because it appeared to have the same first-strike capability attributed to Soviet ICBMs, the MX would, it was feared, create a mutual hair-trigger situation that could lead to a nuclear war that neither side wanted. Each would feel it had to take that risk because if it failed to strike first, its ICBMs might be destroyed.

Even more disturbing was the administration's talk of nuclear warning shots, "protracted" nuclear war, nuclear "war fighting," and "prevailing" in a nuclear war. The Reagan administration, more than its predecessors, speculated about such scenarios publicly, particularly Secretary of State Alexander Haig. Thus the administration's five-year, $1 trillion defense program (which actually totaled almost $2 trillion over Reagan's two terms) sparked an enormous controversy. It conveyed the impression that, by relying too much on military strength, the administration was flirting with disaster, and it reinforced the impression that the United States was largely responsible for the arms race. The momentum of the Soviet Union's arms program since the mid-1960s and its impact on the balance of nuclear and conventional balances often appeared forgotten in the uproar over the administration's rearmament program.

OPPOSITION TO ARMS CONTROL

This uproar was intensified by Reagan's strong opposition to arms control, the centerpiece of both Nixon's and Carter's policies toward the Soviet Union. Rejection of the SALT process reflected the Reagan administration's strong distrust of the Soviets and its conviction that past arms control efforts had led to America's relative decline. Reagan announced that he would postpone any arms negotiations until the

United States could "negotiate from strength." But postponing new arms control talks proved difficult because public opinion equated arms control with a sincere search for peace. The pressure on the administration therefore grew. When negotiations finally began in 1982, the administration claimed it was shifting the emphasis from arms limitation—setting ceilings on missile launchers and warheads—to drastic reductions in both categories. Thus Reagan changed the name of the process from SALT (Strategic Arms Limitation Talks) to START (Strategic Arms Reduction Talks). The administration's real motive for this change, however, was to make its approach politically appealing at home, to deflect domestic criticism, and to weaken the newborn nuclear freeze movement while the buildup continued. The initial arms control proposals were clearly meant to be rejected by Moscow, thereby winning time for the administration.

That is how many Americans saw it too, and Reagan therefore inspired a widespread "peace movement" in the early 1980s. Its adherents ranged from academics to religious leaders, especially the Catholic and Methodist bishops, who in 1993 questioned the morality of nuclear deterrence, a policy based on the threat to use nuclear weapons in order to prevent their use. The bishops condemned not only the use of nuclear weapons, but also their very presence in the arsenals and military doctrines of both superpowers.[6] Yet if such weapons could not be used even in retaliation, how could deterrence be made credible? Was the goal of peace moral but the means of preserving it immoral? In the meantime, antinuclear books and films became popular, climaxing in an ABC-TV movie entitled *The Day After* which depicted the nuclear devastation of an average American city.

In addition to decrying the immorality of nuclear deterrence, the peace movement asserted that nuclear war would mean the end of civilization, the "last epidemic" as a medical association phrased it. This theme was supported strongly by new scientific evidence that the smoke produced by the many fires caused by nuclear attacks would shut out sunlight, plunging the world into darkness for several months and causing a prolonged freeze, or "nuclear winter," leading to the extinction of most plant and animal life. Regardless of who "won" a nuclear war, climatic catastrophe would follow and spread over the globe.[7]

Despite their widespread appeal, the arguments and revelations of the antinuclear movement contained little new. By 1980 the horror of

6. National Conference of Catholic Bishops, *Challenge and Peace: God's Promise and Our Response* (Washington, D.C.: United States Catholic Conference, 1983).

7. See Carl Sagan, "Nuclear Winter and Climatic Catastrophe: Some Policy Implications," *Foreign Affairs* (winter 1983–1984): 257–292.

nuclear war had been common knowledge for thirty-five years—that was, after all, why the United States had adopted a deterrent strategy. And it was the suicidal nature of nuclear arms that had encouraged the belief that nuclear deterrence would prevent an all-out Soviet attack on the United States and preserve peace among the superpowers. Moreover, although deterrence could fail, it had a historical record. The superpowers had not exchanged as much as a rifle shot in Europe where they confronted one another; their nuclear power and their mutual fear of suicide had given Europe thirty-five years without hostilities, its longest period of peace in the twentieth century. Indeed, nuclear weapons had eliminated war among *all* the great powers, not just the superpowers.[8]

Although the antinuclear movement confused the issue of threatening nuclear force to bolster deterrence with its actual use, that confusion did not stop the movement from gaining enormous momentum by 1982. The danger of nuclear war appeared to be the nation's first concern. In New York City three-quarters of a million people turned out for the largest political gathering in American history. For those demonstrators and the others marching, meeting, and debating the nuclear issue across the country, the ultimate goal was to eliminate nuclear weapons, but the immediate goal was to achieve a nuclear freeze. Proposals for a freeze on the testing, production, and deployment of nuclear weapons to stop the arms race were passed (or almost passed) by many town-hall meetings and by voters in ten of the eleven states on whose ballots the proposals appeared in the midterm 1982 election. Congress, especially the Democratic House, reflected this antinuclear mood, and, after coming within two votes of endorsing a nuclear freeze in 1982, it endorsed a modified version of the freeze in 1983. In 1984 all Democratic presidential candidates but one came out in favor of a freeze on building new nuclear weapons.

THE STRATEGIC DEFENSE INITIATIVE

Reagan introduced his Strategic Defense Initiative (SDI) in the midst of this controversy about arms control. The proposal was quickly dubbed "Star Wars" by its critics because of its reliance on sophisticated space-based technologies glimpsed only in movies, such as lasers and particle beams. SDI was intended to render nuclear missiles "impotent and obsolete," presumably protecting America's population. According to official descriptions, SDI would be a "layered" defense using different technologies to destroy approaching missiles during each phase of the ballistic trajectory. Mutual assured survival would replace mutual

8. See John Lewis Gaddis, "The Long Peace: Elements of Stability in the Postwar International System," *International Security* (spring 1986): 99–142.

assured destruction. Was it not better to save lives on both sides, the president asked, than to kill the population of the aggressor in revenge for a first strike?

For the president the SDI plan served several purposes, the first of which was domestic and political. Criticized for increasing the defense budget while cutting social services and assailed for being a warmonger, Reagan was able to seize the initiative with SDI. He could pose as a man of vision who would end the threat of missile attacks and ensure that the population of the United States, of the Soviet Union, and, indeed, of the world would survive. He had gone arms control advocates one better, not merely by stabilizing the balance of offensive missiles but by seeking to banish their life-threatening potential. Reagan became an abolitionist who spoke of a world devoid of nuclear weapons as his ultimate goal. The president clearly was uncomfortable with the deterrent strategy to which all of his predecessors had been committed, and he condoned the addition of new nuclear stockpiles only as a means to hasten arms control efforts. Indeed, at the Reykjavík (Iceland) summit in 1986 Reagan came close to agreeing with Gorbachev to the total elimination of all nuclear weapons within a ten-year period.[9]

Second, SDI's utopian side was matched by a more pragmatic consideration: if it worked, it would outflank the Soviets. For years the Soviets had invested heavily in first-strike missiles, which also were the basis for the Soviet claim to superpower status. SDI now threatened the value of this Soviet investment in ICBMs and claims to equality with the United States. What would be the point of a Soviet attack if its missiles could not penetrate the defensive shield above the United States?

Third, although defense of the population and elimination of all ICBMs were presumably the long-term goals of SDI, the system could potentially defend U.S. land-based ICBMs in the future. A defense against these missiles would relieve the American fear that its ICBMs were vulnerable and increase Soviet uncertainty that they could launch a successful first strike. Thus there would be no point in a Soviet strike in this sense. SDI could make U.S. deterrence more credible.

The SDI plan was denounced by critics for many reasons: it would be enormously expensive; it would accelerate the arms race; it would have to work perfectly the first time it was needed; it would tempt a Soviet first strike if the Soviets felt they were on the verge of becoming "nuclear hostages" to an unassailable United States. In short, SDI would only lead to new arms races, offensive and defensive, in which the defensive technologies, even if they gained the upper hand, would do so only tem-

9. Ironically, it was Reagan's refusal to postpone research on SDI that undermined that agreement.

porarily. Moreover, the system would be so expensive that it would threaten U.S. budgets for other strategic and conventional forces, not to mention domestic priorities. Therefore, it was doubtful that the United States or the Soviet Union would be any more secure. Arms reductions through bilateral negotiations were the better course.

But if the critics were correct, why did the Soviets denounce Reagan's "arms race in space"? Why, after previously walking out of all arms control negotiations, were the Soviets so eager to resume talks? Clearly SDI worried them; they really were as fearful of an American first strike as the Americans had been of a Soviet first strike since the early 1970s. The Soviets perceived SDI to be part of an offensive, not defensive, strategy, a prelude to an American strike that would be launched once the U.S. population could be protected. They also were aware that SDI research and development would result in American technology taking a huge step forward at a time when Soviet technology already was behind. With its domestic economy in shambles, the Soviets could not afford to accelerate the arms race on so great a scale.

The Soviets, then, were eager to delay, if not stop, the deployment of SDI. Meanwhile, the United States continued to worry about the Soviet first-strike capability. A compromise seemed the obvious solution: a drastic cut in Soviet ICBMs in exchange for SDI, or at least a delay of SDI. Reagan, however, refused to turn SDI into a bargaining chip and trade it for Soviet ICBMs. After he walked out of the Reykjavík negotiations, no major arms control agreements were possible. Nevertheless, the president approved the more modest START I agreements.

'ROLLBACK' IN DEVELOPING COUNTRIES

Although President Reagan refocused the attention of American foreign policy on the East-West struggle, the developing countries remained a matter of concern. Among Reagan's top priorities on taking office was a reversal of what he saw as Soviet gains during the 1970s in, among other places, Angola, Ethiopia, Yemen, Afghanistan, and Cambodia after the Vietnam War. The Soviets and their allies had been using force to make inroads in these areas—direct force in Afghanistan, indirect force through proxies elsewhere. And in Central America the Marxist Sandinista government in Nicaragua was seeking to extend its influence to neighboring countries, especially El Salvador.

Past administrations had been committed to containment and had not hesitated to intervene to save a friendly regime from being attacked from outside or from within by the Soviet Union or its friends. But, except for episodic efforts such as Harry Truman's effort to "liberate" North Korea and John Kennedy's Bay of Pigs operation in Cuba, the official policy of the U.S. government had never been to unseat Soviet-supported regimes. Dwight Eisenhower's administration had spoken of the "liberation" of Eastern Europe and the global "rollback" of communism but had never acted on those words; containment remained a fundamentally defensive doctrine. The new Reagan policy, however, was offensive.

Dubbed the "Reagan Doctrine," the policy aimed to reverse Soviet gains. Afghanistan, Angola, and Nicaragua had established Marxist governments that had not yet fully consolidated their power, and all faced resistance movements. The Soviets had justified their expansion in the developing world with the doctrine of "national liberation" and then asserted that communism was irreversible once a society had become Marxist. Reagan now adopted his own national liberation strategy against governments that had not come to power by means of democratic processes. In his eyes such regimes lacked legitimacy. Moscow had placed them in power and, unlike his predecessors (with the partial exception of Jimmy Carter in Afghanistan, where a U.S. program of largely covert assistance for resistance fighters was already in place), he refused to accept Moscow's claim that the civil wars were over once governments were in place. The domestic conflicts were not over until popular governments, acceptable to the people (and presumably to Washington), were in power. In short, the Reagan Doctrine set out to disprove the claim of the Brezhnev Doctrine that once a nation had become part of the Soviet bloc it could never leave.

The rollback strategy was based on certain assumptions: that the Soviet Union had become overextended in the 1970s; that the global balance of military power was increasingly favoring the United States; that the Soviet Union's most critical problems were domestic; that, except for Afghanistan, only peripheral Soviet interests were involved; that the Soviet Union would not want to risk a confrontation with the United States; and that a democratic tide was sweeping across the developing world. In practice, the Reagan Doctrine amounted to little more than bleeding the targeted governments and especially Moscow. If they wanted to stop the hemorrhaging, they would have to negotiate a political solution with the insurgents. The anticommunist forces were not strong enough to overthrow the Marxist regimes, but with American help they could keep the wars going.

As noted, the Reagan administration turned Marxist ideology on its head by arguing that "historical forces" were on the side of Western democracy and capitalism, not communism. For evidence, the administration pointed to Latin America, where during the Reagan years (1981–1989) Argentina, Bolivia, Brazil, Guatemala, Honduras, Peru, and Uruguay had become, at least nominally, democratic, in addition to El

Salvador, Grenada, and Haiti. Whatever the reason for this phenomenon—administration policy, global social and political trends, economic development, or sheer coincidence—the administration expressed its optimism that this was part of an irreversible process. The Soviet bloc, by denying human freedom and dignity to its citizens, was running against the tide of history.

Drawing on the traditional hemispheric preoccupation of the Monroe Doctrine, Reagan identified Central America, South America, and the Caribbean as vital U.S. interests and vowed to turn back any outside (that is, Soviet) incursions into America's backyard. To demonstrate his resolve, Reagan intervened directly on the tiny Caribbean island of Grenada, where a military coup had led to the installation of a Marxist regime in 1983. The U.S. military operation, which ostensibly was designed to liberate American medical students from the island, took longer than expected because of logistical problems and a considerable amount of bungling by U.S. Army, Navy, and Marine forces. But the mission achieved its main objective of eliminating the Marxist regime.

The U.S. invasion of Grenada was intended to raise the risks and the costs for the Soviets and Cubans should they continue to try to extend their political and military control in the Western Hemisphere—and elsewhere. Asserting that it had intervened to prevent Grenada from becoming a "Soviet-Cuban colony," the administration called Grenada a "warning shot" that actually was targeting the Sandinista regime in Nicaragua. The administration was convinced that the Sandinistas, led by Daniel Ortega, harbored ideologically motivated ambitions beyond their own frontiers.[10] Because they also accepted support from Havana and Moscow, they were, in Washington's eyes, a continuing source of instability and tension for the vulnerable states in the region. The Sandinistas' pledge to confine themselves to Nicaragua was regarded with skepticism by those who recalled Ortega's earlier pledges to promote political pluralism, a mixed economy, and a nonaligned foreign policy.

What the Reagan administration sought in Nicaragua was to undo the Sandinistas' increasing monopolization of power and return the country to its immediate post-1979 state when the popular anti-Somoza revolution had produced a new coalition government composed of the major factions—religious groups, entrepreneurs, and large segments of the middle and working classes—that had helped to overthrow the dictator. Once in power, however, the Sandinistas began to consolidate their hold on government, gradually suppressing the voices of criticism. They

10. The Sandinistas derived their name from Cesar Angusto Sandino, the Nicaraguan nationalist who led the resistance against the U.S. occupation of the country in the early 1930s. Sandino was killed by the U.S.-trained Nicaraguan national guard in 1934.

postponed general elections, censored the news media while building an army larger than Somoza's, restricted activities by opposition political parties, extended control over worker and peasant organizations, and strengthened their police and security apparatus. They also turned toward Cuba and the Soviet Union for diplomatic support and economic assistance. But the question was not how *Marxist* the regime would become as it turned against the Catholic Church, the business community, professional organizations, trade unions, and student groups that had helped it to depose Somoza. The question was how *dictatorial* it would become and how closely it would align with Havana and Moscow.

The United States, which initially supported the new regime in Nicaragua with foreign aid, was increasingly distressed by its consolidation of power and militaristic behavior. Thus after Reagan took office, he authorized the formation of an anti-Sandinista army known as the "contras." Trained by U.S. military advisers in neighboring Honduras, the soldiers staged a series of military offenses against the Sandinista regime from Honduras, which received increased U.S. military assistance for these purposes, even though Reagan encouraged the public to view the contras as an indigenous, independent army of "freedom fighters." Later, however, this policy backfired against the Reagan administration and dealt a serious blow to its credibility at home and abroad.

The Reagan administration also placed the Central American country of El Salvador, a country the size of New Jersey with a population of six million, within the context of the superpower conflict. Adapting the Eisenhower administration's "domino theory" of communist expansion to Latin America, Reagan expressed concerns that the Sandinista revolution in Nicaragua would spread to El Salvador, and ultimately the rest of Central America. Furthermore, the threat was defined as applying to the wider U.S. position throughout the world. "If Central America were to fall," the president asked, "what would the consequences be for our position in Asia, Europe, and for alliances such as NATO? If the United States cannot respond to a threat near our own border, why should Europeans or Asians believe that we are seriously concerned about threats to them?"[11] Specifically, Reagan alleged that the Nicaraguan government was shipping weapons to rebels in El Salvador, and he proposed increased U.S. arms transfers to El Salvador to match the reported Sandinista arms transfers.

Whether El Salvador was the right place to take a stand against Soviet communism and its proxies, or whether the revolution should have

11. Ronald Reagan, "Central America: Defending Our Vital Interests," *Current Policy* (U.S. Department of State), April 27, 1983.

been allowed to follow its natural course, was energetically debated in the United States. Critics of the administration's plans, especially the congressional Democrats, argued that the Nicaraguan arms were not the principal cause for the civil war but, rather, the appalling domestic social and economic conditions and political repression. As was the case throughout the developing world (see Chapter 4), the seeds of revolution often were sown in poverty and despair, the byproducts of despotic rule. In the view of these critics, the United States should not support the privileged few who had long exploited the poor. Social justice demanded nonintervention; so perhaps did self-interest if the United States wished to avoid being identified with the losers, as it had been so many times before. The Vietnam War frequently was cited as a reminder of the dangers of supporting the wrong side—an unpopular political elite whose vested interest lay in the preservation of the status quo. In any event, no purely military solution was possible.

Locating a moderate center in El Salvador was the key to the Reagan administration's effort to mobilize support domestically and achieve success. In the developing countries the United States often had appeared trapped between reactionary forces, whose rigid commitment to the status quo only intensified revolutionary sentiment, and radical forces, which tended to be Marxist and to look to Havana and Moscow. The administration was saved from this trap in El Salvador by Napoléon Duarte, who was in power for most of the Reagan years and sought to pursue democratic reforms while preventing the radical left from capturing power. Duarte strengthened the Reagan case for assistance to El Salvador because Reagan could rightfully claim that the United States was not supporting the right wing as an alternative to the radical left. Washington hoped, by sending Duarte economic and military aid and by encouraging domestic reforms, the United States could avoid both another Cuba in Central America, as well as another Vietnam. The fighting, however, continued.

The Salvadoran precedent of support for a democratic center was widely recognized after the events of 1986 in the Philippines, where the United States had long supported the dictator Ferdinand Marcos. But his despotism, economic mismanagement, transparent corruption, and the military's abuses had fueled public discontent and a rebirth of the communist guerrilla force called the Nationalist People's Army. In the absence of basic reforms, it appeared that the guerrillas might defeat the poorly trained and badly led Philippine army. Nevertheless, Marcos refused to heed suggestions for reform and, to prove his legitimacy, called for snap elections. He was confident that he could manipulate and control such elections as he had done before, but in this case the opposition proved overwhelming. The opposition candidate, Corazon

Cojuangco Aquino, was the widow of the popular opposition leader Benigno Aquino, who in 1983 had been assassinated at the airport in the capital of Manila upon returning from exile in the United States. After the assassination, Corazon Aquino, whose tempered manner and conciliatory approach attracted worldwide support, became both a symbol of democracy and a rallying point for the opposition. When it became obvious that he would not win the election, Marcos tried to alter the results with widespread fraud, but, because the election was closely monitored by international observers and the news media, the fraud was clearly visible. Thus Marcos lost his legitimacy even while "winning" another term. The United States encouraged him to step down. When top army commanders defected, Marcos fled to Hawaii and Corazon Aquino became president.

Also in 1986 the Reagan administration helped the Haitian people to oust Jean-Claude "Baby Doc" Duvalier, who had succeeded his father as dictator of the Western Hemisphere's poorest state. The United States first advised Duvalier not to use force against protesting crowds and then furnished him with an airplane to flee to France. Previously, the U.S. government had backed the military juntas in Haiti in the name of communist containment and often had looked the other way as vicious dictators tortured, killed, and otherwise silenced their enemies, real or imagined. The Reagan administration now declared its new policy: "The American people believe in human rights and oppose tyranny in whatever form, whether of the left or the right." [12] Under this variation of Carter's human rights policy, the United States would support those struggling for democracy and oppose not just radical Marxist regimes but also pro-American military dictatorships.

And it did so. In 1987, after considerable turmoil that had flared on and off for years, the military government of South Korea was persuaded to promise free presidential elections. Administration pressure on South Korea, a key U.S. ally and beneficiary of U.S. aid, had been instrumental in the long-awaited transition. Similar pressure on Chile resulted in an election that displaced its military leader, Gen. Augusto Pinochet, and opened the way for the establishment of democratic rule.

EVALUATING THE REAGAN DOCTRINE

Although the Reagan administration invoked its claim of a global pro-democratic tide to support the resistance movements in Afghanistan, Angola, and Nicaragua, the insurgencies it supported in the name of spreading freedom often fell considerably short of that virtue.

12. "President Reagan's March 14 Message to Congress," *New York Times,* March 15, 1986.

Indeed, the administration's emphasis on human rights in many cases was compromised by the absence of moderate factions that had any chance of taking power. For Reagan it became a matter of identifying and supporting the lesser of evils; "authoritarian" regimes that supported Washington were preferable to Soviet-backed "totalitarian" regimes.[13] In Afghanistan the opponents to Soviet rule were Islamic fundamentalists, who, if they won, were more likely to establish an Iranian-style theocracy than a democracy and to fragment the Muslim world further. Still, that they were a genuine resistance movement could not be doubted. In Angola, Jonas Savimbi, the rebel leader representing Angola's largest tribal group, was trained in the People's Republic of China and was quite willing to rely on racist South Africa for help. And in Nicaragua some of the principal contra commanders were former members of Somoza's detested National Guard. Reagan was ultimately pragmatic in these cases; he supported all opponents of the Soviet Union in order to weaken it.

The contrasts between Afghanistan and Nicaragua were instructive. In Afghanistan the resistance to the Soviet-imposed government had genuine popular support. The so-called freedom fighters fought courageously and successfully against the Soviet army despite their general lack of modern weapons. As a result, many nations were sympathetic to the rebels; in fact, the Muslim states were largely united in their condemnation of Moscow. As for the United States, unlike its support for the contra war in Nicaragua, which most states in Latin America and elsewhere opposed, its covert assistance to the Afghan resistance was not condemned by neighboring states. Moreover, at home U.S. assistance in Afghanistan had congressional and popular support.

Lack of congressional and public support for the Nicaraguan contras left Reagan with only one option when the presidents of Costa Rica, El Salvador, Guatemala, Honduras, and Nicaragua agreed to a regional peace plan in 1987. Reagan had to support the Contadora initiative because if the plan failed and if its failure could be clearly attributed to the Sandinistas' unwillingness to open up Nicaragua to genuine democratization, as stipulated by the peace plan, he might regain support for further financial assistance of the contras. But the Democratic-controlled Congress remained disenchanted with the contras, whose ties to the U.S. government were obvious despite administration denials, and used the peace plan as a reason not to fund any more military aid. Such assistance, it was claimed, would only thwart efforts to bring peace to Nicaragua and

13. This controversial distinction was drawn earlier by Jeane J. Kirkpatrick, Reagan's representative to the United Nations, in her article "Dictatorships and Double Standards," *Commentary* (November 1979): 34–45.

the region. Thus the administration's plan to overthrow the Sandinistas seemed doomed to failure. This appeared even more certain after the five Central American presidents, over the protests of the United States, called for the disbandment of the contras, most of them in Honduras, and for general elections in Nicaragua. The presidents made no provision for enforcement, however, so the contras remained a viable force.

Under continuing international pressure, Ortega finally agreed to hold multiparty elections in 1990. Yet he and his military aides were confident about the outcome. They had gradually consolidated power during their ten years in office despite the contras' challenge and expected to exploit their control of the government, including the police and army, to ensure an electoral victory that would give them international legitimacy and eliminate any possible rationale for further U.S. interference. Like Marcos in the Philippines, the Sandinistas were confident they would not lose the general election and have to relinquish their power. But lose they did. Despite Sandinista control of the government and efforts to intimidate opposition candidates and rallies, as well as the holdup of congressionally approved funds for the opposition, Ortega lost to Violeta Chamorro, widow of the anti-Somoza newspaper editor whose assassination had rallied the Sandinista-led revolution that brought down the dictator Somoza.

It was unclear who should have received the credit for the defeat of the Sandinistas: the five Central American presidents led by Costa Rica's Oscar Arias, the Nicaraguan people who had the courage to vote against an oppressive regime, or the Sandinistas themselves for believing they could survive an unpopular draft and a mismanaged economy in a relatively free election. But there was no doubt of the consequences. For the Salvadoran guerrillas, the loss of Nicaraguan political support and military assistance constituted a serious setback to their campaign to overthrow the government or negotiate a favorable settlement that would give them a share of the power. For Fidel Castro, who had served as an idol for the Sandinistas and a source of help and support, it meant further isolation because he was the only remaining revolutionary in Latin America. As for Nicaragua, the solid defeat of the Sandinistas gave that country a second opportunity to build a democracy, to reintegrate the contras into Nicaraguan society, to reconcile political opponents, and to reestablish cordial relations with the United States.

Whether the results of the Nicaraguan elections were attributed to the Reagan Doctrine or not, the doctrine had to be judged at least a partial success. It was a cost-effective means of putting pressure on Moscow, which had to spend an estimated $10–$20 billion a year (compared with less than $1 billion annually for the United States) to preserve the gains it had achieved in the 1970s. In 1988, therefore, a number of the regional conflicts in which the United States and the Soviet Union had been engaged came to an end. In Afghanistan, Gorbachev, realizing that the war was an unending drain and a political embarrassment, withdrew Soviet forces. In Angola, after years of fruitless negotiations, the Cubans agreed to pull out their forces, and the South Africans agreed to pull back their forces and grant independence to neighboring Namibia, which they had governed since World War I. These arrangements were followed by a settlement of the Angolan civil war and a largely effective effort by the United Nations to hasten the region's democratic transition. In Cambodia the Vietnamese agreed to withdraw their army, which had invaded that country earlier and overthrew the pro-Chinese Pol Pot regime, responsible for the genocide of over one million of its own eight million people. Gorbachev had to resolve these regional quarrels because by 1987 it had become obvious that he needed to conserve his resources for investment in the stagnating Soviet economy. The prerequisite was an armistice in the Cold War so that the Soviet leader could greatly reduce spending on the huge Soviet military establishment and unpromising foreign policy involvements. But the Soviet Union did not suffer a set of total defeats, nor did the United States achieve a series of unqualified triumphs. In Afghanistan, Angola, Ethiopia, Mozambique, and Cambodia, Marxist regimes retained power. The United States had compelled the Soviet Union, Cuba, and Vietnam to withdraw, but it had not achieved its declared goal of replacing Marxist regimes with democratic governments.

ABUSES OF THE REAGAN DOCTRINE: THE IRAN-CONTRA SCANDAL

In executing the Reagan Doctrine in Nicaragua, the Reagan administration managed to tarnish the president's reputation. In 1987 Reagan's competence, integrity, and sense of judgment were laid open to question when it was revealed that profits from secret arms sales to Iran, now an anti-American Islamic theocracy, had been used to fund the Nicaraguan contras from late 1984 to 1986, in defiance of a congressional ban on the use of U.S. funds for this purpose. In fact, in an effort to elude Congress the administration had shifted the conduct of the contra war from the Central Intelligence Agency (CIA) to the National Security Council (NSC) staff. Both operations were reputedly run by the CIA director, William Casey, and his point man in the NSC, Oliver North, a marine lieutenant colonel.[14]

14. For a detailed account of this scandal by its chief investigator in the U.S. government, see Lawrence E. Walsh, *Firewall: The Iran-Contra Conspiracy and Cover-up* (New York: Norton, 1997).

Labeled the only "five-star" lieutenant colonel in the U.S. military, North supervised the arms sales made to Iran in the hope that U.S. hostages, seized in Lebanon by pro-Iranian terrorists, would be released. He also directed the raising of private funds for the contras from tax-exempt organizations and from wealthy U.S. citizens and foreign governments. Moreover, North commanded a vast network of arms dealers, ships, and airplanes to supply the contras, for whom he also provided tactical intelligence and advice on how to conduct the war. Under his guidance, then, the NSC became a "shadow government" that organized the secret campaign to direct and fund the contra war effort. NSC staff not only kept any knowledge of what they were doing from Congress, they also lied to Congress. When the "off-the-shelf" operation was discovered, the NSC attempted to cover up its involvement and to minimize the president's role in affair—even resorting to shredding relevant documents or smuggling them out of NSC offices. To make matters worse, when the story broke the president first denied knowledge of many of the details of the Iran-contra activities, making it appear as if his deputies had taken American foreign policy into their own hands.

Public opinion polls showed that most Americans thought Reagan was lying, and the hearings Congress held to look into the matter revealed plainly he was actively involved and informed, especially on the contras. In response, the president suddenly reversed directions and claimed he knew about everything except the diversion of funds, but he argued that the congressional restrictions did not apply to him or his staff. The secrecy with which the Iran and contra operations were carried out, however, suggested that the administration knew very well it was breaking the law even though when Congress had first forbidden military assistance, the administration had claimed repeatedly it was obeying the law. All the participants, once they were caught, claimed to be acting only out of patriotic motives; in several cases, however, their patriotism seemed well greased by private gain.

Reagan was badly damaged by the scandal. He was, after all, the presidential candidate who had accused his opponent, Jimmy Carter, of weakness in dealing with the Iranian hostage situation. Under his own leadership, Reagan had vowed, the United States would "never negotiate with terrorists," let alone sell them weapons. He had consistently projected an image of toughness and confidence, and he had claimed that the nation could "stand tall" again. Many Americans shared this new sense of patriotism and regarded the president as the man who would make them proud again and who could—and did—stand up to the Soviets. But Reagan almost did the impossible by making Carter's hostage policy look good; Carter had not sent arms to Khomeini in the hope that U.S.

IMPACT AND INFLUENCE

OLIVER NORTH

The Iran-contra scandal of 1986 revealed the extreme lengths to which the Reagan administration had gone in order to reverse communist gains in the developing world. As information about the scandal became known, so did the central role played by Lt. Col. Oliver North. A military aide to the National Security Council, North personally negotiated secret arms sales to Iran and used the profits to supply the U.S.-backed "contra" rebels in Nicaragua who were attempting to overthrow that country's communist government.

In testimony to a special congressional committee in 1987, North (pictured here being sworn in) defended his actions and said he was following the orders of senior Reagan administration officials. Two years later he was tried and convicted of destroying government documents vital to the investigation, but his conviction was later overturned on the grounds that he had previously testified on the same charges under a grant of immunity. In the 1990s North remained a highly visible public figure, espousing his conservative views on radio and television talk shows and even making a run (unsuccessful) for the U.S. Senate.

hostages would be returned in exchange. Even President Reagan's admirers and supporters were puzzled. They knew that if congressional investigators had been able to find a "smoking gun" linking the scandal to the

Oval Office, Reagan might, like Nixon before him, have faced impeachment for his violation of federal laws. As it was, he survived the crisis and left office with a clouded reputation. The Iran-contra scandal haunted the administration of Reagan's successor, George Bush.[15]

ALLIANCE POLITICS IN THE LATE COLD WAR

The Reagan administration's early attacks on détente, its preoccupation with rearmament, its reluctance to engage in arms control negotiations, and its vigorous pursuit of the Reagan Doctrine exerted great pressure on the Soviet Union throughout the 1980s. This pressure exacerbated the already strong tensions within the Warsaw Pact countries, where long years of political repression and economic stagnation had left people increasingly frustrated and restive.

Along the way, the renewed Cold War also strained the Western alliance and provoked public demonstrations from Washington to Bonn. Old questions resurfaced about the status of Western Europe as a potential superpower battleground, about the dominant role of the United States in NATO, and about the freedom of each member of NATO to pursue its own foreign policy. But the most important confrontation came over the issue of new Soviet missile deployments, which compelled the United States to propose its own series of new installations of intermediate-range missiles in Europe. With both the NATO and Warsaw Pact alliances wavering, the outcome of the most recent standoff in Europe was very much in doubt: Would NATO disintegrate because of its members' internal differences? Or would the Warsaw Pact succumb to its own deficiencies and to the mounting pressure from the West?

As these and other questions loomed, Reagan's policies produced great volatility on both sides of the iron curtain. What few people anticipated, however, was that this latest round of alliance posturing and self-doubt was a prelude to resolution of the post–World War II division of Europe. The curtain was falling rapidly on the Cold War.

POLAND AND THE RISE OF SOLIDARITY

The first crack in the Soviet empire came in Poland, where in 1980 a labor union, asserting first its economic rights and then its political demands, led the Soviet-backed communist government to impose martial law. This crackdown, reminiscent of past actions in Eastern Europe, further inflamed East-West hostilities.

15. The U.S. government's misunderstanding of Central American politics in general, and Nicaragua in particular, ensured that such foreign policy miscues would be repeated. See Robert A. Pastor, *Condemned to Repetition: The United States and Nicaragua* (Princeton: Princeton University Press, 1987).

It was ironic that it was in Poland, a so-called people's democracy and a communist state that purported to represent and protect the interests of the working class, that a truly spontaneous workers' revolution against their exploiters occurred and threatened the Communist Party's monopoly of power and control. Stimulated by a failing economy stemming from poor political leadership, inefficient bureaucratic planning, and mismanagement, Polish workers demanded the right to form their own independent trade union, which would have the right to strike. Such a demand was unheard of in a communist country where the party claimed to embody the workers' aspirations. In wanting their own union, the Polish workers, and their leader, Lech Walesa, rejected this claim and challenged the party's legitimacy.

After strikes brought down the government, the new political leadership recognized the right of the workers to form their own union, called Solidarity.[16] In effect, this development eliminated the party's monopoly of power. Solidarity then began to issue demands that were not only economic but also political. As the party-controlled government retreated before each demand, the demands increased and the party withdrew further in the face of threatened strikes. With each success, Solidarity grew more militant, publicly asserting that it was "the authentic voice of the working class" and announcing support for other East European workers who might wish to form independent unions. Domestically, the union demanded free elections, free speech, and a voice in government policy, including the running of the economy. Although the Soviets accused Solidarity of provocative behavior—seeking "political power"—they refrained from invading Poland.

This restraint contrasted sharply with earlier Soviet behavior in Hungary (1956) and Czechoslovakia (1968). In those countries the Soviet army had intervened when the Communist Party's monopoly of power was threatened. Yet Poland, where it had not intervened, was far more critical geographically than either country. It was the nation through which every Western invader of Russia had marched and through which the Soviet Union had projected its power into the center of Europe since 1945. As the situation grew more intolerable in Moscow's eyes, leading the Soviet leadership to fear that the Polish "disease" would spread to other East European states, perhaps even to the Soviet Union, the Soviets reacted by holding very visible Warsaw Pact military maneuvers in hope of frightening the Poles. The Soviet Union could afford neither a weakening nor a collapse of its hold on central and Eastern Europe, nor a dilution of controls at home.

16. See Lawrence Goodwyn, *Breaking the Barrier: The Rise of Solidarity in Poland* (New York: Oxford University Press, 1991).

But the risks and costs of intervention also were great. The Soviets recognized that Solidarity was not just a trade union seeking better working conditions; it also represented a well-organized mass movement. In suppressing Solidarity, the Soviets faced the real possibility of a clash with units of the Polish army, the costs of occupation, and the difficulties of pacifying the population and getting it to work. In addition, the cost of paying off Poland's $27 billion debt to the West would be a drain at a time when the Soviet economy was in trouble; the Soviet Union would find it more difficult to maintain the separate détente with America's European allies; and any chance of establishing a better relationship with the new U.S. administration would be jeopardized. No less important, Reagan could exploit a Soviet invasion of Poland to rally the NATO allies. Thus for more than a year Moscow demonstrated remarkable restraint. When the move against Solidarity finally came, it was the Polish military and police who arrested the union leaders and imposed martial law in Poland.

Whether Moscow ordered the intervention or the Polish government acted on its own to forestall Soviet action, there can be little doubt of increasing Soviet pressure on the Polish authorities to crack down on what the Soviets called "counterrevolutionary" elements. Solidarity, by winning the sympathies of almost ten million members, about one-third of the population, was a living refutation of the party's claim of representation; it symbolized the bankruptcy of communism. Unable either to produce a decent standard of living or to tolerate a minimal degree of freedom, communism in Poland had forfeited its legitimacy. The lesson was not lost on other parts of Eastern Europe, where the struggle by Solidarity served as an inspiration and a precursor of greater challenges to come.

THE MISSILE DEBATE IN EUROPE

In Western Europe one almost heard a collective sigh of relief that the Red Army had not invaded Poland. The Polish army's crackdown was considered a domestic affair, not a matter over which détente would be sacrificed. This reaction reflected anxieties in the region about the growing hostilities between East and West, with Western Europeans finding themselves trapped in the middle. Indeed, it had become apparent in the early 1980s that Western Europeans wanted to pursue an independent political policy while still counting on the United States for their defense; they wanted, it was said, to "uncouple" themselves politically from Washington but to remain "coupled" militarily. But even the military relationship was called into question when West European opinion appeared to go back on a decision, collectively agreed to by the United States and Western Europe, to meet the threat of new intermediate-range Soviet missiles (SS-20s) with a new generation of NATO missiles (Pershing IIs) to be deployed in Western Europe.

Since the establishment of NATO, the Europeans had wanted the alliance strategy to emphasize deterrence. Europe had had more than enough wars in the twentieth century. The NATO army, therefore, would serve as a "plate glass"; once the hypothetical Soviet invasion occurred, it would sound the alarm and call in the U.S. strategic forces. The army was not intended to fight a long war like World War II, even when reinforced by 300,000 American soldiers. The presence of the troops emphasized America's stake in Europe and clarified to Moscow that any attack would result in war with the United States. The fear of nuclear retaliation by the United States, it was reasoned, would deter the Soviet Union from invading Western Europe.

After the Soviets' first long-range missile test in 1957, the key question had been: Would the United States risk its own survival for the defense of Europe? Some observers had said no, but most had been uncertain, although U.S. strategic forces at the time had been superior to those of the Soviet Union. After the 1970s and the emergence of strategic parity, the answer to this question had grown even more doubtful. It had been one thing for the United States to attack the Soviet Union when the Soviets could not attack the United States, or when America had a vast strategic superiority; it was quite another to do so when the Soviet Union could retaliate fully. Was America's strategic deterrence still credible? Washington's standard reply was yes, but in Western Europe there was more doubt than ever that this was really so.

The intermediate-range nuclear force (INF) deployments were supposed to reassure the allies, who were troubled by the Soviet SS-20s. Instead of being strengthened by new American resolve, however, the NATO "marriage," in the words of the French foreign minister, came close to a divorce. Huge crowds throughout Western Europe (except in France) demonstrated for months against the proposed deployment of the new missiles, with the greatest opposition in West Germany. There, the Protestant churches, universities, Social Democratic opposition party, and a new political movement, the pro-peace and pro-environment Green Party, were all opposed to the deployment. The street demonstrators' accusations were many: America was stoking the arms race; America intended to fight a war limited to Europe; America was the aggressive party in the Cold War. Moscow was not considered the chief threat. It was Washington, which had defended Western Europe since 1949 and had not yet deployed a single Pershing II, that was charged with being the bigger menace to peace.

Certainly the demonstrators did not represent the majority opinion in their respective countries. In all NATO countries support for the alliance remained generally strong; so did faith in deterrence. Nevertheless, the peace movement reflected widespread concern about Reagan's antidétente foreign policy and an increased fear of war. The Soviets shrewdly exploited the protests. By repeatedly saying they were eager to negotiate the issue, the Soviets appeared reasonable and put the United States on the defensive.

Reagan felt compelled to respond to the demonstrations in Europe and to the Soviet initiative. He proposed a "zero-zero option" whereby the United States would not deploy any of its Pershings and cruise missiles if the Soviets dismantled all of their intermediate-range missiles, which had a maximum range of 1,500 miles, including the SS-20s. It sounded good; all such missiles were to be eliminated. What could be more beneficial for peace and more moral than doing away with a whole class of dangerous weapons? The United States, however, did not expect Moscow to accept this offer. The zero-zero option was a public relations move; by turning it down, the Soviets would enable the U.S. deployment to go ahead as a clearly necessary and defensive move, the street demonstrations would decline, and the blame for the American missile buildup in Europe would be placed at the Kremlin's door.

The intra-NATO "missile crisis," however, had by then done considerable damage to the alliance. For many Europeans, the protests against deployment expressed their concern about Reagan's foreign policy and, more generally, their desire to reduce the risk of war. For many Americans, the protests were a reminder that Europeans did not appear ready to take the measures necessary for their own defense. Although their combined population and industrial output exceeded that of the Soviet Union, America's European allies were still unwilling to increase the size of their conventional forces. They wanted to continue relying on the American strategic deterrent at a time when the superpowers strategically neutralized one another.

In the United States, demands began for the withdrawal of some or all American forces from Europe over a period of several years. Most of the American defense budget allocated for hardware and maintenance was not spent on strategic forces; half went for the upkeep of the more expensive conventional forces whose primary mission was the defense of Europe. When the NATO alliance had been formed, the European nations still vividly remembered their attempts to appease a totalitarian regime, the defeats and suffering of World War II, their postwar collapse, and their need for American protection against the new threat from the East. By the 1970s and 1980s the memory of having appeased Nazi Germany was fading. Indeed, the story of the appeasement was not even a part of the history or consciousness of the new generation that had grown up in a peaceful Europe. Protected by the United States, that generation, like many older Europeans, had seemingly forgotten the realities of international politics and took peace for granted.

Only in France, which had deployed a growing independent deterrent force, was the popular historical association of national independence and pride in the nation's armed forces still alive. There were no massive antinuclear and anti-American demonstrations. French Socialist president François Mitterrand told the West German parliament in 1983, "I'm against the Euromissiles. But I notice two terrible simple things about the current debate: Pacifism is in the West and the Euromissiles are in the East. I consider this an unequal relationship." [17] Such an imbalance, he predicted, would ensure war, not avoid it.

But elsewhere in Western Europe, defense apparently had become an American responsibility. Parties that formerly were stalwart defenders of NATO, such as the British Labour Party and the West German Social Democrats, now deserted the alliance. Given the changes in the four decades after World War II, one had to wonder whether, if NATO had been proposed in the 1980s, there would have been an alliance at all, and if so, which countries would have joined it.

NATO THREATENED FROM WITHIN

By the mid-1980s one thing had become very clear: the intermediate-range nuclear weapons issue was not primarily a military issue but a critical *political* one. The decision to deploy the new generation of ground-based nuclear missiles in Europe had been an alliance decision. But Moscow refused to accept any American deployment and rejected the principle of superpower equality. The Soviets clearly intended to manipulate Europe's fear of war and to encourage divisiveness among the NATO allies, especially between Europe and the United States. Would the alliance survive? The Soviets had no reason to compromise in separate arms control negotiations on this issue; they had every reason to test the strength of the European peace movement in the hope of aborting the American deployment. The Soviets could deploy their missiles and target every European capital, but the United States could not deploy missiles in Europe that could hit the Soviet Union. What Moscow had was not negotiable; what NATO had was.

For NATO, Moscow's attempt to undermine the alliance through the missile debate was the most serious issue it had had to confront since the second Berlin crisis three decades earlier. Both issues had threatened the future of the alliance and its ability to face down intimidation and remain united. Above all, the conflicts involved a struggle for West Germany, NATO's strongest European member whose territory bordered

17. Quoted in Flora Lewis, "Missiles and Pacifists," *New York Times*, November 18, 1983.

the Soviet bloc. Moscow obviously wanted to detach West Germany from NATO; Washington viewed the Bonn regime as critical to its "forward strategy." Given the political stakes for each superpower, should it have been surprising that Soviet-American relations reached a low point in the early 1980s, regardless of who the leaders were? Neither side was willing to compromise in what it regarded as a fundamental test of wills. Despite considerable pressure on Reagan to be more accommodating, he insisted on going ahead with the deployment. When that began during the winter months of 1983–1984, Soviet officials walked out of the arms control negotiations.

For a time, the missile crisis faded as the deployment continued. Then in a complete turnabout, Gorbachev accepted the earlier Reagan proposal for the complete elimination of intermediate-range missiles for both powers. The Soviet leader needed a relaxation of international tensions in order to give priority to domestic affairs and rebuilding the Soviet economy. The administration's determination had paid off. It had not abandoned the deployment, nor, when the Soviets responded by walking out of all arms control negotiations, had it delayed deployment, despite widespread calls to do so. Unable to achieve Soviet goals with threats, Moscow capitulated.

The "zero-zero" solution was a significant achievement that meant trading about 1,400 Soviet warheads for just over 300 U.S. warheads. This move eliminated an entire class of weapons rather than—as in SALTs I and II—placing limits on their deployment. Moscow also accepted intrusive verification procedures to monitor the agreement. More fundamentally, in retrospect the Soviet turnabout was the first sign that the Soviet Union needed a cease-fire in the Cold War. U.S. resolution had paid off, undermining not the NATO position but that of the Warsaw Pact.

It was clear, however, that Europeans' confidence in the United States had weakened severely since Vietnam. During the Nixon-Ford détente years, Europeans had complained about possible U.S.-Soviet deals at Europe's expense; during the Carter years, of vacillation and weakness; and during the Reagan years, of too much machismo or "Ramboism." Europe's fear of war also had risen. Not Soviet behavior but the arms race itself was seen as the critical danger, as was "provocative" American behavior in remote regions that could ignite a head-on clash in Europe. These attitudes translated into growing public doubts about the value of NATO.

The European members of the alliance remained unwilling to reexamine the assumption they had accepted for more than forty years—namely, that the Soviet Union was the naturally dominant Eurasian power against which Western Europe could not mobilize sufficient counterbalancing power without outside help. Such an assumption was demeaning for states that had for centuries been the great powers but that, by the 1980s, found themselves the dependents of an overseas protector. Ironically, their growing skepticism toward NATO coincided with the alliance's victory over the Warsaw Pact.

FROM CONFRONTATION TO CONCILIATION

The tensions of the 1980s may have ruptured the cohesion of both alliances, but, in the end, as Reagan left office in January 1989 U.S.-Soviet relations were better than they had been since the two had been allies against Nazi Germany during World War II. How could that be? How, in a few years, could such a profound transformation of superpower relations have occurred?

The rapidity of the change in the two superpowers' relationship was astounding. The Cold War had spanned more than four decades, exceeding the time that elapsed from the beginning of World War I (1914) to the end of World War II (1945). The transformation of superpower relations was even more surprising because the 1970s had been a period of great confusion and self-doubt for the United States. Having withdrawn from Vietnam without victory, the United States was domestically divided. The Watergate scandal had undermined public trust in the presidency. The U.S. economy and that of the other Western nations had suffered from oil shocks and stagflation in 1973 and again in 1979. The year 1979 was particularly ominous because the Somoza government fell to the Sandinistas in Nicaragua; the Iranians seized the U.S. embassy and fifty-two American hostages; the Soviets invaded Afghanistan; the Vietnamese, after invading Cambodia in December 1978, established a pro-Soviet government there; and a pro-Soviet communist faction seized power in Grenada. In general, the 1970s was a decade to deflate any country's self-confidence. By contrast, the Soviet Union had appeared confident and optimistic about the future course of international politics.

The apparent successes of the Soviet Union were deceptive, however, for two reasons. The first was the failure of the Soviet economy. Its economic growth rate, 5 percent in the 1960s and only 2 percent by the early 1970s, had stagnated by 1980. It was capable only of producing a plentiful supply of weapons and no longer able to supply basic goods and public services. By the late 1980s the Soviets were importing many necessities and basic foodstuffs were being rationed. After harvests failed repeatedly in the 1970s, grains and produce had to be imported from the United States and other countries. The centralized Soviet economy was nearing a breakdown. Gorbachev, who when first appointed general secretary in 1985 had believed that economic growth could be stimulated by more discipline in the workplace, less worker absenteeism and drunkenness, and higher productivity, by 1987 realized the severity of the crisis he faced. The second reason for the Soviet turnabout was the cost of Brezhnev's foreign policy. With a gross domestic product (GDP) half that of the United States and a military budget that the CIA then estimated at 16 percent of GDP (compared with 6 percent for the United States and 3 percent for Western Europe), the civilian economy was starved. In fact, later Soviet figures showed that military spending was between 25 percent and 30 percent of Soviet GDP.

Outside the Soviet Union, Moscow's unrelenting arms buildup and expansionist activities in developing countries had produced fear and suspicion of Soviet intentions. The result was the very encirclement the Soviet Union had long feared. In Asia the growing Soviet threat allowed the United States to play divide-and-conquer, attracting China to the West in a major shift of power. Thus the Soviet Union, like Germany at the turn of the century, had created its own worst nightmare and increased its sense of vulnerability.

The United States played no small role in this scenario. American-supplied weapons raised the price of the Afghanistan intervention, placing victory out of reach, and prolonged the civil war in Angola. Although the administration did not succeed in overthrowing the Sandinistas in Nicaragua, the Soviet effort to sustain that revolutionary faction was the only bargain in an otherwise unending financial drain. The imperial outposts that had looked so promising only ten years earlier had now lost their luster, and support for proxies such as Cuba, Ethiopia, and Vietnam had become prohibitively expensive. Gorbachev had no choice but to appreciate what Marxists always had prided themselves on recognizing: objective reality. The Soviet Union—hampered by a structurally unsound economy, looking at a resurgent U.S. economy (despite its rapidly increasing federal and trade deficits), and surrounded by a strengthened Western alliance—was forced to recognize the need for conciliation with the United States.

The Soviet weakness and consequent desire to end the Cold War first became apparent in 1987 when the Soviet delegates walked back into the INF talks they had earlier walked out of and accepted virtually the entire package of U.S. demands. Even more significant, in a series of pronouncements Gorbachev and his supporters contradicted long-held Soviet doctrine and positions by stating that: (1) the "all-human value of peace" would now take precedence over the class struggle, meaning that the unilateral pursuit of advantage to extend socialism could jeopardize the peace; (2) Soviet (and American) security could not be achieved unless there was "common security," suggesting that if one side armed and then the other responded in kind, as in the past, the initiating side would be left less, not more, secure; (3) force and the threat of force should no longer be instruments of foreign policy; (4) security should be achieved by political means—that is, resolving disputes by compromise; (5) in the future "reasonable sufficiency" would be the new standard by which the Soviet Union would judge the military strength it needed; (6) Soviet forces along the iron curtain would be reorganized in a "nonoffensive defense" so that NATO, whose war plans called for no advance eastward, could feel reassured; and (7) negotiations between NATO and the Warsaw Treaty Organization would likely reduce the levels of troops and arms and, wherever asymmetries favored one side, the stronger power—such as the Soviet Union in tanks and personnel carriers—would reduce them to the level of the weaker side rather than the opposite.

In the developing countries Moscow de-emphasized the revolutionary struggle for national liberation and muted its rhetoric about the future of socialism. In addition, by withdrawing from Afghanistan and helping to resolve several other regional conflicts, Gorbachev reduced Soviet foreign policy costs and diminished the likelihood of new conflicts with the United States and the chances that the current ones would undermine the emerging improvement in U.S.-Soviet relations. More broadly, Gorbachev sought to deprive the American-led coalition encircling the Soviet bloc of an enemy. His "charm offensive," including visits abroad, was very effective in Europe, especially in West Germany where "Gorby" rated far higher as a statesman and peacemaker than either Reagan or his vice president and successor, George Bush. The Soviet leader also normalized relations with China in 1989. Among two of the many dramatic moves made to improve the Soviet image, Moscow confessed that its intervention in Afghanistan had violated Soviet law and international norms of behavior and, after years of denying accusations that it had violated the 1972 ABM treaty, admitted the violation.

Gorbachev therefore changed priorities and launched his program of *glasnost* (openness) and *perestroika* (restructuring) to revitalize Soviet society and the economy. He realized that the two were intimately related: without more openness in Soviet society, without a harnessing of the energies of the Soviet people, long used to suppression and obedience, the Soviet economy would not recover from its stagnation. Gorbachev advocated strengthening civil liberties—more freedom in the press, arts, literature, scholarship, and even in the reexamination of the darker side of Soviet history, long kept secret. He also called for decentralizing the economy, cutting back on the pervasive role of the Moscow-based central planning bureaucracy, and permitting the profit motive and market forces a greater role in stimulating production, including a degree of private ownership and entrepreneurship. And he urged the removal of the Communist Party from the daily management of the economy and other sectors of Soviet life, permitted real but limited competition in party and legislative elections, and allowed the Soviet parliament to assert itself, plus a host of other reforms.

But despite Gorbachev's exhortations and reform efforts, there was strong resistance from the nineteen million party and government bureaucrats who had a vested interest in the status quo. Change threatened their jobs, status, and privileges. Opposition to Gorbachev was further fueled by the fear that any loosening of central controls would be harmful, if not fatal, politically. It was the Russians who in the Soviet Union, as in czarist Russia, had controlled most of the levers of power and were particularly concerned that such a devolution of power away from Moscow might result in more political self-determination by the hundreds of non-Russian nationalities. Economic decentralization would then spill over into political decentralization. In other words, the fundamental structural reforms required by the Soviet Union might threaten not only the party's sole control of power but also Moscow's imperial control over its own vast country. The ongoing unrest in the Baltic republics (Estonia, Latvia, and Lithuania), especially the demands for independence, and similar agitation in Georgia and the central Asian republics, were in this respect very worrisome. This uneasiness was compounded by the successful efforts of the countries of Eastern Europe to throw off their communist yokes. Quite contrary to Marxist analysis, the political system determined the fate of the economy rather than the other way around. The Soviet political system had become the greatest obstacle to economic modernization. That was why, preoccupied at home, Gorbachev needed to end the Cold War.

To many, the dismantling of the Berlin Wall in 1989 symbolized the end of the Cold War.

CHAPTER NINE

The End of the Cold War

The implosion of the Soviet bloc already had begun by the time George Bush became president in January 1989. Mikhail Gorbachev's reforms were rapidly undermining the Communist Party's hold in Moscow, the Baltic states were demanding independence, and the first streams of Eastern Europeans were making their way across the iron curtain with the reluctant assent of their crippled political leaders. Many analysts (including George Kennan, father of the containment policy) proclaimed that the Cold War was effectively over. Others suggested more cautiously that it was coming to a close, perhaps.

President Bush was a lifelong politician who lacked Ronald Reagan's flamboyance and his convictions. But his experience as director of the

Central Intelligence Agency (CIA), ambassador to China, and U.S. representative to the United Nations left little doubt that he was competent in foreign affairs. When he became president, Bush said he would not use the term *Cold War* to characterize America's latest relationship with the Soviet Union. He referred instead to a period of U.S.-Soviet relations "beyond containment" in which the principal task would be to integrate the Soviet Union into the "community of nations." In 1990, however, after referring to the "Revolution of '89" in his State of the Union address, Bush said the changes in Eastern Europe had been so striking and momentous that they marked "the beginning of a new era in the world's affairs." This proclamation proved to be an understatement.

In truth, very few observers, including the most experienced and perceptive analysts of international relations, anticipated the sudden collapse of the Soviet system. Most predicted either a prolonged stalemate between the superpowers, a gradual convergence of the capitalist and communist systems, or, more gloomily, an apocalyptic military showdown. The suggestion that one of the two superpowers would simply disappear from the world map without a shot being fired and virtually without preconditions would have been rejected as sheer fantasy. Napoleonic France, imperial Japan, and Nazi Germany did not just vanish. They had to be defeated on the battlefield, at a horrendous cost.

For Bush, the principal task of American foreign policy would be to manage this historic transition as smoothly as possible and to ensure that the demise of the Warsaw Pact and, later, the Soviet Union would not be overwhelmed by an even greater cataclysm. If that were accomplished, Bush looked forward to a harmonious new era in which the benefits of the Western political and economic system would be extended into the former communist bloc and provide the basis for global stability and prosperity.

BUSH'S MANAGEMENT OF THE SOVIET COLLAPSE

With the benefit of hindsight, what were some of the signs that the Cold War was drawing to a close? At first, the Bush administration was not sure what to believe. In the context of more than forty years of Cold War and of previously dashed hopes that the Cold War was ending, the administration—and especially the president—tended to be cautious. If Gorbachev were to fall and be replaced by a hard-line conservative, the United States did not want to be caught off guard. Nevertheless, Secretary of State James Baker, a holdover from the Reagan team, acknowledged that the "new thinking" in Soviet foreign and defense policies created opportunities for East-West cooperation that were unimaginable a few years earlier.[1] Uncertainty about Soviet reforms was all the more reason to seize the opportunities represented by Gorbachev. Thus after a period of hesitation, the Bush administration followed President Reagan's lead and embraced Gorbachev, whose continuation in power was deemed good for the United States.

Events, already moving rapidly, only accelerated both within the Soviet Union and beyond as the 1980s ended. In these circumstances, predicting what lay ahead for the Soviet Union was risky business because the changes had come so quickly and had been so unexpected. The year 1990 witnessed growing upheaval in Moscow as the communist system, seventy-three years after its inception, began to crack. It became apparent that the Soviet Union was operating from a position of grave weakness and that Gorbachev's foreign policy amounted to a diplomacy of retreat and damage control. The result was that regardless of who held power in Moscow, the United States had a golden opportunity to exploit the shifting balance of power. Any leader of the Soviet Union would face severe domestic constraints on the conduct of foreign policy.

As the "victorious" power in the Cold War, the United States had to give thought to its terms of peace: What kind of post–Cold War world did the United States wish to see? Washington, in short, had to define its own goals. Even if Gorbachev did not survive, the United States needed to take advantage of the time he was in office to ensure that Soviet concessions would be irreversible. Granted, America's influence on Soviet internal affairs was limited, and the ultimate success of the Gorbachev policy of *perestroika* (restructuring) depended on events within the Soviet Union. But if the United States were responsive to Gorbachev's policies and proposals, it could support and assist the process of domestic reform and bolster his position in the Kremlin. Washington's principal recourse, therefore, was to lend its support to the peaceful reform of the Soviet state.

The Soviet Union's negotiating position was very weak—a problem that was to worsen as Eastern Europe defected, ethnic nationalism grew, and communism as a political and economic system was directly challenged inside the Kremlin. Yet Gorbachev would not surrender unconditionally. Thus American leaders simply could not impose their terms on Moscow. Moreover, a victory that humiliated the loser would result in a peace built on sand. World War I had ended with a victor's peace imposed on Germany, but it had lasted only as long as Germany remained weak. After World War II both Germany and Japan were treated in a more conciliatory fashion. Neither, therefore, had been bent on

1. See James A. Baker III, with Thomas M. DeFrank, *The Politics of Diplomacy: Revolution, War, and Peace, 1989–1992* (New York: Putnam, 1995), chap. 5.

revenge. For a durable peace, the Soviet Union also had to find the emerging international order hospitable. The two powers therefore embarked upon complex negotiations about the terms on which the Cold War was to be ended, as well as about the construction and shape of the new balance of power.

The final resolution of the Cold War depended basically on the fulfillment of three conditions: the dismantling of Joseph Stalin's empire in central and Eastern Europe, the detachment of Leonid Brezhnev's outposts in developing countries, and a reduction in arms and a stable nuclear balance. When these conditions were fulfilled, Bush was thrust into the tenuous position of managing the disintegration of the Soviet Union and directing the transition of U.S. bilateral relations toward the largest successor state, Boris Yeltsin's Russia.

DISMANTLING STALIN'S EMPIRE

Events in China during the summer of 1989 served as a prelude to the autumn uprisings in Eastern Europe and suggested that the erosion of communism's appeal and legitimacy had extended to the world's most populous communist state. As in Moscow, dissidents in Beijing were granted greater freedom to express their grievances in public and to exercise some degree of political freedom. After they erected a miniature Statue of Liberty in Beijing's Tiananmen Square, however, the communist government moved in with tanks and brutally quashed the growing rebellion. The worldwide television audience that witnessed these events was understandably horrified by what it saw. China's decrepit regime dismissed the condemnation of foreign governments and intensified its crackdown on pro-democracy activists. When their time came, Eastern Europeans were inspired by the Chinese example to accelerate their own anticommunist revolution and guarantee that it could not be turned back.

One key sign of Soviet willingness to end the Cold War was its acceptance of Eastern Europe's rapid moves away from Communist Party control. The Soviet Union's conquest and Stalinization of Eastern Europe, together with the division of Germany, had split the continent after World War II. This division was at the heart of the Cold War confrontation, and only self-determination for Poland, Hungary, Czechoslovakia, and other Eastern European states could end it. Events in central Europe also were critical because each of the major wars of the twentieth century had broken out there. The disintegration of the Austro-Hungarian Empire had led to the eruption of successive Balkan wars and World War I; Germany's absorption of Austria and Czechoslovakia and its invasion of Poland had sparked World War II; and the de facto Soviet annexation of Eastern Europe had led to the Cold War.

American foreign policy during World War II had been sensitive to Soviet security concerns in Eastern Europe, but the United States also had been committed to national self-determination. President Franklin Roosevelt had presumed that after the war Soviet security could be compatible with democratic freedoms. Where communist parties did well, they could be included in coalition governments, reflecting the popular will. Critical to the president's thinking was the knowledge that smaller countries living in the shadow of the Soviet Union would take Moscow's security concerns into account in formulating their foreign policies. Roosevelt's thinking reflected that of a traditional great power: small nations living within a superior power's sphere of influence do not have to have governments that reflect the latter's ideological and political values. They must, however, be willing to make a virtue out of necessity: to make the best of their geographic situation, to be aware of their constrained freedom and maneuverability, and to acquiesce to the wishes of the regionally dominant power. Finland provided the most concrete example of this relationship.

But Soviet ideology defined security in Marxist terms: the communist regime could be secure only if potential class enemies—including those who frowned upon relations with the capitalist states—were kept out of power altogether. The governments bordering the Soviet Union therefore had to be communist after World War II. Even coalition governments in which the Communist Party controlled the major levers of power—the military and police forces—were unacceptable. Eastern Europe, then, was to become a sphere of dominance, with each country having not only communist governments controlled by Moscow but also ideological conformity. As for the Soviet troops stationed throughout Eastern Europe, they were intended not merely to protect these states from perceived Western threats, but also to assure that these states adhered to Soviet control. Without this military presence, backed up by occasional Soviet interventions, these unpopular governments would not have survived as long as they did.

Could Moscow in the late 1980s separate its ideology from its definition of security? That was the main question in 1989, and the initial answer came in Poland. There, the Communist Party was unable to form a government after its disastrous showing in the free June elections in which the Solidarity labor movement had claimed overwhelming popular support. Because the communists had been repudiated, Solidarity, which had in effect received a mandate to govern, was asked to organize the government. Poland thus formed its first noncommunist—indeed anticommunist—government in the post–World War II era. The military forces, including the security police, were left in communist hands, however, to reassure Moscow about the future course of Poland, a country through which the Germans had twice marched in the twentieth century to invade the Soviet Union. Moreover, Lech Walesa, Solidarity's leader and spokesman, announced that Poland would remain a member of the Warsaw Pact—just the kind of political sensitivity that Roosevelt had had in mind.

Gorbachev appeared willing to accept a noncommunist Poland and a more traditional sphere of influence in Eastern Europe for several reasons. One was his preoccupation with worsening domestic matters. Another was that Eastern Europe had not proved to be a security belt. Instead, the region had added to Soviet *insecurity.* Its people were sullen and resentful of the Soviet-imposed regimes, and they had not forgotten that earlier efforts to rid themselves of these regimes had been suppressed by brute force. Gorbachev did not want to be confronted with an explosive situation that, among other things, would be a major, if not fatal, setback to the reemerging détente with the West. The installation of more acceptable and legitimate governments would avoid this confrontation and thus enhance Soviet security. Furthermore, given the strains on the Soviet economy, he could not afford continued subsidies to Poland and the rest of Eastern Europe to prop up their troubled economies. It made eminent sense, therefore, to unburden his floundering economy. Finally, by accepting a more modest sphere of influence, he could resolve a principal issue that had precipitated and prolonged the Cold War.

The dominoes fell throughout 1989. In Hungary the parliament dropped the word "People" from the country's formal name, and the Communist Party renamed itself the Democratic Socialist Party in order to survive a Polish-style disaster in the upcoming multiparty elections. (Even so, the party was able to keep only 30,000 of its original 720,000 members.) Similarly, Czechoslovakia dropped "Socialist" from its name, and the East German Communist Party also sought to shed its Stalinist skin to better compete in the 1990 elections. In a decision of critical importance, the Hungarian foreign minister opened his country's borders with Austria on September 10, 1989. A free fall then ensued when 200,000 East Germans, mostly young, skilled workers vital to its industry, fled their country—via Czechoslovakia, Hungary, and Austria—for West Germany. These events demonstrated vividly that communism had lost its grip on Eastern Europeans. Indeed, the events of 1989 suggested that the legitimacy of all communist regimes throughout the area was in doubt. Even those who had grown up under communism rejected its philosophy and were now able to say so openly. The direction of these events became obvious during what Zbigniew Brzezinski called the "terminal crisis of Communism." [2]

2. Zbigniew Brzezinski, *The Grand Failure: The Birth and Death of Communism in the Twentieth Century* (New York: Scribner's, 1989).

To make the best of the situation, Gorbachev announced that socialist countries had no right to intervene in each other's affairs; each country was responsible for its own destiny. The clear implication was that the Brezhnev Doctrine was dead. To make the point clearly, in late 1989 Gorbachev paid a symbolic visit to Finland, a country that always had been sensitive to Soviet security interests and yet had maintained a relatively autonomous democracy. He presented Finland as a model of a relationship between a big and little country that were neighbors but had different social systems. Gorbachev also visited East Germany to observe its fortieth anniversary as a communist state. There, by stating the new doctrine of nonintervention, he further propelled the demise of the Warsaw Pact. The process gained even more momentum after Moscow and its four Warsaw Pact allies that had jointly invaded Czechoslovakia in 1968 condemned that invasion as "illegal" and pledged a strict policy of noninterference in each other's affairs. Moscow issued its own declaration of repentance.

Gorbachev's actions were most keenly felt in East Germany, where the exodus of its youth threatened to depopulate the country of sixteen million and undermine its hopes for the future. Mass demonstrations finally led to the removal in December 1989 of its despotic communist leader, Erich Honecker. In what was a genuine people's revolution, Soviet troops stood by instead of propping up the regime, and the new party leader promised radical changes, including free elections in May 1990. Among the first reforms, all restrictions on travel and emigration were lifted, inciting hundreds of thousands of East Germans to scale the Berlin Wall in the hours after that announcement. Altogether, 1.5 million East Germans poured across the wall that first weekend to celebrate. As for the wall itself, entire sections were leveled with sledgehammers, and fragments were taken home as souvenirs. From its construction in 1961, the wall had been the symbol of what the Cold War was all about—tyranny versus freedom. Its collapse on November 9, 1989, exactly fifty-one years after Adolf Hitler unleashed his storm troopers against German Jews, symbolized more than any other event the end of the Cold War.

After the fall of the Berlin Wall, the winds of change swept over Czechoslovakia. What was happening there also had great symbolic importance, although it was not widely noted at the time because of the tumult elsewhere. The great powers had inflicted tremendous injustices on Czechoslovakia, the only central European democracy before World War II. The country was betrayed by France and England in their efforts to appease Hitler in 1938. A decade later, Czechoslovakia was violently transformed into a communist nation by the Soviets. Its efforts to introduce a more democratic form of communism during the Prague Spring of 1968 were crushed by Soviet tanks. The collapse of the communist regime in Prague, therefore, also was a sign of the times.

Everywhere in Eastern Europe—in what Ronald Reagan had once called the "evil empire"—people were saying openly just how evil that empire had been. They demanded not just the reform of communist parties but their removal from office, ending what many saw as a forty-year-long foreign occupation. They also called for free elections and interim governments composed mainly of noncommunists. Only in Bulgaria and Romania did the local communist parties manage to run under new names, promising that they had reformed, and easily win the first free elections after the collapse of the Soviet-supported governments.

The United States responded by expressing support for the new governments of Eastern Europe, and President Bush provided a visible show of support by visiting Poland and Hungary in 1989. Beyond this effort, however, Bush did not want to arouse Soviet security concerns. In fact, Gorbachev, with these concerns in mind, sought a tacit understanding with Bush. The Soviet leader would continue to support, if not encourage, the transformations in Eastern Europe, and he would not resist the changes even if they went further down the road to "decommunization" than he would have preferred. In return, the United States would not exploit the geopolitical transformation then underway in the Soviet empire, nor would it jeopardize Soviet security or add to the humiliation Moscow already was suffering from the popular rejection of communism by its Warsaw Pact allies. Bush also agreed to make concessions—on trade, for example—to help Gorbachev rebuild the Soviet economy and to show some tolerance for his internal problems. Because it was in Washington's interest to manage the changes in the Soviet Union and Eastern Europe peacefully, the Gorbachev-Bush bargain held. This deal even applied for a time to the Baltic republics. Gorbachev considered them part of the Soviet Union and forcefully resisted the secession of Lithuania. The United States, which had never recognized their annexation, did not overtly support their independence movement at this pivotal moment.

The path of nonviolent transformation was chosen not only by the Eastern European rulers but also by the masses, even though they had been exploited and oppressed by the Soviet-imposed regimes for forty years. Only Romania fell into violence as its dictator, Nicolae Ceausescu, sought in vain to buck the trend in the rest of Eastern Europe and stay in power. But he failed; army units defected to the opposition and fought his security forces. Captured as they attempted to flee, Ceausescu and his wife, Elena, were executed after a hasty trial on Christmas Day. With that single exception, nonviolence prevailed. Czechoslovakia's new president, the playwright Vaclav Havel, set the tone by calling on his fellow citizens to act with dignity, honesty, and honor. The slogan of the demonstrators massed in the streets of Prague was "We are not like them."

Equally important, Washington thought it best to allow the transformation of Eastern Europe evolution to occur within the broader European context. Even before the 1989 revolutions the members of the European Community (EC) had decided to revive its movement toward a single market. It was a wise move given the likelihood that U.S. economic problems and a diminished Soviet threat would lead America to shift its attention to the domestic arena. The EC also was mindful of stiffening American economic competition, as well as that of other countries, especially in Asia. A single market and currency, the coordination of foreign and security policies, and other cooperative efforts spelled out in the Maastricht Accords of 1992 represented steps toward a competitive European economy and a possible European confederation.

If the task of helping Eastern Europe was now an additional motive for an enlarged role of the European Community, renamed the European Union (EU) at the Maastricht summit, another and perhaps more important issue was the rebirth of the "German problem." For more than forty years East and West had lived with a divided Germany. Each side preferred a partitioned Germany because such an arrangement would ensure that Germany would not initiate another war. The "terminal crisis" of communism in Eastern Europe, however, ended this division. Thousands of East Germans poured into West Germany every month, further crippling the East German state, its economy, and its social cohesion. Moreover, as the authority of the East German government waned, the calls in East Germany for unification grew stronger every day. To everyone's surprise, the East German election held in March 1990 (earlier than planned given the mounting crisis) was won by the followers of West German chancellor Helmut Kohl, thereby ensuring reunification. The large votes for the Christian Democrats and the Social Democrats, both tied to their West German counterparts, amounted to a death sentence for the German Democratic Republic and an endorsement of a "buyout" by the richer and more powerful West Germans.

But a reunited Germany, even a democratic one, posed all sorts of problems and potential instabilities. In fact, the collapse of the Warsaw Pact and the inevitable, increasingly imminent, reunification of Germany meant constructing a new European balance of power. Western officials insisted that the reunited Germany be a member of NATO. They did, however, offer Moscow several reassurances. First, no Western armies, including German troops assigned to NATO, would be stationed on former East German territory in view of Moscow's certain opposition to the presence of NATO troops on the Polish border. Second, during a three- to four-year transition period, the 380,000 Soviet troops already in East Germany would remain there. Germany also would guarantee its neighbors' borders, renew West Germany's pledge that it would not seek to acquire nuclear weapons, and agree to limit its armed forces to 370,000, below West Germany's 474,000 in 1990 and well below the 667,000 level of the two Germanies.

Gorbachev's initial opposition was based on memories of the German defeat of czarist Russia in World War I and of the twenty million Soviet lives lost repelling the German invasion in World War II. He insisted that a reunited Germany be a neutral, disarmed state. But this was unacceptable to virtually everyone else, and it probably was not even thought by Moscow to be the best solution. The real question was whether a united but neutralized Germany would become once more a nationalistic, dangerously destabilizing force on the continent. Pushed even by his former allies to accept a reunited Germany restrained by the NATO alliance, Gorbachev proposed that Germany be a member of both the Warsaw Pact and NATO. This too was rejected as merely another formula for neutrality. George Bush, who played an active role in the negotiations, felt confident that Moscow eventually would agree to his terms, which were favored by all members of the Western alliance, the West German government, the new East German one, as well as most Warsaw Pact members. The Soviets, having obviously lost the Cold War, were in too weak a bargaining position to insist on anything else.

But Gorbachev, weak or not, continued to resist the Western solution. He realized that when it came, the collapse of East Germany would spell the end of a major Soviet Cold War goal: hegemony over Europe based on neutralizing West Germany. Even more humiliating, a reunited Germany would likely emerge as the financial and economic center of Europe, the dominant power in Eastern Europe, and the principal source of capital and machinery for the Soviet Union.

In July 1990, only four months after declaring that German membership in NATO was "absolutely out of the question," Gorbachev bowed to the inevitable and accepted a reunited Germany in NATO. His acceptance was made easier by the promise of $8 billion in German credits to help the failing Soviet economy. Nevertheless, like his acceptance of a larger number of U.S. troops than Soviet troops in the new Europe, Gorbachev's acquiescence to German membership in NATO was tantamount to Soviet surrender. This event had none of the drama of VE Day and VJ Day, which in 1945 marked the end of the war in Europe and in the Pacific, respectively. Yet history will note July 16, 1990, as the day the Soviet Union gave up, effectively ending the Cold War. Indeed, the

American insistence on Soviet acceptance of Germany's admission to NATO appeared in large part driven by the need to clarify this issue.

The reemergence of modern Europe's central problem—that of Germany—was now imminent. What kind of political and security arrangements could be established to accommodate German power in the new post–Cold War Europe? The two superpowers agreed on a framework for ending the division of Germany. First, merger of the two governing Christian Democratic parties was scheduled for October 1, and formal German reunification was set for October 3. Second, in November the reunification issue would be submitted for formal approval to the thirty-five-nation Conference on Security and Cooperation in Europe (CSCE).[3] Finally, an all-German election of an all-German parliament was set for December 2.

The new year would therefore start with the convocation of the new parliament and the formation of the new government. As for the future, the reunited Germany would assume the role of Europe's most powerful economic actor and, like Japan, the other country vanquished in World War II, would quickly become a principal actor in the post–Cold War multipolar international system. The world hoped, however, that Germany's preponderant size, population, and economic power would be directed not toward fulfilling selfish interests but toward serving as a catalyst for political stability and economic growth throughout Europe and, indeed, within the Soviet Union itself.

DETACHING BREZHNEV'S OUTPOSTS

The second condition to ending the Cold War was Soviet cooperation in resolving regional conflicts in the developing world. As noted earlier, Soviet support for Marxist regimes and insurgencies hindered U.S.-Soviet relations for decades. But now the Soviet Union's desire to avoid trouble with the United States was likely to prevent further challenges.

Gorbachev's reversal of his country's expansionism was dramatic. The Soviets withdrew from Afghanistan and later admitted that the invasion had been a mistake, a result of their foreign policy's overreliance on force. In Angola, after prolonged negotiations failed to achieve the exit of fifty thousand Cuban troops from that country in return for South Africa's withdrawal from Namibia, a deal was struck under which the Cubans would withdraw in return for the independence of Namibia.[4] In Southeast Asia, with Soviet encouragement, Vietnam withdrew

3. The CSCE, now known as the Organization on Security and Cooperation in Europe, comprised sixteen NATO countries, seven Warsaw Pact states, and twelve neutral countries. It was founded in 1975 in Helsinki, Finland, where its signatories promised to respect existing frontiers (including the East German-Polish border) and to respect human rights.

4. South African troops had frequently attacked Angola in pursuit of guerrilla forces operating in Namibia, one of the last African colonies to gain independence.

from Cambodia. Vietnamese forces had invaded Cambodia to overthrow the murderous Khmer Rouge government led by Pol Pot, which had slaughtered more than one million of its own population of eight million. The "killing fields" of Cambodia drew worldwide condemnation.[5] In both Angola and Cambodia, the backing of the Cuban and Vietnamese operations in support of Marxist governments had been costly to the Soviet Union both economically and in terms of credibility. Moscow wanted to cut its losses from these seemingly unending struggles; its overseas empire was proving unmanageable.

Even in the Middle East, Moscow moved initially toward rapprochement with Israel—it had broken diplomatic relations in 1967—and later toward the reestablishment of relations. It also supported the U.S. objective of an Israeli-Palestinian treaty and raised the possibility of increased Jewish emigration from the Soviet Union to Israel. Instead of supporting the more radical parties and obstructing American peace efforts, the Soviet Union indicated that it preferred a new course of partnership with the United States.

But in one important area, Central America, the Soviets continued to supply arms to revolutionary forces despite soothing words about seeking peaceful settlements. Soviet arms shipments to the Nicaraguan government, although reduced, continued; shipments from Cuba and Eastern Europe made up the difference. Soviet-made weapons also reached the communist rebels in El Salvador, who launched a number of attacks in the capital city of San Salvador in 1989.

The Bush administration strongly protested these policies of support as "Cold War relics," calling these countries "Brezhnevite clients" during the informal summit meeting that Gorbachev and Bush held in December 1989 off the Mediterranean island of Malta. Gorbachev denied sending weapons to Central America, but Bush would have none of it. Cuba and Nicaragua were Soviet clients. Washington clearly expected Moscow, which elsewhere had pressured its proxies to resolve their internal and regional differences, to do the same in the Western Hemisphere. Undoubtedly, Cuba's Fidel Castro, who had denounced the Soviet Union's retreat from Marxism-Leninism and considered himself one of the few true remaining communists, would resist counsels of restraint. Even without Soviet arms shipments, Cuba and Nicaragua had enough weapons to ship to the Salvadoran guerrillas.

The more critical issue was the February 1990 election in Nicaragua, which, as noted in Chapter 8, held out the promise of easing regional tensions in Central America. Gorbachev prevailed on the Sandinistas to permit free elections like those held in Eastern Europe. When the San-

5. For elaboration, see Christopher Hudson, *The Killing Fields* (New York: Dell, 1984).

dinistas lost the elections, which were closely monitored by the United Nations and the Organization of American States, the Soviet Union lost yet another overseas client. National reconciliation, disbanding the contras, rebuilding the economy, ensuring a democratic and more just society, and reestablishing good relations with the United States were to be the central tasks of Nicaragua's new government.

The only remaining source of real friction between Washington and Moscow was Cuba. Castro swore that socialism would continue to be practiced on his island even if it had been "betrayed" by Gorbachev and even if it were abandoned virtually everywhere else. Moscow discontinued its massive annual subsidies to Cuba in 1991, which were largely in the form of petroleum and other necessities, announcing that future economic relations between the two countries would be on a trade-only basis. The Soviet military training brigade also would be withdrawn. The Soviet Union, itself seeking economic help from the West, was responding to the Bush administration's insistence that it would not consider providing such assistance while Moscow continued to provide Castro with the equivalent of $5 billion annually. Thus the Soviet retreat from the developing world continued.

REDUCING ARMS AND STABILIZING THE NUCLEAR BALANCE

The third condition for ending the Cold War was a reduction in superpower arms and a stable nuclear balance. A consistent U.S. goal in the evolving new superpower relationship was to provide for a more secure environment through appropriate arms control agreements. More specifically, U.S. policy had three objectives. The first, especially in view of Gorbachev's uncertain tenure, was to reach agreements to reduce strategic and conventional arms; once achieved, such arms reductions would be politically and economically difficult to reverse. The second objective was to reduce the likelihood of surprise attack, a goal that was pursued by both sides through a variety of confidence-building measures. And the third objective was to reduce the burden of defense spending and to realize a "peace dividend" to be spent on domestic needs.[6]

From the beginning of the Strategic Arms Limitations Talks (SALT) process, the long-term objective was to cut drastically the strategic arsenals of both powers. Renamed START (Strategic Arms Reduction Talks) by the Reagan administration to emphasize more ambitious reductions—a 50 percent cut—the treaty was aimed at cutting Soviet land-

6. For Gorbachev, this financial benefit was probably the driving force behind all his arms proposals. As the U.S. budget deficit grew, Bush also wanted to see a reduction in defense spending.

based missiles, which, with their multiple and accurate warheads, were the principal threat to the survival of American intercontinental ballistic missiles (ICBMs). In short, reductions per se were not the objective; the aim was to *stabilize* reductions. By the time Reagan left office, the START negotiations were substantially completed. Each side had agreed to a ceiling of 1,600 delivery vehicles, an aggregate of 6,000 strategic weapons, and a ballistic missile warhead limit of 4,900. Although the overall reduction in strategic forces was closer to 30 percent, the most destabilizing forces—ballistic missiles with multiple warheads—were reduced by 50 percent.

The chief obstacle from the very beginning was the Strategic Defense Initiative (SDI), or the American plan to defend its territory from incoming nuclear missiles (see Chapter 8). The Soviets insisted that they would not reduce their ICBM force until they knew whether they would have to cope with American strategic defenses. But Reagan clung to his vision of SDI, and therefore the Soviets refused to sign the START treaty. To break the deadlock, Moscow announced in 1989 its willingness to sign the treaty on the condition that the United States abide by the 1972 antiballistic missile (ABM) treaty. While the two issues were finally severed, at least formally, START's fate again depended on Washington's decisions about SDI development. The program had lost its main advocate with the end of the Reagan presidency, however, and faced great technical difficulties and increasing congressional disenchantment at the time of a huge federal deficit. Thus support for SDI steadily eroded, and it no longer posed an obstacle to arms control negotiations.

As for conventional forces, after 1987 Gorbachev had talked repeatedly about a shift from an offensive to a defensive military doctrine, as well as sizable military budget cuts as the Soviet Union scaled its forces back to "reasonable sufficiency." He promised and carried out unilateral reductions of Soviet forces, including the withdrawal of troops and tanks facing NATO. For Warsaw Pact forces to shift to a strategy that could repel an attack but not launch a massive surprise attack on NATO was obviously very much in the West's interest. Such a shift would greatly relieve Western fears stemming from the Soviet Union's sizable forces and Soviet military doctrine, and it would be a tangible sign that Soviet intentions had fundamentally changed.

The Conventional Forces in Europe (CFE) negotiations sought to reduce Soviet forces in Eastern Europe and American forces in Western Europe to 275,000. CFE also sought equal numbers of tanks, armored personnel carriers, artillery pieces, and combat aircraft for the two military alliances. But events in Eastern Europe were moving so fast that in January 1990 President Bush called for a further U.S.-Soviet troop reduction in central Europe to 195,000, with 30,000 more American troops outside of that area. Surprisingly, Gorbachev accepted the U.S. proposal, even though this cutback would, for the first time since the war, leave the United States with more troops in Europe than the Soviet Union. Militarily this was unimportant, but politically and psychologically it provided further evidence of Soviet weakness. In any case, the 195,000-troop ceiling was unlikely to be the last word on reductions because of strong domestic pressure in the United States to cut U.S. forces further, to about 75,000.

Such reductions appeared possible because by 1990 the Soviet-led alliance, organized to protect the Soviet-imposed socialist systems, had little to defend as Eastern Europe defected from the Warsaw Pact. In these circumstances, Moscow could no longer count, if it ever could, on the armies of Czechoslovakia, Hungary, Poland, East Germany, Bulgaria, and Romania for any joint military action against the West. In 1990 Moscow agreed to withdraw its forces from Czechoslovakia, Hungary, and Poland by the end of 1992. But this pledge became irrelevant as the Warsaw Pact self-destructed first and was formally buried in 1991.

Would NATO also disappear? That was unlikely, at least in the short run, because the alliance still had several functions. One was to continue to guard the West against the possibility of a renewed Soviet (or, later, Russian) threat. There remained widespread concern that Gorbachev might be overthrown by the old communist guard, which could then reimpose Soviet hegemony in Eastern Europe.[7] Another function of NATO, not spoken of openly for diplomatic reasons, was to restrain the new Germany. After twice calling on American power to defeat Germany, Europeans were unsure that they alone could manage a unified Germany. Retaining NATO would keep American power in Europe. Finally, the United States wanted the NATO alliance to serve as an institutional link through which it could influence the shape of the emerging new order in Europe as the European Union moved toward greater economic and political integration.

Bush's arms control initiatives continued even after the Soviet Union itself dissolved in late 1991. Bush carried on START II negotiations with Russian president Boris Yeltsin. At their June 1992 summit meeting, the two sides agreed to even deeper cuts in nuclear arms, among them the most destabilizing multiple-warhead missiles which had become a headache to strategic planners in Moscow and Washington. The agreement called for both sides to reduce their arsenals to about three thousand missiles by the year 2003, or sooner if the United States could assist the financially strapped Russians in dismantling their weapons.

7. Even after the attempted coup in August 1991 against Gorbachev, which led to the Soviet Union's own demise, Russia, the successor state, retained significant military power.

ENDGAME: THE COLLAPSE OF THE CORE

Between 1989 and 1991 the Soviet Union itself underwent a rapid and profound transformation. With the disintegration of its economy, the political regime lost its legitimacy and was further weakened by internal conflicts between Moscow and a number of Soviet republics. Demands for autonomy, if not independence, erupted in many areas, and ancient ethnic feuds reemerged. These events threatened the integrity of the Soviet state and compelled the regime to move Soviet tactical nuclear warheads out of the Baltics and the volatile southern republics to parts of Russia it considered more secure.

In addition, the Communist Party, showing growing signs of disintegration, was losing its authority to impose decisions on the nation. In the Baltics, Soviet communists were faced with the defection of the Lithuanian Communist Party, which identified itself with Lithuania's demand for independence. In Azerbaijan the Soviet army had to be deployed not only to restore order between the Azerbaijanis and Armenians, but also to prevent the communist government from falling into the hands of the Azerbaijani popular front—much as communist regimes in Eastern Europe had fallen to the opposition groups. In several cities and regions, party officials had to resign because of popular outrage over their corruption and privileges. Indeed, in Moscow, Leningrad, and other cities the emerging democratic political opposition inflicted embarrassing defeats on the communists by winning majorities in local elections.

Gorbachev, alert to popular disenchantment with the party, gradually shifted his base of power from the Communist Party (whose members continued to resist his reforms) to the elected Supreme Soviet and the presidency, a post he held in addition to that of general secretary of the party. A new Congress of People's Deputies was established to promote a more democratic government; elections to this body in May 1989 gave the Russian people their first taste of democracy. Gorbachev went even further by calling on the Communist Party to give up its seventy-year constitutional monopoly of power, although he clearly considered the party to be the most capable of guiding the nation through its turmoil. For the party to remain the political vanguard, however, it would have to earn the Soviet people's trust, and to do this, it would have to restructure itself. Gorbachev even suggested that rival political parties be established. His radical call was persuasive: in February 1990 the party's Central Committee opened the door to opposition parties. The political landscape of the Soviet Union was irreversibly transformed in this "February Revolution."

Equally revolutionary was Gorbachev's embrace of the free market as an alternative to the failed communist economy. Having repudiated

Lenin, Gorbachev now dumped Marx as well. Thus seventy-three years after the Bolshevik revolution, the Soviets reversed themselves; markets would replace bureaucracy, and capitalism would succeed socialism. But Gorbachev, however revolutionary his rhetoric and declarations, hesitated to implement his reforms because they would surely propel the flow of power away from Moscow and the central government he headed. A social explosion might occur as well if the withdrawal of subsidies to industry and to Soviet citizens for rent, food, health care, and education resulted in sharp rises in inflation and unemployment. Moreover, Gorbachev could not discount the old guard's opposition, and he clung to the notion that a communist system could exist alongside a Soviet transition to free markets.

In principle, then, the party had renounced both its political-economic dictatorship and its intellectual heritage, but the real question was whether this had happened too late. Could a political system that no longer enjoyed sufficient political authority or popularity because of many years of growing economic shortages, which now included even bread and cigarettes, take the tough measures required to implement wholesale economic changes? Had Gorbachev become the captain of the Soviet *Titanic* as the party lost control to the Congress of People's Deputies, the legislatures of the republics, the municipal governments, the popular fronts, and the increasingly assertive workers' unions, all of which sought a greater devolution of power and policy?

Gorbachev's strongest challenger for power was Boris Yeltsin, a former Communist Party leader who in May 1990 was elected president of the Russian republic. Russia occupied two-thirds of the territory of the former Soviet Union and had almost half of its population and most of its oil, natural gas reserves, and coal. Yeltsin was quick to sense the popular disaffection with the power and privileges of the Communist Party. Once Gorbachev's protégé, Yeltsin became his fiercest critic and arch rival because the Soviet leader had not, in Yeltsin's judgment, moved quickly enough to change the system.

On the day after his election by the Russian parliament, Yeltsin challenged the system by proposing Russia's economic autonomy and a radical decentralization in which republic law took precedence over Soviet law and the president of the Soviet Union would have no greater authority than the presidents of the fifteen republics. Indeed, not only would Russia claim sovereignty and determine the prices of its natural resources, but it would make its own agreements with the other members of the Soviet Union. And just to make his challenge clear, Yeltsin announced he would seek to make the Russian presidency a popularly elected office, which he won overwhelmingly. By being elected president of the Soviet Union's largest republic, Yeltsin acquired a legitimacy Gorbachev never had.

IMPACT AND INFLUENCE

MIKHAIL GORBACHEV AND BORIS YELTSIN

Amid the collapse of the Soviet Union, the peaceful transfer of power from Mikhail Gorbachev (left) to Boris Yeltsin (right) proved to be an extraordinary achievement. Indeed, Yeltsin's defense of the Soviet leader during the failed coup attempt by communist hard-liners in August 1991 preserved their generally cordial relations even as the Soviet Union was crumbling around them.

Gorbachev, the last leader of the Soviet Union, could not prevent his democratic reforms from weakening the Communist Party's hold over Eastern Europe and, later, the Soviet Union itself. Once out of power, Gorbachev formed a private foundation and continued to advocate "democratic socialism." Meanwhile, Yeltsin remained president of Russia throughout the 1990s, defending his political and economic reforms against challenges from neocommunists and militant nationalists. But Russia suffered under his watch, and economic stagnation, political corruption, and a failed effort to quell a secessionist revolt in Chechnya were largely to blame. Ailing and frustrated, Yeltsin abruptly resigned on the final day of 1999 and yielded power to Prime Minister Vladimir Putin, who was elected to a full term as Russia's president in March 2000.

A few weeks later, Yeltsin, together with the reformist mayors of Moscow and Leningrad, resigned from the Communist Party. Their resignations were symptomatic of growing national disenchantment with the party and Gorbachev's declining popularity. Next, the Ukraine, the Soviet Union's second largest republic and its "breadbasket," with a population of more than fifty million, declared its sovereignty and announced that its laws would supercede those of the Soviet Union. Ukraine also claimed an independent foreign policy role by stating it would be a neutral state, it would not participate in military blocs, and it would ban the production and deployment of nuclear weapons on its territory. Ukraine's action was followed by a similar declaration from Belarus, a small but geographically vital republic located between Ukraine and the Baltic states. Eventually all of the Soviet Union's fifteen republics issued sovereignty declarations, asserting either outright independence or more cautious assertions of their rights. Gorbachev's Soviet Union was crumbling all around him, piece by piece.

By late 1990 Gorbachev had become more and more irrelevant in domestic affairs. Yeltsin was setting the pace and scope of change by supporting the drive for independence of the Baltic republics and by proposing a five hundred-day plan for the transformation of the Russian economy into a market economy. Gorbachev found himself maneuvering between the increasingly radical forces on the left and the forces of reaction on the right, represented by the traditional instruments of Soviet power—the military, secret police, and Communist Party bureaucracy—which had survived all his attempts at reform. They were the elite and therefore had a strong vested interest in the status quo. In the meantime, Gorbachev had his hands full just trying to hold the union together and stem the republics' nationalism. Thus he shifted his original direction and aligned himself with the forces of "law and order." He dismissed many of his former liberal allies in the struggle for *glasnost* and *perestroika,* began cracking down on the Baltic republics, and reimposed censorship.

Gorbachev's new allies, however, tried to limit his power and enhance their own because they felt he was leading the country to chaos and anarchy. Moreover, they despised him because he had retreated from Eastern Europe and had given up the Soviet Union's World War II gains. In response, Gorbachev swung back to ally himself once more with the reformers. He made his peace with the republics and promised the presidents of the nine republics who agreed to stay within the union, including Yeltsin, to turn the Soviet Union into a new voluntary federation that all republics would have the right to join or not join. They also would be free to choose their own form of government and exercise most of the power over their natural resources, industry, foreign trade, and taxes. He promised a new constitution and a newly elected central government.

But just as the new All-Union Treaty was about to be signed, the hard-liners struck. Fearing that their power was waning and that it soon would be too late to do anything about it, they launched a coup in August 1991, arresting Gorbachev while he was on vacation. But the coup plotters failed to understand the effects of the six years of Gorbachev's policies. Led by the popularly elected Yeltsin, who showed enormous courage in condemning the coup, the people of Moscow rallied behind Gorbachev, resisting those who would reimpose the old dictatorship. When units of the military and secret police opposed the coup, it quickly collapsed. This event proved to be the death blow to the Soviet Union.

All the republics now wanted their independence from Moscow and central authority. The three Baltic republics were let go and their independence was recognized by Moscow. At this point, seven of the twelve remaining republics, including Russia, planned to stay together in a loose confederation because they were still economically interdependent, although the agriculturally and industrially important Ukraine would not commit itself to creating a "common economic space" and a single currency, the foundation of a free-market economy.

What was absolutely clear in these times of uncertainty was that the old regime had disgraced itself by the coup attempt. Statues of Stalin and Lenin were toppled and unceremoniously removed from public squares. The old imperial flag designed by Peter the Great once again flew over the Russian parliament, the center of the resistance to the coup. Leningrad was renamed St. Petersburg, its prerevolutionary name, in accordance with the wishes of its citizens. Many said it also was time to remove Lenin's body from the mausoleum in Red Square. But the major victim of the failed coup was the Communist Party. Yeltsin took sweeping measures against the Russian Communist Party, closing all of its offices and newspapers. Gorbachev, acknowledging the mood of the country and trying to salvage some of his authority, ended the party's role as watchdog of the military, secret police, and government bureaucracy, and disbanded its leadership. For all practical purposes, the Communist Party as a governing body was dead. It could no longer block the path to democracy and radical economic reform. The revolution of 1917 had been undone in a stunning sequence of events.

The republics, however, were still grappling with their future. At the moment of decision the seven republics that had endorsed the new union would not commit themselves, leaving its fate in the hands of their national parliaments. When the Ukraine voted on December 1, 1991, for independence and instantly became Europe's fourth largest country, it became clear that nothing could stop the process of Soviet disintegration. With even a weak confederation now dead, Russia was left as the successor state to the Soviet Union. Indeed, this status had become overwhelmingly clear earlier, when in November 1991 the central government declared bankruptcy and Russia assumed its debts and promised to fund what remained of the central government's ministries. In capitalist language, this act constituted a leveraged buyout of the former Soviet Union. Russia also claimed the Soviet Union's permanent seat on the UN Security Council.

The Soviet Union's demise became official on December 8, 1991, when, in an act of desperation to stop the complete disintegration of the nation, the presidents of the three Slavic republics—Russia, Ukraine, and Belarus—established a commonwealth and invited other republics to join. The new Commonwealth of Independent States (CIS) was to assume all the international obligations of the Soviet Union, including control over its nuclear arsenal. Coordinating bodies would be established to decide on cooperative policies in foreign affairs, defense, and economics.[8] Later, the commonwealth agreement was signed by eleven of the remaining twelve Soviet republics after the defection of the three Baltic states; the twelfth republic, Georgia, was consumed by civil war. On December 25, 1991, the red hammer-and-sickle flag that had flown over the Kremlin was lowered for the last time, seventy-four years after the Bolshevik revolution. The Soviet Union literally disappeared from the world's map.

REASONS FOR THE SOVIET COLLAPSE: CONTENDING ARGUMENTS

Throughout his presidency George Bush was dogged by the notion that he lacked a coherent vision of the future of world politics. Furthermore, he was criticized for what seemed to be an overly cautious approach to U.S.-Soviet relations, for his continuing embrace of Gorbachev after the Soviet leader lost legitimacy, and for his resistance to immediate deep cuts in American defense spending. Bush, the lifelong government bureaucrat, manager, and caretaker, presumably lacked the panache to seize such a profound historic opportunity.

Twenty-first century historians probably will be kinder to Bush because a careful review of his performance reveals how skillfully he manipulated one of the crucial turning points in history, not only to the advantage of the United States but also in the interests of global stability. The three-year free fall of the Soviet system was by no means a certainty when Bush arrived in office, and its peaceful course was without precedent. In assisting Gorbachev when he urgently needed outside support, in insisting on German unification on Western terms, and in exploiting the opportunity for drastic nuclear disarmament, Bush successfully navigated the United States and its allies through a complicated phase of international relations toward their ultimate victory in a

8. Internal tensions greatly limited the actual role of the CIS in the 1990s, although the commonwealth remained officially intact into the twenty-first century.

protracted conflict of global proportions. Bush was chastised for adhering to the most "prudent" approach to world politics, but history may suggest that prudence was precisely the approach the world required.[9]

THE CONTENDING ARGUMENTS IN PERSPECTIVE

Immediately after the Cold War ended, the question was raised whether the United States had "won" the war and whether its containment policy had been successful. Or was it more accurate to say that the Soviet Union, plagued by internal problems of its own making, had "lost" the Cold War? This question—not one conducive to a definitive answer—sparked a contentious debate among scholars, journalists, and policy makers.[10] But it was not merely an academic exercise, for the answers to these questions would reveal the central lessons of the Cold War, which in turn would figure in the establishment of guidelines for future American foreign policy.

Advocates of the view that the United States had "won" the Cold War claimed that the Western system of political, economic, and military organization was simply more durable than that of the Soviet Union and its allies. Furthermore, the U.S.-led containment policy successfully combined pressure and patience to overwhelm Soviet capabilities.[11] In other words, containment had worked much as George Kennan predicted it would nearly fifty years earlier, preventing Soviet expansion through the selective application of Western resistance. Conversely, those believing that the Soviet Union had instead "lost" the war diminished the role of the containment policy. If the United States had "won," it was merely because the Soviet Union's flawed system made its demise inevitable. Its excessive centralization of power, bureaucratic planning, and supervision of every detail of Soviet life, economic and otherwise, as well as its command economy and ideological oppression, contributed to its undoing.[12] Furthermore, for some neo-Marxists the demise of the Soviet Union reflected its failed application of Marxist ideals and principles, not the bankruptcy of the political theory.

Both views call for a closer look at the Soviet experience in converting the aspirations of the 1917 Russian Revolution into practice. Seven-

9. A more thorough review of Bush's performance is provided by Michael Beschloss and Strobe Talbott in *At the Highest Levels: The Inside Story of the End of the Cold War* (Boston: Little, Brown, 1993).

10. For a review of these arguments, see Michael J. Hogan, ed., *The End of the Cold War: Its Meanings and Implications* (New York: Cambridge University Press, 1992).

11. See John Lewis Gaddis, *The United States and the End of the Cold War* (New York: Oxford University Press, 1992), 193.

12. See Walter Laquer, *The Dream that Failed: Reflections on the Soviet Union* (New York: Oxford University Press, 1994), 50–76. Also see Charles W. Kegley Jr., "How Did the Cold War Die? Principles for an Autopsy," *Mershon International Studies Review* (summer 1994): 11–41.

ty years after the revolution, the Soviet standard of living was so low that even Eastern Europe, with its own economic problems, appeared affluent by contrast. According to the former Soviet Union's own statistics, about 40 percent of its population and almost 80 percent of its elderly citizens lived in poverty. One-third of its households had no running water. Indeed, the Soviet Union was the only industrialized society in which infant mortality had risen and male life expectancy had declined in the late twentieth century. In Zbigniew Brzezinski's words, "Perhaps never before in history has such a gifted people, in control of such abundant resources, labored so hard for so long to produce so little." [13]

The Soviet economy, which was supposed to have demonstrated the superiority of socialism, sputtered for decades and then collapsed. Deliberately isolating itself from the global capitalist economy, the Soviet Union had intended to build an economy that was self-sufficient and productive, assuring a bountiful life for the workers and peasants who had been deprived for so long. Instead, the centralized command economy meant no domestic competition among firms, and its self-exclusion from the international economy ensured that it remained unchallenged by foreign competition. The Soviet economy thus became a textbook case of what free traders have long argued are the results of state control: inefficiency, lack of productivity, unresponsiveness to consumer needs, and technological stagnation. There was little in the writings of Karl Marx, which had more to do with revolution than communist governance, that provided a solution to this central problem.

Soviet communism was efficient only in producing military hardware. But this, ironically, also contributed to its defeat. As a state with few natural protective barriers, frequently invaded throughout its history, first Russia and then the Soviet Union kept sizable standing forces for its defense. Its twentieth-century experiences with Germany did nothing to relieve the longtime Russian sense of insecurity, fueled by the Marxist conception of politics as a constant struggle and its perception that enemies were everywhere. But whether Soviet expansionism stemmed from a defensive preoccupation with security or from an offensive ideological goal of aggrandizement, Moscow's drive for absolute security left other states feeling absolutely insecure. It is no wonder, then, that such insecurity drove all of the Soviet Union's great-power neighbors (Western Europe, on one side; Turkey, Iran, China, Japan, and South Korea, on the other sides) to accelerate their own defense spending. Furthermore, many Soviet accomplishments, such as its inroads in the developing countries, considered at the time as set-

13. Zbigniew Brzezinski, *Game Plan: A Geostrategic Framework for the Conduct of the U.S.-Soviet Contest* (Boston: Atlantic Monthly Press, 1986), 123. Also see Brzezinski, *Grand Failure.*

backs for the United States, were actually setbacks for Moscow. Cuba in the 1960s, Angola and Ethiopia in the 1970s, and Afghanistan in the 1980s gave the Soviet system a bad case of indigestion. The logic of this thesis—the more the Soviet Union expanded, the greater the cost—was that the U.S.-led containment policy was not an essential ingredient in stopping Soviet expansion. Indeed, it was precisely where containment *failed,* providing an opening for Moscow, that the Soviet Union's burden became too great to bear.[14]

Strobe Talbott, Time's Soviet expert and later a deputy secretary of state in the Clinton administration, asserted that the Soviet threat was a "grotesque exaggeration" and claimed in retrospect, "The doves in the great debate of the past 40 years were right all along." [15] The Soviet "meltdown" in the Cold War was self-inflicted and "not because of anything the outside world has done or not done or threatened to do." Thus American and Western policies had little to do with the Soviet defeat in the Cold War since its cause was purely internal. Characteristic of the revisionist view that has followed every major American war, Talbott's analysis included the following points: there really had been no major danger to this country; the nation's long, intense, and dangerous involvement in the post–World War II world had not been necessary; and the containment policy, instead of playing a key role in the defeat of America's adversary, had merely prolonged the Cold War. Soviet power "was actually Soviet weakness," and the conflict itself "distorted priorities, distracted attention and preoccupied many of the best and the brightest minds in government, academe, and think tanks for nearly two generations." Thus it would have been better to have avoided the "grand obsession" with the "Red Menace," to have remained isolated from the power politics that diverted resources from domestic reforms to military preparations and war. Gorbachev, Talbott claimed, not only helped to show that the Soviet threat was not what it used to be, but "what's more, that it never was."

Soviet communism, a far cry from the worker's utopia envisioned by Karl Marx, surely deserves much of the credit it has been given for abetting its own collapse. But to conclude from this that the containment policy was not necessary, or, if necessary, was not a key ingredient in the Soviet Union's demise, is to differ from the conclusions drawn by its potential victims. As the United States attempted to withdraw from Europe after World War II, countries such as Iran and Turkey, followed by those in Western Europe, pleaded with it to help them. The collapse of the former great powers of Western Europe left the Soviet Union as

14. John Mueller, "Enough Rope," *New Republic,* July 3, 1989, 15.
15. Strobe Talbott, "Rethinking the Red Menace," *Time,* January 1, 1990, 66–71.

the potential hegemon throughout Eurasia. All countries saw their independence and national integrity at stake; America's continued presence was their only protection. Had the United States retreated into isolationism, as it did after World War I, the countries on the periphery of the Soviet Union would have been vulnerable to the same assertion of Soviet power being felt east of the iron curtain.

Western Europe remained the pivotal strategic stake throughout the Cold War. The Soviets repeatedly tried to intimidate these nations, to divide them (especially West Germany from the United States), and to drive the United States back to its shores. But the containment policy made Moscow cautious about expanding its power. From this perspective, the ancient rule of states is a prudent one: power must be met by countervailing power. A balance among states is the only guarantee that they will retain their independence and preserve their way of life. Without containment, the inefficiencies of the Soviet system might not have mattered as much; the Soviet Union would not have had to engage in a costly, ongoing arms competition.

Containment, however, was not aimed just at blocking Soviet domination of Western Europe and the rest of Eurasia. It also was intended to win time for the Soviet leadership to reexamine its goals and moderate its ambitions. Thus the American strategy in the Cold War rested largely and correctly on a tactical assumption of Soviet behavior. As George Kennan had explained years earlier, the United States had

> it in its power to increase enormously the strains under which Soviet policy must operate, to force upon the Kremlin a far greater degree of moderation and circumspection than it has had to observe in recent years, and in this way *to promote tendencies which must eventually find their outlet in either the breakup or the gradual mellowing of Soviet power. For no mystical, messianic movement—and particularly that of the Kremlin—can face frustration indefinitely without eventually adjusting itself in one way or another to the logic of that state of affairs.*[16]

In retrospect, these words were prophetic. The Cold War experience demonstrated the virtue of patience in foreign policy. While interpreting the Soviet threat as the country's paramount concern, Kennan foresaw no quick fixes and recommended no immediate solutions to the problem. To the contrary, he anticipated a prolonged, low-intensity struggle along several distant frontiers. The conflict would be settled most effectively—and most peacefully—through the gradual exposure of contradictions within Soviet society. Soviet communism, in his view, would ultimately *self-destruct* under the weight of these contradictions. In the meantime, the United States would have to pursue a "long-term,

16. George Kennan, *American Diplomacy, 1900–1950* (Chicago: University of Chicago Press, 1951), 127–128. Italics added.

patient, but firm and vigilant containment of Russian expansive tendencies." From Truman to Bush, that is just what U.S. presidents did.

The importance of the containment policy becomes even more evident when it is contrasted to the preceding period of American foreign policy. By failing to take a firm stand against Soviet policy during World War II, after it had become evident that it was impossible to accommodate Soviet interests in Eastern Europe and Asia, the United States had to accept some of the blame for the Cold War that followed. This is not to say that the United States passively accepted Soviet expansionism, but only that it did not oppose Stalin early enough, that it continued to cling to its hope for postwar amity with the Soviet Union despite Soviet behavior in the late stages of the war, and that after hostilities had ceased, it dissipated its strength immediately in a helter-skelter demobilization. Stalin respected American power and was a cautious statesman, but when President Roosevelt informed him that American troops would be withdrawn from Europe after two years, Stalin realized he did not need to concern himself about American protests against Soviet actions in Eastern Europe. Protests were one thing, action another. Not until after the war did the United States act and draw the lines beyond which Soviet expansion would not be tolerated.

The American containment policy, then, played a critical role in the defeat of the Soviet Union. If the United States had not resisted Soviet expansion, Moscow, believing that communism represented the wave of the future, would likely have become even more assertive and aggressive; perceived weakness always invited efforts to expand. For example, when Nikita Khrushchev claimed that the balance of power had turned in favor of the Soviet Union, he precipitated a series of crises in West Berlin and Cuba that stretched from 1957 to 1962. And later, when Brezhnev's Soviet Union attained nuclear parity while also fielding a sizable army and building a growing navy, it exploited America's "Vietnam syndrome," using its own forces and sponsoring clients in Southeast Asia, Africa, Latin America, and Afghanistan. American policy compelled Soviet caution and moderation. If the United States and its allies, especially NATO, had not opposed Soviet expansionist efforts through constant pressure, there would have been no need for Gorbachev to reassess his predecessors' policy and seek an accommodation with the West.

EXCESSES OF THE CONTAINMENT POLICY

Containment was by no means a flawless policy. Once the Cold War began, U.S. misperceptions, like those of Soviet leaders, fed the superpower conflict. For example, Washington frequently exaggerated Soviet military capabilities. Fears of Soviet superiority—the bomber gap in the

1950s, the missile gaps a few years later, the ABM gap in the mid-1960s, and "the window of vulnerability" in the early 1980s—propelled the arms competition already well underway. In addition, the U.S. emphasis on anticommunism meant American policy often was insensitive to the nationalism of the new nations. As a result, the Middle East Treaty Organization (METO) and Southeast Asia Treaty Organization (SEATO) alliances proved weak reeds for containing communism, alienating important states such as Egypt and India which shifted toward the Soviet Union, aggravating regional rivalries, and aligning the United States with discredited regimes such as Nationalist China and Iran. Indeed, in the name of anticommunism Washington often supported authoritarian, right-wing regimes in the developing world; it saw no democratic alternatives to the regimes it backed other than left-wing pro-Soviet or pro-Chinese ones, which were unacceptable.

The U.S. government also consistently exaggerated the monolithic nature of international communism. The fall of Nationalist China, the Korean War, and the communist Chinese intervention in that war transformed the containment policy—which originally was limited to responding to Soviet moves in the eastern Mediterranean and Western Europe—into global anticommunism. The events of 1949 and 1950 led to virulent anticommunism in the United States, with the Republicans (notably Sen. Joseph McCarthy) accusing the Democrats of being "soft on communism" and engaging in paranoid witch hunts. Future Democratic administrations therefore would not be able to exploit the growing differences between the Soviet Union and China; instead, seeking to avoid being charged with the "loss of Indochina," as they had been with the "loss of China," Democratic administrations intervened militarily in Vietnam.

The American penchant for crusading, already demonstrated vividly in two "hot" wars, was not to be denied in the Cold War. America's failure to distinguish between vital and secondary interests—or to discriminate between different communist regimes—resulted in a war the United States could not win, dividing the country deeply and undermining the domestic consensus that had been the basis of the Cold War. Ironically, Vietnam destroyed the aggressive mode of American anticommunism, and U.S. policy shifted back toward a more passive containment of Soviet power—but this time in a de facto "alliance" with China. Finally, as detailed in Chapter 8, the overzealous pursuit of the Reagan Doctrine resulted in the Iran-contra scandal, which raised new doubts about the extent to which the U.S. government would go to fulfill its mission of defeating communism.

A FINAL APPRAISAL

Its shortcomings aside, the American containment policy must be pronounced, on the whole, a success. The expansion of American power and influence in the world has, despite the excesses of the Cold War, been associated with the promotion of democracy. America's World War II enemies, once dictatorial, are today stable, free, and prosperous societies. And its allies, particularly in Western Europe, have benefited from the opportunity to integrate their economies and pursue cooperative foreign relations. If one looks at the societies "liberated" by the Soviet Union during World War II, the contrast is striking. No East European country, until Gorbachev, was granted self-determination by the Kremlin; earlier attempts by East Germany, Hungary, Czechoslovakia, and Poland to move toward greater freedom were crushed by Soviet forces or their proxies. East Germany had to build a wall across Berlin and a barbed-wire fence along its entire border with West Germany to prevent its citizens from escaping.

Over the four decades of the Cold War, the United States acquired many authoritarian allies, mostly in the developing countries, which weakened Washington's moral standing and laid open its foreign policy to the charge of hypocrisy. It would have been preferable, of course, to have democratic allies, but that was not always possible in a world in which most developing countries had never been democratic in the Western sense of the term. Security, both internally and globally, was bound to conflict with democratic development, just as today the values of economic growth and human rights frequently clash. Which value was to be given priority presented a difficult, often agonizing choice both for American leaders and for the leaders of developing countries.

The basic fact remains, however, that the principal thrust of American foreign policy after World War II, as before the war, was to preserve a balance of power that would safeguard democratic values in the United States and other like-minded states. Indeed, this has been a consistent policy since World War I, whether the threat has come from the right or the left. American policy makers in the twentieth century opposed both types of regimes, for they threatened not just U.S. security but, more broadly, the international environment in which democratic values could prosper. This was the crux of U.S. opposition to the Soviet Union: that its great power constituted a threat to Western values and democratic political institutions. Communism, especially as reflected in the Soviet Union that Gorbachev inherited, was antithetical to individual freedoms, whether of speech or religion, to multiparty competition and genuine political choice, and to a distinction between state and society. It was America's power, not simply its democratic ideals, that protected these values.

Indeed, the end of the Cold War was witness not only to the end of the Soviet challenge but also to the defeat of the second totalitarian challenge to Western-style democracy in this century. The Nazis will forever be identified with the concentration camps of Auschwitz, Bergen-Belsen, and Treblinka, where they systematically murdered millions of people, including 6 million Jews, and with the unleashing of World War II, which, before it was over, cost the lives of 17 million soldiers and 34 million civilians. Just as the Nazi system was epitomized by Hitler, the Soviet system remains identified with Stalin and his cruel collectivization of the Soviet peasantry, the deliberate starvation of the Ukrainian peasants in the early 1930s, and the purges and other crimes that claimed the lives, conservatively estimated, of 20 million people and imprisoned and deported 20 million more. Stalin, not Hitler, was the great mass murderer in history; he also was in power twice as long.[17] His ability to impose overwhelming control over such a massive territory had no historical precedent. The defeat of Stalin's successors, therefore, had global significance.

Although the U.S. victory in the Cold War coincided with America's own economic woes, the country still had reason to be proud of its overall record. There had been no nuclear war during the nearly half-century of Cold War in which the United States had led the Western coalition. Soviet expansionist ambitions had been checked. And democracy had emerged in a steadily growing number of countries. Then, after winning the Cold War, the U.S. government refused to gloat, seeking instead to attract the former Soviet bloc as a partner in the process of economic and political reform. While this process would be as complex, difficult, and potentially dangerous as that of containing communism, it would gradually extend the domain of European cooperation and produce a degree of stability not seen before in the twentieth century.

17. See Edvard Radzinsky, *Stalin* (New York: Doubleday, 1996).

Newly elected president Bill Clinton delivers his first major address to a joint session of Congress in February 1993. When Clinton took office the United States held the distinction of being the world's "lone superpower."

CHAPTER TEN

America's 'Unipolar Moment'

The abrupt collapse of the Cold War in the late twentieth century caught most world leaders by surprise and produced new uncertainties about world politics. Despite its perils, the rivalry between the Soviet Union and the United States had become a familiar reality that guided the foreign policies of all countries, large and small. In its absence, once-clear distinctions between friends and foes became blurred. Old alignments were either no longer necessary or, in many cases, no longer advisable. Consequently, future alignments and the source and intensity of new fault lines were hard to distinguish.

A key question during this transition concerned the new balance of power. As noted, global stability traditionally has relied on a stable balance, or equilibrium, among the world's strongest powers and their allies. During the early nineteenth century, the Concert of Europe established a *multipolar* balance of power that produced a "long peace" among the great powers. The dissolution of this balance, beginning with the unification of Germany in 1870, set the stage for two world wars. During the Cold War, the *bipolar* balance between the American and Soviet blocs, which was bolstered by nuclear weapons and threats of "mutual assured destruction," prevented an even more cataclysmic world war.

One thing was clear about the post–Cold War balance of power: the disintegration of the Soviet Union had brought an end to the bipolar order that had persisted since the late 1940s. To many observers, the international system had again become multipolar. The Western Europe states had retained their previous status, and the European Union was taking shape as a single entity. Russia remained a force to be reckoned with. And a host of newly industrialized countries—primarily in East Asia—were emerging as formidable players on the global stage. The United States, in this view, was one of many countries of comparable strength and capabilities. Its foreign policy would have to adapt accordingly.

A more convincing argument was made by those who recognized that, at least for the immediate period, a *unipolar* balance of power would prevail. The United States held a variety of advantages that, when taken together and compared with the aggregate resources of any other single power, marked the arrival of America's "unipolar moment." According to the columnist Charles Krauthammer, who coined the term, "American preeminence is based on the fact that it is the only country with the military, diplomatic and economic assets to be a decisive player in any conflict in whatever part of the world it chooses to involve itself." [1]

The economic statistics speak for themselves. In 1991—the last year of the Cold War—American firms produced $5.6 trillion in goods and services, or 26 percent of the world's output. Japan ranked second in gross domestic product (GDP), yet its output of $3.4 trillion was just three-fifths of the U.S. total. As for Europe, America's GDP exceeded the combined totals of France, Germany, Italy, and the United Kingdom. In all three areas of economic output—manufacturing, agriculture, and services—the U.S. economy set the pace for its competitors. Although foreign commerce contributed only about 10 percent to its GDP, the United States also served as an engine of growth overseas by importing far more goods—worth $506 billion in 1991 alone—than any other country. All of this was especially noteworthy given that the United States was home to less than 5 percent of the world's inhabitants.[2]

1. Charles Krauthammer, "The Unipolar Moment," *Foreign Affairs* (winter 1990–1991): 24.

2. World Bank, *World Development Report 1993* (New York: Oxford University Press, 1993), 239–265.

In terms of military capabilities, American preponderance was even greater. The United States maintained its global presence, with military forces deployed across the Western Hemisphere, Europe, the Middle East, and East Asia. The U.S. Navy patrolled most of the vital sea lanes, and the U.S. Air Force maintained uncontested supremacy of the skies. American military spending of $280 billion in 1991 represented 27 percent of the worldwide total and a much larger sum than the combined totals of its potential adversaries.[3] Although the Soviet Union came close to the United States in defense spending, its status as a viable military competitor had been chronically exaggerated by the CIA. Between 1989 and 1991 its military strength plummeted as the Soviet bloc slowly dissolved, and those forces left were plagued by outdated equipment and sagging morale. Most other countries that maintained large and modern defense forces were longtime allies of the United States. Thus they effectively added to U.S. military power. When the technical superiority of U.S. conventional and nuclear forces was factored into the equation, the United States enjoyed an unprecedented degree of global military might.

Finally, the United States emerged from the Cold War with a stable political system that, despite occasional controversies and scandals, had endured for more than two hundred years. The democratic freedoms offered by the United States were eagerly sought by citizens of other nations who had known only oppression and dictatorial rule. America's vast network of colleges and universities attracted thousands of students from overseas. And its popular culture—expressed in fashion, music, publishing, movies, and television—appealed to a worldwide audience. In this increasingly important area of "soft power," including the less tangible aspects of cultural and political influence, the United States held a sizable advantage.[4]

All of this did not suggest that the unipolar world would necessarily be a stable one, or one of long duration. Simply put, the modern nation-state system had never witnessed such a concentration of the sources of power in a single state. There was, then, no comparable past experience from which to draw informed predictions. The few standard cases for comparison—including the Roman, Ottoman, Spanish, French, British, and Russo-Soviet empires—were hardly global in scope, nor did they possess the many reinforcing elements of "hard" and "soft" power that yielded U.S. predominance in the 1990s. The European empires had, however, imposed a tighter grip over their domains, whereas U.S. influence was generally less direct, taking the form of political and cultural

3. U.S. Arms Control and Disarmament Agency, *World Military Expenditures and Arms Transfers, 1991–1992* (Washington, D.C.: Government Printing Office, 1994), 47–87.

4. Joseph Nye Jr., *Bound to Lead: The Changing Nature of American Power* (New York: Basic Books, 1990), chap. 6.

role modeling or military hegemony rather than conquest and formal occupation. But this difference only worked to further America's advantage. History had proven repeatedly that heavy-handed rulers who ignored the interests of their citizens ultimately became victims of their own tyranny.

These unique features of the American "empire" provoked widely varying expectations. Optimists believed that America's military preponderance would deter other countries from challenging the status quo. Meanwhile, U.S. stewardship of the world economy would strengthen global commitments to private enterprise and free trade.[5] Finally, given its victory in the Cold War the United States would be in a strong position to consolidate the democratic boom of the 1990s. Pessimists, conversely, predicted that American leaders would face an impossible task in calculating how, where, and under what circumstances to exert the country's influence or expend its resources in the turbulent international system. Moreover, because states had always tended to seek a balance against dominant powers, the rise of a global coalition seeking to counter the United States was not out of the question.[6]

Unipolarity also did not mean the United States would face no immediate challenges to its efforts to prevent its domestic base from eroding or to preserve its lead role in world politics. To the contrary, American leaders in the 1990s faced a bewildering array of problems at home and overseas during the first post–Cold War decade. The central point, however, is that the United States confronted these challenges with a superior range of resources. Thus the most compelling question was: How effectively would America bring its predominance to bear in the aftermath of the Cold War?

The remainder of this book seeks to answer this vital question. This chapter explores the domestic transition that occurred within the United States, particularly the intellectual debates, policy innovations, and institutional struggles that unfolded as the post–Cold War dawned. Chapters 11 and 12 then examine the regional issues and conflicts that confronted American leaders in the developing areas and in Europe, respectively. The final chapter returns to the original themes of this book, examines several issues of ongoing concern, and considers how America's experience since the Cold War reflects its enduring style of foreign policy.

5. For an early statement of hegemonic stability theory, see Charles P. Kindleberger, *The World in Depression, 1929–1939* (Berkeley: University of California Press, 1973). Also see Robert Gilpin, *The Political Economy of International Relations* (Princeton: Princeton University Press, 1987), chap. 3.

6. See Christopher Layne, "The Unipolar Illusion: Why New Great Powers Will Rise," *International Security* (spring 1993): 5–51.

GREAT EXPECTATIONS AFTER THE COLD WAR

America's 'Unipolar Moment'

The end of the Cold War not only elevated the stature of the United States, but also gave rise to a new sense of euphoria throughout the West. The world seemed to stand on the verge of a profoundly new era of peace, prosperity, and individual freedom. This hope was based in part on the collapse of the Soviet Union and the anticipated replacement of the Cold War rivalry with Russo-American cooperation. Much of the euphoria also was based on more fundamental expectations that the very forces that historically had fueled international tensions were themselves being transformed. As one scholar declared,

> What we may be witnessing is not just the end of the Cold War, or the passing of a particular period of history, but the end of history as such: that is, the end point of mankind's ideological evolution and the universalization of Western liberal democracy as the final form of human government.[7]

Two forces would presumably characterize the "post-historical" world: democracy and free-market capitalism. Both had already taken hold in many parts of the developing world and were expected in the 1990s to spread across Eastern Europe and the former Soviet Union. To adherents of this view, the expansion of democracy would benefit average citizens while enhancing the prospects for global stability. After all, democracies, while frequently engaging in armed struggles against nondemocratic states, traditionally had engaged in peaceful behavior toward other democratic states. The "democratic peace" they had established with like-minded foreign governments allowed for multiparty elections, observed the rule of law, and respected human rights.[8] In the economic sphere, a market-based world economy would presumably tie nations together in a cooperative search for prosperity. Not only would military conflicts become less frequent, but the powerful nations of the world would be able to confront global problems such as environmental decay, weapons proliferation, population growth, and widespread poverty. Furthermore, economic "globalization" would lift the poorest regions of the world from poverty, thus reducing the economic disparities that had grown ever wider during the Cold War as political leaders engaged in polarized, ideologically driven quarrels over the most effective means to provide for social welfare.

Another part of this equation was the nature of military power in the

7. Francis Fukuyama, "The End of History?" *National Interest* (summer 1989): 4.

8. See Bruce Russett, *Grasping the Democratic Peace: Principles for a Post–Cold War World* (Princeton: Princeton University Press, 1993); and Michael W. Doyle, "Liberalism and World Politics," *American Political Science Review* (December 1986): 1151–1169. For a critique, see Joanne Gowa, *Ballots and Bullets: The Elusive Democratic Peace* (Princeton: Princeton University Press, 1999).

post–Cold War era. Nuclear weapons, it was widely believed, had rendered warfare among the great powers suicidal and thus prohibitive. Large-scale military conflict was destined to become obsolete, just as dueling, once widely accepted, became viewed as "contemptible and stupid" in the nineteenth century.[9] Given the increasingly high costs of conventional warfare and the visible rewards to be expected from growing economic cooperation, war also might become obsolete among developing countries, where most violent conflicts were occurring.

George Bush, the first U.S. president to serve in the aftermath of the Cold War, took all of these factors into account and proclaimed to a joint session of Congress in March 1991 that a "new world order" had arrived. "We can see a new world coming into view, a world in which there is the very real prospect of a new world order, a world where the United Nations—freed from Cold War stalemate—is poised to fulfill the historic vision of its founders; a world in which freedom and respect for human rights find a home among all nations." [10]

For a president who had long been associated with a pragmatic if not conservative approach to foreign policy, Bush's exaltations seemed out of character. But his vision was very much in keeping with the country's traditional idealism and emphasis on moral principles. In predicting the global spread of democracy, Bush recalled the optimism of Thomas Jefferson. In expressing faith in multilateral organizations to uphold widely accepted norms of international behavior, Bush echoed Woodrow Wilson. And in placing the United States at the center of such a reformed world, Bush restated themes advanced by Franklin Roosevelt and John Kennedy. His outlook, then, fit neatly into a mold that was well established by past U.S. presidents. The only difference: for Bush, this long-awaited future had arrived.

Later, President Bush would be taken to task as events demonstrated how *disorderly* the post–Cold War era would actually be. In 1991, however, his heralding of a transformed world seemed appropriate. The Cold War was over; the Soviet Union had disappeared; Germany was finally reunited. Democracies and market economies were taking shape far from the fallen iron curtain, extending to populations that long had been trapped by colonial domination and superpower rivalry. In short, it was a world American leaders had yearned for since the country's founding more than two centuries earlier.

9. John Mueller, *Retreat from Doomsday: The Obsolescence of Major War* (New York: Basic Books, 1989), 10.

10. Quoted in Stanley R. Sloan, "The U.S. Role in a New World Order: Prospects for George Bush's Global Vision," Congressional Research Service Report to Congress, March 28, 1991, 19.

REVIVED DEBATES ABOUT AMERICA'S WORLD ROLE

Even as Bush announced the arrival of the "new world order," debates began about the future role of the United States. One question raised frequently was whether American foreign policy after the Cold War would resemble that of 1918, when the United States retreated into its hemispheric shell after World War I, or that of 1945, when it assumed a strong internationalist posture after World War II. Of central concern was how much attention and resources should be devoted to foreign policy when, for all practical purposes, the nation no longer confronted any formidable military threats.

In Washington and around the country, many people also questioned whether the United States really needed an explicit "grand strategy" in the wake of the Cold War. After all, the U.S.-Soviet rivalry and the bipolar balance of power had been unique in history. Communism had represented a stark challenge to American principles, political institutions, and physical security. In a clear response to that challenge, the United States had implemented George Kennan's containment strategy. But just as clearly, the United States could not pursue a coherent post–Cold War foreign policy in the dark. No great power can survive in the absence of an explicit statement of purpose. Vital interests must be recognized and articulated. Priorities must be established, budgets prepared, and resources deployed in a systematic fashion. Furthermore, allies must be reassured and potential adversaries put on notice by a government speaking with one voice. Otherwise, policy vacillates and drifts, government agencies move in separate directions, and public support is impossible to sustain. Most troubling, challengers to the status quo inevitably exploit the void that results when a great power leads by improvisation.

To address these concerns, policy analysts inside and outside the U.S. government devised an array of possible strategies that clustered around four basic models: a retreat from global leadership, a campaign of liberal internationalism, an effort to maintain U.S. economic and military primacy, and an ad hoc policy of "selective engagement." The first two positions reflected long-held but divergent feelings about America's role in world politics. As noted throughout this book, the country's foreign policy traditionally had lurched between periods of detachment from great-power politics and periods of moral crusading. The third and fourth positions were distinct to the post–Cold War era and suggested a subtle yet significant evolution in the country's approach to world politics that reflected its experience as a great power.

Although America had over the years sought to distance itself from the intrigues and frequent conflicts of the major powers and thereby remain untainted by power politics, isolationism, the first strategy, never meant that the United States would not intervene in "its" sphere of influence in the Western Hemisphere. Nor did it mean that the United States would not be an aggressive player in the world economy. But isolationism did mean that the nation would distance itself politically, diplomatically, and militarily from the affairs of the great powers in Europe and Asia. The nation could best lead by example rather than immersing itself in these and other areas. In keeping with these views, in the wake of the Cold War a large segment of the general public supported a withdrawal from what, for most of the twentieth century, had been a demanding and exceedingly troublesome world beyond the Western Hemisphere.[11]

This appeal was strong, particularly so in light of the nation's traditional fears of open-ended commitments and "entangling alliances." But most policy makers and analysts in the 1990s recognized that the United States, with its absolute and relative strengths in so many categories of power, would find it difficult, if not impossible, to maintain a purely defensive position. After all, a new era of intensifying global economic competition had dawned, computer technologies were uniting the far reaches of the globe, ecological problems were growing more severe, and weapons of mass destruction were falling into unknown hands. For all these reasons, and in view of the risk that a rival power could again cause havoc if the United States let down its guard, policy makers concluded that a revival of American isolationism was out of the question.

An alternative to isolationism was closely related to America's self-image as the "city on a hill." As we have seen, many Americans believed their nation to be an exceptional one whose foreign policy must pursue a moral course, even if other nations did not. It was America's duty to make the world better for its inhabitants and to shape the "new world order" so that the gains from the Cold War could be preserved. Given the human and economic sacrifices borne by the United States during its rise as a great power, America should exploit its hard-fought victory by supporting democracy and improving social welfare throughout the world.

Liberal internationalists, many of whom had embraced Jimmy Carter's "world-order politics" of the late 1970s, believed the time was right for a constructive and activist U.S. role in world politics. The United States was uniquely capable of putting its moral principles into practice. The "peace dividend" stemming from the collapse of the Cold War could be used to ensure the continued spread of democratic institutions, to solve transnational problems such as pollution and the AIDS epi-

11. For an elaboration of this view, see Patrick J. Buchanan, "America First—and Second, and Third," *National Interest* (spring 1990): 77–82. The isolationist view was more fully articulated by Eric A. Nordlinger in *Isolationism Reconfigured: American Foreign Policy for a New Century* (Princeton: Princeton University Press, 1995).

demic, and to hasten the economic growth of developing countries. Furthermore, such a policy could be carried out in conjunction with other states and international organizations. The United Nations, which throughout its history had been plagued by the ideological conflicts of the Cold War, could now realize its potential. And nongovernmental organizations (NGOs) such as Amnesty International, Greenpeace, and Human Rights Watch could play a supporting role in advancing America's humanitarian mission. No other country had this ability to harness global energies for the betterment of humankind.[12]

The third strategy also called for the United States to play an active role in world politics, but one that sought to preserve the gains of the Cold War primarily through the assertion of U.S. power. This so-called "primacy" school presumed that an American withdrawal into an isolationist mode, or an open-ended campaign of global altruism, would tempt potential enemies to challenge America's status as the world's lone superpower. The best hope—for both U.S. security and global stability—was for the United States to prolong its "unipolar moment" by exploiting its military predominance, imposing itself in regional power struggles, and aggressively containing potential challengers. In sum, only through a *pax Americana* could the anarchic world be saved from itself. "A world without U.S. primacy," wrote the political scientist Samuel Huntington, "will be a world with more violence and disorder and less democracy and economic growth than a world where the United States continues to have more influence than any other country in shaping global affairs." [13]

Although few Americans were aware of it, in the aftermath of the Cold War the Bush administration had adopted this goal of maintaining U.S. primacy. "Our strategy must now refocus on precluding the emergence of any future global competitor," the Defense Department concluded in a secret report that was leaked to the press. American leaders "must establish and protect a new order that holds the promise of convincing potential competitors that they need not aspire to a greater role. . . . [The United States] must retain the pre-eminent responsibility for addressing those wrongs which threaten not only our interests, but those of our allies and friends, or which could seriously unsettle international relations." [14] Thus, at least in terms of military doctrine, this

12. This approach, also labeled "cooperative security," was most prominently advanced by Ashton B. Carter, William J. Perry, and John D. Steinbruner in *A New Concept of Cooperative Security* (Washington, D.C.: Brookings, 1992).

13. Samuel Huntington, "Why International Primacy Matters," *International Security* (spring 1993): 83.

14. "Excerpts from Pentagon's Plan: Prevent the Re-emergence of a New Rival," *New York Times*, March 8, 1992, A14.

matter had been settled even before consensus was reached about the country's grand strategy.

The fourth option called for the United States to pursue a middle course in which American leaders would confront and react to problems overseas on a case-by-case basis.[15] This course became attractive to many in light of the country's experience as a world power during the twentieth century. The attempted escape of the United States from great-power politics after World War I only encouraged the fascist challengers to the status quo, who then ignited the Second World War. By contrast, America's escalation of the Cold War from a geopolitical struggle against the Soviet Union into a global anticommunist crusade produced its own calamities. These included the Vietnam War, lost opportunities to drive a wedge between the communist powers, and a host of covert interventions that, once uncovered, created widespread anti-American feelings in the developing world. Thus U.S. leaders should avoid being hamstrung by any single grand strategy, which was unattainable anyway given the complexities of the new era.

As noted, the first two strategies represented well-worn aspects of America's traditional approach to foreign policy. The third and fourth strategies, by contrast, were more consistent with the realist tradition that Americans had long rejected as a vestige of the Old World. By the 1990s, however, realism had become appealing to many Americans because it seemed to eschew moral crusading and frequent interventions in regional disputes of little consequence to the United States. In short, realism sought to restrain America's crusading impulse and shift attention to more mundane considerations common to all states such as self-defense, international stability, and economic growth. The pursuit of these interests did not require American foreign policy to abandon the country's ideals and moral values. They would simply have to be reconciled with the reality of a world of smoldering civil and regional conflicts that could easily reignite in the absence of bipolarity. On these occasions, the United States would have the option either to intervene or to permit the foreign conflicts to run their course. The "national interest" would presumably dictate the appropriate choice.

Each of these strategies for American foreign policy competed for favor in the early 1990s. But, beyond a recognition that some new grand strategy was needed, few policy makers agreed on exactly what that strategy should be. Furthermore, as foreign policy analysts and political leaders quarreled over the proper course, the general public seemed largely indifferent. With the country at peace and facing no serious

15. See Stephen Van Evera, "Why Europe Matters, Why the Third World Doesn't: American Grand Strategy after the Cold War," *Journal of Strategic Studies* (June 1990): 1–51.

threats from overseas, the public wondered, why worry about foreign policy at all?

Into this void came the closely contested presidential campaign of 1992. Bush's popularity ratings were high as he managed the fall of communism, negotiated German unification, and organized a multilateral effort to reverse Iraq's invasion of Kuwait (see Chapter 11). Bush's ratings were so high, in fact, that most top Democratic prospects for the presidency opted not to run. This left the field wide open for Arkansas governor Bill Clinton, who captured the nation's introspective mood and promised to concentrate on domestic problems rather than foreign policy (in fact, he claimed no foreign policy experience). Capitalizing on the broad public support for his domestic platform, Clinton defeated Bush and independent Ross Perot.

Upon taking office, President Clinton reconsidered the basic tenets that had guided American foreign policy in the past. He knew the American people longed to be free of the great-power conflicts that, during the Cold War, had dragged the United States into frequent regional conflicts and close to a cataclysmic showdown with the Soviet Union. Yet Clinton also recognized that the United States had enormous stakes in the rapidly changing international system, particularly in the outcome of political and economic reforms adopted around the world. Thus the president concluded that the United States must play a role in world politics that was commensurate with its stature and resources.

Three other significant assertions by Clinton also shaped his foreign policy. First, the country's primary goal in the mid-1990s would be achievement of strong economic growth, and, more than ever, this growth would depend on a robust global economy. Second, many of the problems neglected during the Cold War—ecological decay, rapid population growth, and political repression (in capitalist as well as communist states), among others—must receive attention in the early 1990s. Finally, international institutions such as the United Nations and World Bank should play a meaningful role in achieving the nation's goals. In his view, these institutions discouraged self-serving behavior among states and encouraged cooperative solutions to problems that crossed political borders. Thus a U.S. policy of "assertive multilateralism" would best serve both the United States and global interests.

Clinton charted a course for American foreign policy that was, by and large, consistent with the spirit of Bush's "new world order" and most closely paralleled the strategy of liberal internationalism. The United States not only would refuse to lapse into isolationism, but also would exploit and extend the advantages that derived from its privileged position in the unipolar world. In so doing, American leaders would look beyond the country's immediate self-interests and collaborate actively with like-minded governments and transnational institutions. By behaving cooperatively and in a nonthreatening manner, the United States would engender trust among the second-tier powers and forestall challenges to its post–Cold War primacy.

CLINTON'S EMBRACE OF 'GEOECONOMICS'

The future of the U.S. economy figured prominently in the foreign policy of President Clinton, who was keenly aware of deep national anxieties about the country's economic outlook. This sense of unease, reflected consistently in public opinion polls, was truly remarkable. One might have expected the American people to feel jubilant after the country's victory in the Cold War. After all, "the Soviet Union wasn't just beaten on points, it was dismembered. Communism wasn't just relegated to second place, it was utterly delegitimized. And all with remarkably little bloodshed." [16]

Many Americans, however, were preoccupied with the country's internal health as smokestack industries fell to foreign competition and the high-technology sector faltered in the 1980s. It was not hard to understand the implications: the loss of America's historic economic vitality meant a decline in the country's status and power in the world. The simultaneous rise of other industrialized states meant a loss of jobs and opportunities to improve America's wage structure and standard of living. As never before, the country had become aware of its dependence on exports for employment and economic growth. Thus with these concerns in mind, Clinton made the U.S. economy the centerpiece of his bid for the presidency. He laid out a program of domestic reforms and emphasized that, without a strong and growing economy accompanied by declining budget and trade deficits, the United States could not afford to play an influential role in world politics.

As Clinton and others acknowledged during this period, the "decline" of the U.S. economy during the Cold War was in many respects inevitable.[17] The overwhelming strength of the U.S. economy just after World War II, when it accounted for half of global production, stemmed from the wreckage of the Western European and Pacific economies. That strength, however, lasted only until these economies recovered; by the early 1990s the U.S. share of global production was about the same as just before World War I. Thus the country's economic predominance

16. Owen Harries, "My So-Called Foreign Policy," *New Republic*, October 10, 1994, 24.

17. Concern over national decline, unusual for a great power but typically American, was reflected in the strong response to Paul Kennedy's *The Rise and Fall of the Great Powers: Economic Change and Military Conflict from 1500 to 2000* (New York: Random House, 1987). It suggested that the United States was on the verge of "imperial overstretch."

after World War II was a historical aberration. Its *relative* economic decline was not a harbinger of economic collapse. On an absolute basis, the U.S. economy continued to grow.

From this perspective, the deep-seated fears of many Americans about the economy were unfounded. Nevertheless, the United States faced many daunting economic problems, some of which were self-inflicted. Many U.S. corporations had become complacent and were unprepared for the sudden burst of overseas competition. In the public sector, the U.S. government had built a military superior to any other and had funded growing social and entitlement programs, but it had refused to approve tax increases to pay for the new programs. Enormous budget deficits were the result. Because almost every part of American society bore some responsibility for the problems confronting the U.S. economy, the president argued that resolution of the problems would require an aggressive national effort. In focusing on domestic problems that went beyond fiscal matters—to include social divisions, deteriorating schools and hospitals, and widespread public cynicism toward government—Clinton confronted a series of issues that had deep historical roots and would thus be difficult to overcome.

THE COURSE OF AMERICA'S ECONOMIC TROUBLES

In the aftermath of World War II, American leaders rarely raised the issue of affordability when responding to a foreign threat or a regional crisis that was of "vital interest" to the United States. A few occasionally asked whether the United States could afford a Marshall Plan or expanded military programs. Yet in the words of President John Kennedy, America could "bear any burden" thought necessary. The nation was wealthy enough, citizens assumed, to support a high standard of living at home and an activist presence abroad.

The 1950s and 1960s were decades of unprecedented economic growth in the United States. Wages rose rapidly as trade unions grew powerful and negotiated sizable annual raises paid by industries that apparently could afford them while still earning handsome profits. In Washington, first Kennedy and then Lyndon Johnson vastly expanded the welfare state in the 1960s in their effort to build a "Great Society." They established new entitlement programs and hiked spending on older programs such as Social Security. Some newer programs, such as Medicare and Medicaid, started small but grew rapidly as their clientele and services multiplied.

The bubble burst for the U.S. economy in the early 1970s. The enormous expense of the Vietnam War combined with the dramatic rise in oil prices produced soaring inflation, interest rates, and unemployment. The economy ceased to grow rapidly as "stagflation" set in. Meanwhile, the war-ravaged industrial economies of Western Europe had recovered and new competitors in East Asia were entering the global marketplace. In the United States, it had become obvious that the country no longer could afford an unlimited supply of both guns and butter. It had to make choices. Richard Nixon first responded in 1971 by suspending the gold standard and ending the U.S. dollar's role as the basis of the world's monetary system. He also extricated the United States from Vietnam, lowered tensions with Moscow, and transformed China from an adversary to an ally, thereby reducing the cost of foreign policy.

In the late 1970s Jimmy Carter tried to revive the economy by reducing military spending and keeping taxes in line with growing entitlement programs. But a second oil shock in 1978–1979 produced a new round of inflation, punctuated by double-digit interest rates and unemployment. The resurgence of Soviet expansionism and anti-American revolutions in Iran and Nicaragua then forced Carter to reverse his military cutbacks. Ronald Reagan accelerated expansion of the military in the early 1980s and simultaneously cut taxes, thereby fulfilling two campaign promises. Yet despite his efforts to reduce domestic spending on social programs and to crack down on "waste, fraud, and mismanagement," government expenditures continued to mount.

Free spending is usually followed by a free fall. The long-term expectation of Reagan's "supply-side" economics was that the U.S. economy, stimulated by lower taxes, would grow as rapidly in the 1980s as it had during the 1950s and 1960s. But the American economy had changed greatly since the 1960s. Although American agriculture was the most bountiful in the world, by the mid-1980s its overseas markets were shrinking. Other industrialized countries and many developing states such as India, China, Thailand, and Indonesia had become food exporters. More important, traditional American industries such as steel and automobile manufacturing were caught off guard as the newly industrialized countries (NICs) produced superior goods at less cost and thereby increased their shares of export markets. Thus in addition to the growing budget deficits recorded in Washington, which surpassed $100 billion in the early 1980s and reached $290 billion by 1992, a string of trade deficits plagued the U.S. economy. The annual trade deficits with Japan and China alone averaged $80 billion by the mid-1990s.

The reasons for the twin deficits of the eighties and early nineties were similar to those for the overall deterioration of American industry: low capital investments in nonmilitary research and development; the preoccupation of corporate leaders with quarterly profits and dividends to the detriment of long-term growth; and the decline of the American labor force, a byproduct of lower educational standards. In addition, there was a lack of corporate enterprise. During the 1980s, capital investment and modernization took second place to merger mania and hostile takeovers. Although this shuffling of paper was profitable financially for a small group of investment bankers and lawyers, it added little to economic growth. As for American consumers, despite the stagnation of their disposable incomes they continued to spend freely, often with credit cards, thereby draining the economy of an essential pool of national savings. Finally, much of American industry was moving overseas, especially to developing countries, where it could gain access to new markets and lower labor costs. Corporate leaders considered these policies rational, but they contributed to growing unemployment in the United States and other problems that could not be attributed simply to economic cycles. It appeared that "structural problems"—a euphemism for intensified global competition—threatened the U.S. economy, and they would not recede on their own.

But not all of the blame for America's economic lethargy could be directed inward. The economies of East Asia and Western Europe were expanding rapidly, and those of Eastern Europe and Latin America also were heating up. As more countries enacted economic reforms based on private enterprise and open markets, they joined the fast-paced competition in export markets and attracted record volumes of private investment. Leading economists heralded the arrival of economic globalization, meaning that a single, integrated worldwide market had replaced national and regional markets. Increasingly, commerce would have no political boundaries; firms would compete not only with others within their country but also with those based overseas. A typical corporation in the "globalized" economy would have its headquarters in the "home" country but engage in research and development, production, marketing, and sales all over the world. "There is coming to be no such thing as an American corporation or an American industry," wrote the economist Robert Reich, who became secretary of labor in the Clinton administration. "The American economy is but a region of the global economy." [18]

Some observers argued that economic globalization would gradually weaken the authority, if not the sovereignty, of nation-states. Even though just such an outcome was eagerly sought by early U.S. leaders who had longed for a world dominated by economic rather than political competition, many contemporary Americans worried that the United States would lose control of its own destiny if global economic forces were truly allowed to dominate. Suddenly, the social and economic protections afforded by the U.S. government seemed at risk, along with the

18. Robert B. Reich, *The Work of Nations: Preparing Ourselves for 21st Century Capitalism* (New York: Knopf, 1991), 243.

country's political clout. As a result, many Americans looked to Washington for relief from the transformed world the United States had played a major role in creating.

RESPONSES BY THE CLINTON ADMINISTRATION

The superior production capacity of the United States underwrote its victory in World War II and its successful Cold War campaign against the Soviet Union. But economic stagnation in the 1980s and early 1990s raised the critical question of whether the economy could still support a foreign policy that maintained 300,000 U.S. soldiers in Western Europe, defended Japan and South Korea, policed the Persian Gulf and the Middle East, and retained the traditional sphere of influence in Latin America. Could the United States do all this while supporting ever-growing domestic programs and keeping up with interest payments on the national debt, the fastest-growing area of federal spending?

Upon taking office, Clinton declared that for America to compete more effectively with the outside world the U.S. government would have to "reinvest" in its domestic base—that is, take a more active role in reforming the national health care system, improving the quality of American schools, and restoring the country's basic infrastructure such as roads and bridges. Furthermore, he sought to ease the long-standing antagonism between the federal government and many large industries. Toward this end, the president met in 1993 with leaders from the U.S. automobile industry and proclaimed a "new partnership" between the federal government and auto makers. These two groups would act as allies rather than adversaries in promoting economic growth, much as their counterparts had done in Japan. In promoting his own version of "industrial policy," Clinton was prepared to play by many of the same rules as his competitors.

The president also was determined to see U.S. economic relations assume the same institutional prominence as its diplomatic and military relations. Clinton elevated the status of the U.S. trade representative and gave his secretaries of the Treasury (Lloyd Bentsen), commerce (Ron Brown), and labor (Robert Reich) unprecedented power to shape the nation's foreign policy. He also created a National Economic Council to coordinate economic relations and serve as a counterpart to the National Security Council (NSC). Even the NSC, established early in the Cold War, was expanded to include top economic advisers.

Among Clinton's other priorities in foreign economic policy was expansion of the U.S. role in regional trading blocs. The early 1990s witnessed a wave of regional economic integration, much of it based on the success of the European Union, which had linked its member states together in a single economic market (see Chapter 12). By removing barriers to trade and investment within the blocs, by encouraging the movement of workers and services across national borders, and by unifying health and safety regulations, these states hoped to increase economic efficiency and raise overall levels of production.

The first such achievement for the United States was the passage in 1993 of the North American Free Trade Agreement (NAFTA). Devised and negotiated by the Bush administration, NAFTA was aimed at reducing or eliminating the tariffs that had limited trade among the United States, Canada, and Mexico. American critics of NAFTA charged that it would encourage U.S. manufacturers to relocate their factories in Mexico, where labor was far cheaper, thereby crippling American firms and their surrounding communities. Others claimed NAFTA would reward Mexico's one-party government for its longtime neglect of its impoverished population. NAFTA supporters countered that in Mexico the treaty would stimulate economic growth, relieve poverty, and move the country toward democracy, all while creating new markets for American goods. They further argued that trade with Canada, the largest export market for the United States, had been severely limited by cross-border restrictions. Finally, they proclaimed NAFTA to be consistent with the laissez-faire principles of free markets that the United States had long espoused. In the end, the pro-NAFTA forces prevailed; the treaty passed narrowly in Congress and went into effect on the first day of 1994.

The United States also became actively involved in a second, but more loosely knit, regional organization known as Asia-Pacific Economic Cooperation (APEC). The Pacific market had emerged as the most dynamic area of economic exchange for the United States; it was growing faster and producing more jobs than Europe. According to the president, Asian export markets had become the "lifeblood" of U.S. economic growth. Political divisions ran deep among APEC members, however, thereby limiting progress on economic reforms. Nevertheless, the organization provided potential avenues for political as well as economic reforms, and, significantly, leaders of the Pacific region's most powerful states—including the United States, Japan, China, and Russia—became enthusiastic supporters of APEC.[19]

Overall, this move toward regional integration in global trade relations both resulted from and contributed to the market-driven world economy sought by the United States throughout its history. A further

19. Economic integration already had moved forward among Asian states in 1992, when Brunei, Indonesia, Malaysia, the Philippines, Singapore, and Thailand—all members of the Association of Southeast Asian Nations (ASEAN)—committed themselves to creating a free trade area by 2003. In addition, several countries in South America formed an economic alliance known as Mercosur that sought to rival the European, North American, and Asian blocs.

step in this direction was taken late in 1994 when Congress ratified the latest General Agreement on Tariffs and Trade (GATT), approved by most other member states earlier that year. The agreement reduced tariffs on most products sold overseas and was hailed by Clinton as the "largest tax cut in world history." Passage of GATT, which had seemed assured, briefly was placed in doubt after several members of Congress criticized its provisions for a World Trade Organization (WTO) to monitor trade practices and enforce compliance. The criticisms were silenced, however, after Clinton assured Congress that the United States would not surrender its sovereign authority to the WTO. In fact, the United States would be in a strong position to use the WTO as a vehicle to promote its own economic agenda. After Clinton's Republican rivals finally endorsed the agreement, the latest GATT accord was ratified easily and the WTO became a fixture of world politics.

EAST ASIA'S ECONOMIC 'MIRACLE'

Major challengers of the United States in the rapidly integrating global economy were the countries of East Asia. Led by Japan and the "four tigers"—Hong Kong, Singapore, South Korea, and Taiwan—these newly industrialized countries (NICs) enjoyed the world's most rapid rates of economic growth in the 1980s and early 1990s. Unlike the developing countries in Latin America and Africa that had sought to insulate themselves from the capitalist "core" in the United States and Western Europe, the NICs plunged into global trading markets, welcomed foreign investments, and aggressively located their own manufacturing firms in Western countries. Between 1965 and 1990, Japan and the four tigers increased their share of world trade from 7 percent to 16 percent, nearly reaching the share of global trade attained by all the other developing countries combined.[20] In addition, East Asia attracted nearly all of the private investments that were flowing from industrialized states to developing regions.

The East Asian states became more competitive in large measure by violating the terms of the "liberal international economic order" promoted by the United States under the Bretton Woods regime (see Chapter 3). Japan, in particular, was widely viewed as a culprit given its status as a role model and "engine of growth" for the other NICs, many of which hoped to repeat Japan's success story. Since the 1950s, the Japanese government had actively supported the expansion of its key industries, particularly automobiles and consumer electronics, by providing them with generous tax breaks, research funding, and protection from

20. World Bank, *The East Asian Miracle: Economic Growth and Public Policy* (New York: Oxford University Press, 1993), 38.

foreign competitors. This collusion between Japan's public and private sectors was epitomized by the Japanese Ministry for International Trade and Industry (MITI), which included a small group of top government and corporate leaders.[21] Within MITI, this small group of leaders decided which manufactured goods Japan would mass produce for export, where the exports would be targeted, and how Japanese industries could be protected from foreign competition. These practices incited charges of *neomercantilism* from the United States, Japan's primary export market, which was unable to sell its products in Tokyo at competitive prices. Relations between the two countries suffered as a result, especially after the Cold War when Japan's strategic role as an East Asian bulwark of containment had lapsed. As Japan annually recorded trade surpluses over the United States in excess of $40 billion, and as the United States struggled with chronic trade deficits and a soaring national debt, many Americans suggested that Tokyo's days as a "free rider" should end.

The East Asian version of industrial policy was troubling to American leaders and workers, who feared that the combination of lower wages, government subsidies, and import restrictions would damage American industries. These critics, however, conveniently overlooked the fact that the U.S. government had engaged in many of the same practices during its rise as a regional and then global economic power. Indeed, such a strategy was openly advocated in the country's earliest years by Alexander Hamilton, the first secretary of the Treasury, who believed America's "infant industries" should be carefully protected through government controls. The critics also forgot that the United States had condoned the protectionist practices of many East Asian governments during the Cold War because those governments served as essential agents of the U.S.-led anticommunist crusade. If "cheating" in the global marketplace was required to strengthen East Asia from the appeals of communism, that was the price the United States was willing to pay. Therefore, just as foreign leaders' warnings of communist insurgencies prompted the United States to look the other way while they imposed authoritarian rule, the same kinds of warnings produced U.S. deference on economic matters.

To those who felt threatened by the East Asian economic "miracle" in the aftermath of the Cold War, all of this was beside the point. Not only did the policies of the East Asian governments violate the sacrosanct American creed of free markets, they also were widely seen as taking jobs away from American workers and threatening the country's economic

21. See Chalmers Johnson, *MITI and the Japanese Miracle: The Growth of Industrial Policy, 1925–1975* (Palo Alto: Stanford University Press, 1982). Also see Jeffrey A. Hart, *Rival Capitalists: International Competitiveness in the United States, Japan, and Western Europe* (Ithaca: Cornell University Press, 1992), chap. 2.

prosperity. The critics' complaints demonstrated that the new era of geoeconomics often would depart from the "harmony of interests" envisioned by the eighteenth-century Scottish economist Adam Smith. Territorial disputes, ideological conflicts, and political power struggles remained facts of life in a world still dominated by nation-states. Thus American leaders, with the Cold War winding down, stepped up their efforts to retaliate against unfair competitors, primarily those in East Asia. Under the 1988 Omnibus Trade and Competitiveness Act, the president was required to identify the most flagrant violators and provide means for retaliation. Although the United States rarely employed the act and instead settled for a system of "managed trade" with Japan, the legislation conveyed a strong message that America's patience was wearing thin.

These economic tensions also extended to U.S. relations with China, one of the world's fastest-growing economies. Under Deng Xiaoping, who had replaced Mao Zedong in 1978, China's government remained firmly in the grip of the Communist Party. Deng, however, had departed from Mao's command economy. First, he opened up Chinese agriculture to private farms that could earn profits from surplus production. Second, Deng allowed private industries, funded largely by foreign investment, to flourish in the numerous "enterprise zones" created along China's coastline. Taking advantage of the country's massive labor pool, Deng oversaw a rapid economic expansion in which China's gross national product grew at an average rate of nearly 10 percent in the 1980s and early 1990s.

The contrast between Deng's reforms and those of Mikhail Gorbachev in the Soviet Union during the 1980s was revealing. Gorbachev had sought to reform the ossified Soviet political system through *glasnost* and *perestroika,* but he had kept the country's command economy largely intact. Deng, by contrast, opened and greatly expanded the Chinese economy while refusing to consider meaningful political reforms. In the end, Gorbachev's politically based strategy proved suicidal, while Deng's economic strategy left its communist government with ample power to prevent "counter-revolution." The implications were clear: whereas effective economic reforms could improve living conditions in the absence of democratic rule, political reforms combined with economic stagnation invited popular backlash and jeopardized the state's very existence.

Even after Richard Nixon's recognition of the communist government in Beijing, the United States frequently condemned China's repressive system of rule and systematic violations of human rights, particularly the crackdown on pro-democracy activists during and after the 1989 Tiananmen Square uprising. American leaders after the Nixon years tried to link China's most-favored nation (MFN) trade status, which provided it with open access to American consumers, to its progress in respecting human rights. But officials in Beijing insisted that their domestic behavior would not be tailored to satisfy Americans. Their defiance grew only stronger as the Chinese economy boomed in the early 1990s. Clinton, who was well aware of the economic value of Sino-American trade, was trapped by American policy.

When push finally came to shove, Clinton backed down on his political demands and announced in 1994 that human rights no longer would be linked directly to China's MFN status. The carrot of continuing trade would better elicit reforms in China than the stick of trade sanctions, asserted Clinton. But China's treatment of its political dissidents became even harsher after Clinton's "engagement" policy (described in the next section) was announced. The policy remained a sore point for congressional critics, human rights groups, and even the State Department, which through its annual survey of human rights kept up a steady barrage of criticism toward China. But neither these criticisms nor the continuing trade imbalances that favored China deterred Clinton from maintaining closer economic ties with Beijing.

PROMOTING DEMOCRACY AND SUSTAINABLE DEVELOPMENT

By the time the Cold War collapsed, urgent global problems such as environmental decay, rapid population growth, and the growing gap between rich and poor were demanding immediate attention. Attempts to address these problems and the effort to consolidate global democratic reforms became part of a distinct post–Cold War global agenda. Clinton, who as a presidential candidate called for greater attention to global problems along with a heightened emphasis on economic issues, seized on these aspects of "low politics" once in office. His variant of liberal internationalism recalled John Kennedy's Alliance for Progress and Jimmy Carter's world-order politics, both of which emphasized cooperative North-South relations, human rights, and the interdependence of all countries in the modern world. Now, though, this approach would be applied for the first time in the absence of superpower tensions.

A POLICY OF DEMOCRATIC 'ENLARGEMENT'

Long before Clinton took office, the United States had sought to promote the expansion of democratic rule overseas. The roots of this longtime American quest can be traced to Thomas Jefferson's "empire of liberty," to the widespread presumption of America's "manifest destiny," and to Woodrow Wilson's pledge to make the U.S. role in World War I a mission "for democracy, for the right of those who submit to authority to have a voice in their own government, for the rights and liberties of small nations. . . . and to make the world itself free." The renewal of this democratic crusade after the collapse of the Soviet Union was, then, merely the continuation of an existing practice. "No national security issue is more urgent, nowhere is our country's imperative more clear," candidate Clinton declared in 1992. "I believe it is time for America to lead a global alliance for democracy as united and steadfast as the global alliance that defeated communism." [22]

The Clinton administration's pledge to emphasize political reforms not only extended a long national tradition of promoting democracy, but also recognized undeniable political trends that had been under way for a decade. By the time of Clinton's election, more countries than ever had adopted representative governments, permitted the formation of multiple political parties, established the rule of law, and allowed for basic political and civil rights. Competitive elections were held for the first time across Latin America during the Reagan and Bush years and throughout Eastern Europe after the Cold War. Although most African governments remained under autocratic control, South Africa took a giant step toward democracy by dismantling its racist system of apartheid and permitting free elections in April 1994. The rise to power of Nelson Mandela, who had spent much of his life in South African prisons, was just one more symbol of the global reach of democracy.

It was in this environment that the Clinton administration sought to make the promotion of democracy the centerpiece of its foreign policy. Echoing George Kennan, the intellectual founder of containment, Clinton national security adviser Anthony Lake asserted in 1993:

> The successor to a doctrine of containment must be a strategy of enlargement—enlargement of the world's free community. . . . We must counter the aggression—and support the liberalization—of states hostile to democracy. . . . The United States will seek to isolate [non-democratic states] diplomatically, militarily, economically and technologically.[23]

Secretary of State Warren Christopher cited U.S. involvement in Eastern Europe, southern Africa, the Middle East, and Latin America as evidence of the administration's determination to match its words with deeds. Commitments of Western aid to Russia and its neighbors—at a time when public support for U.S. foreign aid had descended to record lows—were viewed as a critical component of this effort. Administration officials also pointed out that the United States, which had always

22. Bill Clinton, "A Strategy for Foreign Policy," *Vital Speeches of the Day,* May 1, 1992, 421.

23. Anthony Lake, "From Containment to Enlargement," Department of State Dispatch, September 27, 1993, 658–664.

portrayed itself as the world's "beacon of democracy," could not stand by while countries sought to consolidate democratic institutions in the face of internal upheaval. Driven by this logic, the Clinton White House proceeded to identify "rogue states"—including Cuba, Iran, Iraq, Libya, and North Korea, among others—which it felt threatened the foundations of democratic rule, and then sought to punish them through economic sanctions, diplomatic exclusion, and occasional military coercion. America's allies were expected to follow suit.

The Clinton administration faced an uphill battle, however, in arousing public and congressional support for its democratization campaign. Many Americans questioned whether the effort was actually vital to U.S. security and economic interests. Furthermore, the targets of the democratization strategy were scattered throughout the world, often in remote areas with little or no tradition of representative government. Already, internal revolts had upended democratic regimes in many countries, which then succumbed to ethnic rivalries and military rule. In most of the countries that maintained authoritarian rule through their armed forces, elections were largely a sideshow. Finally, in several Eastern European countries many former communists were being elected to leadership positions, demonstrating that the ballot box was no guarantee that leaders favorable to the United States would come to power.

Clinton also confronted charges that the United States was observing double standards in its most recent campaign of democratization. Violations of human rights by the Chinese government were subordinated to the primary goal of expanded economic ties. Meanwhile, Saudi Arabia and Egypt, loyal friends of the United States—one the source of oil, the other a strong supporter of Arab-Israeli peace—were ruled by repressive governments. And Turkey, which was engaged in a brutal crackdown of its Kurdish minority, continued to receive generous allotments of U.S. military aid, not to mention full partnership in NATO. But the United States would not be denied its self-appointed democratic mission in its own way. After all, it had succeeded in defeating fascism during World War II and the world's most powerful communist state in the Cold War—campaigns not undertaken merely to resurrect a stable balance of power but also to liberate world politics from the scourge of tyranny. In this context, obstacles to democratization in the more benign setting of the 1990s did not appear insurmountable, and occasional exceptions by the United States would not significantly undercut the general policy of democratic enlargement.

SUPPORT FOR SUSTAINABLE DEVELOPMENT

Beyond his policy to support democracy, Clinton embraced the global effort to promote "sustainable development" in the developing countries. Sustainable development was a loosely knit concept that combined political reforms, environmental protection, population control, and market-based economic growth. Chronic problems in developing countries, where most of the world's people lived and where population growth was most rapid, could no longer be ignored by the industrialized nations. Their problems were becoming transnational in scope, spilling into neighboring countries and threatening global security. Solving these problems, Clinton proclaimed, would require cooperative action and sacrifice on an equally universal scale—and strong leadership by the United States.

Like the democratization policy, plans to promote sustainable development preceded Clinton's arrival in office, and they originated from many sources outside the United States. The impetus for sustainable development came in June 1992 during the UN Conference on Environment and Development, at the time the largest single gathering of world leaders in history. *Agenda 21,* the concluding statement of the "Earth Summit," constituted a call to arms to pursue this goal. The eight hundred-page manifesto recommended annual spending of more than $125 billion in dozens of areas such as pollution control, education, health care, poverty relief, technology transfer, and the empowerment of women. According to the preamble to *Agenda 21,* "peace, development, and environmental protection are interdependent and indivisible."[24]

Many of these provisions had been rejected earlier by President Bush, who had been more concerned about his fading reelection prospects in the summer of 1992 and virtually had to be dragged to the Earth Summit. Once there, Bush provoked worldwide criticism by refusing to sign the Biodiversity Convention, designed to protect woodlands and habitat that were hard-hit by accelerating development. Bush believed the treaty unfairly restricted the access of American companies to the tropical forests of Latin America and Asia and imposed excessive demands (more than $200 million initially) on wealthy countries to aid equatorial states that would lose revenue if development halted in these sensitive areas. The United States stood alone in opposing the treaty, which was approved by 153 other governments. Back on the campaign trail, Bush's defiance of the Earth Summit and the estrangement of the United States from the revived environmental movement provided strong ammunition for Clinton, who made the unpopular U.S. stance one of the few foreign policy issues of his campaign.

Once elected, Clinton adopted *Agenda 21* as a prototype for his environmental proposals of 1993 and 1994. Vice President Al Gore, a self-

24. United Nations Conference on Environment and Development, *Agenda 21* (New York: United Nations, 1992).

proclaimed environmentalist, was designated to oversee the effort.[25] In the State Department a new position was created—under secretary of state for global affairs—symbolizing the administration's concern for these issues. Clinton also signed the Biodiversity Convention and restored funding for the UN Population Fund, which had been suspended by Bush and Reagan. In 1994 the Clinton administration set forth its "Strategies for Sustainable Development" which proposed multilateral efforts in six areas: protecting the environment, stabilizing world population growth, protecting human health, providing humanitarian assistance, encouraging economic growth, and "building democracy." [26] In all these areas the United States pledged to work closely with the UN and other international organizations, as well as a growing number of private groups. These programs were brought together in the Peace, Prosperity, and Democracy Act of 1994, a wide-ranging bill supported by Clinton and a Congress then dominated by the Democratic Party.

For a brief time, it appeared that Clinton's "pragmatic neo-Wilsonian" foreign policy, as it was described by Anthony Lake, would be enacted into law. But this was not to be. Clinton's window of opportunity slammed shut in November 1994 after midterm congressional elections reversed the political tide and brought an entirely different agenda to Washington.

DOMESTIC CHALLENGES TO CLINTON'S FOREIGN POLICY

It was not upheavals abroad that provoked the challenge to Clinton's foreign policy in the second half of his first term. The backlash began at home, within the U.S. government, for reasons only marginally related to foreign policy. Despite the administration's progress in reducing the federal deficit and stimulating economic growth, public opinion polls suggested widespread distrust of the federal government. The extremism of regional militia groups served as a potent expression of growing public disenchantment with "business as usual" in Washington. On another and more personal level, this sentiment was directed toward Clinton himself. Beset by scrutiny of his role in the Whitewater land development venture while governor of Arkansas, charges of sexual harassment, and other "character issues," Clinton was viewed with skepticism by the general public and many members of Congress.

25. Gore outlined his environmental views in *Earth in the Balance: Ecology and the Human Spirit* (New York: Plume, 1993).

26. U.S. Agency for International Development, *Strategies for Sustainable Development* (Washington, D.C.: Department of State, 1994), 4.

IMPACT AND INFLUENCE

JESSE HELMS

The conventional wisdom "politics stops at the water's edge" certainly did not apply to American foreign policy after November 1994, when the Republican Party captured control of Congress. The new congressional leaders quickly challenged President Bill Clinton, a Democrat, on many aspects of his foreign policy, leading to bitter policy debates and reversals.

Sen. Jesse Helms, chairman of the Senate Foreign Relations Committee, aggressively opposed Clinton's foreign policy of liberal internationalism. A staunch conservative from North Carolina, Helms demanded a lower American profile in world politics. He then used his personal clout—along with Congress's many constitutional powers—in overseeing deep cuts in the U.S. foreign aid budget, curbing U.S. involvement in the United Nations, imposing new sanctions against Cuba, and advocating the rejection of several arms control treaties. Meanwhile, Helms demanded increases in military spending and an assertive stance toward Russia, China, and other foreign powers. His self-proclaimed "hard-ball" political tactics deepened the divisions between Congress and the White House that prevented the United States from facing the post–Cold War world with a united front.

This widespread distrust was accompanied by the revival of the Republican Party in many state governments, particularly in the South, where a historic realignment in state legislatures had been under way for more than a decade. While many observers expected Republican Party gains in the midterm elections, few predicted that the elections of 1994 would produce a historic resurgence of the Republican Party—its first claim to majority status in both houses of Congress since 1954. The Republicans, who held just 176 of the 435 House seats before the elections, won 231 seats to capture majority control. On the Senate side, the Republican Party increased its share from 43 to 52 of the 100 seats—a solid, if not veto-proof, majority. Thus the remainder of Clinton's first term would feature a reversal of the pattern of divided government experienced by Reagan and Bush: now a *Republican* Congress would offset a *Democratic* White House.

Republican leaders in Congress favored a foreign policy that departed from Clinton's in several respects. In general, they sought a more modest role for the United States because the Soviet threat had disappeared and because no other power comparable to the Soviet Union had emerged in its absence. In the Republican view, American policy should be based on tangible self-interests rather than ambiguous global concerns and on strong military defenses rather than on foreign aid and a reliance on international organizations. Congressional Republicans followed the lead of Sen. Jesse Helms, an outspoken critic of Clinton's foreign policy who became chairman of the powerful Senate Foreign Relations Committee in January 1995. Within five months, Helms introduced legislation for a "new" State Department that included major cutbacks in foreign affairs spending, particularly foreign aid, which Helms charged was being poured down a "rathole" overseas. Helms and his Republican allies proposed increased spending on the U.S. military as a more appropriate means to achieve the country's goals in the post–Cold War world.

By the end of 1995 Helms was holding much of U.S. foreign policy hostage, including nearly four hundred foreign service promotions, thirty ambassadorial nominations, more than a dozen treaties and international agreements, and many daily functions of the State Department. Moreover, as Helms made clear, until Clinton agreed to the Republicans' demands to restructure the State Department, the Foreign Relations Committee would remain recessed indefinitely and many routine operations of U.S. foreign policy would cease. As a result, the State Department had to furlough many of its Washington-based staffers and temporarily halt processing the nearly thirty thousand visa applications received daily. The U.S. government stopped paying utility bills at many foreign embassies, and the funding needed to operate the State Department's computer and cable services was suspended. "The day-to-day foreign policy business on Capitol Hill has ground to a halt," reported the *New York Times*. [27]

27. Elaine Sciolino, "Awaiting Call, Helms Puts Foreign Policy on Hold," *New York Times*, September 23, 1995, 1A.

The showdown between the White House and Congress not only reflected national ambivalence about America's post–Cold War role; it also illustrated the limitations imposed on any president's foreign policy powers when the United States is not at war or faced with a military crisis. Congress generally holds sway in more tranquil periods, primarily through its "power of the purse" and its role in ratifying treaties. In these times, it is not only the balance of power overseas, but also the balance of power *within* the U.S. government that becomes a driving force in its foreign policy. From the standpoint of foreign diplomats, the United States becomes a two-headed monster whenever the two political parties control separate branches of government. The president may conduct state visits, command the armed forces, and assume other functions of a head of state, but presidential promises must always be taken with a grain of salt. Treaties negotiated with the United States are signed with the knowledge that Congress may likely tear them up. And in the first term of the Clinton administration promises to "enlarge" the sphere of democracy and resolve global problems were hollow if funds were not provided to put the promises into practice.

Shaken by the Republican victories of November 1994, Clinton placed his "neo-Wilsonian" foreign policy on the back burner. What little fervor he had demonstrated previously—most of the real passion for enlargement and sustainable development had come from his subordinates—was all but extinguished after the elections. Thus when the Republican Congress demanded the ouster of UN Secretary General Boutros Boutros-Ghali of Egypt, Clinton complied. When Congress expressed doubts about the 1993 Chemical Weapons Convention, which had been signed by dozens of other governments, Clinton removed the treaty from the table. And when Congress demanded a larger defense budget than was requested by the Joint Chiefs of Staff, along with deep cuts in foreign aid that greatly reduced the U.S. contribution to sustainable development, Clinton again conceded. Rarely in American history had a president so passively relinquished his control over American foreign policy.

The growing schism between Clinton and Congress revealed that the debate over America's role in the post–Cold War world was far from resolved. Both aspects of the American style of foreign policy—detachment from the "outside world" and moral crusading—found expression in the debate and in the country's actions throughout the world. Meanwhile, the military doctrine of global primacy remained in place as U.S. armed forces were repeatedly, but selectively, sent into battle to support the country's declared goals. Taken together, these actions suggested that, of the four competing grand strategies summarized earlier in this chapter—renewed isolationism, liberal internationalism, global primacy, and selective engagement—a peculiar course was ultimately adopted: all of the above. It was not surprising, then, that the United States became widely viewed as an erratic and unpredictable power in the heyday of its "unipolar moment."

A Somali woman runs across a field as U.S. Army helicopters land outside the town of Afgoi, where armed bandits had prevented the delivery of food aid. The U.S. mission in Somalia, aimed at restoring political order, was later abandoned after U.S. and UN troops were killed in fighting between rival militias.

CHAPTER ELEVEN

Old Tensions in a New Order

The mid-1990s in the United States saw the euphoria surrounding the end of the Cold War quickly succumb to partisan bickering and a congressional assault on President Bill Clinton's leadership. Overseas, an outbreak of conflicts raised doubts about the president's global ambitions. Ethnic and religious disputes sparked violence across the developing world, challenging ruling elites and threatening regional power balances. Meanwhile, the jockeying continued among the great powers for power and strategic advantage. Western leaders expressed concerns about the sluggish reform movement in Russia, lest the country slip back into its old dictatorial ways and expansionism. They also grew increasingly anxious about China's growing military strength and assertiveness after the Sino-American partnership, which in large measure was directed against the Soviet Union, became null and void after the Cold War.

Taken together, these problems demanded a coherent response by the United States, whose historic vision of a more democratic and peaceful world was under assault. But such a response became less likely amid the political war being waged between Clinton and Congress. Their struggle, which culminated in Clinton's impeachment by the House of Representatives in December 1998, boosted the level of public cynicism to record levels, infuriated U.S. allies who looked to Washington for leadership, and tempted potential adversaries to exploit America's internal divisions.

As conflicts erupted in many parts of the developing world and in Europe, where renewed fighting broke out in the Balkan peninsula and Russia's reforms faced unending challenges (see Chapter 12), U.S. leaders were forced to make difficult choices about their ability—and willingness—to intervene in the regional disputes, many of which dated back centuries. Their decisions played a vital, if not decisive, role in the outcome of the conflicts. More important, the responses by the United States signaled to the rest of the world how America would handle its responsibilities as the world's preeminent power.

SOURCES OF GLOBAL FRAGMENTATION

Among those who felt the "end of history" was at hand after the Cold War, the defining trend in world politics was the technological revolution that was rapidly drawing the far reaches of the world closer together. This process of global *integration,* described earlier, was welcomed for several reasons: world leaders would increasingly recognize and solve problems that crossed national boundaries; integration would discourage self-serving and nationalistic behavior; nongovernmental organizations would mobilize global public opinion and highlight human rights and environmental concerns; economic globalization would increase prosperity; and the spread of democratic rule would reduce the likelihood of war.

It was not long, however, before the equal but opposite forces of global *fragmentation* raised doubts about these rosy scenarios. The reason: the shift in the global balance of power had produced a volatile and violent international order.[1] Bipolarity had been relatively stable because of its very simplicity. Watching each other constantly, the superpowers maintained the balance, always aware of the danger of nuclear war and its suicidal potential. Consequently, there was no third world war; after the 1962 Cuban missile crisis there were no comparable crises between the superpowers; and despite tensions, Europe experienced the longest period of peace in the twentieth century. All of this changed with the

1. See Benjamin Barber, *Jihad vs. McWorld: How Globalism and Tribalism Are Reshaping the World* (New York: Times Books, 1995), chaps. 10–14.

collapse of the Soviet Union, leading some analysts to express nostalgia for the Cold War.[2]

The breakdown of bipolarity wrought instability and encouraged fragmentation in three distinct ways. First, the retreat of the Soviet Union revived the nationalist, ethnic, and religious tensions that had accompanied the breakup of the Austro-Hungarian, Russian, and Ottoman (Turkish) empires after World War I but that were kept largely in check during the Cold War. The breakup of the Soviet Union into fifteen republics produced armed clashes between Armenia and Azerbaijan, a war of secession in the Russian province of Chechnya, civil war in Tajikistan, and new tensions between Russia and its formidable neighbors in China and India. The end of communist rule in Yugoslavia sparked a new and ghastly round of religious warfare. In fact, the reemergence of the fault lines separating ethnic and religious groups in many parts of the world suggested that a "clash of civilizations" was imminent.[3]

A second consequence was that aspirants to regional hegemony felt free to pursue their aggressive designs. It was no longer the case that each superpower, dominant in its own sphere of influence, could restrain its clients and prevent local conflicts. Expansionist middle powers were now free to fill the void left by the superpowers. Iraq's invasion of Kuwait in 1990, described later in this chapter, was unthinkable so long as the Soviet Union remained a key regional player that wished to avoid a confrontation with the United States. Similarly, the resurgence of ethnic conflict across Africa and the escalation of tensions between India and Pakistan coincided with the withdrawal of the great powers.

Finally, the fragmented world order tested the resilience of U.S. alliances. Organized to counter the power of the Soviet Union and China, these alliances gave priority to common interests in collective security. With the Cold War over, NATO's mission became unclear as other security arrangements were devised for the European Union. The fears of U.S. leaders that NATO would become obsolete explained much of their enthusiasm for its eastward expansion. Meanwhile, the web of multilateral alliances created by the United States across the Pacific Ocean had long ceased to exist in any meaningful sense, and the durability of its bilateral ties to several nations in East Asia was thrown into question. The United States reaffirmed its regional presence by extending its security pact with Japan in 1996 and keeping its troops in South Korea. But it was doubtful the emerging powers of the Pacific Rim would indefinitely accept their status as de facto protectorates of the United States.

2. See John Mearsheimer, "Why We Will Soon Miss the Cold War," *Atlantic Monthly,* August 1990, 33–50.

3. Samuel Huntington, "The Clash of Civilizations?" *Foreign Affairs* (summer 1993): 22–49.

The contradictory forces of global integration and fragmentation had far deeper roots than the Cold War and its aftermath.[4] Advances in transportation and communication had been making the world "smaller" for centuries. By the same token, the outbreak of civil wars was a logical result of the spread of democracy and its calls for self-determination, which first became a strong political force during the Enlightenment era of the eighteenth century. The end of the Cold War, however, ruptured the geopolitical basis for world order and allowed both forces to find full expression.

For James Woolsey, Clinton's first director of central intelligence, all of this boiled down to a simple metaphor: although the Soviet "dragon" had been slain, America now existed in a "jungle filled with a bewildering variety of poisonous snakes."[5] This newer environment was potentially menacing to the United States in several ways. While the "snakes" were just as deadly, they were more numerous and difficult to identity. In practical terms, then, the United States had to concern itself not only with other major powers, but also with the behavior of the terrorist groups, drug cartels, organized crime syndicates, and black market weapons dealers who threatened the world of the early 1990s. In other words, the United States would have to guard itself against threats that could take several forms and come from any direction.

WAR AND PEACE IN THE MIDDLE EAST

The first trouble spot to disrupt the "new world order" was the Middle East. Ample and inexpensive oil flows from the Persian Gulf had powered the twentieth century's industrial revolution. But after the Arab members of the Organization of Petroleum Exporting Countries (OPEC) embargoed oil shipments to the United States in 1973 and provoked a second oil shock in 1978, the West recognized all too well its dependence on Middle East oil and its vulnerability to future disruptions of oil flows. In the 1990s the absence of a superpower rivalry left a power vacuum in the Middle East that one regional leader, Iraq's Saddam Hussein, attempted to fill. Saddam's bid for hegemony effectively produced the first post–Cold War world crisis. Meanwhile, the peace process between Israel and its Arab neighbors inched forward between spasms of violence and political crisis.

4. See John Lewis Gaddis, "Toward the Post–Cold War World," *Foreign Affairs* (spring 1991): 102–122.
5. Quoted in Loch Johnson, "Reinventing the CIA," in *U.S. Foreign Policy after the Cold War*, ed. Randall B. Ripley and James M. Lindsay. (Pittsburgh: University of Pittsburgh Press, 1997), 135.

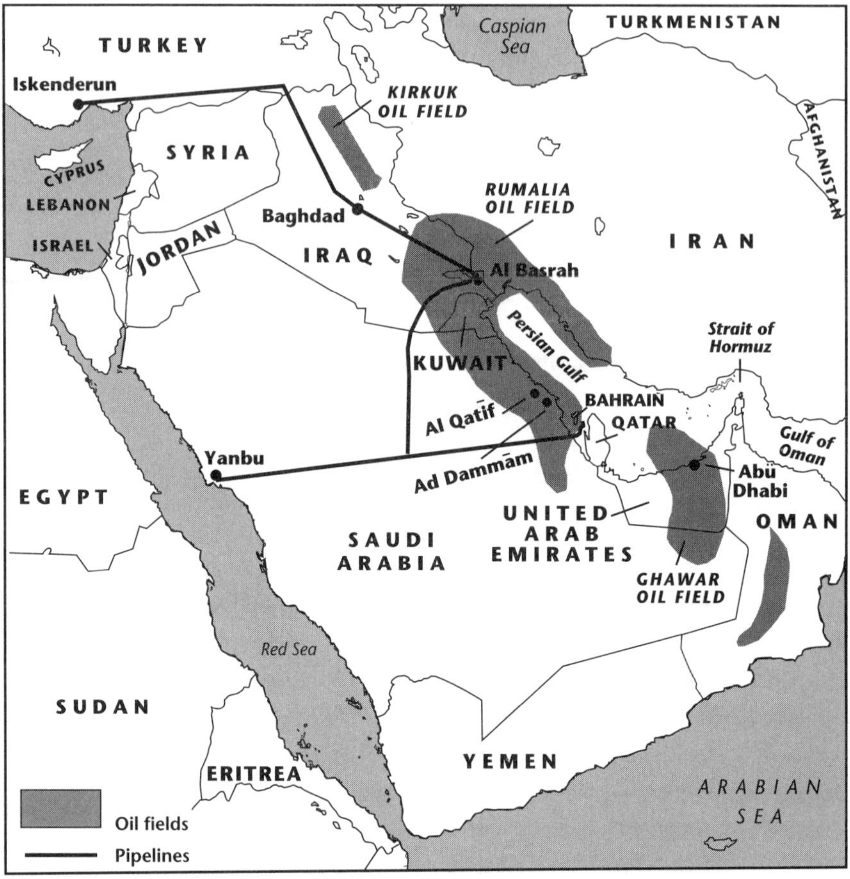

THE PERSIAN GULF, WITH KEY OIL FIELDS AND PIPELINES

IRAQ'S CHALLENGE IN THE PERSIAN GULF

The year 1990 found Saddam Hussein at least $80 billion in debt from his eight-year war with Iran and unable to compel OPEC to cut its production levels, thereby forcing oil prices higher and replenishing his treasury, Taking matters into his own hands, on August 2, 1990, Saddam ordered his battle-tested army to invade his oil-rich neighbor, the emirate of Kuwait. The Iraqi army quickly overran the largely undefended Kuwaiti capital. With his troops poised on the border of Saudi Arabia and many Arab neighbors afraid of him, Saddam then sought to intimidate the Persian Gulf oil kingdoms and assert his dominance over the entire region, goals he had failed to achieve in his costly war against Iran.

At the time, there was no one in the Middle East to oppose Saddam's bid for power. Egypt, traditionally the leader of the Arab states, had lost that status when it made peace with Israel. Moreover, in an era in which "petrodollars" produced political and military power, Egypt, without oil reserves, was weaker than the Persian Gulf states. Syria, another frequent rival for Arab leadership, was left isolated with the disappearance of its patron in Moscow. Saddam reasoned that by establishing Iraq as the dominant power in the region, he could launch his campaign for regional hegemony against the moderate Persian Gulf oil kingdoms and rival Arab states.

As Iraqi forces massed near Saudi Arabia's border in the summer of 1990, the possibility that Saddam might soon control 40 percent of the world's oil reserves and dictate the terms of OPEC production forced an aggressive response. Japan and the Western powers froze Iraqi assets in their countries and those of the deposed government of Kuwait. This measure was accompanied by an embargo on Iraqi oil and other economic sanctions, to be enforced by a naval blockade of the Persian Gulf. The two key questions were whether Iraq's customers would honor the embargo long enough to bankrupt the Iraqi economy and whether Saddam ultimately would succumb to the economic sanctions or allow his people to suffer indefinitely, like Fidel Castro in Cuba. Meanwhile, the United States proceeded with its largest troop buildup (dubbed Operation Desert Shield) since the Vietnam War; 250,000 troops were deployed to deter an Iraqi attack on Saudi Arabia. American officials hoped the prospect of war with the UN coalition—composed mainly of U.S., British, and French forces and those from several Arab states—would persuade Saddam to withdraw from Kuwait.

The stakes in this confrontation were clear: possible Iraqi control over oil production and prices, the stability of moderate Arab regimes and Israel, and the durability of the post–Cold War balance of power. Having rhetorically accepted the challenge, the United States could not afford to back down. If it did so, it would endanger its security, its economic growth as well as that of its major trading partners, and its status as the world's lone superpower after the Cold War. If the Arab allies and Israel were neglected in their moment of peril, they might not trust the United States again. Thus the stage was set for a showdown.

The United Nations gave Saddam a deadline of January 15, 1991, to withdraw from Kuwait. If he refused, he would be ejected by force. The unanimity within the UN Security Council was remarkable and clearly demonstrated how great-power politics had changed with the end of the Cold War. Previously, the council's five permanent members—the United States, Soviet Union, Great Britain, France, and China—had agreed on virtually nothing and the two superpowers had vetoed any call for collective action. But with Mikhail Gorbachev clinging to power in the Soviet Union and seeking accommodation with the West, the great powers were for once able to cooperate. Saddam, hoping to disrupt this marriage of the great powers, instead provided a rationale for the UN to test its long-dormant system of collective security. As his tactics became more ruthless, they infuriated world opinion and stiffened the resolve of the UN coalition.

The unprecedented UN solidarity was not matched within Congress, however, which insisted that President George Bush gain its assent before he used force. Many members, still haunted by memories of Vietnam, argued that economic sanctions would be sufficient to dislodge Iraq. Their arguments were shared by thousands of peace activists, who held candlelight vigils and public demonstrations to denounce the impending war. With the UN deadline nearing and the U.S. troop deployment increasing to nearly 500,000, Congress held a historic debate about the Iraqi challenge and narrowly approved the military operation. When the January 15 deadline passed with Iraqi forces still in Kuwait, the United States and coalition partners transformed Operation Desert Shield into Operation Desert Storm.

The massive air assault that began on January 17 sent Saddam's forces fleeing for cover. Allied air forces flew more than 100,000 sorties, devastating Iraqi targets from the front lines to Baghdad. In the first phase they took out Iraqi command-and-control posts, airfields, communications centers, and other military installations. In the second phase they destroyed the bridges and roads being used to supply the Iraqi forces in Kuwait. Cut off, those forces were then subjected to constant pounding. Their poorly concealed tanks and armored personnel carriers were destroyed by laser-guided U.S. missiles, which either killed the Iraqi soldiers or left them stranded in the desert. Not until February 24 did the coalition's tank forces launch their ground attack across the Saudi border.

The results of this military response exceeded the expectations of the most optimistic military planners. Within one hundred hours, the ground forces had surrounded the Iraqis, most of whom surrendered at the beginning of the ground assault. Once feared as the world's fourth largest fighting force, these troops were only too glad to throw down their arms in return for food and water from the coalition tank commanders. Facing almost no opposition, the coalition convoys rolled toward Kuwait City, past burning oil fields set ablaze by Iraq's retreating forces. When the first wave of liberation forces, mostly from Arab countries, reached the Kuwaiti capital, they were greeted and embraced by cheering mobs. The Gulf War had lasted forty-three days. More than 100,000 Iraqis were killed in the blitzkrieg; coalition casualties were limited to less than 200. In the end, Saddam was forced to revoke his annexation of Kuwait and withdraw what was left of his occupation force.

The war, however, did not result in Saddam's removal from power; that had not been the goal of the UN. Indeed, had the tank columns

IMPACT AND INFLUENCE

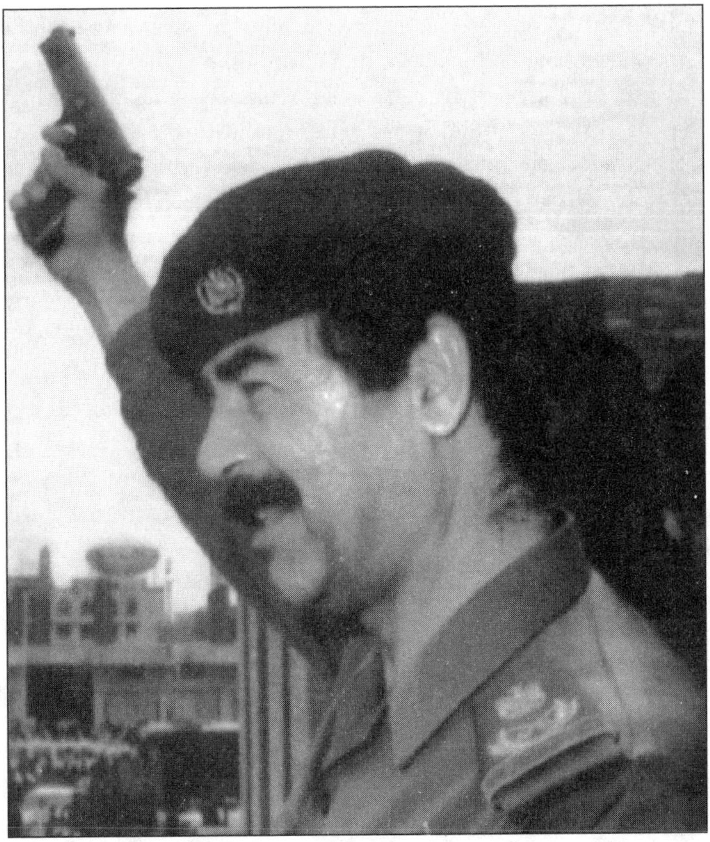

SADDAM HUSSEIN

For all of its advantages as the world's "lone superpower" after the Cold War, the United States could not prevent hostile foreign leaders from sparking regional conflicts and prompting intervention by U.S. military forces. Among these leaders, Iraqi president Saddam Hussein caused the first post–Cold War crisis by invading Kuwait in 1990 and threatening to seize control of the Persian Gulf's vast oil supplies.

Hussein originally achieved prominence as a leader of the Baath Party, an Arab nationalist movement. After taking power in Iraq in 1979, he quickly prepared its army to invade neighboring Iran and topple its newly installed Islamic government, which he viewed as a threat. The ensuing Iran-Iraq War produced hundreds of thousands of casualties. It was soon followed by another conflict, this time arising from Iraq's invasion of Kuwait, which was reversed by a UN coalition led by the United States. After his defeat, Hussein remained firmly in power despite harsh UN economic sanctions against Iraq and repeated efforts by the United States and its allies to destroy Iraq's military arsenal.

rolled on to Baghdad, the coalition likely would have come apart. The Arabs wanted to ensure that Saddam would no longer pose a threat to his neighbors, but they were against his overthrow. And Washington wanted no part in governing a nation in civil war, which appeared likely in the wake of Saddam's defeat. Iraq's Kurds and Shiite Muslims, constituting the majority of the country's population, rebelled in separate regions against Saddam, a Sunni Muslim. But they were not strong enough to defeat the remnants of Saddam's Republican Guard, many of whom were saved at the last moment by the abrupt cease-fire.

Despite Saddam's undisguised brutality toward his own people, the United States and its allies did not want to see Iraq disintegrate. They expected the country to maintain its pivotal role in the Middle East balance of power, a role not possible if it were partitioned. More important, they did not want the surrounding countries, especially Iran and Syria, to carve up the country in their own bids for regional dominance. The United States was charged with inciting Iraqi dissidents to unite against Saddam, then ignoring the rebels once they were engaged in battle. But the realities of the regional power balance overrode those criticisms.

After the war, Saddam defied a series of international demands, making it clear that despite the coalition's victory he would remain a threat. In late 1994 he displayed his capacity to menace the Persian Gulf region at will when he again massed troops on the Kuwaiti border, this time to protest continuing UN sanctions against Iraq. The United States, now led by President Clinton, responded by mobilizing its remaining forces in the Persian Gulf and deploying thousands of additional troops to the region. Saddam then again backed down and ordered his Republican Guards to return to their bases. Two years later, he sponsored attacks against the Kurdish populations of northern Iraq, a region declared off-limits by the UN and occupied by a U.S.-led relief force. After the United States responded with air strikes against Iraqi military installations, Saddam withdrew once more. His economy ravaged by economic sanctions, he remained passive until Iraq was allowed to renew oil production in December 1996 so it could pay for urgently needed shipments of food, medicine, and other necessities.

Overall, then, despite the coalition's spectacular success in routing Iraq from Kuwait in 1991, Saddam remained firmly in power and demonstrated repeatedly his ability to create havoc. He recognized Iraq's importance to the strategic interests of the Western powers. And he openly exploited his freedom to inflame the region at the time and place of his choosing. As he did so, Saddam wore down the UN coalition that had formed at the time of the Kuwait crisis. Two factors aided his divide-and-conquer strategy. First, the United States was steadily losing support within the UN Security Council. Among the permanent members, Russia and China were growing more supportive of Iraq—less because of their affinity for Saddam than because of their desire to curb U.S. influence. Their defiance of U.S. positions was joined by France, whose leaders used any opportunity to display their independence from Washington. French officials also hoped to capitalize on their previous economic ties with Iraq once the UN sanctions were lifted, although this ulterior motive was adamantly, if not convincingly, denied. Many rotating members of the Security Council also opposed the hard-line U.S. position, particularly former Arab members of the anti-Iraqi coalition. Only Great Britain, led by Prime Minister Tony Blair, remained loyal to the United States in the Security Council.

Saddam also was aware of Clinton's faltering domestic support, particularly within the Republican-controlled Congress. Even within the Clinton administration, splits were widely reported among Secretary of State Madeleine Albright, Secretary of Defense William Cohen, and National Security Adviser Sandy Berger. The president's ability to lead was further impaired by the deepening White House scandals that ultimately triggered a congressional effort remove him from office. Although Saddam remained secluded and his whereabouts were unknown, he obviously kept up with current events in Washington. The Iraqi leader's repeated provocations were timed to coincide with the crisis points in the president's legal struggles at home.

In 1997 Saddam directed his wrath toward the United Nations Special Commission (UNSCOM), which had been given the difficult task of ensuring that Iraq dismantled its chemical, biological, and nuclear weapons programs. The role of UNSCOM was vital because Iraq had used biological weapons against its own Kurdish population. There also was evidence that Iraq had since the 1980s filled missile warheads with botulism, anthrax, and other deadly agents. The fears that Iraq was secretly storing such weapons and would use them if given the opportunity were therefore justified. Saddam had acceded to the creation of UNSCOM but soon resisted inspections of Iraqi military installations, which frequently were conducted without warning. A cat-and-mouse game quickly ensued, with UNSCOM agents arriving at suspected Iraqi weapons facilities only to find they had been recently vacated. Saddam turned up the heat late in 1997 by expelling the U.S. members of UNSCOM, whom he accused of dominating the inspections and conspiring with the U.S. Central Intelligence Agency to overthrow him. The second expulsions in February 1998 led Clinton to threaten a punitive military strike. But this was averted at the last moment by UN Secretary General Kofi Annan, who flew to Baghdad and received Saddam's assurances that Iraq would allow UNSCOM inspections. Saddam then reneged on this pledge, and another military strike was ordered by Clinton in November. With the assault hours away, Iraq again reversed course and announced it would comply with U.S. demands. And again, Clinton canceled the attack.

Clinton was clearly losing this standoff with Iraq. His lack of political support at home and overseas left him with little room to maneuver. More than anything, Clinton feared he would be condemned for launching a military attack on Iraq at a time when Saddam was widely perceived as seeking reconciliation. Political concerns took precedence over military strategy, and in the political sphere Clinton's hand was growing weaker every day. His concessions to Iraq only stiffened Saddam's resolve and energized the anti-American coalition within the UN. Furthermore, Clinton's waffling infuriated the UNSCOM inspectors, who grew tired of being used as pawns in the conflict.

Finally, in December 1998 Clinton ordered a four-day aerial bombardment of Iraqi military headquarters, intelligence agencies, and weapons plants. The attacks, conducted by U.S. and British air forces, destroyed most of their targets. But they did nothing to reduce Saddam's power or slow the erosion of U.S. support among other major powers. Russia, China, and France all denounced the use of force and Clinton's decision to act without the approval of the UN Security Council. The president was further charged with authorizing the attack to save his political skin at home. The timing of the December 16 attacks was certainly suspicious. On the very next day the House of Representatives was scheduled to begin debate on impeaching Clinton for his role in an affair with a White House intern.[6]

The standoff with Iraq dragged on with no resolution in sight. Saddam had achieved his goals of fragmenting the anti-Iraqi coalition and ending the UNSCOM inspections. But Iraq remained the target of UN economic sanctions, which could not be lifted without the consent of the U.S. government. Thus Saddam's next objective was to isolate Washington within the Security Council in the hope that a compromise could be reached that would allow Iraq to regain its economic livelihood. Continued bombing attacks by U.S. and British forces in 1999 proved self-defeating in this respect. Far from forcing Iraqi compliance, the attacks merely added to the "sanctions fatigue" among UN members and provoked sympathy for Saddam, despite his flagrant atrocities and thwarting of the UN's will. It became more likely that Saddam would outlast

6. The impeachment debate was delayed by just one day. After Clinton's impeachment by the House of Representatives, the Senate failed to convict the president in January 1999. Clinton was, however, severely wounded by the scandal for the remainder of his presidency.

the U.S.-led sanctions and emerge from the struggle as a hero to the Iraqi people.

MOMENTUM TOWARD AN ARAB-ISRAELI PEACE

In the wake of Operation Desert Storm, the United States judged the time right for a new effort to gain a comprehensive peace between Israel and its neighbors. The oil kingdoms owed Washington a favor for saving them from Saddam Hussein. Syria, deprived of Soviet patronage and protection, also seemed ready for a settlement. Moreover, shortly after the Gulf War Israel's hard-line Likud government, which had a cool relationship with the United States, was replaced by a more accommodating Labor Party government headed by Yitzhak Rabin.

The unexpected breakthrough came in September 1993 when the Palestine Liberation Organization (PLO) and Israel agreed to mutual recognition. In the historic Oslo Declaration of Principles, which was facilitated by the Norwegian government, the PLO abandoned its call for the destruction of Israel and renounced terrorism. In return, Israel would withdraw from the Gaza Strip and the West Bank town of Jericho and allow the Palestinians to govern themselves. It was assumed that, over time, Palestinian control over education, health, social services, taxation, and tourism would be extended over the West Bank except in the areas settled by the Israelis. It also was assumed that the Palestinians would keep order, police themselves, and, in particular, end the *intifada* (holy war) against Israel and its supporters. If these expectations were realized, the two sides eventually would hold "final-status" talks about whether the Palestinians would be allowed to establish a state of their own.

Why did these two deadly enemies finally decide to negotiate their differences? For one thing, the end of the Cold War deprived the PLO of a strong political supporter—the Soviet Union. For another, the Gulf War had left the organization almost broke; PLO leader Yasir Arafat had made the disastrous decision to support Iraq against the oil kingdoms that had provided the PLO with most of its funds. Even earlier, however, the spontaneous outburst of the *intifada* among West Bank Palestinians, frustrated by the continued Israeli occupation and Arafat's inability to solve their problems, had demonstrated his declining influence. In response, Arafat had established a "Palestinian authority" in the occupied areas, thereby suggesting a two-state solution instead of Israel's elimination. For their part, the Israelis were tired of the conflict and the costs—physical, economic, and human—of the six-year-old *intifada.* But more than that, they too were worried about the increasing support among Palestinians for extremists. If Israel could achieve a stable peace, the country's economy would prosper, especially with the large influx of skilled Russian immigrants who were fleeing the anti-Semitism that was flourishing once more in their homeland. Talks with the PLO had therefore become inevitable, and the hope was that these would lead to a comprehensive peace agreement.

Despite the opposition of extremists in Israel, the Middle East peace process edged further forward in 1994 when Israel resolved its major differences with Jordan. Under the terms of this second agreement, both countries acknowledged the right of the other to exist, bringing their de facto state of war to an end. In addition, Jordan's King Hussein and Rabin agreed on the boundaries between the two states and divided control over underground water reservoirs and other natural resources; they also established the basis for bilateral trade and tourism. As part of the treaty, the United States agreed to forgive Jordan's foreign debt, which had soared after years of economic stagnation.

Syria was another story. Earlier, Clinton had failed to bring Syria into the peace process, even after visiting Damascus and meeting personally with Syrian leader Hafez al-Assad, long considered by the U.S. government to be a primary sponsor of international terrorism. Assad conceded little to Clinton while enjoying the enhanced prestige and legitimacy that attended the presidential visit. The fact that Clinton would go to Damascus without a set of previously negotiated agreements spelling out Syria's contributions to the peace process suggested an unwillingness to pressure Assad and wishful thinking that Syria's strongman would reciprocate American goodwill—an unlikely occurrence.

The United States had hoped that Israel and Syria would agree on a peace accord that would incorporate Syria and Lebanon, Syria's satellite, and produce peace on the northern border of Israel. Since the 1967 Six-day War, Israeli troops had occupied the Golan Heights region connecting the three countries as well as a strip of southern Lebanon, where Hezbollah (Party of God) guerillas supported by Syria had menaced Israel. Both areas served as staging grounds for attacks by Islamic militants on Israel and would have to be brought under control. If Syria could be brought into serious negotiations and would cooperate in order to regain the Golan Heights, the elusive goal of a comprehensive treaty with all of Israel's neighbors along with the PLO would be within reach. But despite news reports that Rabin and Assad both privately endorsed the principle of a return of the Golan Heights to Syria in return for Syria's recognition of Israel, no such agreement was concluded.

Suddenly, just as in the past, the progress toward Arab-Israeli peace was shattered by violence and tragedy. On November 4, 1995, Rabin was assassinated by a Jewish extremist who admitted killing the Israeli leader in order to halt the peace process. After mourning the loss of Rabin,

GOLAN HEIGHTS AREA: Occupied by Israel in 1967. Unilaterally annexed by Israel in 1981.
WEST BANK AREA: Unilaterally annexed by Jordan in 1950. Occupied by Israel in 1967. Currently portions under Palestinian control.
GAZA STRIP: Occupied by Israel in 1967. Currently under total Palestinian control.
SINAI PENINSULA: Returned to Egypt by Israel in 1982.
LEBANON
GOLAN HEIGHTS
SYRIA
Haifa
Sea of Galilee
Haifa
Nazareth
Jordan River
Tel Aviv
WEST BANK
Ammān
Jericho
Mediterranean Sea
Jerusalem
Gaza
GAZA STRIP
Hebron
Dead Sea
Beersheba
ISRAEL
EGYPT
SINAI PENINSULA
JORDAN
NEGEV
Gulf of Aqaba

ISRAEL AND OCCUPIED TERRITORIES

Israel was shocked by another wave of violence in the midst of an election campaign to select a new leader. In the spring of 1996 Palestinian terrorists staged four suicide bombings in nine days, killing fifty-nine Israelis and wounding more than two hundred. In the subsequent vote, Israelis, suddenly doubtful about the peace process, elected a new prime minister, Benjamin Netanyahu, head of the rival and more conservative Likud Party and an outspoken critic of the peace process. Netanyahu pledged to bring "peace with security" to Israel, meaning he would not support further concessions to the Arabs without explicit guarantees that Israel's security would be protected on all fronts.

When these guarantees were not forthcoming, Netanyahu delayed the withdrawal of Israeli troops from the West Bank and from Hebron, a city in the heart of the occupied territories. As each side accused the other of trying to scuttle the agreements, a new round of bloody attacks occurred in the spring and summer of 1996. Each massacre and the inevitable counterattacks that followed diminished the prospects for a Middle East settlement. With the peace process on the verge of collapse, Israel, under great pressure from the United States and other countries, agreed in January 1997 to withdraw from Hebron, a concession that at least temporarily restored the lost momentum. But Netanyahu's insistence on building new Jewish settlements in East Jerusalem, home to many Palestinians, led to another round of violence. Despite the best efforts of the United States, a resolution of the Arab-Israeli conflict remained elusive.

A peculiar characteristic of Middle East diplomacy is that breakthroughs often occur when the prospects for peace seem most remote. This was certainly the case in October 1998 when Israel and the PLO revived their peace talks and moved closer to final-status negotiations for Palestinian statehood. The United States hosted the talks at the Wye River Plantation in Maryland, where Netanyahu, under pressure from the United States and his political opponents at home, agreed to transfer 13 percent of the occupied territories to the Palestinians. Arafat, in turn, provided stronger guarantees that the PLO would outlaw terrorism, prevent the flow of illegal weapons, and create a police force to maintain order in the Palestinian zones. The Wye River Memorandum also called for the two sides to work together on economic development in the West Bank and Gaza and to hold regular meetings on regional security.

Netanyahu paid the ultimate political price by signing the accords. His concessions to the PLO cost him the support of his allies in the Likud Party, leading to his electoral defeat in May 1999 to Ehud Barak, head of the Labor Party. In his campaign, Barak had made a "true, lasting peace" between Israel and its neighbors his top priority. His election as Israel's prime minister fueled the momentum toward a final agreement with the PLO. Barak also moved closer to a deal with Assad in Syria, whose assent was vital to any comprehensive peace.

All four leaders involved in the negotiations had much to gain by a settlement. Barak would be viewed as a savior whose appeals for reconciliation between Israel and its Arab neighbors had secured the peace. Palestinian statehood also would represent a personal triumph for the aging Arafat, who had long been criticized for his autocratic control of the PLO and his defiant negotiating style.[7] Assad, in poor health, was eager to reclaim the Golan Heights and gain an Israeli withdrawal from southern Lebanon. He succeeded in his latter goal but died in June 2000 with the Golan Heights still under Israeli control. As for Clinton, a Middle East accord would help establish his historic legacy beyond the scandals and other controversies that had nearly destroyed his presidency. In this respect, personal ambitions combined with collective exhaustion from the Arab-Israeli struggles to bring a peaceful settlement within reach. Lingering suspicions, however, assured that progress toward an accord would be slow and uncertain.

THE PLIGHT OF 'FAILED STATES'

Among the most notable trends in world politics after World War II was the steady rise in the number of nation-states—from fifty-five in 1946 to nearly two hundred by the turn of the millennium. Most of the new countries were created from former European colonies in Africa and southern Asia. Others, such as the Czech Republic and Slovakia, emerged after the Cold War in Eastern Europe. Still others were carved out of the former Soviet Union. This proliferation of nation-states dramatically changed the face of world politics during the late twentieth century. The new countries, often located in the world's poorest areas, received large volumes of foreign aid from wealthier nations and accepted their help in the complicated task of "state building." Yet despite some progress in their living conditions, these developing countries remained generally hostile to the industrialized North. In the UN, the new states united with other developing countries to form a majority in the General Assembly, which served as a forum to express their grievances against the United States and other industrialized nations.

This resentment steadily intensified during the Cold War, when many developing countries became the battleground of the superpower conflict, illustrating a popular aphorism that "when two elephants fight, the

7. On the internal political struggles within the PLO, see Hillel Frisch, *Countdown to Statehood: Palestinian State Formation in the West Bank and Gaza* (Albany: State University of New York Press, 1998).

grass suffers." The ideological nature of these conflicts polarized the developing countries and often pitted neo-Marxist revolutionaries against right-wing military juntas, which became ever more repressive when challenged for power. Neither a middle class nor a moderate political center was possible under these circumstances. Frequently, extremists on both sides received modern weaponry from the superpowers or their allies, which further inflamed the conflicts.

In this respect, the end of the Cold War was welcomed by the most impoverished nations, which were still reeling from the punishing economic distress in the 1980s, widely labeled the "lost decade" of development. By the late 1990s, however, the social and economic problems plaguing many poor countries had only worsened. Contrary to widespread expectations, the accommodation between Washington and Moscow had produced lower levels of foreign aid to the world's poor; indeed, the United States had all but eliminated aid to "non-strategic allies." Instead, U.S. policy makers called on the developing countries to seek private investments to boost their economies. But this was unlikely where poverty and political unrest prevailed. In contrast to the flood of foreign investment that flowed to the newly industrialized countries of East Asia, the poorest states received barely a trickle.

Some observers suggested dismantling what was left of the most desperate developing countries and putting them under UN trusteeship. Such a response was highly unlikely, but it revealed the depths to which many of these countries had fallen. Indeed, in many areas the post–Cold War era witnessed the emergence of the "failed state":

> From Haiti in the Western Hemisphere to the remnants of Yugoslavia in Europe, from Somalia, Sudan, and Liberia in Africa to Cambodia in Southeast Asia, a disturbing new phenomenon is emerging: the failed nation-state, utterly incapable of sustaining itself as a member of the international community. . . . [T]hose states descend into violence and anarchy—imperiling their own citizens and threatening their neighbors through refugee flows, political instability, and random warfare.[8]

These crises raised questions about the arrangements that had created these countries in the first place, particularly those in Africa whose ethnic groups overlapped the state boundaries drawn by the colonial rulers. For the United States, which had sought support from these impoverished states to counter Soviet influence in the region, their plight was suddenly remote to its strategic self-interests. Yet Americans could not escape the disturbing scenes of warfare and starvation appearing on their television sets daily and crying out for action by the world's

8. Gerald B. Helman and Steven R. Ratner, "Saving Failed States," *Foreign Policy* (winter 1992–1993): 3. Also see I. William Zartman, ed., *Collapsed States: The Disintegration and Restoration of Legitimate Authority* (Boulder: Lynne Rienner, 1995).

richest and most powerful country. Yet what form, if any, this help should take remained unclear.

SOMALIA AND CENTRAL AFRICA

One of the first states to arouse international attention was the impoverished country of Somalia, located along the Horn of Africa at the entrance to the Red Sea (see the map "Africa Today" in Chapter 4). During the Cold War, the Soviets had supported the government of Somalia because its larger neighbor to the north, Ethiopia, was aligned with the United States. But when a pro-Soviet military regime came into power in Ethiopia, Somalia's ruler switched sides as well. Gen. Muhammad Siad Barre became a loyal client of the United States despite his ruthless oppression of the Somali people. All of this perversely made sense in the context of Cold War rivalry. But when the Cold War ended and Barre was overthrown, Somalia became embroiled in a war of succession among rival factions. The government ceased to function and chaos prevailed. Widespread starvation followed when the rival militias prevented farmers from planting new crops, disrupted the activities of nomadic traders, and killed most of the nation's livestock. An estimated 300,000 Somalis died of starvation; another 2 million were in immediate danger.

After months during which the world looked the other way, media attention compelled a Western response through the United Nations. More than 27,000 troops, at first mainly American, were dispatched in late 1992 to provide order and food. After they had accomplished the mission of Operation Restore Hope, the U.S. forces were to be withdrawn and replaced by a temporary contingent of UN forces. Saved by the foreign intervention, a "restored" Somalia would then be able to chart its own course.

Unfortunately, the reality in Somalia was not so simple. It soon became clear that, once the outside forces were withdrawn, the Somali warlords would resume their struggle for power, leading to renewed killing and hunger. Thus in 1993 the UN mission changed its mission from one of humanitarian relief to one of rebuilding Somalia's political and economic structures. But the country's principal warlord, Gen. Mohammed Farah Aidid, who controlled Somalia's capital, Mogadishu, resisted the enlarged UN mission because it called for his own removal and disarmament. In the fighting that followed, twenty-four Pakistani peacekeepers were ambushed and killed. Later, more UN troops were killed, including U.S. soldiers who were deployed to capture the elusive general. As the number of U.S. casualties mounted—and after a slain U.S. soldier was dragged through the streets of Mogadishu before cheering crowds and television cameras—demands began for the withdrawal of U.S. troops. Clinton responded by accelerating their departure, and the United Nations suspended the mission in the spring of 1995.

How did the Somali operation go so tragically wrong? The international peacekeepers, initially dispatched for the humanitarian purpose of feeding the people, ignored the political situation that had created the hunger in the first place. Food shortages had not stemmed from a natural disaster; they were man-made. Indeed, it should have been clear from the beginning that resolving the anarchic political situation was a prerequisite to resolving the humanitarian crisis. But that was not clear; what was thought at the outset to be a short mission ended up taking two and a half years, underlining the fact that there was no such thing as an apolitical, purely humanitarian intervention. A lasting solution to the Somali conflict was possible only through internal reconciliation undertaken by the Somalis themselves. Thus a worthy, moral effort to help Somalia turned into an open-ended, futile commitment, after which Somalia remained in the grip of civil war for the rest of the decade.

In the waning days of the Somalia debacle, the world was confronted with an even more grotesque humanitarian nightmare in the African state of Rwanda. In 1994, over a period of less than three months, violence between the Hutus, who dominated the government, and the minority Tutsi population had resulted in more than 800,000 casualties, mainly Tutsi. This death toll far exceeded that in Bosnia, where the killing of about 200,000 Muslims by the Serbs had been labeled genocide (see Chapter 12). Because the multilateral response had proved unworkable in Somalia, a concerted peacekeeping effort in Rwanda was out of the question. For this reason, the UN was largely silent in the face of the Rwandan tragedy.

The responsibility for outside intervention fell on the French government, which considered francophone Africa within its sphere of influence even after its colonial control had ended.[9] But by the time French troops intervened in Rwanda, it was too late. Rwanda's rivers were choked with corpses, many horribly hacked to death with machetes. The subsequent victory of the Tutsi army and the establishment of a Tutsi-led government then provoked one of the world's greatest human migrations. Fearing vengeance, the Hutus virtually emptied Rwanda—half a million fled to Burundi, another half million to Tanzania, and a million to Zaire. This relentless flow of refugees overwhelmed local and international efforts to help and led to widespread deaths from starvation, cholera, dehydration, and exhaustion.

9. Although Rwanda was a Belgian colony, it had been incorporated into France's sphere of influence after its independence.

Personal apologies by President Clinton in 1998 for the lack of a U.S. response did nothing to relieve the suffering of the Rwandans. Nor did the UN's admission in December 1999 that it made "serious mistakes" in failing to prevent the catastrophe.[10] But for all of their admissions of guilt and pledges to act more decisively in the future, the United States and the UN could not escape the central reality: Rwanda had been deemed irrelevant by most non-African countries and unworthy of their sacrifice. Under the spell of the "Somalia syndrome," Clinton had signed a presidential directive in May 1994 that had placed strict conditions on U.S. support for UN peacekeeping. These conditions included: a clear threat to U.S. security, substantial public support for intervention, participation by other countries under UN supervision, and an assurance that long-term "nation-building" would not be necessary. Given these restrictions, a repeat of the Rwandan episode would likely elicit the same nonresponse by the United States.

The regional conflicts in Africa widened in the late 1990s with no end in sight. Violent attacks and reprisals between the Tutsi-led government of Burundi and the majority population of Hutus raised the prospect of another Rwandan-style bloodbath. The fighting there provoked yet another exodus of refugees, mostly to eastern Zaire, where the corrupt regime of the ailing dictator Mobutu Sese Seko battled its own insurgency. Thousands of Hutu refugees were trapped in the crossfire between rebel forces, led by Laurent Kabila, and Mobutu's army. Mobutu had virtually no support among Zaire's civilian population, and, unlike during the Cold War, he could not count on military assistance from the U.S. government, which declared during the rebellion that "the era of Mobutuism is over." The rapid advance and victory of Kabila's forces in May 1997 were therefore unstoppable.

Upon seizing control of the capital of Kinshasa, Kabila restored the country's original name—Democratic Republic of the Congo—and sought international recognition. His new regime, however, proved to be no more democratic or effective in improving living conditions than Mobutu's dictatorship. To the contrary, Kabila presided over Africa's newest failed state. His country was overrun by ethnic conflict that produced thousands of new casualties, ghastly human rights abuses, and intervention by half a dozen neighboring countries. Described by Madeleine Albright as "Africa's first world war," the conflict raged well into 2000 despite the proclamation of a cease-fire that was later ignored.

These events in Africa proved how difficult the process of political and economic development would be in countries recovering from colo-

10. See United Nations, *Independent Inquiry into the Actions of the United Nations during the 1994 Genocide in Rwanda* (New York: United Nations, 1999).

nial rule and the intervention by the Cold War superpowers. The conflicts also revealed the inability of outside actors—whether governments or relief organizations—to prevent atrocities and humanitarian nightmares. In fact, many critics charged that foreign aid programs were designed to promote the self-interests of the donors themselves, not to relieve suffering in developing countries, and that relief agencies like CARE, UNICEF, and the U.S. Agency for International Development were most concerned with enhancing their own stature.[11] As these criticisms mounted, sub-Saharan Africa reverted to its status before the Cold War when it was off the radar screen of American foreign policy.

HAITI

The Clinton administration was confronted with yet another crisis in the failed state of Haiti, the poorest country in the Western Hemisphere. Ruled by the U.S.-backed Duvalier dictatorship until 1986, the Haitian people had their first taste of democratic elections in 1990 when they elevated the Reverend Jean-Bertrand Aristide to the country's presidency. But Aristide's proposed reforms, including his plans to demilitarize the country and redistribute wealth, resulted in his overthrow six months later by the military. With Aristide in exile in the United States, Haiti's military leaders, led by Gen. Raoul Cédras, launched a campaign of terror across the island, killing, torturing, and imprisoning those who had fought for reforms and who continued to resist the new rulers. As a result, thousands of Haitians constructed makeshift boats and fled to the United States. In his final months in office, President Bush announced that the United States was unprepared to accommodate these "boat people" and ordered the U.S. Coast Guard to turn them back. His decision angered many human rights groups, as well as candidate Bill Clinton, who declared that as president he would allow the Haitians to seek asylum in the United States.

But just as in other areas of foreign policy, Clinton's position on Haiti changed once he took office. Suddenly he shared Bush's reservations about absorbing the mass emigration of Haitians. While continuing to demand Aristide's return to Haiti and denouncing the military rulers, Clinton announced he would not allow Haitian refugees to enter the United States. Instead, a UN-sponsored economic embargo was imposed on Haiti, but it proved to have little effect on the political and social crisis. In July 1993 Clinton and the Haitian leadership reached an agreement that would have brought about Aristide's return to power in exchange for amnesty for Cédras and other military leaders. When the

11. Michael Maren, *The Road to Hell: The Ravaging Effects of Foreign Aid and International Charity* (New York: Free Press, 1997).

270 U.S. and Canadian peacekeepers arrived in Haiti on the U.S.S. *Harlan County* to oversee the transition back to civilian rule, they were greeted at the waterfront by armed demonstrators who denounced their arrival. The ship then beat an ignominious retreat. An angry and disappointed Aristide publicly condemned the Clinton administration's reversal and was joined by many liberals on Capitol Hill, including members of the Congressional Black Caucus who saw a racial bias in Clinton's acceptance of Cuban refugees, while Haitians, of African origin, were turned back in open waters.

The tentative American response to disorder in Haiti became a symbol of the Clinton administration's general lack of resolve in foreign policy. The *New York Times,* which supported most of Clinton's domestic initiatives, expressed dismay at his reversals in handling the deepening crisis in Haiti: "After months of vacillating from one policy to another, America faces the troubling prospect that Mr. Clinton is drifting into using troops in Haiti because he wants to compensate for other policy embarrassments and does not have a better idea." [12] Clinton also was condemned by conservatives, aghast at his retreat at the first sign of opposition by a weak and corrupt military regime and at the squandering of U.S. prestige, which had been elevated by America's Cold War victory and its more recent military defeat of Iraq.

The turmoil in Haiti continued into the fall of 1994 even while Haitian refugees were being diverted to an overcrowded settlement camp on the Guantánamo naval base in Cuba, then to temporary facilities as far away as Panama City. Clinton finally concluded that the Haitian problem could only be resolved by U.S. military intervention, and he issued a public ultimatum to the Cédras junta. His threat of war was widely denounced in the United States, where congressional opponents demanded time to debate and vote on the impending invasion, but Clinton had gone beyond the point of no return. As American warplanes were preparing to leave for the capital Port-au-Prince, Clinton dispatched to Haiti a high-level mission, headed by former president Jimmy Carter, to confront Cédras, offer him a final opportunity to leave peacefully, and prevent a military clash. Cédras accepted the offer, but only after being notified that the invasion was imminent.

The military assault on Haiti was then transformed into a "semi-permissive occupation" by twenty thousand U.S. troops, and it extended well into 1995. As in Somalia, the United States was thrust into the role of state builder. Aristide was returned to power, and he was succeeded peacefully the next year by René Préval in elections that, although closely monitored, were widely boycotted by Haiti's political parties and its

12. "Which Haiti Policy?" (editorial), *New York Times,* July 7, 1994, A18.

largely illiterate citizens. Stability on the island depended on the presence of U.S. troops, a steady stream of Western foreign aid, and the deployment in March 1996 of six thousand UN peacekeepers. By the end of 1999, any hopes that Haiti could be converted into a stable and democratic country had vanished. The country's unemployment rate hovered around 60 percent and almost all foreign investment had been withdrawn. Haiti's government was so paralyzed it could not pass the minimal legislation needed to permit $500 million in aid to be sent to the island. Faced with an impossible task, U.S. troops abandoned Haiti, and they were joined by police training personnel and human rights monitors from the UN and Organization of American States. The warring factions were left to their own devices.

NUCLEAR BRINKMANSHIP IN SOUTH ASIA

Growing regional tensions and the absence of superpower-induced restraint also afflicted South Asia in the decade after the Cold War. The problem reached especially alarming proportions when India and Pakistan conducted underground nuclear tests in May 1998. In doing so, both governments incurred worldwide wrath, diplomatic isolation, and economic sanctions. But this was a price they were willing to pay in return for their entry into the "nuclear club."

The roots of this conflict extended deep into the historical animosities between Muslims and Hindus in the region. These differences exploded into violence after India, once the "crown jewel" of the British empire, was granted independence in 1947. Rather than exist as a minority within a Hindu-dominated India, members of the rival Muslim League sought their own state. The creation of Pakistan in 1956 came with immense bloodshed as nearly one million people were killed and another twelve million were displaced from their homes. The mutual distrust between India and Pakistan sparked two more wars and constant border skirmishes, particularly in the Kashmir region of northern India, whose majority Islamic population was claimed by Pakistan.

Greatly complicating matters, both countries had become entangled in the Cold War—Pakistan as a U.S. ally, India on the side of the Soviet Union.[13] In return for their allegiance, both governments received massive volumes of military aid from the superpowers. A regional arms race quickly ensued, with India testing a nuclear "device" in 1974 and Pakistan rushing to acquire its own nuclear weapons. The growing military

13. The India case was noteworthy because the Indian government, under the leadership of Jawaharlal Nehru, had declared itself a leader of the "nonaligned movement" in the 1950s.

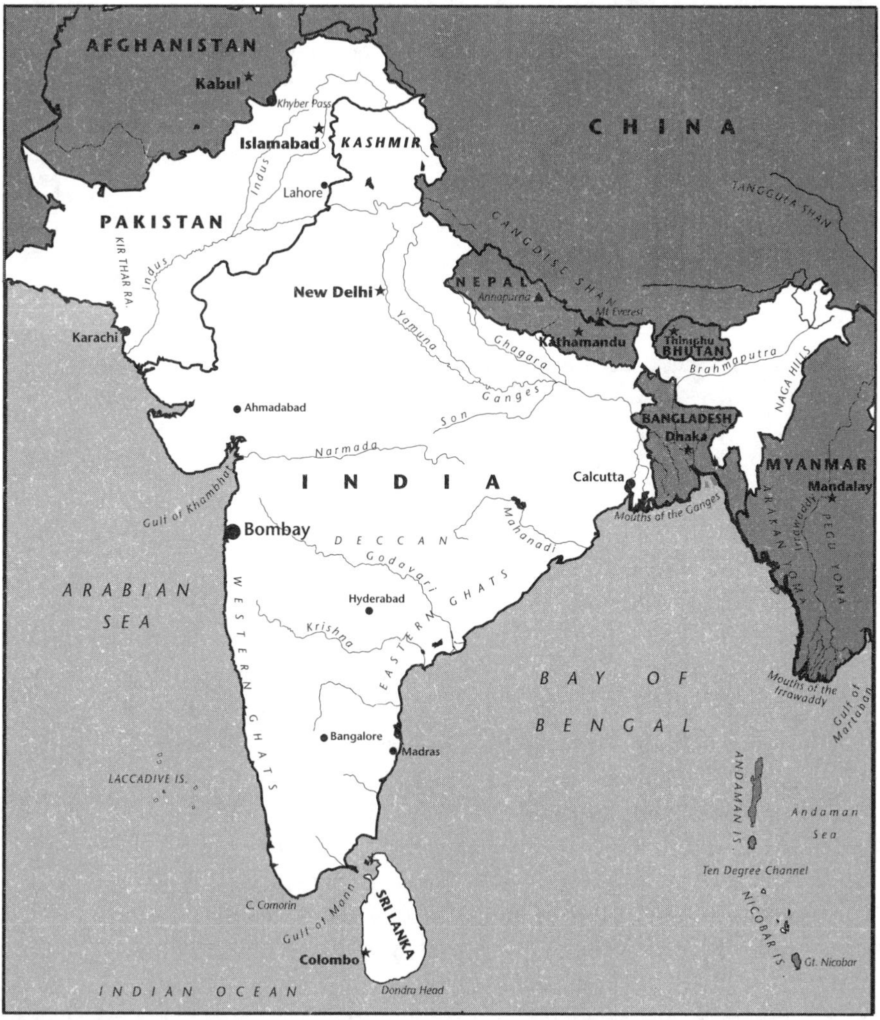

SOUTH ASIA

strength of both countries stood in stark contrast to their economic stagnation and chronic political unrest.

In few areas of the world did the power politics of the Cold War so contaminate regional relations as in South Asia. For the Soviet Union, India served the dual function of blunting the U.S. presence in South Asia and countering China, which had sought to restrain Moscow's ambitions in the region. Since independence, India's government had been mired in a chronic border dispute with China and had fought a short war against Mao Zedong's forces in 1962. China had prevailed in that struggle, but the border tensions remained unresolved. As for the United States, Pakistan played a key role in the U.S. effort to contain the Soviet Union in South Asia. Pakistan became particularly useful in the 1980s as a transit point for covert U.S. military shipments to the *mujahidin* in Afghanistan seeking to oust the Soviet-sponsored regime that took power in 1979. But while India and Pakistan served as valuable pawns for the superpowers, they became more and more threatening to each other.

In the 1970s and 1980s the United States tried to discourage Pakistan from becoming a nuclear power by approving sales of modern jet fighters, missiles, and munitions to the country's dictator, Gen. Mohammed Zia ul-Haq. Much of this weaponry was funded by U.S. assistance; the rest only added to Pakistan's crippling international debt. After Pakistan defied American wishes and continued developing nuclear weapons, the United States suspended its weapons sales. But this action was too little too late. The fact that both India and Pakistan had become de facto nuclear powers was widely known long before their tit-for-tat detonations in the spring of 1998.

The end of the Cold War deprived India and Pakistan of any leverage they had to expand their military arsenals. Both countries, already armed to the teeth, looked to other arms exporters to provide them with additional weaponry. The only question was how they would employ their military might at a time when their citizens remained in poverty. Domestic politics thus played a key role in fueling tensions as leaders on both sides of the hotly contested border deliberately inflamed nationalist passions in order to enhance their popularity. Indian prime minister Atal Bihari Vajpayee, elected in March 1998, became a hero among Hindu nationalists for his nuclear show of force. "The nuclear tests have given the government an aura of credibility and decisiveness," one Indian scholar observed. "It is difficult to think of any decision in India's recent history that has had such overwhelming public support." [14] The Indian tests also played into the hands of Pakistan's autocratic premier, Nawaz Sharif, who resisted international pleas for restraint. In ordering the Pakistani tests, Sharif declared a state of emergency that enabled him to clamp down even more harshly on his political opponents at home.

The nuclear tests raised the stakes of South Asia's power struggle. But even more worrying, they also imperiled global efforts to prevent the spread of nuclear weapons. In particular, the addition of India and Pakistan to the nuclear club greatly weakened the nuclear Non-Proliferation

14. Pratap Bhanu Mehta, "Exploding Myths," *New Republic*, June 8, 1998, 18.

Treaty (NPT) that had been extended indefinitely by 168 governments in 1995. Although the two South Asian states had refused to sign the NPT, it was hoped they would eventually succumb to international pressure. But the result was just the opposite. The nuclear tests by India and Pakistan raised anxieties elsewhere and tempted potential proliferators to cross the nuclear threshold.

The world, then, had to adjust to the new reality of seven self-proclaimed nuclear powers.[15] Far from backing down in the face of global pressure and sanctions, India's National Security Council announced in August 1999 a military doctrine of "minimum credible deterrence," complete with a triad of ground-, sea-, and land-based nuclear missiles. Indian officials then approved a 28 percent increase in military spending early in 2000, the largest single-year increase in the nation's history. And in Pakistan, Sharif's campaign of political repression backfired as he was driven from power in October 1999 in a military coup. The new military regime, however, was in no mood to disarm its nuclear program at a time when India was flaunting its arsenal and promising new deployments. Efforts by President Clinton to defuse the regional arms race—including an extended trip to both countries in March 2000—failed to produce concessions by either side.

LESSONS FROM THE REGIONAL CRISES

The regional conflicts just described collectively deflated the euphoria that followed the end of the Cold War. Many members of Congress—including Clinton's allies in the Democratic Party—openly doubted that the United States had vital interests in the failed states. But they generally supported the humanitarian interventions in the early 1990s, which appealed to the nation's historic sense of mission and moral responsibility. Support for U.S. involvement quickly evaporated, however, when it became clear the United States could not resolve the underlying problems in these countries—or when U.S. interventions clashed with domestic priorities. As for India and Pakistan, it is doubtful that the United States could have prevented the two bitter rivals from raising the stakes of their dispute, and their nuclear tests compounded the rising sense of global disorder felt by Congress, administration officials, and the general public.[16] For many Americans, a retreat from the chaotic

15. Israel also maintained a nuclear capability, making it the eighth nuclear power, but this well-known fact was not confirmed by the Israeli government. It also was believed that North Korea maintained a small nuclear arsenal after its weapons program was "frozen" in 1994.

16. For an elaboration, see Stanley Hoffmann, *World Disorders: Troubled Peace in the Post–Cold War Era* (Lanham, Md.: Rowman and Littlefield, 1998).

struggles overseas became more appealing. They could then enjoy the unprecedented prosperity that had overtaken the country.

Although at this time the restraints on U.S. intervention were fewer than ever, it had become clear that the United States could not solve the many political, economic, and social problems in developing countries that were sparking widespread violence after the Cold War. America's vast military arsenal was of little or no use in most trouble spots; constructive, long-term solutions were required. Moreover, in most cases these were civil wars, not disputes between states—a fact that reinforced the lesson that home-grown solutions, not ones imposed by other states, were needed. This stubborn reality challenged the long-held view among many Americans that, once the United States committed its military forces to battle, their overwhelming strength would subdue any foe. The Vietnam trauma had previously thrown this presumption into doubt. But this time, many people assumed, the righteousness and selflessness of the American cause were irrefutable, and the country had never been more capable of asserting itself throughout the world.

Even in the more purified atmosphere of the 1990s, however, the limits of U.S. military power were again revealed. The failed military interventions reminded American leaders that they must pay attention to the interests at stake in any conflict—as well as the cost, level of public support, likelihood of success, and existence of a coherent exit strategy. These preconditions became part of the so-called "Powell doctrine," named after Gen. Colin Powell, chairman of the Joint Chiefs of Staff under Presidents Bush and Clinton. In the early days of the Persian Gulf crisis, Powell had urged Bush to extend the economic sanctions against Saddam Hussein rather than unleash Operation Desert Storm. But once Bush ordered military action, Powell sought to defeat Iraq quickly with overwhelming force, then quickly withdraw American forces from the region. As for Somalia, Powell had warned that it would be a reckless operation with predictable consequences. His warnings were dismissed by Bush and Clinton, who were convinced that good intentions coupled with superior military force could solve virtually any problem overseas—a view deeply embedded in the country's traditional approach to foreign affairs. The failure of the Somali mission quickly exposed their delusions.

More generally, the frustrations stemming from the regional conflicts forced Pentagon officials to rethink the military doctrines that had been aligned in the early 1990s with Clinton's foreign policy of liberal internationalism. Les Aspin, Clinton's first secretary of defense, had streamlined U.S. defense forces as part of his "bottom-up review" of the Pentagon completed in 1994.[17] Aspin's successor, William Perry, found these cutbacks insufficient, and he announced in 1996 that "preventive defense" had become the new military doctrine. The Pentagon's new priorities included preventing weapons proliferation, supporting democratization, and promoting "confidence-building" measures between governments. But preventive defense seemed too abstract and remote from the sense of invulnerability shared by many Americans. Moreover, the strategy diverted the Pentagon's attention from its core mission of protecting U.S. interests at home and in strategically vital regions such as Europe, the Middle East, and East Asia. As a result of these concerns, Perry was replaced in Clinton's second term by William Cohen, a former Republican senator whose pledges to pursue a more modest and self-interested military policy were well received.

The regional conflicts also demonstrated the limits of multilateral intervention and peacekeeping. As in the early 1930s, when the League of Nations failed to resist Japan's invasion of Manchuria, pledges by UN members to act collectively in the 1990s turned out to be hollow. The reasons for this were eerily similar to the League of Nations precedent: the primacy of national self-interests over transnational concerns; unresolved disputes among the great powers; and doubts about the world body's political and military leadership. While hardly alone, the United States was the most conspicuous in turning away from the UN. "Assertive multilateralism" had been a cornerstone of Clinton's early foreign policy, and the UN had been embraced as a bulwark against aggression in the post–Cold War era (see Chapter 10). After the honeymoon, however, the marriage became strained. The UN was viewed with suspicion—if not contempt—by congressional leaders, who controlled the country's purse strings and refused to meet its financial obligations to that organization.[18]

While the lessons from the regional conflicts prescribed a healthy dose of moderation for U.S. military policy, in other respects the wrong lessons were learned. The failure of the humanitarian interventions, combined with more general misgivings about Clinton's foreign policy, provoked a general backlash against U.S. activism in the developing areas. As the pendulum swung toward the other extreme—global *disengagement*—Congress cut deeply into the State Department's budget and closed dozens of foreign embassies, consulates, and missions. Many for-

17. As part of this force reduction, the Pentagon closed dozens of military bases and sought to create smaller, but more technologically advanced, defense forces that could prevail in two major conflicts at the same time. See Michael Cox, *U.S. Foreign Policy after the Cold War: Superpower without a Mission?* (London: Pinter, 1995), chap. 4.

18. In late 1999 the United States began to pay off its overdue financial commitment to the UN, which amounted to more than $1 billion, but only after being faced with the loss of its vote in the General Assembly.

eign aid programs to the poorest countries of Africa, southern Asia, and Latin America were eliminated.[19] As a result, the United States deprived itself of a key resource with which to address the underlying problems in the poor countries and contribute to constructive, peaceful, and long-term change. The fact that the world's most prosperous country scaled back its foreign service and virtually dismantled its foreign aid program—at a time when its defense budget was returning to Cold War levels even without a serious foreign threat—sent a clear but troubling message about Washington's future intentions.

Collectively, the recurring crises in developing areas defied easy explanation and could not be placed neatly into a single paradigm of world politics, despite the best efforts of the Clinton administration to do so. In the absence of such an orienting principle, both aspects of America's national style of foreign policy—its missionary zeal and its desire for detachment from "foreign entanglements"—returned to the fore. But the ambiguous new order demanded a firm restatement of American purpose that would reconcile the competing requirements of global leadership and self-restraint. As Henry Kissinger observed in 1994,

> Indiscriminate involvement in all the ethnic turmoil and civil wars of the post–Cold War world would drain a crusading America. Yet an America that confines itself to the refinement of its domestic virtues would, in the end, abdicate America's security and prosperity to decisions made by other societies in faraway places over which America would progressively lose control.[20]

As during the Cold War, most violent conflicts during the 1990s occurred in the developing world. But in Europe, the focus of the next chapter, the breakdown of bipolarity also produced renewed tensions. A spreading religious war in the Balkan peninsula threatened the process of regional integration that was rapidly drawing the Western European states toward confederation. Meanwhile, Russia's transition to democracy and capitalism confronted a variety of obstacles. While these problems were largely internal, the prospect of civil war and renewed Russian militarism raised fears far beyond Moscow. Despite its internal divisions and lack of an overriding grand strategy, the United States would be thrust into a major role throughout Europe even as the crises in the developing world persisted.

19. As a percentage of economic output, U.S. foreign aid spending was by 1995 the lowest of all industrialized countries. Michael O'Hanlon and Carol Graham, *A Half Penny on the Dollar: The Future of Development Aid* (Washington, D.C.: Brookings, 1997), 25.

20. Henry Kissinger, *Diplomacy* (New York: Simon and Schuster, 1994), 833.

British prime minister Tony Blair (left) and German chancellor Gerhard Schroeder (right) greet a crowd of European Union delegates during the EU's 1999 summit meeting in Cologne, Germany. The two leaders represented a generational shift in Europe and a new era in the region's political, economic, and military order.

CHAPTER TWELVE

The Shifting European Landscape

After the Cold War the United States continued to maintain a visible presence on the European continent, hoping to exploit the gains stemming from the collapse of the Soviet Union and to prevent the emergence of new fault lines. The U.S. effort, however, yielded contradictory results. As Europeans became stronger and more unified, they also grew wary of their American caretaker and sought to become more self-sufficient. Above all, they hoped to regain their place among the great powers after being trapped for nearly a half-century in the middle of the East-West struggle.

America's preoccupation with Europe was, of course, nothing new. It always had viewed a stable Europe as essential to its security. Specifically, a *balance* among the European powers was required to prevent a single country from dominating the continent and, in turn, threatening the United States. Throughout the nineteenth century, this geopolitical concern led U.S. leaders to avoid alliances with the European powers, a strategy clearly laid out in President George Washington's Farewell Address (1796) and in the Monroe Doctrine (1823). American detachment from the great powers of Europe was further justified on moral terms: the European monarchs had brazenly denied their citizens fundamental political rights and routinely placed them in harm's way in their deadly game of power politics. The United States, by contrast, would remain true to its democratic principles by refusing to play this game. This strategy worked so long as the Concert of Europe maintained a balance of power and the British navy protected the Atlantic sea lanes. But American fears that one country would try to dominate the European continent were affirmed in the two world wars, which forced the United States to abandon its policy of "splendid isolation" once and for all.

As the Cold War set in, American foreign policy makers faced a dilemma in contemplating future relations with Europe. With the United States the strongest world power in 1945 and with the Soviet Union quickly emerging as its chief rival, U.S. isolation from Europe *even in peacetime* was no longer conceivable. This dilemma led the United States to prolong its presence in Western Europe, where it sought to enmesh those states in a variety of international organizations that would reward regional cooperation, suppress nationalism, and discourage self-serving economic and security policies.

This strategy of European "institutionalism" served the vital function of strengthening Western Europeans against the Soviet Union, but it also contained a logic that extended beyond the Cold War. It was not surprising, then, that President George Bush and his successor, Bill Clinton, adhered to this strategy throughout the 1990s amid rapidly changing circumstances in Europe. As this chapter describes, the Western European states edged closer toward a confederation by creating the European Union (EU), complete with a common currency. Meanwhile, their neighbors in Eastern Europe were rebuilding their political institutions and economies largely along the lines of the EU states. The North Atlantic Treaty Organization (NATO), far from dissolving along with the Soviet Union, expanded into Eastern Europe and became embroiled in "out-of-area" conflicts. All the while, the Russian government lurched from crisis to crisis, keeping tensions at a high level all across Europe.

First Bush and then Clinton tried to play a stabilizing role as Europe adjusted to the new strategic landscape. Both presidents knew that a democratic Europe that embraced free markets not only would benefit

Europeans, but also would make the United States more secure. Yet the United States could not prevent conflicts from breaking out in the Balkan peninsula and within the former Soviet Union. Nor could it prevent its European allies from erecting new military structures and devising new strategies that would, if fully implemented, amount to a declaration of independence from Washington. "The EU is no longer merely a client of the United States and now often takes the lead on major issues in international gatherings," wrote an official in the European Parliament. "This can have advantages or disadvantages for U.S. policy, but whatever the outcome, it is a new fact of political life that Washington must now consider." [1]

WESTERN EUROPE: FROM COMMUNITY TO UNION

The integration of Western Europe into a more cohesive European Union brought those states closer together and provided them with a forum in which to resolve their long-standing political differences. In 1992 the twelve members of the European Commission ratified the Maastricht Treaty, which created the European Union and moved the alliance beyond economic integration to include goals such as a unified legal code and a common foreign policy.[2] In 1995 three previously neutral countries joined the European Union—Austria, Finland, and Sweden—bringing its full membership to fifteen.[3] With the EU growing in both numbers and responsibilities, a system of "dual sovereignty" emerged. Although the member states retained ultimate political control over their territories and citizens, they transferred an ever-growing share of their authority to the EU's central government in Brussels. By 2000 it appeared that the historic visions of a "United States of Europe," long dismissed by skeptics, might actually come to pass.

From the standpoint of Washington, Europe's gradual move toward confederation was both welcome and potentially troubling. As noted, American leaders had long encouraged regional integration as a means of defusing the bitter rivalries among the European powers. The Truman administration explicitly made regional cooperation a condition for Marshall Plan funding and military aid. But a revitalized Europe could very well seek to detach itself from the United States and chart an independent course. In fact, as some Europeans saw it in the 1990s, Ameri-

1. Christopher Piening, *Global Europe: The European Union in World Affairs* (Boulder: Lynne Rienner, 1997), 102.

2. The twelve countries were: Belgium, Denmark, France, Italy, Germany, Greece, Luxembourg, the Netherlands, Portugal, Spain, Switzerland, and the United Kingdom.

3. Another fourteen countries had formally applied for EU membership by 2000. Of these, seven were given top priority for membership: Cyprus, the Czech Republic, Estonia, Hungary, Malta, Poland, and Slovenia.

THE EUROPEAN UNION

cans frequently overstepped their bounds and meddled in the region for selfish reasons. With Europe fully recovered from World War II and free of the Soviet threat, these critics urged the EU to exploit its new strength and assert its interests more strongly, even if such gestures meant alienating the United States.

Changes in the European landscape also produced a changing of the political guard. The new generation of leaders that took power in the 1990s sought to put the Cold War behind them and enter the new millennium with a clean slate. These leaders included Prime Minister Tony Blair of Great Britain, President Jacques Chirac of France, and Chancellor Gerhard Schroeder of Germany. All three supported the continued push toward European integration, and they used their political advantages within the EU to pressure the smaller states to follow along. The leaders of the "big three" European governments had something else in common: they were appalled by the disabling conflict between Bill Clinton and the U.S. Congress, irritated by the resulting stalemate in U.S. foreign policy, and determined to pursue their own interests with or without the United States.

The greatest leap forward in European integration came in January 1999 with the introduction of a common currency, the "euro." [4] A national currency represented one of the central pillars of sovereignty and was, therefore, closely guarded by political leaders. This was especially true in Europe, where the nation-state system was devised in the seventeenth century. But the presence of many national currencies, all with different and wildly fluctuating values, became a nuisance after the Europeans created a single internal market. A common currency would be the most efficient way to do business.

The euro, however, came at a hefty price: each government was forced to relinquish its fiscal and monetary authority and rein in public spending, reduce debts, and lower inflation. Welfare programs were scaled back and government subsidies reduced in all eleven participating countries. In the past, external pressures to undertake such reforms incited charges of imperialism, and austerity measures often sparked demonstrations or riots when spending cuts increased unemployment or reduced popular social services. But European leaders willfully accepted these curbs on their autonomy in exchange for the promise of greater prosperity.

Internal harmony among the European economies did not mean their chronic trade disputes with the United States would suddenly vanish. Quite the contrary, these disputes became even more contentious,

4. Four EU members did not immediately adopt the common currency. The governments of Britain, Denmark, and Sweden decided not to participate, and Greece did not meet the economic requirements for entry. For the eleven other member states of the EU, the euro became the basis of foreign exchange in 1999 and was scheduled to begin circulation in 2002.

only this time U.S. trade negotiators faced a united front in Europe instead of separate foreign ministries. In 1999 the growing strains between Washington and the EU led to a "banana war" in which the United States imposed 100 percent tariffs on many European goods in retaliation for the EU's refusal to import bananas from U.S.-based corporations. A second dispute over the sale of aircraft engines prompted U.S. officials to ban Europe's supersonic Concorde from landing in the United States. Meanwhile, European investors ignored the U.S.-led economic embargo against Cuba and other sanctions that targeted Castro's trading partners. Taken together, these problems made it clear that a united Europe, whose population and economic output exceeded that of the United States, could become a formidable rival in the intensifying competition for world markets.

The EU's pursuit of a "common foreign and security policy," called for in the Maastricht Treaty, was even more ambitious than its adoption of a common currency. By pledging to pool their diplomat corps and military forces, EU members seemed prepared to surrender the last and most vital element of their national sovereignty. But large, familiar hurdles to an all-European foreign policy remained. While the nationality of the armed forces would become irrelevant, that of the military leadership would not. Which of the major powers would lead the all-European forces? What roles would the other EU members play in the command structure?[5] Furthermore, it was never clearly established how the Europeans would pay for such a military force, or, more fundamentally, what the substance of a "common" foreign policy would actually be.

These ambiguities had little effect so long as the United States ran things from Washington—and from NATO headquarters in Brussels. The alliance not only spared Europeans a perilous decision over military leadership, but also allowed them to skimp on military spending, thus freeing up funds for the more generous social programs favored by European citizens. In the wake of the Cold War, however, a growing number of Europeans, particularly the French, associated NATO with American hegemony. Thus France moved forward on a joint defense force with Germany that would bring the common foreign policy to life. Its efforts, if successful, threatened to make the United States a victim of its own success. "Where the mark, the franc, the lira, and the guilder are headed, armies, fleets, and air squadrons will eventually follow," one scholar observed. "A Europe moving toward real economic integration

5. France and Germany already had sparked a political crisis by clashing at the last minute over the leadership of the European Central Bank. The German-backed candidate, Willem Duisenberg, was finally appointed in May 1998, but only after agreeing to "retire" halfway through his eight-year term and be replaced by the French candidate.

may be a less reliable and less predictable partner for the United States—or perhaps not even a partner at all." [6]

JUMP-STARTING DEMOCRACY IN EASTERN EUROPE

The fate of the "transition" countries of Eastern Europe also was of great importance to the United States. This region had long been viewed as a fulcrum in the power balance between East and West. Russian and German armies had twice turned Eastern Europe into a bloodbath in the world wars. The same nations then served as Soviet pawns in the Cold War, enduring decades of political repression and economic decay under communist rule. For all the major powers, then, the fate of the wide-ranging reforms undertaken in the early 1990s in Eastern Europe had implications that extended well beyond that region.

Because most Eastern European governments lacked historical experience with either democratic rule or market economics, they faced enormous difficulties in instituting reforms. But the demise of the Cold War suggested better times lay ahead. Francis Fukuyama's vision of the "end of history," outlined in Chapter 10, was therefore welcomed by most Eastern Europeans, whose histories had largely consisted of foreign conquest and domination.

The newly liberated Eastern European states quickly put into place the variety of institutional components required of democratic goverments. They wrote and approved constitutions that provided for basic political and civil rights, and they established modern legal codes and court systems to assure that the rule of law prevailed. They also created legislatures in which elected leaders from competing political parties could debate and enact the new laws. By and large, their efforts to build the structural foundations of democracy, mostly from scratch, were fruitful. But the success of these political reforms depended on the progress of the simultaneous economic reforms that sought to replace the centrally planned economies of the Soviet era with those based on private enterprise. This task, though, proved quite difficult in many parts of Eastern Europe and threatened the region's move toward democratic rule.

The problems came from several sources. First, the cost of rebuilding these economies turned out to be far greater than expected. Economic conditions after the Cold War were dismal throughout Eastern Europe. The landscape was blighted by decaying factories, crumbling roads, outdated utilities, and widespread environmental damage. Moreover, school systems had fallen into disrepair, course materials were out of

6. Ronald Steel, "Eurotrash," *New Republic,* June 1, 1998, 12.

date, and teachers were paid barely enough to survive. It soon became clear that educating and training the productive workforce required for long-term economic growth would take many years, possibly more than a generation.[7]

Second, many citizens of Eastern Europe were demoralized by the half-century of communist rule that had deprived them of political power and the prosperity enjoyed in the West. These citizens had little experience in forming independent trade unions, rival political parties, and other mass movements—and no experience at all in campaigning for elected positions of their own. As a result, they often were unprepared to manage the demands of political leadership that came with their freedom from Soviet rule. The widespread layoffs and cutbacks in social services that followed from the "structural adjustments" produced mass protests against national leaders, many of whom had been exalted as saviors during Eastern Europe's rise against communism.

A third problem was that most countries in Eastern Europe were not immediately attractive to large-scale foreign investment, which at the time was flowing primarily to the United States, Western Europe, and the newly industrialized countries of East Asia. Private investors and multinational corporations generally adopted a wait-and-see attitude toward the former communist countries. Only Poland, Hungary, and the Czech Republic received large volumes of foreign investment. Elsewhere, what little private capital was invested was quickly withdrawn at the first sign of trouble.

The fourth obstacle to reform became evident long after the transitions had begun. Throughout Eastern Europe the most powerful government officials often were former communists who had, at least rhetorically, rejected communism and embraced free markets. In practice, however, these former members of the communist *nomenklatura* exploited their status and connections to ensure for themselves a sizable share of the public enterprises that were placed in private hands. But once they obtained control over these industries, the former communist technocrats were no better able to stimulate productivity and economic growth than they had been during the Cold War. "Crony capitalism" prolonged the economic stagnation of many Eastern European economies and failed to improve living standards.

In extolling the virtues of capitalism during the Cold War, U.S. leaders had ignored the widespread practice of crony capitalism in countries such as Japan, South Korea, Indonesia, and Mexico. In these countries a small number of economic elites received generous treatment from gov-

7. These problems persisted despite a massive inflow of aid funds from the EU to Eastern Europe. See Karen E. Smith, *The Making of EU Foreign Policy: The Case of Eastern Europe* (New York: St. Martin's Press, 1999).

ernment officials, many of whom sat on corporate boards and had personal interests in the firms they regulated. Business leaders, in turn, routinely served on government advisory boards, deepening the cozy relationship between the public and private sectors. It did not take long for the same patterns of behavior to take hold across Eastern Europe in the 1990s. As a result, economic and political power remained tightly concentrated, often among the same elites who controlled these societies during the communist era. The masses, by contrast, remained on the sidelines. Their initial euphoria over the coming of private enterprise yielded to the familiar feelings of isolation, betrayal, and cynicism they had long known under communist regimes.

By 2000, only Poland and Hungary (and, to a lesser extent, the Czech Republic) had emerged as prosperous market economies that could compete effectively with their counterparts in Western Europe. Poland, with by far the largest level of economic output in Eastern Europe, had introduced economic reforms quickly, through "shock therapy." After several sluggish years, the Polish economy grew in the late 1990s at an annual rate of more than 5 percent, while inflation and unemployment rates fell steadily. In Hungary more than $17 billion in foreign investments fueled a similar economic resurgence. Given this progress, it was no coincidence that these countries quickly rose to the top of the EU's list of members-in-waiting and were welcomed into NATO (described in the next section).

The smaller economies in Eastern Europe continued to struggle. Economic output in Bulgaria and Romania declined throughout the 1990s, forcing their leaders to rely on emergency aid from the International Monetary Fund (IMF) to prevent their economies from collapsing. Meanwhile, government corruption and organized crime undermined public confidence in the reform efforts. Many people in these countries became nostalgic for the communist regimes of the Cold War era, which at least assured them of jobs and a minimal level of income. Thus in 1994 the Bulgarian Socialist Party gained control of the national legislature. In Romania the most popular political party was the National Salvation Front, led by high-ranking members of the former Communist Party.

In sum, the first decade after the Cold War produced a growing split among the countries of Eastern Europe—between the "haves" and the "have-nots." While the more prosperous countries became part of the integrated Western economy and gained early admission into Western political and military arrangements, the others lapsed into mass demonstrations, strikes, and ideological debates reminiscent of the Cold War. In these countries the "end of history" was nowhere in sight.

NATO'S ENDURANCE AFTER THE COLD WAR

Beyond the economic realm, the future of European military security remained uncertain after the Cold War. Of central concern was the status of NATO, which had accomplished its stated mission of protecting the Western European states from possible Soviet aggression. In view of this achievement, many observers felt the alliance should be disbanded. But to others, including Presidents Bush and Clinton, NATO remained useful in confronting potential new threats to its members on both sides of the Atlantic Ocean.

Confusion over NATO's future reflected widespread misunderstandings about its past. Contrary to official proclamations, containing the Soviet bloc was not the only purpose served by NATO during the Cold War (see Chapter 3). Its broader functions were aptly summarized by Lord Hastings Ismay, its first secretary general, when he pointed out that NATO was needed "to keep the Americans in, the Russians out, and the Germans down." Only the second function was directly related to the Cold War; the first and third had deeper roots. These functions, combined with nagging doubts about Russia in the 1990s, propelled the alliance into a new and ambiguous future.

The military "umbrella" offered by the United States was critical to NATO's founding and eagerly welcomed by Western European leaders. Not only did the U.S. presence created by NATO fortify the front lines of the Cold War, it also stifled the chronic *internal* rivalries that had twice thrust the region into world war. Protected by the alliance, Western Europeans were able to focus their energies on economic recovery and political cooperation. In this sense, the United States provided "a sense of reassurance to the Europeans that they would not otherwise have and thereby helped make security relations, and also political and economic relations, within Western Europe more stable than they would otherwise be." [8]

Germany also figured prominently in the NATO equation. Through NATO, German leaders rejoined the Western European community without provoking new fears of expansionism. In so doing, German chancellors from Konrad Adenauer to Gerhard Schroeder also sought to strengthen Germany's fragile democracy and ensure its success in a country with a dictatorial history. The alliance, in effect, adopted a policy of "double containment" of Germany and Russia. But, as in the case of America's role as a regional caretaker, the need to keep Germany "down" was rarely mentioned publicly.

8. Robert J. Art, "Why Western Europe Needs the United States and NATO," *Political Science Quarterly* (spring 1998): 12.

NATO, then, provided for the collective *defense* of Western Europe against foreign attack and for the region's collective *security* against its own self-destructive tendencies. Both roles, as it turned out, remained valid after the Cold War. Developments in Russia, described later in this chapter, were hardly reassuring to the other European states. Nor was Germany's emergence as the EU's economic powerhouse. NATO was thus seen as a guarantor against another German-Russian collision (like that before World War I) or further collusion (like that before World War II). The alliance also could soothe tensions between other members. For example, disputes between Greece and Turkey over the control of Cyprus and other matters simmered during and after the Cold War. Those and other points of contention required a continued and pervasive U.S. presence in Europe.

An immediate rationale for NATO's continued survival was found in the desire of the former Soviet bloc states to become part of the "West." Thus the question quickly became not whether the alliance should disband, but whether it should *expand.* The timing for "enlargement" (the term favored by military planners) seemed right given the new power vacuum in Eastern Europe created by the abolition of the Warsaw Pact. Unless NATO stepped in to fill this vacuum, countries such as Poland and Hungary would have to build independent military forces. They also might be tempted to create another regional bloc. Neither scenario was appealing to NATO members, nor to Eastern Europeans themselves who saw NATO as a steppingstone to EU membership.

The decision to expand NATO beyond its sixteen members was complicated by Russia, whose leaders always had feared encirclement by hostile neighbors. Thus any move to add the Eastern European states to NATO threatened to inflame Russian nationalism and isolate moderates. This development would, in turn, introduce pressures for Russia to rearm and divert resources badly needed to ensure the success of its political and economic reforms. Clinton and other NATO leaders arrived at a compromise solution in October 1993. Under the rubric of a "Partnership for Peace," the former Warsaw Pact members and Soviet republics were invited to become junior partners of NATO. In this capacity, they would participate in some NATO deliberations and training exercises. But they would not receive the security guarantees of full members. If the "partnerships" proved successful, these auxiliary states would be considered for full membership.[9]

9. Twenty-five countries had agreed to join the partnership by 2000: Albania, Armenia, Austria, Azerbaijan, Belarus, Bulgaria, Estonia, Finland, Georgia, Ireland, Kazakhstan, Kyrghyzstan, Latvia, Lithuania, Macedonia, Moldova, Romania, Russia, Slovakia, Slovenia, Sweden, Switzerland, Turkmenistan, Ukraine, and Uzbekistan.

Russian president Boris Yeltsin first rejected the partnership concept but soon recognized the futility of his position. He then insisted, also in vain, that Russia receive preferential treatment given its military strength and permanent membership in the UN Security Council. Yeltsin further protested NATO's plans to invite Poland, Hungary, and the Czech Republic to join the alliance as its first new full members. Exploiting the tensions within NATO, the Russian president warned all Europeans about subjecting themselves to continued U.S. military control. He declared that a "cold peace" was setting in between Moscow and Washington and suggested that it would thaw only after suspension of the proposed eastward expansion of NATO.

The United States and its NATO allies dismissed Yeltsin's thinly veiled threats, which were attributed to his need to appease nationalists at a time when his hold on power was tenuous. Instead, they moved forward on their plan to add the three Eastern European countries to NATO membership by 1999, the fiftieth anniversary of the alliance's founding, and to leave the door open for other new members. Faced with the inevitable, Yeltsin again softened his stance. Instead of blocking NATO expansion, he successfully negotiated a separate treaty that would prevent the placement of foreign troops or nuclear weapons in Eastern Europe. The Russian-NATO Founding Act of 1997 called for military cooperation rather than competition between the former Cold War adversaries. Under the agreement, Russia would be given a "voice, but not a veto" over NATO policy.

Yeltsin's surrender on NATO expansion revealed the depths to which his country had fallen. One need only consider how Washington would have reacted if the Soviet Union had won the Cold War and then invited Mexico and other Latin American countries to join the Warsaw Pact. In reality, NATO's offer not to place nuclear weapons in the Eastern European states was hollow since it could be quickly withdrawn in a crisis. Yet Russia still accepted the face-saving agreement and reaped the rewards: billions of dollars in continued economic aid from the West. Having attained Russia's compliance, NATO welcomed Poland, Hungary, and the Czech Republic into its fold in March 1999. The expansion was quickly approved by all the European states and Canada. In the United States, even the Senate, which had opposed Clinton on nearly every foreign policy issue, approved the expansion by a vote of 80–19. To Secretary of State Madeleine Albright, Europe had taken a giant step toward becoming "whole and free."

But what was to be the mission of the enlarged NATO? Its new "Strategic Concept" omitted the previous objective—to preserve a "strategic balance in Europe"—yet it failed to outline a coherent future role. If, as the document proclaimed, the meaning of regional security would be broadened beyond military concerns, how would the alliance solve the vast array of political and social problems it would then confront? And how exactly would the alliance conduct a global crackdown against weapons of mass destruction, as Albright had proposed? No clear answers to these questions were forthcoming for the uncomfortable reason noted above: the real driving forces behind NATO's endurance—restraining Russia and Germany while preserving a dominant U.S. military presence in Europe—were too politically sensitive to acknowledge openly.

Yet another question raised during the expansion debate—whether NATO would intervene in "out-of-area" conflicts beyond the borders of its member states—was answered by NATO jet fighters. At the very time of the anniversary celebration they were bombing Yugoslavia in southeastern Europe. This was the second round of NATO assaults on the former communist country, which had become embroiled in a brutal civil war in the aftermath of the Cold War. The protracted conflict in the Balkan peninsula, long known as the "tinderbox of Europe," put NATO and its hazy new mission to the ultimate test.

'ETHNIC CLEANSING' IN THE BALKANS

The violent disintegration of Yugoslavia in the 1990s served as a frightening example of how the removal of Cold War restraints could unleash nationalistic rivalries. Yugoslavia, created in the aftermath of World War I, was a diverse federation of ethnic and religious groups—mainly Serbs (Eastern Orthodox), Slovenes and Croats (Catholic), and Bosnians and Albanians (Muslim). During the Cold War, the country was held together under a communist regime headed by Marshall Josip Tito, who relied on Marxist ideology and a monopoly of political power to suppress these deep and bitter divisions. But Tito's makeshift arrangements began crumbling soon after his death in 1980. They collapsed altogether in 1989 along with the communist regimes in other Eastern European states. Ancient religious hatreds quickly returned to the surface, and Yugoslavia's descent into a spiral of violence soon followed.[10]

The dominant Serbs, who still controlled the capital of Belgrade and the country's formidable armed forces, opposed Yugoslavia's disintegration and sought instead to create a Greater Serbia that would include

10. For an account by the former U.S. ambassador to Yugoslavia, see Warren Zimmerman, *Origins of a Catastrophe: Yugoslavia and Its Destroyers—America's Last Ambassador Tells What Happened and Why* (New York: Times Books, 1996). For another historical perspective, see Robert D. Kaplan, *Balkan Ghosts: A Journey through History* (New York: Vintage Books, 1993).

YUGOSLAVIA AND SUCCESSOR STATES

territories occupied primarily by non-Serbs. After the provinces of Slovenia and Croatia declared independence in 1991 and were immediately recognized by the European Community, the Yugoslav army intervened in both territories. Serbian troops inflicted great damage on Slovenia and Croatia but were unable to prevent the secession of the two new states, both of which were promptly admitted to the United Nations. The Serbs then directed their military campaign to the heart of Bosnia and Herzegovina (referred to as Bosnia here), the most multinational of the Yugoslav provinces, which also had declared its independence from Belgrade. There, the Bosnian Serbs launched a self-described campaign of "ethnic cleansing" that consisted of driving Muslims from their communities in order to expand Serbian territory. Masked paramilitary forces burned and looted villages, tortured and starved non-Serbs in concentration camps, raped Islamic women, and besieged the Bosnian capital, Sarajevo, for three years, depriving its citizens of food, water, and electricity.

These actions appalled outside observers and drew widespread condemnation. Many Americans, including presidential candidate Bill Clinton, called in 1992 for military intervention in Bosnia. In view of the expectations of the post–Cold War world, such aggression "would not stand," as Bush had stated at the height of the Persian Gulf crisis. Horrified onlookers charged that the systematic expulsion of Muslims constituted genocide, which was explicitly prohibited by the UN Charter, and they called on all countries to intervene and prevent the mass slaughter, which was based ethnic or religious differences. Charges of widespread war crimes went both ways because Croat and Muslim forces also committed atrocities against the Serbs—a familiar pattern in the region's history.

Opponents of intervention in the Balkans argued that this was a civil conflict, not an international war, despite the establishment of new states recognized by the European Community and United Nations. The Pentagon asserted that any military intervention to separate the combatants and restore order would entail a massive commitment of between 200,000 and 400,000 troops, heavy fighting, and extensive casualties. Moreover, the foreign troops probably would have to remain in the treacherous mountain territory for many years, and no coherent "exit strategy" was evident. Most important, the conflict appeared to be contained within the Balkan peninsula, posing little threat to the great powers, especially the United States. The Bush administration generally adopted this cautious view and pursued a negotiated outcome. Likewise, once elected, Clinton soon retracted his earlier calls for outside intervention and pressed for a diplomatic solution, preferably mediated by the newly reorganized European Union. Later he would be gravely disappointed when the EU member states, preoccupied with regional integration and plagued by conflicting allegiances in the Balkans, failed to take a united stand.

An international arms embargo imposed on Yugoslavia in the early days of the conflict favored the Serbs because the Yugoslav army—well equipped from its years of association with a communist dictatorship—supplied the Bosnian Serbs with weapons from its arsenal. The Muslims, by contrast, could not acquire sufficient arms to protect themselves. Nevertheless, European leaders opposed lifting the embargo, arguing it would only broaden the violence and endanger their own peacekeeping forces, which were protecting so-called "safe havens" in the remaining Muslim-held areas. The arms embargo continued into 1995, along with an economic boycott against the Serbian regime in Belgrade.

When Clinton occasionally advanced proposals for multilateral military action—and for lifting the arms embargo against Bosnia—he was opposed by most Western European governments and many influential members of the United Nations, including Russia, a traditional ally of the Slavic Serbs. Most experts in the Defense Department also opposed a military response because, in their view, air strikes would have little effect without the deployment of large U.S. ground forces. Within Congress and among the general public, domestic issues were of greater concern than the seemingly intractable problems in the Balkans. In short, many Americans asked the same question: If the Europeans did not feel sufficiently threatened by events in Bosnia to intervene in their own backyard, why should the United States, an ocean away?

For all these reasons, Clinton was unwilling to assert himself and demand action as Bush had done in Kuwait. Instead, he wavered, sometimes threatening to intervene with air power and to lift the arms embargo, at other times retracting these positions, citing allied reluctance to go along as his reason for inaction. But, if anything, Clinton was a savvy politician, and he knew that if the United States intervened unilaterally, the war would soon become "America's war." Like President Lyndon Johnson in Vietnam, he might become stuck in military quicksand, jeopardizing his domestic priorities, stimulating a peace movement, and endangering his chances for reelection in 1996.

Meanwhile, the United Nations pressed forward with a plan to partition Bosnia along ethnic lines, but the Serbs continued shelling Muslim enclaves that the UN had promised to protect. UN peacekeepers provided the besieged Muslims with medicine and food, but only the threat of air strikes against Serbian positions in the mountains surrounding Sarajevo temporarily brought relief to that city and other safe havens. Serbian defiance resumed, however, when the few air strikes authorized by the UN and undertaken by NATO revealed that the foreign powers did not have the will to stop the Serbian aggression. To deter future air attacks, the Serbs seized hundreds of UN peacekeepers and placed them around bombing targets as human shields. They accomplished their goal of displacing the Muslims from their homes throughout Bosnia and succeeded in humiliating the UN by demonstrating that its peacekeeping forces never had a peace to keep. In a final turn of the screw, the Serbs overran the Muslim safe havens of Srebenica and Zepa in July 1995. While UN peacekeepers watched, they separated Muslim families and herded thousands of men and boys into concentration camps, where they were later executed and buried in mass graves.

IMPACT AND INFLUENCE

SLOBODAN MILOSEVIC AND RADOVAN KARADZIC

As civil war swept across Yugoslavia in the 1990s, prompting two U.S.-led military interventions, the UN formed a special tribunal to punish those who had committed brutal atrocities against civilians. By 2000 the list of indicted war criminals included two prominent Serbian leaders, Slobodan Milosevic (left) and Radovan Karadzic (right).

Milosevic, president of Yugoslavia since 1997, had previously ruled the country's largest province, Serbia. In both positions he financed campaigns of "ethnic cleansing" against non-Serbs. His indictment in May 1999 for his role in Kosovo marked the first time a sitting head of state had been formally charged with war crimes. Karadzic, who had led the Serbian crackdown against Muslims and Croats in Bosnia-Herzegovina, was indicted in 1995 on charges of mass murder, rape, and torture of civilians. Both men remained free long after the indictments were issued, however, and Milosevic continued to serve as president of Yugoslavia. Nearly one hundred suspects had been indicted by the UN tribunal since its inception in 1993. The UN also established a tribunal to investigate suspected war crimes during the 1994 genocide in Rwanda.

THE DAYTON ACCORDS

Suddenly in late 1995 a shift in the regional balance of power transformed this situation. The Croatian army, showing surprising strength, launched a successful ground attack against the Serbs, depriving them of many of their earlier territorial gains. Muslim forces joined in the counteroffensive, which produced a new flood of refugees, this time Serbs fleeing the Croats and Muslims. Recognizing the shifting power balance and outraged by the most recent Serbian atrocities, NATO launched a sustained bombing campaign against Serbian munition dumps, bridges, and air defenses that further weakened the Serbs. By this time, the multilateral economic sanctions against Belgrade had begun taking their toll and forced Serbian president Slobodan Milosevic to assert his authority over the Bosnian Serbs.

In this improved climate, American leaders seized their opportunity to negotiate a deal among the Balkan rivals. Despite the violence and the deepening mutual hatreds, each of the factions had strong reasons to end the fighting: for the Serbs, to consolidate the Bosnian Serb gains before they were lost or reversed and to end the economic sanctions; for the Croats, to secure their independent state and the safety of their nationals in other areas; and for the Muslims, to relieve the suffering of their people and to create a Bosnian state with strong Muslim representation. Forced to negotiate face to face at a U.S. Air Force base in Dayton, Ohio, leaders of the three factions signed a complex agreement in November 1995 that led to a cease-fire in 1996. Under the Dayton Accords, nearly sixty thousand NATO troops were deployed to the region as part of Operation Joint Endeavor. Once in place, they separated the armed factions, protected civilian populations, and delivered economic assistance to the war-ravaged Bosnian communities. Bosnian leaders then created a new government led by a three-member presidency, one from each ethnic group, to be chosen by the Bosnian people in national elections.

Implementation of the Dayton Accords, however, was fraught with problems. All three factions harbored deep resentments from the war, and the elections held in September 1996 brought Serb and Croat representatives to power who openly called for the secession of their respective territories from Bosnia and the creation of a Muslim mini-state around Sarajevo. The third member of the presidency, a Muslim, received the most votes and became its chairman. His calls for a "Greater Bosnia" led by Muslims were predictably rejected by the other leaders.

Shortly after his reelection in November 1996, Clinton extended the NATO mission in Bosnia through June 1998, a move that surprised no one and was followed by longer extensions of the foreign presence. NATO troops, accompanied by Russian peacekeepers, would continue to separate the combatants in three zones supervised by the United States, Great Britain, and France, respectively. Clinton argued that the troops were still needed to buy time for the new civilian-led government to take full control. In addition, NATO forces were attempting to disarm Bosnia's warring factions and, if this failed, to provide weapons and training for Muslim and Croat forces in order to create a balance of power in the region. The United States and Western European governments formally put the Bosnians on notice: continue the peace process or face new economic sanctions and the withdrawal of the peacekeeping force.

Left open to question, however, was the ultimate exit strategy of the NATO mission. Could it successfully provide the basis for long-term peace in Bosnia and leave the country to a patchwork national security force? Or, more likely, would it be forced to extend its mission indefinitely and acknowledge the permanent partition of Bosnia? If so, would the Western powers agree to police another Cyprus or Korea indefinitely? Even the Clinton administration would not guarantee the success of this mission, which continued into 2000. Interestingly, the only aspect of the Dayton Accords acceptable to critics was the provision for NATO withdrawal if the Bosnian factions could not eventually come to terms.

The Bosnian war revealed critical shortcomings in the system of collective security that was supposed to guarantee peace in the post–Cold War era. The United Nations was incapable of harnessing a united response to aggression, much less ending and punishing such transparent "ethnic cleansing." This failure of the UN reflected the failure of the Western great powers. Western Europeans, until forced into action, were deeply divided by the crisis. The European Union, which at the same time was trying to create a "common foreign and security policy," proved especially impotent. Given this record, it was doubtful that the externally imposed peace would provide a basis for long-term reconciliation.

THE KOSOVO SHOWDOWN

Tragically, the Balkan wars did not end in Bosnia. As many feared, Milosevic simply redirected his military machine against another Yugoslav province, Kosovo. The province held great symbolic value to Belgrade despite its chronic poverty and small Serbian population, for it was there that Serbian armies made their last stand against the Ottoman Turks in the 1389 Battle of Kosovo. After the Serbian defeat, most Kosovars converted to Islam. The remaining Serbs adhered to Christianity and submitted to five centuries of repressive rule by the Ottoman Empire, all the while plotting their revenge. They received their first chance when Kosovo was folded into the new federation of Yugoslavia after World War I. The Serb-dominated government immediately sought to settle the score, ejecting the majority population of ethnic Albanians from Kosovo and repopulating their villages with Serbs. But this early round of ethnic cleansing was cut short by the Second World War as the region again became a battleground for the great powers.

Tito allowed the conflict in Kosovo to smolder during the early stages of the Cold War and even permitted the region's autonomy under the new Yugoslav constitution of 1974. But Milosevic had other ideas once he assumed power fifteen years later. He quickly rescinded the new constitution, nullified the rights of Kosovar Albanians, and installed Serbs in key provincial offices. Yet Serbs, because of their mass exodus from Kosovo over a period of centuries, made up only about 10 percent of the province's population; ethnic Albanians made up the other 90 percent. In this respect, the crackdown that began in 1989 was doomed from the start. The Kosovars responded by declaring independence and organizing a defense force that became known as the Kosovo Liberation Army (KLA). Their appeals for statehood, however, were drowned out—first by the jubilation that attended the collapse of the Soviet Union, and then by the eruption of violence elsewhere in Yugoslavia.

Western leaders knew that Kosovo was a ticking time bomb even as the first battles were fought in Slovenia and Croatia. Military officials were particularly anxious about Kosovo because of its southern location and proximity to other fragile, ethnically mixed states such as Macedonia and Bulgaria. A major eruption in Kosovo, it was feared, could extend into Greece, whose Christian population supported the Serbs, then tempt intervention by Turkey funded by its Islamic allies in the Middle East. This nightmare scenario prompted the UN to deploy in 1993 a small force to Macedonia, which had seceded from Yugoslavia a year earlier. But the UN "firewall," which included a token contingent of 300 U.S. troops, was largely symbolic and did nothing to prevent the conflict from spreading into Kosovo.

To Milosevic, revenge in Kosovo was the only way to overcome his humiliating defeats in Slovenia, Croatia, and Bosnia. His paramilitary troops forced Albanian families from their homes, seized their possessions, and then set entire villages on fire. The KLA responded by conducting raids against the small population of Serbs, primarily police and government officials. In February 1999, attempting to prevent a full-scale war, the United States and European powers brought the rival factions together in Rambouillet, France. The deal proposed by the mediators—the retreat of Serbian forces from Kosovo, the introduction of a NATO-led peacekeeping force, and renewed autonomy (but not independence) for Kosovo—appealed to neither the Serbs nor the Kosovars. Under intense pressure from U.S. and European leaders, the Kosovar delegation agreed to the deal anyway, but only because Milosevic's rejection of the accords was a foregone conclusion.

With the Rambouillet accords in tatters, the NATO powers faced little choice but to act on their threats to respond with military force. Withholding military intervention would have revealed their threats as empty. Furthermore, in doing nothing NATO ran the risk of undermining the alliance at the very time it was seeking new life—and new members—

after the Cold War. The threatened NATO bombardment, code-named Operation Allied Force, began in late March. President Clinton, under pressure from domestic critics and many anxious European leaders, publicly ruled out a ground offensive.[11] In gaining support for the intervention by minimizing the risk of NATO casualties, however, Clinton and his NATO counterparts provided cover for Milosevic to create the very cataclysm NATO sought to avoid: the wholesale destruction of Kovovo and the displacement of more than one million ethnic Albanians.

The events that followed were ghastly, but familiar. Thousands of Muslim men were systematically rounded up, tortured, and murdered. Serbian troops systematically raped Muslim women, often in front of their children. Homes and businesses were pillaged and burned to the ground. Entire cities such as Pec and Djakovica, and even Kosovo's capital, Pristina, were reduced to ashes. Those who escaped the onslaught were stripped of their identification papers and sent wandering into the mine-filled mountain passes out of Kosovo. Many elderly refugees fell to their deaths along the way, their unrecovered bodies compounding the horror of the survivors. Other refugees were separated from their families, stuffed into locked trains, and shuttled to refugee camps in Albania and Macedonia that could not adequately feed or house them, nor provide them with the medical care they urgently needed. Although seemingly random and spontaneous, and contrary to Serb claims that the exodus was caused by the NATO bombing, the campaign of terror had been "meticulously organized and aimed, from the outset, at expelling huge numbers of people." [12]

Clinton soon confronted the consequences of NATO's decision to adopt a bombing campaign based on gradual escalation rather than an immediate and overwhelming destructive force that would have inflicted real pain on the civilian population. Based on the successful experience in Bosnia, the president had wrongly assumed that a modest show of NATO muscle—lasting just two or three days—would again drive Milosevic to the bargaining table. But this time the pinprick attacks on Serbian artillery and command centers only accelerated the gutting of Kosovo. Clinton therefore had only one option: to intensify the bombing campaign by directing NATO air strikes against the heart of Serbia. Early on, however, a series of targeting errors by NATO bombers, including the destruction of passenger trains and of the Chinese embassy in downtown Belgrade, left scores of civilians dead and prompted wide-

11. The German government, in particular, insisted that ground forces be avoided. The mere prospect of introducing ground troops to Kosovo was certain to incite a backlash against Chancellor Schroeder's new administration.

12. John Kifner, "How Serb Forces Purged One Million Albanians," *New York Times*, May 29, 1999, 1A.

spread condemnation. Such mistakes were to be expected given that pilots were prevented from flying below 15,000 feet, within the reach of Serbian antiaircraft missiles. But by this point the NATO barrage and its commitment to a final victory were irreversible.

After lengthy internal negotiations, the NATO states finally acknowledged in May that ground forces might be required to support the air campaign. The alliance also assented to a renewed ground campaign by KLA forces that would flush Serbian forces from their concealed positions in Kosovo and expose them to a crippling round of NATO attacks. As in Bosnia, where aerial attacks had been bolstered by the Croat-Muslim counteroffensive, the military campaign in Kosovo finally produced results. Repeated attacks on Belgrade's electrical grid, which literally "turned off the lights" in the Yugoslav capital, were especially helpful in demonstrating NATO's heightened resolve. Faced with another defeat and under pressure by Russian officials to end the war, Milosevic agreed in June to withdraw the Serbian forces and allow the displaced Kosovars to return to the remnants of their communities.

This latest round of the latest Balkan ordeal achieved the general objectives of the NATO powers. Serbia's ten-year campaign of terror and intimidation finally was brought to an end, and fears of a widened conflict beyond Yugoslavia were dispelled. In gaining Milosevic's final surrender, Western leaders had delivered their message that ethnic cleansing in Europe was a thing of the past. In defeating Serbia without a single NATO casualty, Clinton and his European counterparts had prevented their domestic opponents from mobilizing against the war, challenging their leadership, and threatening the future of the alliance.

In other respects the NATO victory was partial and highly qualified. Kosovo was "liberated," but it would remain—at least in name—a part of Yugoslavia. Milosevic and his top military aides remained in power, even after being indicted by a UN court for crimes against humanity. The returning Kosovars faced the difficult task of creating a system of self-rule within Yugoslavia—a task possible only with the assistance of the fifty thousand NATO and UN troops. The mission of the peacekeepers, who confronted resistance by Serbs as well as many militant Kosovars, would be dangerous, its long-term prospects uncertain. For all of these reasons, the end of the conflict was greeted more with relief than celebration by the victors.

As for the European governments, the Kosovo intervention clearly showed them how far they had to go to attain any semblance of a common foreign policy. Serious divisions had emerged—and remained unresolved—regarding the gravity of the Balkan crisis and the risk it actually had posed to Western Europe. In tactical terms, it was significant that U.S. aircraft had carried out most of the estimated six thousand bombing missions, and that nearly every target had been identified by U.S. intelligence sources. The European states, by contrast, had had little to offer in the way of skilled manpower and weapons systems. "The Kosovo war was mainly an experience of Europe's own insufficiency and weakness," German foreign minister Joschka Fischer observed. "We as Europeans never could have coped with the Balkan wars that were caused by Milosevic without the help of the United States. The sad truth is that Kosovo showed Europe is still not able to solve its own problems." [13]

With this in mind, the European Union decided in December 1999 to create a strike force of sixty thousand troops by 2003 that would respond to crises not requiring NATO (or U.S.) involvement. Javier Solana, the retiring secretary general of NATO, was appointed the EU's first "high representative for foreign affairs and security." Despite these well-publicized moves, it remained highly doubtful that Europeans would be willing to fund such a military force, or that they would overcome their chronic differences over its command structure. Nevertheless, the lesson of the Yugoslav wars was inescapable: the European powers remained unable to take concerted action in a military crisis and remained utterly dependent on the United States to keep the peace in their own region.

In the end, the Balkan wars revealed the extent to which the post–Cold War system had strayed from the "new world order" so widely proclaimed less than a decade earlier. The credibility of the United Nations was especially damaged by the conflicts. During the Kosovo crisis, the United States and its NATO allies were forced to sidestep the UN Security Council, which had played a key role in legitimating the expulsion of Iraq from Kuwait. The certainty of Russian and Chinese vetoes persuaded the Western powers to press ahead without the UN's blessing. While their decision ultimately led to the Serbs' expulsion from Kosovo, it dashed for the foreseeable future any remaining hopes that the world body would live up to the great expectations that had prevailed after the Cold War. Power politics had once again proven insurmountable in the Balkan peninsula, with ominous implications for other trouble spots in the twenty-first century.

U.S.-RUSSIAN RELATIONS UNDER STRESS

One of the most bizarre episodes of the war in Kosovo occurred after the fighting had ended and the peace treaty had been signed. Before

13. Quoted in Ivo H. Daalder and Michael E. O'Hanlon, "Unlearning the Lessons of Kosovo," *Foreign Policy* (fall 1999): 137.

dawn on June 12, 1999, an armored column of Russian troops entered the smoldering ruins of Pristina, the capital city. The soldiers were cheered by the remaining Serbs in the city as they rolled toward the airport, where they took up their position as an occupying force.

But there was a problem: the Russians were not supposed to be in Pristina; they were supposed to be at their peacekeeping posts in Bosnia. Their surprise arrival several hours ahead of the NATO contingent—including British, French, Italian, and U.S. troops—stole the spotlight from the very forces whose military campaign had brought about Milosevic's surrender of Kosovo. Russian leaders, in stark contrast, had consistently *opposed* the bombing campaign and promised to veto any UN effort to prevent the ethnic cleansing of Kosovar Albanians. The Russian "liberation" of Pristina was, therefore, a farce. But it offered the Russian troops and their leaders in Moscow a brief moment of glory, along with a barely concealed sense of satisfaction that they had beaten the NATO powers to their prize.

This misplaced show of force illustrated just how decrepit Russia had become during its torturous period of transition after the Cold War. Eight years of political and economic crises produced almost daily political struggles in Moscow, a declining economic output, and a string of military challenges inside and beyond Russia's borders. Were it not for a steady supply of economic aid from Western countries, Boris Yeltsin's faltering regime—and his democratic reforms—would likely have collapsed long before the Kosovo conflict and its surreal aftermath. Yet Yeltsin somehow managed to remain in power until after the Balkan wars, and his country retained the one source of power that could not be denied: a massive nuclear stockpile. As a result, Russia continued to preoccupy American leaders into the new millennium.

INTERNAL CHALLENGES TO REFORM

The collapse of communist rule exposed deep fault lines within the former Soviet Union. Just as the breakup of the Ottoman and Austro-Hungarian empires contributed to the onset of World War I, and just as the dismantling of the European colonial empires after 1945 set off violence between and within many new states, new possibilities for conflict appeared after the Soviet Union fractured into fifteen republics, all claiming sovereignty. The Baltic states of Estonia, Latvia, and Lithuania reclaimed their pre–World War II independence. Because the Russians had long controlled both the czarist and communist states, ethnic Russians were left scattered throughout the Commonwealth of Independent States (CIS), the loose-knit group of twelve non-Baltic republics formed after the fall of the Soviet Union. In addition to the Russians, dozens of other ethnic groups inhabited the vast frontiers of the CIS.

COMMONWEALTH OF INDEPENDENT STATES, 1992

This intermingling of ethnic groups inflamed the hatreds between the Russians and the peoples they had long dominated, particularly Muslims living in the southern tier of CIS states. In Russia the revival of ethnic tensions gave xenophobic nationalists and former communists, bent on destroying the liberal state and market economy the reformers were trying to create, a strong emotional issue with which to bring down Yeltsin's centrist regime. Moldova and Georgia (a non-CIS state) immediately faced secessionist movements. Ukraine was internally divided between its own ethnic group and a sizable Russian population. Belarus, Turkmenistan, and Uzbekistan came under dictatorial rule. Tajikistan was engulfed in civil war. And Armenia and Azerbaijan fought a costly war over an enclave—Nagorno-Karabakh—seen as the rightful possession of both states.

But Russia remained a potentially formidable military power with the ability to destroy the fragile political arrangements that were emerging in the 1990s. The Russian government continued to command an army of more than 1 million soldiers, 200,000 of whom remained outside its borders within the CIS. Yeltsin instituted ambitious political and economic reforms, but they proved difficult to impose on a society that had never been exposed to democracy or the free market. Prominent communists, elected under the old Soviet constitution, still dominated the legislature and state bureaucracy, and they blocked the Russian president's reform efforts. Also opposed to Yeltsin's efforts were Russian nationalists, who shared the communists' resentment at the loss of empire and status, and a powerful "mafia" that exploited the vast black market in Russia's largest cities.

Boris Yeltsin was caught in the middle of a political cyclone.[14] In September 1993 the Russian president dissolved the Russian parliament whose members were elected under the Soviet system and opposed many of his political and economic reforms. The dissidents then called for armed insurrection against Yeltsin and barricaded themselves within the "White House," as the building that housed the parliament was known. Yeltsin, faced with growing unrest on the streets of Moscow, responded by declaring a state of emergency and ordering Russian troops to shell the White House, which had served as a symbol of democracy and resistance to the communist regime prior to the collapse of the Soviet Union. More than a hundred people were killed in the assault, and the leading political opponents were arrested. Yeltsin quickly introduced a new constitution that greatly enhanced his powers while calling for elections to a new bicameral federal assembly. These actions, he argued, were necessary to ensure the success of Russia's experiment with democracy.

The elections that followed in December, however, only made matters worse for the Russian president. Extremists from both the right and the left dominated the new federal assembly. The most outspoken nationalist, Vladimir Zhirinovsky, pledged to restore the old Russian empire, even suggesting he would gain the return of Alaska. As conditions worsened across the country, many Russians welcomed his appeals and longed openly for the more "orderly" system under Lenin, Stalin, and Brezhnev.

In the United States and Western Europe, questions were raised about the continuing flow of Western aid to Russia. Should the new Russia be left to wallow in its economic misery, perhaps to emerge some day as a resentful state—like Germany after World War I? Or should Russia's for-

14. On the debilitating effect of Russia's internal politics, see Lilia Shevtsova, *Yeltsin's Russia: Myths and Reality* (Washington: Carnegie Endowment for International Peace, 1999). Also see Dimitri K. Simes, *After the Collapse: Russia Seeks Its Place as a Great Power* (New York: Simon and Schuster, 1999).

mer adversaries furnish the support Russia needed to grow economically and become politically stable—in much the same way the United States helped Germany after World War II? The Western powers adopted the latter course and agreed that Russia should receive economic assistance, but only so long as the money was used effectively. They demanded that Yeltsin's political reforms move forward and that Russian leaders hold inflation in check and stop subsidizing inefficient or Mafia-controlled industries. Even though they were faced with their own economic problems, Western leaders, led by the German government, promised Russia more than $30 billion in aid. Meanwhile, the International Monetary Fund approved an additional $10 billion in low-interest loans to Russia—a transparent effort to revive Yeltsin's standing as he campaigned for reelection in 1995.

Living conditions continued to deteriorate for most Russians as doubts about the durability of Yeltsin's reforms spread across the country. Russia's economic output had fallen by nearly 20 percent in the first four years of reform, and the rampant inflation of 1993–1994 consumed much of the national savings. Russian soldiers went unpaid for months and in some cases relied on the charity of private citizens for survival. But with his $10 billion in IMF credits, a quarter of which were made available immediately, Yeltsin restored many social programs and launched an aggressive, Western-style political campaign. By the time national elections were held, Yeltsin had regained enough support to defeat his communist and nationalist challengers.

The Russian president could not, however, prevent Russia's continued slide into disarray. Economic output finally increased by 1997 but then plunged again in 1998 amid a collapse of the ruble, renewed inflation, and a Russian default on its foreign debt payments. Much of the Russian economy had been reduced to barter transactions by this time. Tax collection was sporadic and selective, and government regulators routinely supplemented their meager incomes by demanding bribes. The practice of "crony capitalism" that was sweeping across Eastern Europe became an art form in Russia, where former communists gobbled up huge public industries such as the Gazprom energy consortium and kept the profits for themselves. Meanwhile, Yeltsin fueled a recurring political crisis by sacking four prime ministers between March 1998 and August 1999. His behavior became ever more erratic as he battled not only his domestic enemies but a series of health problems that left him frail and often incapacitated.

UNREST IN THE 'NEAR ABROAD'

Yeltsin's problems were further aggravated by turmoil in the "near abroad" region of central Asia, home to the largely Islamic states of the

CIS whose people had struggled against Russian domination ever since the Cossacks first entered the Caucasus Mountains in the sixteenth century. The sparse and impoverished Muslim population had succumbed to the brute strength of czarist Russia, and during the Cold War it suffered even worse repression as captive members of the Soviet Union. Given this history, it is no wonder that the liberated republics of central Asia welcomed the collapse of the Soviet Union and seized their opportunity to be finally free of Moscow's control.

Of particular concern to Russia was the possibility that other Islamic powers in the region, including Iran and Turkey, would exploit the vacuum created by the Soviet Union's demise and attempt to impose their own hegemonic designs on the region. All of central Asia seemed up for grabs in the 1990s as militant Islamic groups seized control of Afghanistan and civil wars raged in neighboring CIS republics. In the meantime, the United States and European powers quietly pursued their own interests in the rich oil fields of the Caspian Sea and sought to construct pipelines out of the area that would not be subject to Russian control.

Yeltsin faced the immediate threat posed by the rise of Islamic movements within Russia itself. This threat quickly became real in the territory of Chechnya, which had long struggled against Moscow's hegemony.[15] After Chechen leaders declared in 1994 that "our independence is forever," Yeltsin sent Russian troops to the Chechen capital, Grozny, and the Russian air force bombed residential neighborhoods. But his poorly organized and under-equipped troops faltered against the more determined Chechens, who drew support from neighboring Islamic states and continued to press their case for independence into the late 1990s.

Of particular importance to Russia was the dangerous precedent that Chechnya, a relatively small territory, would set for other dissatisfied ethnic groups if its demands for independence were met. Yet nothing the Russian troops did was sufficient to overcome the Chechen fighters, whose defiance in the face of a stronger enemy was reminiscent of the Afghan *mujahidin.* The Chechens stood firm, held elections in January 1997, and then issued an even more explicit declaration of independence. Humiliated by these events, Yeltsin unleashed another attack against the Chechens in 1999. The military campaign served as the only rallying point for the Russian people, who were otherwise demoralized and destitute after years of stalled economic reforms.

The United States clung to Yeltsin throughout this ordeal, viewing the Russian leader as the best and perhaps only hope for the country's

15. See Anatol Lieven, *Chechnya: Tombstone of Russian Power* (New Haven: Yale University Press, 1998).

peaceful reform. While Clinton and Yeltsin bickered over issues such as NATO expansion and Yugoslavia, they agreed on the basic designs of the new Russia. And they knew that Russia would need continued infusions of aid—accompanied by exceptional patience—from the West in order to prevent a catastrophe. From the standpoint of U.S. leaders, only Yeltsin could keep bilateral arms control talks from coming apart and prevent Russia's nuclear technology from being sold to the highest bidders. The latter was especially important to the United States. It had spent nearly $3 billion between 1992 and 1999 to "denuclearize" Belarus, Kazakhstan, and Ukraine, and to remove other weapons of mass destruction from across the former Soviet Union. But more work was needed to prevent the sale of nuclear technology, which had become an attractive prospect to the cash-starved economies of the region. Clinton was therefore restrained in criticizing Yeltsin. After first condemning the crackdown in Chechnya, Clinton defended the Russian leader's sovereign right to keep the province and only asked that Yeltsin avoid excessive force.

Clinton's hands-off stance could not disguise Russia's military humiliation in Chechnya, or the futility of its effort to defeat the nationalists. Even after Russian tanks had reduced Grozny to a pile of rubble, the Chechens merely retreated into the surrounding mountains to begin plotting their next offensive. But Clinton did provide Yeltsin with the diplomatic cover he needed to continue his attacks, which finally subdued the rebels, at least for the moment. The amity between Washington and Moscow infuriated Yeltsin's opponents and a large segment of the general public. To Russian nationalists, Yeltsin had diminished their country's prestige by becoming addicted to Western aid and political support. Meanwhile, neocommunists condemned the Russian president for falling prey to the capitalist designs of the IMF and multinational banks.

In the face of these attacks, and seizing his chance to shape his own succession, Yeltsin abruptly resigned on the last day of 1999 and transferred power to his latest prime minister, Vladimir Putin. The former KGB officer had become a hero for leading the most recent crackdown in Chechnya, despite the mission's tactical failures which were not reported in the Russian press. Putin also had just consolidated his political power in parliamentary elections, giving him a distinct advantage in the March 2000 presidential elections, which he won easily after pledging to revive Russia's economy at home and in world markets, root out corruption, and strengthen the military forces.

While such a brazen power play would have been widely condemned in the United States, Yeltsin's timely resignation received little fanfare within or outside Russia. The mere fact that power had been transferred peacefully was considered a major achievement—and a source of relief. Nevertheless, the prospects for Russia in the post-Yeltsin era were highly uncertain. The country did not have the luxury of reverting to either its feudal or communist pasts, when territorial expansion and foreign domination overcame the effects of domestic oppression, corruption, and incompetence. This formula proved the undoing of both political systems and left Russia a top-heavy military power with a decaying economic base and a sullen, resentful population. The last communist leader, Mikhail Gorbachev, had recognized that the public must be energized and empowered, but his political reforms only brought about the final repudiation of the Soviet Union. When Yeltsin's turn came in 1992, he could not overcome the root rot that had devoured the Soviet Union. The aging Russian leader kept his tenuous hold on power only by resorting to many of the same autocratic measures that had sustained his predecessors. None of this would work for Russia in the future, under Putin or any other Russian leader, because, as one historian aptly noted,

> at the end of the twentieth century international power rests not on the extent of territory a state controls but on its level of economic and technological developments. Politically, economically, and morally the age of territorial empires is over: crossing frontiers with armies is no longer a permissible road to national aggrandizement. . . . Thus Russia, no matter how organized politically, must first become rich if she wishes again to be powerful; and getting rich, with the handicap of a Soviet legacy, will take no small length of time.[16]

Given this stubborn reality, the United States remained patient with Russia into the twenty-first century. Russia was simply too large, too well stocked with nuclear weapons, and too politically volatile to be ignored. Put more positively, a democratic Russia with a vibrant economy would be a force for global stability. For different reasons, U.S. leaders had no choice but to maintain their close contacts with the Eastern European governments, which still claimed allegiance to the democratic values long espoused by the United States even as their economic reforms came under fire. America's vision of democratic governance and market economics had finally been given its chance on the dividing line between East and West. This was no time for the United States to retreat into its hemispheric shell, despite the appeal this course held among many Americans.

The upheavals of the 1990s also compelled an ongoing U.S. presence in Western Europe. As described earlier, the EU states proved unable to resolve the Balkan crises without the United States, and they remained

16. Martin Malia, *Russia under Western Eyes: From the Bronze Horseman to the Lenin Mausoleum* (Cambridge: Belknap Press, 1999), 417.

dependent on NATO as their ultimate source of military security. But this dependence did not stop Europeans from planning other military arrangements and pursuing a common foreign policy, often with U.S. encouragement. Nor did it prevent them from complaining about the "hyperpower" in Washington, a term often used by European critics of the United States. The outcome of all these struggles would shape the transatlantic relationship well into the twenty-first century.

Protesters confront police during the World Trade Organization's 1999 conference in Seattle. Environmental and human rights groups joined with U.S.-based trade unions to disrupt the WTO conference, which became a major foreign policy embarrassment to the Clinton administration.

CHAPTER THIRTEEN

Into the Twenty-first Century

The United States entered the twentieth century as a rising industrial power that remained, deliberately, outside the circles of great-power diplomacy. American leaders stood by as the Concert of Europe was created in 1815, as the revolutions of 1848 swept across the continent, and as the European powers scrambled for African colonies in the 1890s. With its considerable freedom to maneuver, the United States extended its sphere of influence throughout the Western Hemisphere and its territorial reach across the Pacific Ocean. The American dream of permanent isolation from power politics proved impossible, however, after Germany provoked total war in Europe in 1914 and again in 1939, and after Japan attacked Pearl Harbor in 1941.

Once it defeated the Axis powers, the United States faced yet another threat, this time from its wartime ally the Soviet Union and its dictator, Joseph Stalin, who was imposing puppet regimes across Eastern Europe and predicting the "inevitable" victory of communism over capitalism.

The containment strategy adopted by the United States in 1946, originally intended for the Soviet Union, was extended to China after Mao Zedong signed a friendship treaty with Stalin in 1950 and the two leaders tacitly approved North Korea's invasion of South Korea. As in the case of Germany, the actions of the communist powers threatened the United States, whose security, economic vitality, and democratic values could not be sustained in a world filled with "despotic utopias." [1] This was particularly true as colonialism yielded in the 1960s to dozens of new but impoverished countries whose leaders—often resentful and hostile toward the West—sought revolutionary cures to the ills facing their people.

In the end, the American political system, based on individual rights and limited government, proved superior to the collectivist schemes of fascism and communism. Meanwhile, the market-driven American economy brought greater prosperity than the centralized control of the communist states. Thus the "American century," which began during World War II, outlasted the Cold War.

With the United States secure and prosperous in the 1990s, many Americans approached foreign affairs with the same wariness exhibited by the nation's earliest leaders. Public opinion polls consistently registered a longing for the nation to turn its energies away from foreign entanglements and toward the resolution of long-neglected domestic problems. But other Americans, including a majority of the business and political elite, felt the United States should exploit its status as the lone superpower to seek a more stable, peaceful, and prosperous world. Meanwhile, officials in the Central Intelligence Agency and the Pentagon worried that poisonous "snakes" lurked overseas and called for the United States to prevent the rise of any challengers to its primacy.

In short, the new era revived old controversies about America's role in the system of states—controversies that were often suppressed as the country fended off the totalitarian challenges of the twentieth century. Advocates of U.S. withdrawal from great-power politics once again clashed with liberal internationalists who urged America to save the anarchic and war-prone international system from itself. Nowhere was this disconnect more visible than in the struggle between the executive and legislative branches of government, which produced a spiral of political stalemates and policy reversals. As U.S. allies watched with dismay and as adversaries watched with amusement, the United States entered the twenty-first century a divided and uncertain power.

1. Paul Johnson, *Modern Times: The World from the Twenties to the Eighties* (New York: Harper and Row, 1983). Also see Tony Smith, *America's Mission: The United States and the Worldwide Struggle for Democracy in the Twentieth Century* (Princeton: Princeton University Press, 1994).

All this could be considered a harmless, perhaps even an endearing episode in America's democratic "experiment" were the stakes not so immense. The first years of the twenty-first century will witness key leadership changes in the United States and Russia. Their relations, which deteriorated steadily during the 1990s, remain pivotal to global stability. China's future direction also will affect the United States and the precarious power balance along the Pacific Rim. Meanwhile, tensions between the United States and a more unified Europe will likely provoke disputes over trade, security arrangements, and "out of area" military interventions. Long-term solutions to the conflicts in the Balkans, the Middle East, Korea, and South Asia will be elusive, if not impossible, in the absence of strong and coherent U.S. leadership.

In addition to these regional questions, American leaders will face many problems overseas that have little to do with geography. New democracies will continue to be put to the test, along with the claim that democratic states are by nature peaceful toward one another. Soaring population growth and environmental deterioration will increasingly strain the world's "carrying capacity" while the AIDS epidemic claims millions of new victims. Drug cartels, Mafias, and black market arms dealers will seek continued profits from a world in flux. Finally, the United Nations will again try to make sense of its global mission after seeing its campaign of sustainable development thwarted and the Security Council ignored by the Western powers in Kosovo.

As America falls into the patterns of the past, its leaders will no doubt recognize that the current period is unique in one critical respect: never before has any single country possessed such immense power in the absence of a formidable adversary. The United States is, then, a central *component* of the international system, not a second-tier state that can take or leave the vagaries of world politics as it did before the world wars. American preeminence carries with it an inescapable measure of responsibility.

History demonstrates how timidity by great powers only invites challenges to the status quo that eventually must be confronted at great cost. The rise of Germany in the early 1900s exploited the decline of three empires and the turmoil in revolutionary Russia. Germany's resurgence in the 1930s and Japan's regional conquests were abetted by the false promises of the League of Nations and the disarmament and declared neutrality of the United States. For his part, Stalin quickly seized on the void in Eastern Europe after World War II, and his successors sought to extend Marxism-Leninism to developing countries recently freed from colonial rule. The lesson is clear that world politics, as nature itself, abhors a vacuum.

REALISM VERSUS MORALISM: THE CURRENT DEBATE

As we have seen, the turbulent international system of the post–Cold War era did not wait patiently for the United States to resolve its latest identity crisis. Upheavals in several regions shattered the widely anticipated "new world order" and forced American leaders to respond, often inconsistently, in the absence of an overriding redefinition of national purpose. At some point, however, they had to confront the central question: What would be the role of the United States in the post–Cold War world? Containing communism could no longer serve as a rationale for intervention, nor could the bipolar division of power that had compelled the United States to respond to nearly every Soviet provocation, regional conflict, and civil war. Yet a foreign policy based on hemispheric isolation would not be viable in an era of economic integration and global interdependence.

In the debates over U.S. grand stragegy, two general worldviews vied for supremacy. At one pole were the realists, whose outlook supplanted isolationism and prevailed during the Cold War. They envisioned a United States motivated by consistent, well-defined national interests, rooted in its need for self-preservation in a hostile system of nation-states. Realism provided a clear set of orienting principles: the central role of power, the primacy of national interests versus transnational concerns, the frequency of conflict, and the necessity for self-reliance.

But whereas realists could agree on these principles, their prescriptions for American foreign policy often diverged. While most realists opposed the proliferation of weapons of mass destruction, threats to regional power balances, and the rise of another great power in Eurasia, they could not agree on which country, group, or situation presented a specific threat to American or broader Western interests, let alone on the means to cope with such threats. Thus there were significant differences in policy preferences among realists, who otherwise shared certain philosophical views and a sense of caution about the American role in the world.[2]

The opposing view remained that of traditional moralism, which animated American foreign policy before the world wars and fueled its sense of destiny. In this view, moral imperatives rendered American foreign policy distinct from the "power politics" of Old World diplomacy. Its advocates continued to equate the country's national values—individual liberty, religious tolerance, human rights—with universal values.

2. For an elaboration of this view, see Barry R. Posen and Andrew L. Ross, "Competing Visions for U.S. Grand Strategy," *International Security* (winter 1996–1997): 5–53.

IMPACT AND INFLUENCE

MADELEINE ALBRIGHT

Among the most forceful proponents of an activist U.S. world role after the Cold War was Secretary of State Madeleine Albright, the first woman to hold the post and the highest-ranking woman in the U.S. government. As the world's "indispensable nation," she argued, the United States was duty bound to promote democratic freedoms far from its borders, even through the use of military force.

Albright's personal history profoundly shaped her world view. Her family fled Czechoslovakia in 1939 after Adolf Hitler's takeover of the country, and three of her Jewish grandparents later died in German concentration camps. Upon Hitler's defeat, Albright's family returned home, but soon became refugees again when the Soviet Union seized control of the government in a 1948 communist coup. The daughter of a Czech diplomat, Albright served during Clinton's first term as U.S. ambassador to the United Nations. Her calls for U.S. participation in several UN peacekeeping missions resulted in frequent clashes with Republican leaders in Congress. Yet she remained well respected on Capitol Hill and was easily confirmed as secretary of state in 1997.

In the country's early history, adherence to such values meant excluding the United States from the corruptive world of *realpolitik*.

Given America's unparalleled strengths after the Cold War, advocates of moral activism felt the United States was in a favorable position to project these values overseas, not simply its military power and economic wealth. Such presumptions informed Bill Clinton's "neo-Wilsonian" foreign policy and later inspired Secretary of State Madeleine Albright to declare the United States the world's "indispensable" nation.

In practice, moral concerns led to U.S. interventions in Somalia, Haiti, and Yugoslavia—and to the Clinton administration's early support for the UN campaigns of sustainable development and international peace-keeping.

THE CNN REVOLUTION AND FOREIGN POLICY

This moralistic impulse fed on the satellite images conveyed by news networks, many of which featured grisly pictures of the effects of famine, military carnage, and violations of human rights in other countries. These images often promoted activism in cases that otherwise were only marginally relevant to American interests.

During his tenure in the Oval Office, George Bush admitted that he was influenced by television's ability to bring pictures of human suffering and misery into American homes. Such pictures appeared after the victory over Iraq, when Saddam Hussein persecuted the Kurdish minority that had rebelled during the war and sought to secede from the country. The televised footage of more than a million Kurdish refugees, from the very young to the old, fleeing their homes with whatever they could carry and living in the mountains in the bitter winter cold, was wrenching to a global television audience. The subsequent moral outrage created public pressure to act, leading to an American-led relief effort and a declaration that the Kurd-held regions of northern Iraq were off-limits to Iraqi forces.

Televised images of the famine in Somalia also were instrumental in rallying an international response. But when some of the American soldiers sent to Somalia on a humanitarian mission were killed or injured—all before the television cameras—public and congressional pressure to withdraw became intense. In response, Clinton ordered a hasty retreat. Ironically, then, television brought the United States into the Somalia nightmare, and television forced it out. Meanwhile, in nearby Sudan a less-visible but more deadly civil war dragged on between the ruling Arab population in the north and the black population in the south. Nearly two million Sudanese died in that struggle—more than the combined death tolls of Rwanda and Yugoslavia—but the lack of television coverage ensured that no large-scale foreign intervention would be forthcoming.

Recognition of human suffering—whether from dictatorial rule, natural disasters, or ethnic violence—is crucial for any great power that aspires to make constructive change beyond its borders. But such recognition does not in itself constitute a sufficient basis for action. Political leaders also must determine their country's stakes in these distant problems, and more important, their capacity to solve them. Failing to do so will only compound the devastation and promote calls for renewed isolation. As George Kennan recently observed, "If American policy from here on out, particularly policy involving the use of our armed forces abroad, is to be controlled by popular emotional impulses, and especially ones provoked by the commercial television industry, then there is no place not only for myself, but for the responsible deliberative organs of our government." [3]

BEYOND THE CLINTON DOCTRINE

The early debates about the Balkan crisis vividly illustrated the tensions underlying America's post–Cold War foreign policy, especially the use of force. For George Bush, the criterion was whether vital interests—that is, strategic or material assets valuable to the United States—were involved. Such interests were present in the Persian Gulf; they were not so clear in Yugoslavia. There, the stakes were largely humanitarian, as they were in Somalia and Haiti, but in these two countries the initial assumption was that the United States could satisfy its moral urges at a relatively minor cost. Moral principles, however, could not be so easily upheld in the "tinderbox of Europe." Military intervention might not be successful given the complexity of the struggle and the region's inhospitable terrain and climate. And even if the fighting could be stopped, the chances for long-term reconciliation among the warring parties were remote. An extended—and possibly endless—peacekeeping presence by outside forces would thus be likely.

The paradox and irony in the situation were tremendous. The very people who had opposed going to war against Saddam Hussein were by and large the same people who favored intervention in Yugoslavia. If only Yugoslavia had oil, some of them said. That was a very revealing comment because it suggested that the United States would have intervened sooner had there been material interests at stake. For liberals advocating intervention in behalf of the Muslims, however, such intervention was essential precisely because material interests were *not* involved. Neither oil nor strategic position should sully America's cause. What did America stand for if not democracy and human rights?

Thus American public opinion, so crucial in shaping its conduct overseas, was turned upside down. After the Vietnam War, many liberals had rejected John Kennedy's inaugural pledge that the United States would "pay any price, bear any burden, meet any hardship, support any friend, oppose any foe to assure the survival and the success of liberty." The war had turned many of them into foes of military intervention and pushed many others toward pacifism and isolationism. America's moral standing, in their view, had been irreparably damaged by that conflict.

3. George Kennan, *At a Century's End: Reflections 1982–1995* (New York: Norton, 1996), 297.

The post-Vietnam problem, then, was not how to contain Soviet expansion but how to *restrain* U.S. power. Most liberals therefore opposed every post-Vietnam use of force until Bush asked Congress for authorization to go to war against Iraq—a resolution that passed the Senate by only three votes.

If fighting against Saddam Hussein was not a pure cause, fighting for the Muslims in the remnants of Yugoslavia apparently was. And in such desperate areas as Somalia and Haiti, where political disintegration had produced brutal violence and widespread human suffering, American military preeminence could, for once, be put to good use. Thus the post-Vietnam doves transformed themselves into hawks, and many of their most vocal advocates assumed powerful positions in the Clinton administration. Within a short time, the equation of humanitarian crises with U.S. national interests had become the closest approximation to a Clinton Doctrine.

An American foreign policy based on moralism, however, could not ultimately be sustained. Human rights and democratization may have been deemed major concerns by the U.S. government, but not all foreign countries were of equal importance to the United States. If a government's inhumane treatment of its own people became the principal reason for U.S. intervention, where would American leaders draw the line? Why not intervene in other areas where civil wars and attendant cruelties were occurring—in Sudan, Rwanda, Congo, Liberia, Azerbaijan, Sri Lanka, or dozens of other places? "Our planet will be filled with barbarism for a long time to come," said one distinguished historian. "In many cases we must accept the sad necessity of living with tragedies that are beyond our power to control and our wisdom to cure. We cannot right every wrong or reverse each adversity. There cannot be an American solution to every world problem." [4]

This central lesson was driven home by the anti-American backlash in Somalia, the remoteness of the ethnic rivalries in Africa, the failure of the mission in Haiti, and endless confrontations with "rogue states." Faced with its own limitations, the United States was forced to draw the line by not stepping into the bloodbaths in central Africa and Sudan. The Clinton Doctrine, which had at first lent nearly unqualified support for humanitarian interventions, steadily became more modest. In its revised form, strong domestic support—from Congress and the general public—would be a prerequisite for military interventions, which meant that a successful outcome had to be virtually guaranteed. More directly, any loss of American lives would be unacceptable in regions not vital to American security.

4. Arthur Schlesinger Jr., "How to Think about Bosnia," *Wall Street Journal*, May 3, 1993, A16.

Clinton's insistence that the upheaval in Kosovo represented more than a humanitarian concern was contradicted by his painstaking effort to keep NATO forces out of harm's way in the conflict. Indeed, even the capture of three U.S. soldiers became a national crisis and prompted calls for withdrawal. The intense effort to secure their release, ultimately successful, was rare in wartime but logical under the terms of the revised Clinton Doctrine. Although the high-altitude bombings ordered by Clinton led to numerous targeting errors and civilian casualties, the fact that no Americans or other NATO personnel were killed kept the mission from becoming a political liability to the president. The practical limits of America's most recent moral crusade had been clearly established.

Taken together, developments in the 1990s tested the assumptions of both realism and moralism. The rise of geoeconomics and interdependence did not square with many realist assumptions. Nor did the political infighting in Washington that prevented the United States from facing the world as a "unitary" actor. As in the past, realists neglected the differing values held by foreign governments and instead reduced interstate behavior to crude measures of military strength. This failure of realism to distinguish between despotic and democratic powers, a throwback to the amoral school of *realpolitik* long rejected by Americans, seemed even more perverse given the nation's experience of the twentieth century.

Meanwhile, the practical difficulties of resolving entrenched civil wars and global problems frustrated moralism. The revival of ethnic and religious blood feuds, and the persistent competition among nation-states for advantage, shattered the visions of growing solidarity that were widely held after the Cold War and prompted the liberal internationalism of the early Clinton administration. Events in the 1990s made it stubbornly clear that power struggles would remain a defining element of world politics, that the nation-state was hardly withering away, and that the moral ambitions of the United States would often be frustrated.

THE GLOBALIZATION BACKLASH

A key assumption guiding American foreign policy after the Cold War was that the "smaller" world made possible by the forces of global integration would encourage common solutions to social, political, and economic problems. New computer technologies, satellite and cable television, and expanded transportation networks had brought the world's diverse populations closer together and created, for the first time, a global marketplace. With more information in more hands, governments would find it harder to control minds and dictate behavior, furthering the cause of democracy. Fateful decisions regarding public welfare would be shared not only among government leaders, but also among private interest groups, corporations, and international organizations.

If for every action there is an equal and opposite reaction, it should not have been surprising that globalization sparked opposition in the late 1990s. Critics charged that an integrated world threatened cultural diversity, imperiled the global environment, and prevented local and national leaders from controlling events within their territories. Moreover, a single world economy would give free reign to multinational corporations and effectively make the world safe for McDonalds, Wal-Mart, Toyota, and Shell. These concerns provided the normative basis for the backlash against the phenomenon. The economic crisis that beset East Asia in the late 1990s (described in the next section) further suggested that an integrated world economy would produce perils as well as prosperity. All of this greatly complicated the task of American leaders, many of whom had embraced globalization as the realization of the country's historic vision.

EAST ASIA FROM BOOM TO BUST

In the 1980s the economies of East Asia became role models for developing countries that sought to spur economic growth by immersing themselves in global markets (see Chapter 10). The region's civil societies had long been valued for their emphases on education, discipline, and family values, and the governments of East Asia had been praised in financial circles for maintaining fiscal discipline, encouraging high rates of savings, and improving living standards. This record contrasted sharply with that of other developing regions, where state intervention and isolation from trade and capital markets had become the standard, if ineffective, means of achieving economic growth.

The bubble burst, however, in 1997. The East Asian economic "miracle" suddenly gave way to a severe crisis that spread to other regions and threatened to slow or reverse worldwide economic growth. Problems were first reported in Japan, East Asia's engine of growth, which faced falling demand for its exports, rising debts, and an unstable currency. In July 1997 Thailand's government devalued its currency and prompted the rampant withdrawal of capital from the country. South Korea and Indonesia then caught the "Asian flu" as banks recalled outstanding debts, many of which could not be repaid. The Russian economy soon afterward plunged into economic chaos, currency devaluation, and a default on its foreign debts. As the crisis spread toward Brazil and other newly industrialized countries, economic globalization took on a new and darker form. The high level of interdependence among the world's market economies, once thought to be a blessing, had turned out to be a curse as well.

The crisis originated from two closely related sources. The first of these involved structural problems within the East Asian countries themselves; they were ill equipped to handle the rapid economic growth and inflows of foreign capital. Rapid growth inflated expectations of even greater prosperity, producing a building boom that quickly exceeded the level of demand. As a result, many of the huge office towers erected from Bangkok to Jakarta stood empty. In the overheated real estate market of Japan, the land underneath the Imperial Palace in downtown Tokyo was said to be worth as much as all of California. Making matters worse, a small group of government bureaucrats, bankers, and industrialists practiced the same crony capitalism that had plagued Russia and Eastern Europe since the fall of communism. Their intimate ties paved the way for rampant corruption and poorly enforced regulations, particularly in the critical banking sector.

These internal problems set the stage for disaster when combined with the second source of trouble: the massive and largely uncontrollable flow of foreign capital into East Asia. More than $200 billion poured into the region in the mid-1990s as private investors, bond traders, and currency speculators sought to share in the economic boom.[5] But at the first signs of economic stress, these same investors just as quickly pulled their money out. Large-scale capital flight compounded the economic calamity and forced Western governments, along with the International Monetary Fund, World Bank, and Asian Development Bank, to provide more than $100 billion in emergency relief to Thailand, South Korea, and Indonesia. The relief efforts, modeled on the $40 billion bailout of the Mexican economy in 1994, were required to prevent an even worse "contagion" effect in other areas.

The United States was hardly an innocent bystander in this crisis. The Clinton administration's strenuous efforts to permit the free flow of capital across national borders played a key role in triggering both the huge influx of foreign capital into East Asia and the subsequent exodus of foreign investments from the region. Clinton's secretary of the Treasury, Robert Rubin, pushed for lifting the controls on capital as part of his strategy to exploit opportunities in a selected group of "big emerging markets," most of which were in East Asia. In Rubin's view, restrictions on cash flows stood in the way of a truly integrated global economy. His pitch was well received within other industrialized states, particularly by business leaders, and most restrictions were lifted. In 1996

5. Organization for Economic Cooperation and Development, "OECD News Release: Aid and Private Flows Fell in 1997," June 18, 1997.

alone, foreign investors pumped $93 billion into just five countries: Indonesia, Malaysia, the Philippines, South Korea, and Thailand. It was no coincidence, then, that these countries became the primary victims of the regional economic crisis—and the first to line up for relief from Western governments.[6]

In return for the bailouts, the East Asian governments were forced to comply with a broad array of demands imposed by the aid lenders. They had to reform their financial institutions, root out corruption, dismantle national monopolies, reduce government spending and subsidies, and provide "safety nets" for labor and other domestic groups victimized by the economic crisis. The governments' agreement to these demands represented a profound concession of political autonomy that contrasted sharply with their previous insistence on self-sufficiency. But by this point the East Asians had little choice. Without outside help, their economies would have been set back for decades. Even with the aid, which finally stemmed the region's free fall in 1999, East Asia had lost its luster as the world's economic "miracle."

NEW STRAINS IN SINO-AMERICAN RELATIONS

The turmoil in East Asia coincided with rising tensions between the United States and China. In March 1996 yet another military confrontation nearly erupted in the Taiwan Straits over the first free presidential election to be held in the island's history. Chinese leaders still considered Taiwan a part of China and feared that the new elected leaders would declare political independence. Beijing resorted to gunboat diplomacy as the elections approached, holding live-fire war games in the straits and "testing" intermediate-range missiles, aimed to fall just short of Taiwanese ports. The United States, which maintained a bilateral military pact with Taiwan dating from the Cold War years, responded by deploying two aircraft carriers to the region in a show of support for its ally. Despite all the commotion offshore, the elections were held and the reformist leader and incumbent president, Lee Teng-hui, became Taiwan's first freely elected leader. After the election, the Chinese and American fleets withdrew from the area. But their latest round of brinkmanship added to the enmity created by numerous trade disputes and human rights issues.

Among these issues was the proposed sale of Chinese nuclear technology to Pakistan in a direct challenge to U.S. antiproliferation policy. Once again, officials in Beijing curtly dismissed the American complaints, as they did earlier when China considered a similar sale to Iran.

6. Nicholas D. Kristof and David E. Sanger, "How U.S. Wooed Asia to Let Cash Flow In," *New York Times*, February 16, 1999, 1A.

By the mid-1990s Clinton's policy of Chinese "engagement" had taken on a recurring pattern: the United States would openly criticize Chinese behavior, China would dismiss Washington's allegations, and business would then continue as usual. Far from becoming more compliant, Chinese leaders were growing increasingly defiant of the United States.

China's future course became more uncertain after the death in February 1997 of Deng Xiaoping, the reformist leader who had succeeded Mao Zedong two decades earlier. Deng's successor, Jiang Zemin, followed the same formula of economic reform that had proven so effective in the past, while continuing to crush political dissent and flout international human rights standards. Jiang dispelled any doubts about his iron rule by cracking down on the China Democracy Party, formed by dissidents after Clinton's visit to China in June 1998. The Chinese Communist Party led by Jiang maintained its monopoly of political power, continued to deny even modest freedoms of speech and assembly, and ensured that any potential rivals were locked away in Chinese prisons. Meanwhile, frequent state visits between Jiang and Russian leaders produced tirades against U.S. imperialism that were reminiscent of the Cold War.

These developments raised new doubts about the long-term direction of China. A growing number of observers predicted a "coming conflict with America" and argued that Beijing had come to see the United States "not as a strategic partner but as the chief obstacle to its own strategic ambitions."[7] According to this view, as China became stronger and as its leaders increasingly appealed to nationalism as a substitute for communism, the country would assert what it considered to be its rightful place as Asia's dominant power. In working toward that end, Chinese leaders would use whatever means were available, including the acquisition of nuclear secrets from U.S. weapons laboratories and other sources.[8]

Clinton's more optimistic view was shared by American business leaders, who were enthralled with the prospect of virtually unlimited profits to be made in a country with more than 1.2 billion people. The president, therefore, clung to his strategy of engaging China and even endorsed China's entry into the World Trade Organization (WTO). Clinton once again insisted that China's presence in such institutions would elicit cooperative behavior. But his familiar refrain ignored the

7. Richard Bernstein and Ross H. Munro, "The Coming Conflict with America," *Foreign Affairs* (March–April 1997): 19.

8. A congressional investigation in 1999 revealed widespread evidence that China had acquired classified information about the most modern U.S. thermonuclear weapons and delivery systems. Some of this information was allegedly stolen from U.S. laboratories, but even more technical information was acquired from public sources and through the purchase of "dual-use" nuclear technology on the open market—often from U.S. corporations.

past failures of the engagement policy to extract even modest concessions from Beijing.

The president's high hopes for Sino-American relations faced two serious obstacles during his last year in office. The first involved Taiwan, where a new round of elections in March 2000 led to the defeat of the Nationalist Party and the election of Chen Shui-bien, who had openly called for Taiwan's independence. Renewed tensions between Beijing and Taipei once again placed Clinton in the political crossfire. The second obstacle was Congress, which was far more inclined than the president to challenge the Chinese government. Leading members of Congress were not eager to approve a new trade bill with Beijing—and provide U.S. support for China's entry into the WTO—that would be considered a breakthrough for the Clinton administration. Fittingly, their willingness to support the bill came only after Clinton was abandoned by his allies in the Democratic Party.

OPPOSITION TO THE WTO AND IMF

The WTO held particular allure for Clinton as the embodiment of globalization. The president had long argued that the WTO, with 135 members in 1999, would bolster a world economy based on private enterprise and free trade. Through the WTO, he predicted, trade disputes would be resolved in an orderly fashion, agreements would be reached on transnational cash flows, and clear standards would be established for labor and environmental protection. Most important, the WTO would become enmeshed with other international organizations, ensuring political stability and harmony among the nations of the world.

Directly challenging this logic, however, was a vast network of local, national, and transnational interest groups that resisted the push for globalization. Widely dispersed but closely connected through the Internet, these groups had little in common except their shared disdain for the WTO. Many environmental activists viewed it as an agent of global warming and deforestation. Labor unions saw their jobs being shipped away by WTO bureaucrats. The leaders of developing countries feared that new labor standards would deny them the opportunity to compete with the industrialized states. And self-styled anarchists alleged that the WTO represented a stepping-stone toward an oppressive world government.

Distracted by domestic upheavals and regional conflicts, Clinton was oblivious to this rising tide of antiglobalization. He had assumed all along that the growing networks of nongovernmental organizations would play a key role in *advancing* rather than opposing the globalist cause. Nor did Clinton appreciate the deep divisions between rich and poor countries over issues such as labor standards and the costs of environmental protection, or the strained trade relations between the United States and European Union that were engulfing the WTO. The president also disregarded the lesson from the East Asian economic crisis that unfettered capital flows often caused more problems than they solved. Clinton's ignorance on all these points led him to make a fateful decision that overrode the warnings of his closest advisers: to host the annual meetings of the WTO in Seattle, Washington.

The conference in December 1999 was a fiasco from start to finish. First, Clinton aides waited until the last minute to invite foreign leaders to the meetings. Thus by the time the aides tried to arrange a "Millennium Round" of trade negotiations, most foreign leaders had other plans. Second, Clinton failed to achieve even a minimal consensus among other countries on the agenda, which ensured that the conference would lack not only heads of state but also any sense of focus. Third, by the time the meetings began, the widespread protests nearby were overwhelming the Seattle police, who had ignored the problems at the most recent WTO summit in Geneva, Switzerland, and therefore failed to take the necessary precautions against the ensuing civil disobedience. Storefronts were smashed and looted, police were pelted by rocks, and hundreds of protesters were injured or arrested in the melees. Many WTO delegates, including Secretary of State Madeleine Albright and UN Secretary General Kofi Annan, were forced to remain in their hotels for much of the conference, unable to pass through the chaos outside the conference center.

Clinton then expediently added insult to injury. When the streets were finally cleared and a plenary session was convened, the president embraced the demonstrators' calls for reform and berated the WTO delegates. The president strongly criticized the trade body for operating secretly—a legitimate concern, but one that had not seemed to bother Clinton earlier. In appeasing the dissidents, Clinton also contradicted his earlier claims that the WTO was itself an agent of reform, particularly in areas such as labor rights which were widely denied in developing countries. The president thus managed not only to sponsor the "battle in Seattle," but also to alienate many WTO delegates. As a result, the WTO entered the new millennium a beleaguered organization, its many years of momentum suddenly frozen.

During this period, disillusionment also set in at the International Monetary Fund, whose actions before and during the economic crisis in East Asia were widely criticized.[9] In encouraging the tidal wave of private investments in East Asia which then proved unable to absorb the

9. See Steven Radelet and Jeffrey Sachs, *The Onset of the East Asian Financial Crisis* (Cambridge: National Bureau of Economic Research, 1998).

funds, the IMF helped to spark the economic wildfire. And in providing vast sums of aid after the bottom had fallen out, the IMF rewarded the same state bureaucrats and foreign investors whose reckless behavior had produced the crisis. Under the terms of its aid, the IMF was ensured of eventual repayment; the East Asian countries were left to pick up the pieces. The painful readjustments fell most heavily on the laborers, property owners, and small merchants who had nothing to do with the economic meltdown. This experience was similar to that in Russia and many parts of Eastern Europe where IMF funds effectively rewarded government corruption and ineptitude.

The failures of the IMF led to the resignation of its managing director, Michael Camdessus, and his replacement in March 2000 by Horst Köhler of Germany. Although Köhler's appointment did not settle the debates over the IMF's role, two points were clear. First, the IMF would play a more modest role in the coming years than it had in the past. Other organizations, including the World Bank and UN agencies, would assume greater responsibility for promoting global development. Second, IMF officials would have to rectify their internal problems before their global ambitions could be reached. In particular, the IMF would have to suspend its past practice of making major funding decisions—many of which involved billions of dollars—behind closed doors. Thus the IMF, which had demanded that its aid recipients undertake political as well as economic reforms, would itself have to become more democratic.

More generally, the turmoil within the IMF and WTO provided ample evidence that the honeymoon for globalization was over. It was ironic that the same forces that propelled the trend—computer technologies, large corporations, and transnational interest groups—also were instrumental in the backlash against globalization. All of this ensured that future tensions between the contrary trends of global integration and fragmentation would be inescapable.

UNFINISHED BUSINESS AFTER THE MILLENNIUM

American foreign policy is by nature a work in progress. Relations between the United States and other governments, even its closest allies, are rarely smooth; they continually oscillate between periods of amity and discord. The same principle applies to ongoing efforts by the United States to advance its interests in dozens of issue areas. Among these, efforts to promote global democratization, impose and enforce economic sanctions, and control weapons of mass destruction emerged as national priorities during the Cold War and continued to occupy American leaders in its aftermath. All three undertakings, however, proved highly troublesome. An array of problems overseas hindered the task of policy makers, as did the divisions between the White House and Congress. As a result, American leadership in all these areas was questioned both at home and overseas, and the nation's ambitious goals often proved beyond its reach.

THE LIMITS OF 'BUILDING DEMOCRACY'

As described in Chapter 10, both Presidents Bush and Clinton proclaimed the promotion of democracy a continuing foreign policy priority of the United States after the Cold War. Bush famously included global democratization among the key elements of his envisaged "new world order." And Clinton, otherwise more interested in domestic affairs, declared the "enlargement of the democratic community" to be a centerpiece of his foreign policy. Both presidents cited the complementary relationship between political reforms and global economic integration. And both adopted the view that a world made up of democratic states would be more peaceful. Top officials in the State Department shared these views and sought to put the policy, labeled "Building Democracy," into practice.

This campaign was designed not merely to support the creation of new democracies, but also to consolidate gains that had been made since the beginning of the democratic boom in the 1980s. According to Freedom House, a nonprofit group whose annual reports were closely followed by political leaders, the number of electoral democracies increased from 69 in 1989 to 117 a decade later. A record 2.4 billion people, or 40 percent of the world's population, lived in "free" countries by 1999, and another 1.6 billion people lived in countries considered by Freedom House to be "partly free." These and other trends strongly indicated that electoral democracy had become "the world's predominant form of government." [10]

Beyond setting an example for other countries, however, the extent to which the United States contributed to the democratic boom is difficult to determine. Pressures for political reform come from many sources, and the ability of any outside actor to induce fundamental change in governance is greatly limited. In this respect, the lesson of history is clear: the desire for democratic freedoms must come from within a society, not only from external pressure. If the conditions for democracy are absent, no amount of external support or coercion is likely to make a difference. Indeed, the prospects for democracy are strengthened when political leaders and their citizens make this profound transition on their own.

10. Adrian Karatnycky, ed., *Freedom in the World, 1998–1999* (Piscataway, N.J.: Transaction Publishers, 1999), 3–5, 7.

The U.S. effort also was hamstrung by several other factors. First, during the Cold War the U.S. government had often violated its own democratic principles and left itself exposed to charges of hypocrisy. In equating democratization with anticommunism and in supporting dozens of military dictatorships that denied fundamental freedoms to their citizens, the United States became widely mistrusted overseas, particularly within developing countries where the need for political reform was greatest. Moreover, the polarized societies that resulted from the intrusion of Cold War tensions made the task of creating democratic institutions all the more difficult. Memories of U.S. interventions in behalf of authoritarian rulers, and the feelings of resentment these produced, persisted long after the Cold War.

Second, regional security concerns continued to preoccupy U.S. leaders after the Cold War. When these concerns clashed with the democratization policy, most conspicuously in the Middle East, strategic considerations prevailed. Israel and Egypt, for example, retained their status as the primary recipients of U.S. foreign aid. But Israel, while widely considered a democratic state, often repressed Palestinians living in the occupied territories. In Egypt, the government of Hosni Mubarek routinely committed abuses and "dominated the political scene to such an extent that citizens [did] not have a meaningful ability to change their government." [11] Despite these problems, the annual infusions of U.S. aid to both governments were not threatened. Moreover, in Jordan new aid programs were established for its unelected government in an effort to advance the Arab-Israeli peace process.

A third and related problem involved the frequent clashes between U.S. concerns for global democracy and its own economic self-interests. This tension was most visible in U.S. relations with China, which maintained one of the world's most repressive governments while expanding its economic ties to Washington. The message sent in this case was that American concerns for democracy and human rights were limited not only by security concerns, but also by the costs the United States would have to bear in upholding its proclaimed standards.

The fourth problem was that the United States had long adhered to a conception of democracy that was based on narrowly defined political rights as opposed to the broader notions of economic and social rights favored by most other governments and international organizations. Indeed, the functional relationships among the strictly *political* components of democracy—representative government, constitutionalism, separation of powers, and political participation—were themselves

11. Department of State, *Egypt Country Report, 1995* (Washington, D.C.: Department of State, 1996).

unclear, a point made evident by the emergence of "illiberal democracies" in many developing countries.[12] For example, the elected government of Ethiopia routinely persecuted journalists and political opponents, and the Iranian parliament, also elected, imposed harsh restrictions on free speech and women's rights. These and other cases demonstrated that the very meaning of democracy was highly elastic and largely in the eyes of the beholder.

A final obstacle to U.S. democratization policy concerned the meaning and limitations of national sovereignty in the fragmenting world of the 1990s. For more than 350 years the nation-state system had extolled sovereignty as a vehicle for maintaining internal stability and preserving peace between states. This principle, however, came under increasing attack after the Cold War when the rights of repressed minority groups to determine their political fate, as democratic rule implied, clashed with the rights of existing states to maintain order and prevent disintegration. As a growing number of critics saw it, national sovereignty should be denied to political leaders who routinely violated human rights or committed crimes against humanity. In their view, even former rulers should be held accountable for their past actions in international courts.[13]

The dilemma for American foreign policy was most keenly illustrated in the Indonesian territory of East Timor. Its people sought independence from Indonesia following the departure in May 1998 of Suharto, the country's longtime ruler whose forceful annexation of East Timor in 1976 had been condemned worldwide. Urged on by the UN, the new Indonesian government of B. J. Habibie permitted a referendum on statehood in August 1999. Not surprisingly, the East Timorese people voted overwhelmingly for independence. A violent crackdown by Indonesian authorities followed and threatened to overturn the popular will.

The United States, like other countries, was then faced with a crucial question: Should the Indonesian claim of sovereign rule prevail over East Timor's widely recognized quest for freedom? In the end, Clinton and most other world leaders concluded that the logic of democracy and self-rule could not be denied. They supported the separatists, and an

12. Fareed Zakaria, "The Rise of Illiberal Democracy," *Foreign Affairs* (November–December 1997): 22–43.

13. This point was made most clearly by the October 1998 arrest of Gen. Augusto Pinochet on charges that he committed crimes against humanity during his reign as Chile's military dictator between 1974 and 1990. Great Britain's detention of the former Chilean leader—requested by a Spanish judge who was supported by transnational human rights groups—had no precedent in legal history. The case against Pinochet, who was declared unfit to stand trial and released in March 2000, revealed the extent to which traditional principles of sovereignty were being eclipsed by global standards of human rights.

independent East Timor was placed under the watchful eye of UN peacekeepers, led by a contingent from neighboring Australia. But their judgment only begged more vexing questions: If the captive peoples of East Timor were to be granted sovereignty, what about those in the Chinese territory of Tibet who had been conquered by communist forces shortly after Mao Zedong took power and whose spiritual aspirations had been brutally denied for a half-century? And what about the embattled population of Chechnya, which fought throughout the 1990s to be free of Russian rule? The Tibetan and Chechen uprisings were in many ways identical to the one that received global support in East Timor.

The Clinton administration could not provide a consistent response to these questions. While the United States owed its own existence to the right of self-determination, U.S. leaders had resisted just such a claim by the Confederacy during the nation's own civil war in the 1860s. Moreover, Clinton was reluctant to jeopardize relations with Russia and China by supporting nationalist revolts in those countries. The double standard was obvious but unavoidable. Claims to sovereignty would be resolved not by their intrinsic merits but by calculations of global power relations. Absolute principles would be subordinated to the relative morality of power politics. And as a great power the United States would have to play by the rules, despite its long-standing claims of moral superiority. Thus while Clinton prevented his relations with Russia and China from unraveling, his coveted stature as a defender of freedom was further diminished.[14]

Faced with these ambiguities, the Clinton administration found that its central challenge was to convince a skeptical Congress and public that global democratization was as vital to U.S. national interests—and as worthy of the country's financial sacrifice—as communist containment during the Cold War. This proved to be a losing proposition. Foreign aid, the primary means of supporting democratization, had become less popular than ever among the general public, and aid spending by the United States plummeted from nearly $12 billion in 1992 to less than $7 billion five years later.[15] When the large annual aid packages to Israel, Egypt, and other "strategic allies" were excluded from this total, little aid was left to support democratic transitions elsewhere. Instead, American leaders turned to the IMF, which disbursed far more money to developing countries—and was controlled largely by the United States, its primary benefactor. But these funds were generally provided to recipients

14. This was far from the first time the principle of sovereignty had been manipulated by the great powers. See Stephen D. Krasner, *Sovereignty: Organized Hypocrisy* (Princeton: Princeton University Press, 1999).

15. Organization for Economic Cooperation and Development, *Development Cooperation* (Paris: OECD, 1994, 1999)

only after they had succumbed to political and economic crises. By then, the task of building democracy had become doubly difficult.

RETHINKING ECONOMIC SANCTIONS

After World War II the United States frequently turned to economic sanctions in order to achieve its foreign policy goals. By the late 1990s U.S. sanctions were in place against more than seventy-five foreign governments that ruled more than two-thirds of the world's population. American officials demanded that these governments meet widely varying demands, including greater respect for human rights, increased access to U.S. exports, improved environmental protection, and cooperation in global efforts to prevent terrorism and weapons proliferation. If its demands were not met, the U.S. government vowed to punish these states by closing its markets to their goods, freezing their assets in U.S. banks, withholding aid and private investments, canceling air links, or taking other retaliatory measures.

Economic sanctions were appealing because they seemed to offer a nonviolent form of coercion that would elicit the changes in behavior sought by the United States. In this respect, sanctions seemed a logical extension of Clinton's "geoeconomic" approach to foreign relations. Unfortunately, sanctions proved to be very blunt instruments because targeted states rarely gave in to U.S. pressure. Cuba, for example, weathered four decades of U.S. economic sanctions without a change in government. Sanctions against Iraq made Saddam Hussein more determined to thwart America's will after his withdrawal from Kuwait. The governments of Libya, Iran, and other "rogue states" garnered sympathy—and economic support—from other nations that opposed U.S. economic coercion. Meanwhile, a cutoff of U.S. aid to Pakistan, which was designed to force its leaders to suspend their nuclear programs, merely hastened that country's move to join the nuclear club.

Not only did economic sanctions usually fail to achieve their goals, they also often victimized ordinary citizens who had nothing to do with government policies. Meanwhile, despotic rulers continued to live comfortably, and U.S. sanctions often penalized the United States as much, if not more than, the offending states. According to a government study, during the 1980s and 1990s sanctions led to more than $7 billion in lost U.S. exports and more than 178,000 lost jobs for U.S. workers.[16] Given this record, many Americans wondered just who were the real "victims" of U.S. sanctions.[17]

16. Congressional Budget Office, *The Domestic Costs of Sanctions on Foreign Commerce* (Washington, D.C.: Government Printing Office, 1999), 43.

17. For a recent assessment, see David A. Baldwin, "The Sanctions Debate and the Logic of Choice," *International Security* (winter 1999–2000): 80–107.

The Cuban case was the most controversial. After the United States failed to overthrow Fidel Castro in 1962, Cuba was placed under a strict U.S. economic embargo that remained in force into the new millennium. Concerned that Havana's growing influx of outside capital would undermine this embargo, U.S. officials announced in 1996 new measures to penalize foreign companies whose commerce with Cuba involved properties that had been seized from American firms after the 1959 revolution. The Helms-Burton law (named after Republican senator Jesse Helms of North Carolina and Democratic representative Dan Burton of Indiana) not only angered Castro, but also infuriated many U.S. trading partners who declared they would not allow Washington to impose its sanctions on them. Thus they ignored the U.S. embargo and exploited Castro's new-found openness to foreign investment. Many Americans also opposed a policy of economic isolation that failed to force cooperation from Castro while giving foreign investors free reign on the island.

These doubts about U.S. policy toward Cuba reached a new high in early 2000. This time the issue arose from an unlikely source: a six-year-old boy. In November 1999 Eliàn Gonzàlez and his mother tried to flee Cuba for the United States in a makeshift raft. When the raft sank off the coast of Florida, his mother and ten other Cubans drowned, but Eliàn was rescued. The boy was placed in the care of relatives in Miami and quickly became entrapped in a political tug of war. The Clinton administration ruled that Eliàn should be returned to the custody of his father in Cuba, who was divorced from his mother. But the boy's relatives in Miami refused to surrender him to federal authorities, prompting an extended custody battle in U.S. courts. The controversy yielded yet another public relations coup for the aging Castro. More important, the controversy provided new evidence that the U.S. policy of isolating Cuba—at a time when the United States was "engaging" China and other U.S. adversaries—was doomed to repeated frustrations, embarrassments, and, ultimately, failure at dislodging the island's communist government.

ARMS CONTROL IN LIMBO

One other piece of unfinished business from the Cold War years involved the dangers posed by weapons of mass destruction. In many ways the collapse of the Soviet Union created new opportunities for the spread of nuclear, chemical, and biological weapons. An immediate concern was that the vast nuclear arsenal and related technologies of the former Soviet Union would fall into unknown hands. It also was feared that "rogue states" and terrorist groups would take advantage of regional power vacuums and seek to gain the upper hand by acquiring or using such weapons.

In promoting arms control, the United States faced several obstacles. Many congressional leaders, whose support was required for most arms control treaties, raised old concerns about the reliability of foreign governments in honoring the treaties. In practice, these legislators used arms control as leverage in gaining concessions from the White House in other areas, many of which had little or nothing to do with foreign policy. Further complicating matters, many foreign governments openly questioned the credibility of the United States, which maintained the world's largest nuclear arsenal and, since the Cold War, had earned more in global arms markets than all other exporters combined.[18]

The most immediate issue was the nuclear stockpiles of the United States and Russia. In January 1996 Congress ratified the START II agreement, which Bush and Russian leader Boris Yeltsin had signed four years earlier. START II required both countries to reduce the number of their long-range nuclear warheads to between 3,000 and 3,500 by 2003, a two-thirds cutback in such warheads since the peak of the Cold War. In addition, the treaty banned long-range nuclear weapons with multiple warheads, one of the most destabilizing components of the nuclear arms race. Clinton and Yeltsin agreed in March 1997 to move forward on START III, which would require even deeper cuts in their nuclear stockpiles.

But the Russian parliament, unhappy about NATO expansion and the alliance's interventions in Yugoslavia, had not yet ratified START II. Moreover, after Clinton announced he would seek to deploy a missile defense system in violation of the antiballistic missile (ABM) treaty of 1972, it became unclear whether the parliament would ever approve the treaty. Clinton, who had earlier praised the ABM treaty for preventing a full-scale global arms race, bowed to domestic pressure and reversed his position. A "limited" defense system, he claimed, would be designed to repel incoming missiles from rogue states such as Iraq and Libya, not from Russia. But his argument proved unconvincing to Russian legislators. When they finally ratified START II in April 2000, they warned Washington that the treaty would be scrapped—and START III talks cancelled—if the U.S. government went ahead on a missile defense system.[19] Clinton's reversal also infuriated other governments, which feared that a repudiation of the ABM treaty would trigger a new round of nuclear proliferation. America's allies, it appeared, would have to devel-

18. The United States received 50.1 percent of global income from arms exports in the first three years of the post–Cold War era. U.S. Arms Control and Disarmament Agency, *World Military Expenditures and Arms Exports, 1995* (Washington, D.C.: Government Printing Office, 1996), 16.

19. A Congressional Budget Office study released in April 2000 estimated that the cost of such a missile defense system would be approximately $49 billion through 2015.

op their own nuclear defenses—a costly enterprise with uncertain prospects—since the "limited" U.S. shield would not protect them.

Even when Clinton aggressively pursued arms control, his actions often backfired. In North Korea, for example, its Stalinesque dictator, Kim Il Sung, had threatened to build nuclear weapons. Faced with this challenge, Clinton dispatched former president Jimmy Carter to Pyongyang in June 1994 for meetings with Kim. After the meetings, Kim pledged to "freeze" his nuclear program. But the price for maintaining peace with North Korea was incredible: an agreement that the United States, South Korea, and Japan would pay nearly $5 billion for the construction of two nuclear power generators that would not yield plutonium; a free supply of oil for eight to ten years; and diplomatic relations with the United States and Japan. What did the United States receive in return for reviving North Korea's failing economy? Kim merely promised to allow inspections of North Korea's weapons plants within eight years and shut down a plutonium reprocessing plant—promises he had made years earlier and then broken.

American leaders also had to assume that Kim Il Sung's successor—his son Kim Jong Il, who assumed power upon his father's death in July 1994—would respect the agreement. But this was unlikely in view of North Korea's next round of demands. When the United States sought to inspect several underground military installations in 1998, Kim Jong Il demanded an additional $300 million. When it was refused, North Korea launched a three-stage missile over Japan and into the Pacific Ocean, a clear provocation meant to symbolize the country's continued status as a regional military power. This behavior was particularly appalling given that North Korea's economy had shrunk by half since the collapse of the Soviet Union, leading to mass starvation and calls for Western aid.

As complex as the situation was in Korea, the worst blow to Clinton's arms control agenda came not from enemies abroad but from the U.S. Senate, which rejected the Comprehensive Test Ban Treaty (CTBT) in October 1999. In signing the treaty in 1996, Clinton had called it "the longest-sought, hardest-fought prize in the history of arms control." More than 150 foreign governments had also pledged to support the test-ban treaty, which was based on the premise that a ban on testing would prevent would-be proliferators from building the weapons in the first place. But ratification was another matter. For the ban to take effect, all forty-four countries believed capable of building and testing at least one crude bomb had to ratify the agreement. Yet only twenty-four states had ratified the testing ban when it came before the Senate. Great Britain and France stood alone among the nuclear powers in ratifying the CTBT, which remained mired in the legislatures of the United States,

Russia, and China. The leaders of India and Pakistan, the newest nuclear powers, had refused to sign the treaty. Final acceptance by other governments was therefore crucial in coaxing India and Pakistan out of the nuclear club and discouraging others from gaining entry.

In the United States, the general public and a large number of prominent nuclear physicists supported the CTBT. Clinton, however, was unaware that opposition to the treaty was growing, primarily among the conservative Republicans who controlled Congress. Its opponents predicted that hostile foreign leaders would exploit American restraint and threaten the United States when its guard was down. But the primary motive of Clinton's opponents was political: the treaty gave them a golden opportunity to humiliate the president on the world stage. The Senate defeat of the CTBT marked its first repudiation of a major treaty in eighty years and its first rejection of a nuclear treaty. The refusal of the world's foremost nuclear superpower to join the moratorium on nuclear testing sent a strong signal to would-be nuclear powers: If the United States reserved for itself the right to test these weapons, why shouldn't others have the same right?

Clinton's failure to detect and counter the opposition to the treaty was similar to his lapse that led to the WTO debacle. In both cases, signs of discontent were clearly visible, but not to the president, even though his keen sense of the political landscape had generally served him well in the past. By the end of 1999, however, Clinton was exhausted from fending off impeachment and managing the conflicts overseas. Once he finally realized the strength of his opposition, it was too late; his stinging defeat was unavoidable.

The primary casualty in this episode, however, was not the president; it was the country's prestige, which was battered by the rejection of a widely supported global treaty for reasons of domestic politics. To make matters worse, the United States refused to sign, let alone ratify, a global ban on land mines that entered into force in March 1999 with support from ninety governments, including all the major Western European governments and Japan. Thus the United States, which had proclaimed weapons proliferation a primary threat to international security after the Cold War, was widely viewed as an outcast. In no other area of foreign policy did the country fail more gravely to live up to its global responsibilities.

FUTURE PROSPECTS FOR AMERICAN LEADERSHIP

For all of its problems at home and overseas, the United States today retains to retain its stature as the world's preeminent power. Recurring upheavals in Russia, confusion over the future governance of Europe,

East Asia's economic slump, and the profound contradictions in China's political and economic system have all extended America's global primacy into the twenty-first century. If anything, the United States has become even more formidable due to its prolonged economic expansion and improved fiscal performance.

It is not enough, however, for any country to simply amass a considerable degree of international influence. How such a country *exercises* that influence—toward the greater security and betterment of its citizens, as well as those beyond its shores—is the true test of leadership. Given its many advantages, the United States is uniquely capable of shaping the political, economic, and social currents of the world. On a more basic level, it can seek to maintain a degree of stability in the turbulent international system. "Political order is not sufficient to explain economic prosperity, but it is necessary," observed Joseph S. Nye Jr., a political scientist and assistant secretary of defense in the Clinton administration. "Analysts who ignore the importance of this political order are like people who forget the importance of the oxygen they breathe. Security is like oxygen—you tend not to notice it until you begin to lose it, but once that occurs there is nothing else that you think about." [20]

In this respect, the frenzy of partisan politics that overwhelmed Washington in the late 1990s was particularly ominous. The diversion of the nation's attention from global concerns led to an erratic, unpredictable foreign policy. Policy makers sent confusing signals abroad by simultaneously adhering to a military doctrine based on global primacy while slashing funds for diplomacy and foreign aid. Most troubling, foreign policy often was reduced to a pawn in the domestic power struggle. As the United States grew more isolated, its ability to exploit its many advantages and to promote constructive change overseas steadily eroded.

To understand more clearly the faltering performance of the United States, it is helpful to reconsider its Constitution, which was devised in large part to inhibit—rather than promote—the efficient exercise of government power. The complicated system of checks and balances, combined with explicit curbs on presidential power, was intended to prevent the rise of a tyrannical state or an autocratic ruler. At the same time, the Framers' blueprint for governance deliberately allowed "for longstanding institutional rivalries and jealousies, for personal ambitions and rivalries on both ends of Pennsylvania Avenue, for perceptions and misperceptions by executive and legislative officials, and for other

20. Joseph S. Nye Jr., "The Case for Deep Engagement," *Foreign Affairs* (July–August 1995): 91.

irrational and personal factors that often crucially influence the policy-making process."[21]

These problems generally faded when the United States was at war or faced imminent threats from overseas. But in peacetime, including most of the post–Cold War period, the internal contradictions proved irresistible. Thus the same instruments of democratic governance that enabled the United States to flourish in its early years also produced the domestic upheavals of the 1990s that prevented the nation from forging a coherent foreign policy. To the drafters of the Constitution—whose political system was designed for a small and fragmented republic, not a global superpower—such an outcome was a reasonable price to pay for democratic rule. There is little doubt they would make the same bargain today, even in the transformed global environment and with the heightened stature of the United States.

American foreign policy, therefore, will likely exhibit the same dysfunctions in the years to come. Government positions on global issues will often reflect political stalemate rather than consensus, and a long-term grand strategy will remain elusive in the absence of a clear threat from overseas. In such an environment, policy makers will be forced to lead by improvisation, allowing regional crises to dictate their agendas. So long as American citizens remain ambivalent about the nation's world role, the United States will maintain its schizophrenic approach to world politics that historically has veered between detachment from the outside world and a penchant for global crusading. The result will be far from optimal, but entirely consistent with the American style of foreign policy.

21. Cecil V. Crabb Jr. and Pat M. Holt, *Invitation to Struggle: Congress, the President, and Foreign Policy*, 4th ed. (Washington, D.C.: CQ Press, 1992), 298.

Appendix A
U.S. Administrations since World War II

President	*Secretary of State*	*Secretary of Defense*	*National Security Adviser*
Harry Truman 1945–1953	Edward Stettinius James Byrnes George Marshall Dean Acheson	James Forrestal Louis Johnson George Marshall Robert Lovett	
Dwight Eisenhower 1953–1961	John Dulles Christian Herter	Charles Wilson Neil McElroy Thomas Gates	
John Kennedy 1961–1963	Dean Rusk	Robert McNamara	McGeorge Bundy
Lyndon Johnson 1963–1969	Dean Rusk	Robert McNamara Clark Clifford	McGeorge Bundy Walt Rostow
Richard Nixon 1969–1974	William Rogers Henry Kissinger	Melvin Laird Elliot Richardson James Schlesinger	Henry Kissinger
Gerald Ford 1974–1977	Henry Kissinger Donald Rumsfeld	James Schlesinger Brent Scowcroft	Henry Kissinger
Jimmy Carter 1977–1981	Cyrus Vance Edmund Muskie	Harold Brown	Zbigniew Brzezinski
Ronald Reagan 1981–1989	Alexander Haig George Shultz	Caspar Weinberger Frank Carlucci	Richard Allen William Clark Robert McFarlane John Poindexter Frank Carlucci Colin Powell
George Bush 1989–1993	James Baker Lawrence Eagleburger	Richard Cheney	Brent Scowcroft
Bill Clinton 1993–	Warren Christopher Madeleine Albright	Les Aspin William Perry William Cohen	Anthony Lake Samuel Berger

Appendix B
Chronology of Significant Events

1945 Yalta Conference seeks to organize postwar world.
World War II with Germany ends.
World War II with Japan ends after two atomic bombs are dropped.
President Franklin Roosevelt dies, and Vice President Harry Truman succeeds him.
United Nations is established.
Soviet military forces occupy Poland, Romania, Bulgaria, Hungary, and Czechoslovakia.

1946 United States confronts the Soviet Union over Iran, and Moscow withdraws its troops.
Winston Churchill, Britain's wartime prime minister, delivers "iron curtain" speech at Fulton, Missouri, warning of Soviet threat.
George Kennan, a Foreign Service officer, provides the government with the analysis that becomes the basis of the containment policy of Soviet Russia.

1947 Truman Doctrine commits the United States to assist Greece and Turkey.
Plan for the economic recovery of Western Europe is devised by Secretary of State George Marshall, formerly U.S. chief of staff and architect of victory during World War II.
India becomes independent from British colonial rule.

1948 Soviet coup d'état takes place in Czechoslovakia.
Soviets blockade all ground traffic from West Germany to West Berlin and the Western airlift starts.
Vandenberg resolution of U.S. Senate commits American support for the Brussels Pact of self-defense.
Marshall Plan is passed by Congress.
North and South Korea are established.
The state of Israel is established and receives immediate U.S. recognition.
Truman wins upset election.
Stalin expels Yugoslavia's Tito from communist bloc.

1949 North Atlantic Treaty Organization (NATO) is formed.
Soviet Union ends Berlin blockade.
East and West Germany are established.
Soviet Union explodes atomic bomb.
Nationalist China collapses and People's Republic of China (PRC) is established.
U.S. troops are withdrawn from South Korea.
Truman announces Point Four foreign aid program for developing countries.

1950 Soviet Union and communist China sign thirty-year treaty of mutual assistance.
North Korea attacks South Korea by crossing the thirty-eighth parallel.
United States intervenes in behalf of South Korea.
Communist China intervenes after U.S. forces advance into North Korea toward China's frontier.
Sen. Joseph McCarthy begins his attacks on government for treason and "coddling communism."

1951 Gen. Dwight Eisenhower is appointed Supreme Allied Commander in Europe and Truman sends U.S. forces to Europe.
U.S.-Japanese mutual security pact is signed.

Truman fires Gen. Douglas MacArthur in Korea for proposing that the United States attack communist China.
European Coal and Steel Community (ECSC) is formed.

1952 Eisenhower is elected president.
Greece and Turkey join NATO.
Britain tests its first atomic weapon.

1953 Joseph Stalin dies.
Armistice negotiated along thirty-eighth parallel in Korea.
Soviet Union intervenes in East Germany to quell revolt.

1954 United States explodes first hydrogen bomb.
France is defeated at Dienbienphu in Indochina.
United States threatens to intervene in Indochina.
Vietnam is partitioned at the seventeenth parallel at the Geneva Conference.
Southeast Asia Treaty Organization (SEATO) is formed.
U.S.-Korean pact is signed to prevent a renewal of the war.
U.S.-Nationalist China defense treaty is signed.
Central Intelligence Agency overthrows Guatemala's left-wing government.

1955 Communist China shells the Nationalist Chinese (Taiwanese) islands of Quemoy and Matsu.
Formosa resolution authorizes Eisenhower to use force, if necessary, to protect Taiwan against a possible communist Chinese invasion.
Middle East Treaty Organization (Baghdad Pact) is formed.
West Germany joins NATO, and Soviets establish "their NATO," called the Warsaw Treaty Organization.

1956 United States withdraws offer to help finance Egypt's Aswan High Dam.
Egypt nationalizes the Suez Canal.
Suez War breaks out after Israel attacks Egypt, and France and Britain intervene.
UN forces are sent to Egypt to keep the peace between Israel and Egypt.
Soviets suppress Hungarian revolt and almost intervene in Poland.
Soviet leader Nikita Khrushchev attacks Stalin at twentieth Communist Party Congress.

1957 Soviet Union tests intercontinental ballistic missile (ICBM).
Soviets launch two *Sputniks*, or satellites, into space.
British test hydrogen bomb.
Eisenhower Doctrine commits the United States to assist Middle East countries that resist communist aggression or states closely tied to the Soviet Union, such as Egypt.

1958 United States lands marines in Lebanon, and Britain lands paratroopers in Jordan after Iraqi revolution.
Soviet Union declares it would end the four-power occupation of Berlin and turn West Berlin into a "free city."
European Economic Community (Common Market) is established.
First of several Berlin crises erupts.
Communist China shells Quemoy and Matsu again.

1959 Khrushchev visits Eisenhower for Camp David meeting over Berlin issue.
Fidel Castro seizes power in Cuba.
Central Treaty Organization (CENTO) replaces the Baghdad Pact.

1960 Soviets shoot down U.S. U-2 spy plane over the Soviet Union.
Paris summit conference collapses over U-2 incident.
The Congo becomes independent from Belgium, causing the first superpower crisis in sub-Saharan Africa.
UN forces sent to the Congo to help resolve the crisis.
France becomes an atomic power.
John Kennedy wins presidential election.

1961 Kennedy launches abortive Bay of Pigs invasion of Cuba.
Kennedy proposes Alliance for Progress for Latin America.
Soviets send Yuri Gagarin into orbital spaceflight.
Kennedy holds summit conference with Khrushchev in Vienna.
Kennedy sends first military advisers to South Vietnam.
Soviets build Berlin Wall.

1962 U.S. sends John Glenn into orbital spaceflight.
In Cuban missile crisis, the United States blockades Cuba to compel the Soviets to withdraw their missiles.
Chinese-Indian frontier conflict erupts.

1963 French president Charles de Gaulle vetoes Britain's entry into the Common Market.
"Hot line" established between the White House and the Kremlin for direct emergency communications.
Atomic test-ban treaty is signed.
President Kennedy is assassinated, and Vice President Lyndon Johnson succeeds him.

1964 Congress passes Gulf of Tonkin resolution, raising the U.S. commitment to the defense of South Vietnam.
Khrushchev falls from power and is replaced by Prime Minister Aleksei Kosygin and Communist Party Secretary Leonid Brezhnev.

1965 United States starts bombing North Vietnam and sends American land forces into South Vietnam.
Protests against the war start.
United States intervenes in the Dominican Republic.
War erupts between Pakistan and India.

1966 People's Republic of China becomes a nuclear power.
France withdraws its forces from NATO's integrated command structure but remains a member of the alliance.

1967 Six-day War between Israel and its Arab neighbors takes place.
Greek colonels seize power in Greece.

1968 Tet offensive in South Vietnam escalates demand for U.S. withdrawal from Vietnam.
Johnson withdraws from presidential race.
Richard Nixon elected president.
Vietnamese peace talks begin in Paris.
Nuclear Non-Proliferation Treaty is made.
Soviet Union intervenes in Czechoslovakia to quell revolt.

1969 Brezhnev Doctrine is proclaimed, asserting the right of Soviet Union to intervene in Soviet sphere to suppress "counterrevolution."
Antiballistic missile (ABM) deployment is narrowly approved by Senate.
United States tests multiple independently targeted reentry vehicle (MIRV).
Negotiations on Strategic Arms Limitation Treaty (SALT) begin.
"Vietnamization" program starts. South Vietnamese are to do more of the fighting while the United States begins troop withdrawal.
Ho Chi Minh dies.
United States lands men on moon.
Lt. William Calley Jr. stands trial for My Lai massacre of civilians in South Vietnam by U.S. troops.
First of several Sino-Soviet border clashes occurs.

1970 West Germany, East Germany, the Soviet Union, and Poland conclude treaties recognizing Poland's western border and acknowledging Germany's division into East and West Germany.
Senate repeals Gulf of Tonkin resolution.
U.S. invasion of Cambodia causes widespread student protests, which escalate after National Guard kills four students at Kent State University.
Chile elects a Marxist, Salvador Allende, president.

1971 India and Pakistan go to war over the Bangladesh (East Pakistan) secession effort.
People's Republic of China joins the United Nations.
Four-power Berlin settlement is reached, ensuring Western access to Berlin.

1972 Nixon visits communist China, beginning a process of normalizing relations after two decades of hostility.
North Vietnam invades South Vietnam.
Nixon retaliates by expanding air war against North Vietnam and blockading the harbor of Haiphong.
Nixon visits Moscow for summit conference with Soviet leaders; signs SALT I and ABM treaty.
Watergate affair starts when police arrest five men who had broken into Democratic Party headquarters.
Soviets buy enormous quantities of U.S. grains, raising domestic prices in the United States.
Paris peace talks, close to success, break down, and the United States bombs North Vietnam heavily during Christmas season.
Nixon reelected president in a landslide that carried every state but Massachusetts.

1973 Henry Kissinger is appointed secretary of state while remaining the president's national security adviser.
Vietnamese peace agreement is signed.
United States and China establish liaison offices, or informal embassies, in Washington and Beijing.
Yom Kippur War breaks out in Middle East.
Arab members of the Organization of Petroleum Exporting Countries (OPEC) embargo oil to the United States because of U.S. support for Israel.
Britain, Denmark, and Republic of Ireland join Common Market, increasing membership to nine countries.
OPEC quadruples oil prices.

U.S.-Soviet Mutual and Balanced Force Reductions talks in Europe start.
West and East Germany exchange recognition and ambassadors, acknowledging Germany's division into two countries.
Congress passes the War Powers Resolution over Nixon's veto.
Vice President Spiro Agnew resigns and Gerald Ford succeeds him.
Allende is overthrown by military in Chile.

1974 India explodes "peaceful" nuclear device.
Congress asserts right to veto large arms sales to other nations.
Annual Nixon-Brezhnev summit conference further reduces small numbers of ABMs the United States and Soviet Union are allowed by SALT I.
Kissinger negotiates first agreements between Israel and Egypt and Syria as part of his "step-by-step" diplomacy intended to achieve a comprehensive regional peace.
Nixon visits Egypt, Syria, and Israel.
Nixon resigns and Ford becomes unelected president; New York governor Nelson Rockefeller becomes vice president.
Ford and Brezhnev set Vladivostok guidelines for SALT II negotiations.

1975 Soviet Union rejects American-Soviet trade agreement because of the Jackson-Vanik amendment.
South Vietnam collapses and a unified communist Vietnam is established.
Cambodia falls to Cambodian communists.
Cambodians seize U.S. merchant ship *Mayaguez*, and the United States reacts forcefully to free crew and ship.
SEATO dissolves itself.
Helsinki agreements, including Western recognition of Europe's division (and Soviet domination in Eastern Europe), arrived at by Western and Eastern states.
Congress passes arms embargo against Turkey.
Lebanese civil war erupts.
Francisco Franco dies and King Juan Carlos starts to lead Spain to democracy.
In Angola three major factions struggle for control as Portugal grants independence.

1976 Soviet-Cuban forces in Angola win victory for Marxist-led faction over pro-Western factions.
Syrian forces intervene in Lebanon.
Mao Zedong dies.
Jimmy Carter elected president.

1977 Carter announces U.S. withdrawal from South Korea (to be reversed later).
Carter sends letter to leading Soviet dissident, and another dissident visits the White House.
Soviets denounce Carter's human rights campaign as violation of Soviet sovereignty.
Carter submits new SALT II plan to Soviet Union, which quickly rejects it because it is not based on Vladivostok guidelines.
Carter halts plans to produce B-1 bomber and instead chooses to deploy air-launched cruise missiles on B-52 bombers.
United States and Panama sign Panama Canal treaties.
Somalia expels Soviet advisers and denounces friendship treaty with Soviet Union.
Soviet-Cuban military help for Ethiopia grows.

Menachem Begin is elected prime minister in Israel.
Egyptian president Anwar Sadat pays historic visit to Israel, offering peace and friendship. Other Arab states denounce him.

1978 Soviet-Cuban military intervention in Ethiopia's war against Somalia forces latter out of Ogaden.
Soviet-inspired coup occurs in Afghanistan.
Camp David meeting of the United States, Israel, and Egypt arrives at "framework for peace" between two former enemies. Other Arab states denounce framework because it did not provide for a Palestine solution.
Senate approves sale of jet fighters to Israel, Egypt, and Saudi Arabia.
Panama Canal treaties approved by Senate.
Carter postpones neutron bomb (tactical warhead) production.
United States ends arms embargo on Turkey.
Rhodesian prime minister Ian Smith announces "internal solution" to the race problem—the formation of a black-led government.

1979 Shah Mohammad Reza Pahlavi leaves Iran.
United States officially recognizes the People's Republic of China. United States suspends formal relations with Taiwan government and ends mutual defense treaty.
China invades Vietnam to punish it for the invasion of Cambodia.
Shah's regime in Iran replaced by Islamic republic led by Ayatollah Ruhollah Khomeini.
U.S. embassy in Tehran seized and employees held hostage by militant Islamic students after shah is hospitalized in United States for cancer treatment.
United States freezes Iran's financial assets in United States and boycotts Iranian oil.
Oil prices shoot upward as Iranian oil production drops and world supplies tighten.
SALT II treaty signed by Brezhnev and Carter at Vienna summit conference.
Soviets send 80,000 troops into Afghanistan to ensure survival of pro-Soviet regime.
NATO decides to deploy 572 theater nuclear weapons to counter Soviet "Eurostrategic" missile buildup.

1980 U.S. mission to rescue hostages in Tehran ends in disaster before it reaches embassy.
SALT II "temporarily" withdrawn from Senate by Carter after Soviet invasion of Afghanistan.
Carter embargoes shipments of feed grain and high technology to Soviet Union and declares United States will boycott summer Olympic games in Moscow.
Carter Doctrine commits United States to security of Persian Gulf oil-producing states if they are externally threatened.
United States organizes rapid deployment force to back up the Carter Doctrine.
Iraq attacks Iran.
Ronald Reagan elected president.

1981 U.S. hostages released moments after Reagan assumes presidency.
Reagan declares United States will not allow Saudi Arabia to become "another Iran."
Begin reelected in Israel.
Sadat assassinated in Egypt.

Reagan decides on large program to rebuild U.S. military power, including 100 MX missiles and 100 B-1 bombers.

Polish government imposes martial law.

United States imposes economic sanctions on Poland and on Soviet Union, believed to be behind Polish crackdown.

1982 Reagan announces economic assistance plan for Caribbean Basin (the Caribbean and Central America) as he supports El Salvador's government against rebel forces and attempts to isolate the Sandinistas in Nicaragua despite congressional criticism.

Israel invades Lebanon, attempting to destroy the Palestine Liberation Organization (PLO).

U.S. marines are sent into Beirut as part of a multinational peacekeeping force to supervise the PLO's leaving.

China and the United States sign agreement on the reduction of U.S. arms sales to Taiwan.

Brezhnev dies and is succeeded by Yuri Andropov, former head of the Soviet secret police.

Argentina invades the British Falkland Islands, long claimed by Argentina. Britain reconquers the islands.

United States imposes—and later lifts—sanctions on U.S. and European companies selling equipment to the Soviets for building of a natural gas pipeline to Western Europe.

Secretary of State Alexander Haig resigns.

1983 Reagan denounces the Soviet Union as an "evil empire."

Bipartisan Scowcroft Commission recommends deployment of 100 MX missiles and eventual replacement of missiles equipped with MIRVs with mobile, smaller missiles with single warheads. Congress accepts these recommendations.

Catholic bishops in pastoral letter deplore nuclear deterrence for its immorality. French bishops endorse deterrence as "service to peace."

Two hundred forty-one marines killed in suicide truck-bomb attack on their barracks in Beirut.

Soviet Union shoots down Korean 747 jetliner with 269 passengers aboard after it strays into Soviet airspace.

U.S. forces, together with troops from six Caribbean states, invade the island of Grenada. They depose the Marxist government, return Cuban worker-soldiers to Cuba, and withdraw.

United States begins deployment of Pershing II and ground-launched cruise missiles in Europe. Soviet Union responds by breaking off all arms control talks.

1984 Bipartisan Kissinger Commission recommends extensive economic and military assistance to Central America to combat domestic poverty and Soviet-Cuban intervention. Congress critical of administration policy.

Andropov dies and Brezhnev's confidant, Konstantin Chernenko, succeeds him.

Reagan is reelected.

United States pulls marines out of Lebanon.

Napoléon Duarte wins Salvadoran presidency, defeating right-wing candidate.

Congress cuts off all military assistance to the contras in Nicaragua.

Latin American debtor countries meet at Cartagena to discuss the debt problem and repayment.

United States declares Iran a supporter of international terrorism.

1985 Chernenko dies and is succeeded by Mikhail Gorbachev.

Africa, especially Ethiopia, which is engaged in a civil war, suffers from widespread starvation.

Christian Democratic Party, led by Duarte, wins majority in Salvadoran National Assembly.

Various terrorist groups hijack a TWA plane flying from Athens to Rome, seize an Italian cruise ship, and attack Israel's El Al passengers at the Vienna and Rome airports.

Reagan orders limited economic sanctions against South Africa; Congress imposes harsher sanctions in 1986.

Reagan and Gorbachev hold their first summit conference in Geneva, Switzerland.

1986 Ferdinand Marcos in the Philippines and Jean-Claude Duvalier in Haiti are forced to flee their respective countries, and the Reagan administration proclaims its new human rights policy, opposing dictatorships of the left and right.

Congress approves $100 million for the Nicaraguan contras.

The United States attacks Libya for terrorist acts. Syria is shown to be involved in terrorism, and Britain breaks diplomatic relations with Syria after abortive attempt to blow up Israeli airliner.

World's worst nuclear accident takes place at Chernobyl in the Ukraine. Sweden breaks news of radioactivity coming from the Soviet Union.

Reagan and Gorbachev meet in Iceland, and Reagan refuses to trade limitations in Strategic Defense Initiative (SDI) research for deep cuts of Soviet strategic missiles and a mutual elimination of all intermediate-range missiles in Europe.

United States exceeds SALT II limits and declares that the unratified 1979 treaty is no longer "operational."

Iran-contra scandal breaks.

OPEC's oil price falls to $9–$10 a barrel, but then stabilizes at $18 a barrel.

Spain and Portugal join the European Economic Community.

U.S. dollar is allowed to drop substantially against Japanese yen and West German mark to improve U.S. exports and reduce huge trade deficit, but action proves ineffective.

1987 Congressional hearings into Iran-contra scandal raise doubts about Reagan's effectiveness for the remainder of his term.

The United States and the Soviet Union agree to a worldwide ban on short- and intermediate-range missiles, the so-called double zero option, ending years of tension over Soviet SS-20 missile deployment.

The United States reflags Kuwaiti oil tankers in the Persian Gulf and escorts them with U.S. warships to protect them from possible Iranian attacks.

Five Central American presidents devise a plan for peace in their area. The contras and Sandinistas are to negotiate an end to the civil war, and the Sandinista government commits itself to hold general election by spring 1990.

Palestinians in December begin the *intifada*, or uprising, protesting both the continued Israeli occupation of the West Bank and opposition to a Palestinian state, and, more indirectly, the PLO failure to seek a diplomatic solution.

Gorbachev at the seventieth anniversary celebration of Bolshevik Revolution denounces Stalin's historical legacy and defends his program of *perestroika*.

1988 George Bush elected president.

Gorbachev, at first national party conference since 1941, proposes to restructure Soviet government with strong presidency, selected by a more popularly responsive Supreme Soviet.

U.S. Navy shoots down Iranian commercial jetliner with 290 people aboard over Persian Gulf.
Iran and Iraq agree to a cease-fire in their eight-year-long war.
Panama's strongman, Gen. Manuel Noriega, is indicted for drug running by two Florida grand juries.
The right-wing Arena Party wins majority in Salvadoran Legislative Assembly.
PLO and Yasir Arafat declare the right of all states in the region to live in peace with secure boundaries; proclaim a Palestinian state in the West Bank and the Gaza Strip; recognize Israel; and reject terrorism.
The Soviet Baltic republics assert their desire for autonomy, if not independence; ethnic clashes in the southern Soviet Union between Azerbaijanis and Armenians lead to increasing violence.
Gorbachev makes dramatic announcement at UN of unilateral military reductions, including sizable cuts in troop levels and tanks (50,000 and 1,000 respectively), and other offensive weapons of the forces facing NATO.

1989 Gorbachev elected president of the Soviet Union, an alternative base of power to the Communist Party.
Free elections in Poland result in repudiation of the Polish Communist Party. Solidarity forms first noncommunist government in Eastern Europe.
Hungary allows emigration to the West. Mass demonstrations in East Germany protest regime celebrating its fortieth year; cabinet resigns. Hard-line Communist Party leaders are replaced.
Czechoslovakia and Bulgaria follow the reformist path of Poland, Hungary, and East Germany. Only in Romania does government resist and use force, but its leader, Nicolae Ceausescu, is nevertheless overthrown and executed.
Soviet Union withdraws its troops from Afghanistan.
Gorbachev in neutral Finland states that the Soviet Union has no moral or political right to interfere in the affairs of its neighbors. Statement effectively repudiates Brezhnev Doctrine.
The Ayatollah Khomeini dies in Iran.
Huge pro-democracy demonstrations in Beijing are violently suppressed by the communist leadership.
Berlin Wall is opened, beginning process of German reunification.
Panamanian general Noriega voids result of national election. Coup led by Panamanian officers fails. Noriega declares Panama to be in a state of war with the United States, which then invades Panama, overthrows Noriega, and brings him to the United States for trial.
Cuban troops begin withdrawal from Angola based on multilateral agreement under which Namibia achieves its independence.

1990 Lithuanian Communist Party breaks from the Soviet party and speaks for independent Lithuania.
Armenians and Azerbaijanis continue feud while local Communist Party loses control to the Azerbaijani popular front. Gorbachev sends in the Soviet army to restore order and keep the party in power.
Gorbachev, in a revolutionary statement to a plenum of the Communist Party, renounces the constitutionally guaranteed communist monopoly of power and declares his support for an eventual multiparty system as well as private enterprise.
Eastern European free elections in the spring produce noncommunist governments, except in Romania and Bulgaria, where the communists, under a new name, win by large majorities.
Iraqi troops invade neighboring Kuwait, provoking condemnation and economic sanctions by the United Nations.

After East German election in March, East and West Germany begin negotiating reunification. On July 1 they create a financial and economic union. Two weeks later Gorbachev agrees that a reunited Germany can choose to join NATO. On October 3 the two Germanies unify. In November the Conference on Security and Cooperation in Europe endorses Germany's unity. On December 2 elections in both Germanies produce the first postwar all-German parliament.

Soviet Union's two largest republics, Russia and the Ukraine, declare their sovereignty and assert that their laws are superior to those of the Soviet Union. Other republics follow.

Nicaraguan government agrees to free election and loses to rival coalition. The contras disband.

1991 All-German parliament and government are sworn in.

Iraq, refusing to withdraw from Kuwait, is forced out in forty-three days by the U.S.-led UN coalition.

United States and Soviet Union sign a Strategic Arms Reduction Talks (START) agreement, reducing strategic weapons by 30 percent.

Warsaw Treaty Organization formally dissolved. Soviet troops leave Hungary and Czechoslovakia.

Boris Yeltsin, Gorbachev's rival, becomes the first elected leader of the thousand-year-old Russian republic.

Coup against Gorbachev is launched by political opponents. Yeltsin defies the coup attempt and it fails. Gorbachev survives, but his authority declines further as Yeltsin establishes his primacy versus Soviet leaders.

Estonia, Latvia, and Lithuania are granted independence. After efforts to establish a confederation founder, Russia, Belarus, and Ukraine declare the Soviet Union dead and form the Commonwealth of Independent States. Other republics are invited to join.

European Free Trade Association, consisting of Austria, Switzerland, Sweden, Finland, Liechtenstein (neutrals during the Cold War), and Norway and Iceland (NATO members), establishes a common free trade area with the European Community (EC).

Soviet Union dissolves. Gorbachev resigns and cedes Kremlin to Yeltsin.

Slovenia and Croatia secede from Yugoslavia. Serb-dominated Yugoslav army resists secessions by force.

1992 Government of El Salvador reaches accord with Farabundo Marti Liberation Front (FMLN), ending decade of civil war.

U.S. government begins forcible repatriation of Haitian refugees. Establishment of joint military force for Commonwealth of Independent States.

UN peacekeeping troops intervene in Balkans. Voters in Bosnia-Herzegovina approve independence by referendum. European Community and United States recognize Bosnia-Herzegovina along with independent Croatia and Slovenia. United Nations offers membership to all three countries; Yugoslavia expelled by General Assembly.

Nineteen European states approve European Economic Area (EEA) to create flee-trade zone beyond the borders of the EC.

Members of the EC ratify the Maastrict treaty, designed to move the now-named European Union beyond economic integration toward creation of a common foreign and security policy.

U.S. Senate and Russian Supreme Soviet ratify START agreement.

France and Germany create 35,000-member joint defense force to serve as nucleus of regional security system for Western European Union.

U.S. and German governments announce G-7 plan to provide Russia with $24 billion in economic assistance upon Russia's entry into the International Monetary Fund.

NATO announces final removal of all ground-based tactical nuclear weapons from Europe.

Asia-Pacific Economic Cooperation (APEC) group announces program of liberalized and expanded trade within region.

Philippine government gains control of Subic Bay Naval Base from United States, ending century of American presence in country.

Bill Clinton elected president on platform of domestic reform.

1993 European Union initiates single market.

United States and Russia approve new START treaty calling for deeper cuts in strategic arsenals; they also sign military cooperation agreement providing for joint exercises and greater consultation in crises.

Terrorist bomb damages World Trade Center, killing six people and forcing the evacuation of 50,000.

North Korean government announces withdrawal from Nuclear Non-Proliferation Treaty (NPT).

United States pledges to accelerate efforts to restore deposed Haitian leader Jean-Bertrand Aristide to power. UN Security Council imposes economic sanctions against military regime.

United States endorses Vance-Owen plan to partition the former Yugoslavia along ethnic lines. United States airdrops relief supplies to besieged Bosnian Muslims. United Nations declares Sarajevo and other cities in Bosnia-Herzegovina to be "safe areas."

Twelve American soldiers are killed in Mogadishu, Somalia. Clinton orders reinforcements and sets timetable for U.S. withdrawal from Somalia.

Israel and Palestinian Liberation Organization sign peace treaty.

U.S. Congress ratifies North American Free Trade Agreement (NAFTA).

South African government approves new constitution, abolishing apartheid and setting agenda for national elections.

1994 United States and Japan reach agreement on future bilateral trade. For China, United States suspends linkage between bilateral trade and that country's behavior in human rights. Trade ties with Vietnam renewed as well.

Assassination of Rwandan president sparks civil war between Hutu and Tutsi tribes, resulting in more than 500,000 casualties.

North Korean government rejects U.S. and UN demands that it allow foreign inspection of its nuclear facilities. Kim Il-Sung dies and is replaced by his son, Kim Jong-Il. After protracted talks, North Korean government agrees to freeze nuclear program in exchange for U.S. economic and technological assistance.

GATT's Uruguay Round concludes. Multilateral trade agreement passed by member states.

Cuban refugees launch new boatlift to Florida coast. U.S. and Cuban governments reach agreement on future emigration levels.

Scandinavian states (except Norway) agree to join European Union.

United States begins "semi-permissive" occupation of Haiti. Military regime yields power to American troops and parliament disbands. Gen. Raul Cédras, leader of the military junta, is exiled to Panama; Aristide resumes leadership.

Iraqi armed forces mass along Kuwaiti border. U.S. forces are deployed to Persian Gulf to deter invasion.

Israel and Jordan sign peace agreement.

United Nations announces plans to withdraw from Somalia by March 1995; cites continuing clan warfare as reason for suspension of efforts.

Midterm elections bring collapse of Democratic majority in U.S. Congress.

1995 Russian troops reclaim control over Chechen capital of Grozny after secession attempt. Chechen rebels retreat to surrounding hillsides and continue fight for independence.

Mexican economy is battered by devaluation of peso. Fiscal crisis results in massive loan guarantees from foreign countries, including $10 billion from United States, to prevent further weakening of Mexican economy.

NATO launches air strikes against Serbian forces after Serbs seize "safe havens" in Srebenica and Zepa and attack civilians in Sarajevo.

U.S. marines are deployed to Somalia to oversee evacuation of UN peacekeeping forces.

Massacre of Israeli citizens by Islamic terrorists threatens to undermine peace accord between Israel and PLO. Israeli prime minister Yitzhak Rabin assassinated, succeeded by Benjamin Netanyahu of rival Likud Party.

Muslim and Croatian forces launch successful offensive against Serbs, changing balance of power in region. All sides convene in Dayton, Ohio, and agree to cease-fire, temporary NATO occupation, and formation of new Bosnian government.

United States threatens trade war against China over Beijing's alleged violations of international copyright laws.

Republican majority in U.S. Congress promotes "National Security Restoration Act" calling for increased defense spending, cutbacks in foreign aid, and reduced support for UN peacekeeping efforts. President Clinton vetoes congressional measures.

1996 Congress ratifies START II accord with Russia.

Taiwan holds first democratic elections. United States deploys naval forces to region in response to Chinese military provocations in Taiwan Straits.

Control over peacekeeping mission in Haiti transferred from United States to United Nations. Réné Préval elected president in closely monitored but widely boycotted elections.

United States deploys naval forces to free foreign nationals that are trapped in Liberia.

President Clinton and Russian president Boris Yeltsin meet in Moscow together with leaders of Western industrial democracies.

Yeltsin reelected as president of Russia, forming coalition with former general Alexander Lebed to defeat communist leader Gennady Zyuganov. Lebed later fired as national security adviser after challenging Yeltsin's foreign and domestic policies.

Iraq intervenes in Kurdish-held territories considered off-limits by Western powers. United States responds with aerial attacks on Iraqi military installations.

Clinton signs Comprehensive Test Ban Treaty and encourages other states to enter agreement that prevents nuclear testing.

Ethnic violence spreads from Rwanda and Burundi to other parts of Central Africa. Massive refugee population threatens political stability in region.

Clinton calls for NATO expansion by 1999 with likely new members to include Poland, Hungary, and the Czech Republic. Russia declares NATO expansion a threat to its security and seeks separate treaty with alliance.

Muslim leader elected to lead tripartite government in Bosnia. NATO peacekeeping mission extended until June 1998.

Clinton is elected to second term, defeating former senator Robert Dole.

U.S. government, dissatisfied with pace of reform in United Nations, leads effort to prevent UN Secretary-General Boutros Boutros-Ghali from gaining second term. Ghana's Kofi Annan, favored by the United States, is elected secretary-general.

1997 Madeleine Albright is confirmed as U.S. secretary of state, William Cohen as secretary of defense, and Bill Richardson as ambassador to the United Nations. Samuel Berger replaces Anthony Lake as national security adviser. George Tenet is confirmed as CIA director after Lake, Clinton's first choice, withdraws his nomination amid widespread opposition.

Chinese leader Deng Xiaoping dies, leading to uncertain period of political transition.

United States rejects authority of World Trade Organization over threatened U.S. economic sanctions against Cuba. European leaders protest Helms-Burton sanctions but do not retaliate.

Clinton and Boris Yeltsin meet in Helsinki, Finland, and agree to new round of nuclear weapons reductions, labeled START III.

Israel announces plans for new Jewish settlements in East Jerusalem, setting off violent demonstrations by Palestinians and new threats to peace process.

British Labour Party leader Tony Blair replaces Conservative John Major as prime minister.

Congress ratifies Chemical Weapons Convention, previously signed by most other governments.

Zaire's government headed by Mobutu Sese Seko falls to rival forces led by Laurent Kabila. Country becomes the Democratic Republic of Congo, and the new regime is immediately recognized by the U.S. government.

Czech Republic, Hungary, and Poland are invited to join NATO. Russian government approves security charter with NATO that calls for consultations and limited security cooperation.

Chinese government assumes control over Hong Kong, a former British colony.

United States grants political asylum to two high-ranking North Korean diplomats after their defection.

NATO troops seize illegal weapons from Bosnian police forces suspected of planning coup against government.

1998 Pope John Paul II, visiting Cuba for the first time, criticizes Fidel Castro's communist government, its restrictions against the Catholic Church, and the ongoing U.S. economic sanctions against Cuba.

Attacks by the Kosovo Liberation Army against Serbian police prompt a military crackdown in the Yugoslav province of Kosovo, whose majority population of ethnic Albanians seeks independence.

President Clinton visits six African countries and denounces past U.S. support for dictatorships on the continent.

With assistance from U.S. mediators, a landmark peace settlement is reached in Northern Ireland that paves the way for greater self-government in the British-held territory.

Eleven Western European countries agree to adopt a common currency, the euro, which would become the basis of foreign exchange in 1999.

Underground nuclear tests conducted by India and Pakistan provoke worldwide condemnation.

Suharto, Indonesia's long-reigning military dictator, relinquishes power after thirty-two years.

Clinton visits China and vows to maintain close economic ties between the two countries while pressing Beijing to improve its human rights record.

Iraqi leaders suspend cooperation with United Nations weapons inspectors.

U.S. embassies in Kenya and Tanzania are bombed in terrorist attacks. The United States retaliates by bombing suspected terrorist bases in Sudan and Afghanistan.

East Asian economic crisis spreads to Russia, prompting the collapse of the ruble and a default on foreign debts.

North Korea fires a three-stage ballistic missile over Japan as a demonstration of its military capabilities.

German chancellor Helmut Kohl is defeated in national elections by Gerhard Schroeder, head of the Social Democratic Party.

Gen. Augusto Pinochet, the former Chilean dictator, is arrested in London at the request of a Spanish judge who hopes to try Pinochet on charges of crimes against humanity. Pinochet is placed under house arrest for more than a year, then ruled unfit to stand trial.

Israel and Palestinian leaders meet at Wye River Plantation in Maryland to begin "final-status" negotiations on possible Palestinian statehood.

American bombers strike Iraqi military headquarters, intelligence agencies, and weapons plants in response to Saddam Hussein's defiance of United Nations weapons inspections.

U.S. House of Representatives votes to impeach President Clinton for his role in a White House sex scandal. The president remains in office after the U.S. Senate fails to convict him in 1999 on charges of perjury and obstruction of justice.

1999 On its fiftieth anniversary the North Atlantic Treaty Organization (NATO) expands to include the Czech Republic, Hungary, and Poland.

NATO bombers conduct aerial assaults against hundreds of targets in Serbia. Yugoslav president Slobodan Milosevic responds by expelling more than one million ethnic Albanians from Kosovo. Continued NATO bombings force Milosevic to allow refugees to return and place Kosovo under the supervision of UN and NATO peacekeepers.

Ehud Barak, leader of Israel's Labor Party, is elected as prime minister and pledges to seek a "true, lasting peace" between Israel and its neighbors.

Report by the U.S. Congress charges the Chinese government with conducting a "systematic" espionage campaign to obtain classified information on U.S. nuclear weapons technology.

Nelson Mandela completes five-year term as president of South Africa and is replaced by Thabo Mbeki of the African National Congress.

Residents of East Timor vote overwhelmingly to secede from Indonesia. An attempt by the Indonesian government to prevent secession with military force prompts the United Nations to deploy peacekeepers to East Timor.

Russian troops escalate their crackdown against separatists in Chechnya.

U.S. Senate rejects the Comprehensive Test Ban Treaty signed by Clinton in 1996 and by the leaders of more than 150 foreign governments.

The United States and China sign a landmark trade agreement. Clinton endorses China's entry into the World Trade Organization (WTO) and seeks congressional support for permanent normal trade relations between the United States and China.

Annual meetings of the WTO are disrupted by protesters in Seattle.

United Nations admits to making "serious mistakes" in not responding to 1994 genocide in Rwanda and Burundi.

U.S. troops, along with human rights monitors from the UN and Organization of American States, abandon peacekeeping mission in Haiti.

European Union creates "strike force" of 60,000 troops to respond to security threats that do not require NATO involvement.

Russian president Boris Yeltsin provokes repeated political crises by firing four prime ministers between March 1998 and August 1999. Yeltsin abruptly resigns on New Year's Eve and names Prime Minister Vladimir Putin as his successor on an interim basis.

2000 The citizenship status of Elián González, a six-year-old Cuban refugee who survived a November 1999 escape to Florida, fuels tensions between the United States and Cuba.

Vladimir Putin is elected as Russia's president.

Clinton visits India and Pakistan in an effort to defuse tensions between the two newest nuclear powers.

Voters in Taiwan elect Chen Shui-bian president. While campaigning, he called openly for the nation's independence from China.

World Bank and International Monetary Fund announce new reforms during annual meetings in Washington, D.C., in response to public pressure.

Leaders of North Korea and South Korea agree to hold the first-ever summit meeting between the two countries, which technically remain at war.

Seven African presidents seek assistance from the UN Security Council in halting a civil war in the Democratic Republic of the Congo. Turmoil in Sierra Leone also requires intervention by UN peacekeepers.

U.S. government pledges more than $1 billion to Colombia to support its effort to stem the flow of illegal narcotics.

Russian legislators ratify START II and the Comprehensive Test Ban Treaty, but threaten to abrogate both treaties if the United States builds an antiballistic missile system.

European Union endorses Chinese entry into World Trade Organization. U.S. Congress votes to establish permanent normal trade relations with China.

Israeli troops withdraw from buffer zone in southern Lebanon, which they had occupied since 1978.

Syrian leader Hafez al-Assad dies. His 34-year-old son, Bashar, is selected as the nation's new president.

Select Bibliography

All of the entries in this bibliography are books. Readers who wish to keep up with the journal literature on American foreign policy will find the articles in *Foreign Affairs*, *Foreign Policy*, and *International Security* useful and relevant.

AMERICAN SOCIETY AND STYLE IN FOREIGN POLICY

Almond, Gabriel A. *The American People and Foreign Policy.* New York: Praeger, 1960.

Boorstin, Daniel J. *The Genius of American Politics.* Chicago: Phoenix Books, 1953.

Brands, H. W. *What America Owes the World.* New York: Cambridge University Press, 1998.

Dallek, Robert. *The American Style of Foreign Policy.* New York: Knopf, 1983.

Hartz, Louis. *The Liberal Tradition in America.* New York: Harvest Books, 1955.

Hofstadter, Richard. *The Paranoid Style in American Politics.* New York: Vintage Books, 1967.

Hunt, Michael H. *Ideology and U.S. Foreign Policy.* New Haven: Yale University Press, 1987.

Kennan, George F. *American Diplomacy, 1900–1950.* Chicago: University of Chicago Press, 1951.

Lippmann, Walter. *U.S. Foreign Policy: Shield of the Republic.* Boston: Little, Brown, 1943.

Lipset, Seymour Martin. *American Exceptionalism.* New York: Norton, 1996.

McDougall, Walter A. *Promised Land, Crusader State.* Boston: Houghton Mifflin, 1997.

McElroy, Robert W. *Morality and American Foreign Policy.* Princeton: Princeton University Press, 1992.

Morgenthau, Hans J. *In Defense of the National Interest.* New York: Knopf, 1951.

Nichols, Bruce, and Gil Loescher, eds. *The Moral Nation.* South Bend.: University of Notre Dame Press, 1989.

Osgood, Robert. *Ideals and Self-Interest in America's Foreign Relations.* Chicago: University of Chicago Press, 1953.

Owen, John M., IV. *Liberal Peace, Liberal War.* Ithaca: Cornell University Press, 1997.

Perlmutter, Amos. *Making the World Safe for Democracy.* Chapel Hill: University of North Carolina Press, 1997.

Potter, David M. *The People of Plenty.* Chicago: Phoenix Books, 1954.

Smith, Tony. *America's Mission.* Princeton: Princeton University Press, 1994.

Stoessinger, John G. *Crusaders and Pragmatists.* 2d ed. New York: Norton, 1985.

Thompson, Kenneth W. *Traditions and Values in Politics and Diplomacy.* Baton Rouge: Louisiana State University Press, 1992.

Trubowitz, Peter. *Defining the National Interest.* Chicago: University of Chicago Press, 1998.

von Vorys, Karl. *American National Interest.* New York: Praeger, 1990.

Weigel, George. *American Interests, American Purpose.* New York: Praeger, 1989.

Whitcomb, Roger S. *The American Approach to Foreign Affairs.* Westport, Conn.: Praeger, 1998.

White, Donald W. *The American Century.* New Haven: Yale University Press, 1996.

AMERICAN FOREIGN POLICY DURING THE COLD WAR

Aron, Raymond. *The Imperial Republic.* Cambridge: Winthrop, 1974.

Bell, Coral. *The Diplomacy of Détente.* New York: St. Martin's Press, 1977.

Brzezinski, Zbigniew. *Game Plan.* Boston: Atlantic Monthly Press, 1986.

Cingranelli, David Louis. *Ethics, American Foreign Policy, and the Third World.* New York: St. Martin's Press, 1993.
Dukes, Paul. *The Last Great Game.* New York: St. Martin's Press, 1989.
Fulbright, J. William. *The Arrogance of Power.* New York: Vintage Books, 1967.
___. *The Crippled Giant.* New York: Vintage Books, 1972.
___. *Old Myths and New Realities.* New York: Vintage Books, 1964.
Gaddis, John Lewis. *The Long Peace.* New York: Oxford University Press, 1987.
___. *Russia, the Soviet Union and the United States.* New York: Wiley, 1978.
___. *Strategies of Containment.* New York: Oxford University Press, 1982.
___. *The United States and the Origins of the Cold War, 1941–1947.* New York: Columbia University Press, 1972.
___. *We Now Know: Rethinking Cold War History.* New York: Oxford University Press, 1997.
Halle, Louis J. *The Cold War as History.* New York: Harper and Row, 1967.
Hoffmann, Stanley. *Gulliver's Troubles, or the Setting of American Foreign Policy.* New York: McGraw-Hill, 1968.
___. *Primacy or World Order.* New York: McGraw-Hill, 1978.
Kumamoto, Robert D. *International Terrorism and American Foreign Relations, 1945–1976.* Boston: Northeastern University Press, 1999.
Larson, Deborah Welch. *Origins of Containment.* Princeton: Princeton University Press, 1985.
Leffler, Melvyn P. *A Preponderance of Power.* Stanford: Stanford University Press, 1992.
Leffler, Melvyn P., and David Painter, eds. *The Origins of the Cold War.* New York: Routledge, 1994.
Lucas, Scott. *Freedom's War.* New York: New York University Press, 1999.
McNamara, Robert S. *Out of the Cold.* New York: Simon and Schuster, 1989.
Mandelbaum, Richard, and Strobe Talbott. *Reagan and Gorbachev.* New York: Vintage Books, 1987.
Moskin, Robert J. *Mr. Truman's War.* New York: Random House, 1996.
Muravchik, Joshua. *The Uncertain Crusade.* New York: Hamilton Press, 1985.
Oberdorfer, Don. *From the Cold War to a New Era.* Baltimore: Johns Hopkins University Press, 1998.
Osgood, Robert, et al. *America and the World.* Baltimore: Johns Hopkins University Press, 1970.
Rodman, Peter W. *More Precious than Peace.* New York: Scribner's, 1994.
Schlesinger, Arthur, Jr. *The Imperial Presidency.* Boston: Houghton Mifflin, 1973.
Schulzinger, Robert D. *The Wise Men of Foreign Affairs.* New York: Columbia University Press, 1985.
Scott, James M. *Deciding to Intervene.* Durham: Duke University Press, 1996.
Skidmore, David. *Reversing Course.* Nashville: Vanderbilt University Press, 1996.
Smith, Gaddis. *Morality, Reason, and Power.* New York: Hill and Wang, 1986.
Steel, Ronald. *Pax Americana.* New York: Viking Press, 1967.
Tillema, Herbert K. *Appeal to Force.* New York: Crowell, 1973.
Tucker, Robert W. *The Purposes of American Power.* New York: Praeger, 1981.
Yergin, Daniel. *Shattered Peace.* Boston: Houghton Mifflin, 1977.

AMERICAN FOREIGN POLICY AFTER THE COLD WAR

Art, Robert J., and Seyom Brown, eds. *U.S. Foreign Policy: The Search for a New Role.* New York: Macmillan, 1993.
Brawley, Mark R. *Afterglow or Adjustment?* New York: Columbia University Press, 1999.
Brzezinski, Zbigniew. *Out of Control.* New York: Scribner's, 1993.
Callahan, David. *Between Two Worlds.* New York: HarperCollins, 1994.

Chace, James. *The Consequences of the Peace.* New York: Oxford University Press, 1992.
Chase, Robert, et al., eds. *The Pivotal States.* New York: Norton, 1999.
Cox, Michael. *U.S. Foreign Policy after the Cold War.* London: Pinter, 1995.
Cyr, Arthur I. *After the Cold War.* New York: New York University Press, 1997.
Deitchman, Seymour J. *On Being a Superpower.* Boulder: Westview Press, 2000.
Fry, Earl H. *America the Vincible.* Englewood Cliffs, N.J.: Prentice Hall, 1994.
Gaddis, John Lewis. *The United States and the End of the Cold War.* New York: Oxford University Press, 1992.
Garten, Jeffrey E. *A Cold Peace.* New York: Times Books, 1992.
Garthoff, Raymond. *The Great Transition.* Washington, D.C.: Brookings, 1994.
Gray, Colin. *War, Peace, and Victory.* New York: Simon and Schuster, 1990.
Hoffmann, Stanley. *World Disorders.* Lanham, Md.: Rowman and Littlefield, 1998.
Hogan, Michael J., ed. *The End of the Cold War.* New York: Cambridge University Press, 1992.
Hutchings, Robert L., ed. *At the End of the American Century.* Baltimore: Johns Hopkins University Press, 1998.
Hyland, William G. *Clinton's World.* Westport, Conn.: Praeger, 1999.
Johnson, Chalmers. *Blowback: The Costs and Consequences of American Empire.* New York: Metropolitan Books, 2000.
Kanter, Arnold, and Linton F. Brooks, eds. *U.S. Intervention Policy for the Post–Cold War World.* New York: Norton, 1995.
Kegley, Charles W., Jr., and Gregory A. Raymond. *A Multipolar Peace?* New York: St. Martin's Press, 1994.
Kennan, George. *At a Century's End.* New York: Norton, 1996.
Kennedy, Paul. *Preparing for the Twenty-First Century.* New York: Random House, 1993.
Lieber, Robert J., ed. *Eagle Adrift.* New York: Longman, 1997.
Maynes, Charles William, and Richard Williamson, eds. *U.S. Foreign Policy and the United Nations.* New York: Norton, 1996.
Muller, Steven, and Gebhard Schweigler, eds. *From Occupation to Cooperation.* New York: Norton, 1992.
Muravchik, Joshua. *The Imperative of American Leadership: A Challenge to Neo-Isolationism.* Washington, D.C.: American Enterprise Institute, 1996.
Myers, Robert J. *U.S. Foreign Policy in the Twenty-First Century.* Baton Rouge: Louisiana State University Press, 1999.
Nau, Richard. *The Myth of America's Decline.* New York: Oxford University Press, 1990.
Nielson, Jonathan M., ed. *Paths Not Taken.* Westport, Conn.: Praeger, 2000.
Nolan, Janne E. *An Elusive Consensus.* Washington, D.C.: Brookings, 1999.
Nolan, Janne E., ed. *Global Engagement.* Washington, D.C.: Brookings, 1994.
Nye, Joseph S., Jr. *Bound to Lead.* New York: Basic Books, 1990.
Payne, Richard J. *The Western European Allies, the Third World, and U.S. Foreign Policy.* New York: Greenwood Press, 1991.
Ripley, Randall B., and James M. Lindsay, eds. *U.S. Foreign Policy after the Cold War.* Pittsburgh: University of Pittsburgh Press, 1997.
Rubenstein, Alvin Z., ed. *America's National Interests in a Post–Cold War World.* New York: McGraw-Hill, 1994.
Rubenstein, Alvin Z., et al., eds. *The Clinton Foreign Policy Reader.* Armonk, N.Y.: Sharpe, 2000.
Ruggie, John Gerard. *Winning the Peace.* New York: Columbia University Press, 1996.
Russett, Bruce M. *Grasping the Democratic Peace.* Princeton: Princeton University Press, 1993.
Scott, James M., ed. *After the End.* Durham: Duke University Press, 1998.
Steel, Ronald. *Temptations of a Superpower.* Cambridge: Harvard University Press, 1995.
Treverton, Gregory F. *America, Germany, and the Future of Europe.* Princeton: Princeton University Press, 1992.

Tucker, Robert W., and David C. Hendrickson. *The Imperial Temptation.* New York: Council on Foreign Relations, 1992.
Von Hippel, Karin. *Democracy by Force.* New York: Cambridge University Press, 2000.
Wiarda, Howard J. *Cracks in the Consensus.* Westport, Conn.: Praeger, 1997.
Yankelovich, Daniel, and I. M. Destler, eds. *Beyond the Beltway.* New York: Norton, 1994.

DIPLOMATIC HISTORIES

Ambrose, Stephen E. *Rise to Globalism: American Foreign Policy since 1938.* 7th ed. rev. New York: Penguin, 1993.
Bagby, Wesley M. *America's International Relations since World War I.* New York: Oxford University Press, 1999.
Bailey, Thomas. *A Diplomatic History of the American People.* 10th ed. Englewood Cliffs, N.J.: Prentice Hall, 1980.
Bemis, Samuel. *A Diplomatic History of the United States.* 4th ed. New York: Holt, 1955.
Clarfield, Gerard. *U.S. Diplomatic History.* 2 vols. Englewood Cliffs, N.J.: Prentice Hall, 1992.
Ferrell, Robert H. *American Diplomacy.* 4th ed. New York: Norton, 1988.
Fleming, D. F. *The Cold War and Its Origins, 1917–1960.* 2 vols. Garden City, N.Y.: Doubleday, 1961.
Hogan, Michael J., ed. *Paths to Power.* New York: Cambridge University Press, 2000.
Jentleson, Bruce W., and Thomas G. Paterson, eds. *The Encyclopedia of U.S. Foreign Relations.* 4 vols. New York: Oxford University Press, 1997.
Jones, Howard. *The Course of American Diplomacy.* 2d ed. Chicago: Dorsey Press, 1988.
Kissinger, Henry. *Diplomacy.* New York: Simon and Schuster, 1994.
Kunz, Diane B., ed. *The Diplomacy of the Crucial Decade.* New York: Columbia University Press, 1994.
McCormick, Thomas J. *America's Half-Century.* 2d ed. Baltimore: Johns Hopkins University Press, 1995.
Melanson, Richard A. *American Foreign Policy since the Vietnam War.* 3d ed. Armonk, N.Y.: Sharpe, 2000.
Nielson, Jonathan M., ed. *Paths Not Taken.* Westport, Conn.: Praeger, 2000.
Paterson, Thomas G. *Meeting the Communist Threat.* New York: Oxford University Press, 1989.
Pratt, Julius W. *A History of United States Foreign Policy.* New York: Prentice Hall, 1955.
Rappaport, Armin. *A History of American Diplomacy.* New York: Macmillan, 1975.
Schulzinger, Robert D. *American Diplomacy in the Twentieth Century.* 3d ed. New York: Oxford University Press, 1994.
Walker, Martin. *The Cold War.* New York: Henry Holt, 1994.

REVISIONIST INTERPRETATIONS AND DEBATES

Alperovitz, Gar. *Atomic Diplomacy.* New York: Vintage Books, 1967.
Barnet, Richard. *Roots of War.* New York: Atheneum, 1972.
Campbell, David. *United States Foreign Policy and the Politics of Identity.* Minneapolis: University of Minnesota Press, 1992.
———. *Writing Security.* Rev. ed. Minneapolis: University of Minnesota Press, 1998.
Gardner, Lloyd. *Architects of Illusion.* Chicago: Quadrangle Books, 1970.
Johnson, Robert H. *Improbable Dangers.* New York: St. Martin's Press, 1994.
Kolko, Gabriel. *The Roots of American Foreign Policy.* Boston: Beacon Press, 1969.
Kolko, Gabriel, and Joyce Kolko. *The Limits of Power.* New York: Harper and Row, 1972.
Kwitny, Jonathan. *Endless Enemies.* New York: Penguin, 1984.
LaFeber, Walter. *America, Russia, and the Cold War, 1945–1980.* 5th ed. New York: Knopf, 1985.
———. *The New Empire.* Ithaca: Cornell University Press, 1963.

Lens, Sidney. *The Forging of the American Empire.* New York: Crowell, 1971.
Maddox, Robert J. *The New Left and the Origins of the Cold War.* Princeton: Princeton University Press, 1973.
Melanson, Richard A. *Writing History and Making Policy.* Lanham, Md.: University Press of America, 1983.
Parenti, Michael. *Against Empire.* San Francisco: City Lights Books, 1995.
___. *The Sword and the Dollar.* New York: St. Martin's Press, 1989.
Paterson, Thomas G. *On Every Front.* New York: Norton, 1979.
___. *Soviet-American Confrontation.* Baltimore: Johns Hopkins University Press, 1973.
Sanders, Jerry W. *Peddlers of Crisis.* Boston: South End Press, 1983.
Tucker, Robert W. *The Radical Left and American Foreign Policy.* Baltimore: Johns Hopkins University Press, 1971.
Weldes, Jutta. *Constructing National Interests.* Minneapolis: University of Minnesota Press, 1999.
Williams, William Appleman. *The Tragedy of American Diplomacy.* New York: Norton, 1988.

AMERICAN MILITARY STRATEGY

Binkin, Martin. *Who Will Fight the Next War?* Washington, D.C.: Brookings, 1993.
Blight, James G., and David A. Welch. *On the Brink.* New York: Hill and Wang, 1989.
Boll, Michael M. *National Security Planning.* Lexington: University of Kentucky Press, 1988.
Brown, Harold. *The Strategic Defense Initiative.* Boulder: Westview Press, 1987.
Caldicott, Helen. *Missile Envy.* New York: Bantam Books, 1986.
Callahan, David. *Unwinnable Wars.* New York: Hill and Wang, 1997.
Carter, Ashton B., and William J. Perry. *Preventive Defense.* Washington, D.C.: Brookings, 1999.
Flournoy, Michele A. *Nuclear Weapons after the Cold War.* New York: HarperCollins, 1993.
Freedman, Lawrence. *The Evolution of Nuclear Strategy.* 2d ed. New York: St. Martin's Press, 1989.
Gaddis, John Lewis, et al., eds. *Cold War Statesmen Confront the Bomb.* New York: Oxford University Press, 1999.
George, Alexander L., and Richard Smoke. *Deterrence in American Foreign Policy.* New York: Columbia University Press, 1974.
Glynn, Patrick. *Closing Pandora's Box.* New York: Basic Books, 1992.
Gray, Colin. *Nuclear Strategy and Nuclear Planning.* Philadelphia: Foreign Policy Research Institute, 1985.
___. *The Soviet-American Arms Race.* Lexington, Mass.: Lexington Books, 1976.
Herken, Gregg. *Counsels of War.* New York: Oxford University Press, 1987.
Jervis, Robert. *The Illogic of American National Strategy.* Ithaca: Cornell University Press, 1984.
Kaplan, Fred. *The Wizards of Armageddon.* New York: Simon and Schuster, 1983.
Kapstein, Ethan, ed. *Downsizing Defense.* Washington, D.C.: CQ Press, 1993.
Kissinger, Henry A. *Nuclear Weapons and Foreign Policy.* New York: Harper and Brothers, 1957.
Lake, David A. *Entangling Relations.* Princeton: Princeton University Press, 1999.
Landau, Saul. *The Dangerous Doctrine.* Boulder: Westview Press, 1988.
Luttwak, Edward N. *The Pentagon and the Art of War.* New York: Simon and Schuster, 1985.
Marolda, Edward J., and Robert J. Schneller Jr. *Shield and Sword.* Washington, D.C.: Naval Historical Center, 1998.
Nolan, Janne E. *Guardians of the Arsenal.* New York: Basic Books, 1989.
Payne, Keith P. *Strategic Defense.* Lanham, Md.: Hamilton Press, 1986.
Powaski, Ronald E. *March to Armageddon.* New York: Oxford University Press, 1987.

Powell, Robert. *Nuclear Deterrence Theory.* New York: Cambridge University Press, 1990.
Sagan, Scott D., and Kenneth N. Waltz. *The Spread of Nuclear Weapons.* New York: Norton, 1995.
Schwartz, William A., and Charles Derber. *The Nuclear Seduction.* Berkeley: University of California Press, 1990.
Smoke, Richard. *National Security and the Nuclear Dilemma.* 3d ed. New York: Random House, 1992.
Talbott, Strobe. *Deadly Gambits.* New York: Knopf, 1984.
Woodward, Bob. *The Commanders.* New York: Simon and Schuster, 1991.

AMERICAN POLICY IN WESTERN EUROPE

Allin, Dana H. *Cold War Illusions.* New York: St. Martin's Press, 1995.
Burwell, Frances G., and Ivo H. Daalder, eds. *The United States and Europe in the Global Arena.* New York: St. Martin's Press, 1999.
Calingaert, Michael. *European Integration.* Boulder: Westview Press, 1996.
Carpenter, Ted Galen. *Beyond NATO.* Washington, D.C.: Cato Institute, 1994.
Dean, Jonathan. *Ending Europe's Wars.* New York: Twentieth Century Fund, 1994.
Freedman, Lawrence, ed. *Europe Transformed.* New York: St. Martin's Press, 1990.
Goldgeier, James M. *Not Whether but When: The U.S. Decision to Enlarge NATO.* Washington, D.C.: Brookings, 1999.
Gompert, David C., and F. Stephen Larrabee, eds. *America and Europe.* New York: Cambridge University Press, 1997.
Harrison, Glennon J. *Europe and the United States.* Armonk, N.Y.: Sharpe, 1994.
Holmes, John W. *The United States and Europe after the Cold War.* Columbia: University of South Carolina Press, 1997.
Kaplan, Lawrence S. *The Long Entanglement: NATO's First Fifty Years.* Westport, Conn.: Praeger, 1999.
Kapstein, Ethan B. *The Insecure Alliance.* New York: Oxford University Press, 1990.
Laquer, Walter. *The Dream that Failed.* New York: Oxford University Press, 1994.
Lundestad, Geir. *Empire by Integration, 1945–1997.* New York: Oxford University Press, 1998.
Mandelbaum, Michael. *The Dawn of Peace in Europe.* New York: Twentieth Century Fund, 1996.
Padoa-Schioppa, Tommaso. *The Road to Monetary Union in Europe.* New York: Oxford University Press, 1994.
Sherwood, Elizabeth. *Allies in Crisis.* New Haven: Yale University Press, 1990.
Stokes, Gale. *The Walls Came Tumbling Down.* New York: Oxford University Press, 1993.
Tow, William T. *The Limits of Alliance.* Baltimore: Johns Hopkins University Press, 1990.
Treverton, Gregory F. *America, Germany, and the Future of Europe.* Princeton: Princeton University Press, 1990.
Tucker, Robert W., and Linda Wrigley. *The Atlantic Alliance and Its Critics.* New York: Praeger, 1983.
Yost, David. *NATO Transformed.* Washington, D.C.: U.S. Institute of Peace Press, 1998.

AMERICAN POLICY IN EASTERN EUROPE AND THE FORMER SOVIET UNION

Amsden, Alice H., Jacek Kochanowicz, and Lance Taylor. *The Market Meets Its Match.* Cambridge: Harvard University Press, 1995.
Blaney, John W., ed. *The Successor States to the USSR.* Washington, D.C.: CQ Press, 1995.
Brown, J. F. *Hopes and Shadows.* Durham: Duke University Press, 1994.
Burg, Steven L. *War or Peace?* New York: New York University Press, 1996.
Dawisha, Karen, and Bruce Parrott. *Russia and the New States of Eurasia.* New York: Cambridge University Press, 1994.

Denitch, Bogdan. *Ethnic Nationalism.* Minneapolis: University of Minnesota Press, 1994.
Dobbs, Michael. *Down with Big Brother.* New York: Knopf, 1997.
Dunlop, John B. *The Rise of Russia and the Fall of the Soviet Empire.* Princeton: Princeton University Press, 1993.
Fromkin, David. *Kosovo Crossing.* New York: Free Press, 1999.
Goldman, Marshall I. *Lost Opportunity.* New York: Norton, 1994.
Goodby, James E. *Europe Undivided.* Washington, D.C.: U.S. Institute of Peace Press, 1998.
Judah, Tim. *Kosovo: War and Revenge.* New Haven: Yale University Press, 2000.
Kaplan, Robert D. *Balkan Ghosts.* New York: St. Martin's Press, 1993.
Keep, John. *Last of the Empires.* New York: Oxford University Press, 1996.
Malia, Martin E. *Russia under Western Eyes.* Cambridge: Belknap Press, 1999.
Mayers, David A. *The Ambassadors and America's Soviet Policy.* New York: Oxford University Press, 1995.
Midlarsky, Manus I., John A. Vasquez, and Peter V. Gladkov. *From Rivalry to Cooperation.* New York: HarperCollins, 1994.
Remnick, David. *Resurrection.* New York: Random House, 1997.
Rieff, David. *Slaughterhouse.* New York: Simon and Schuster, 1995.
Satter, David. *Age of Delirium.* New York: Knopf, 1996.
Simes, Dimitri K. *After the Collapse.* New York: Simon and Schuster, 1999.
Waller, J. Michael. *Secret Empire.* Boulder: Westview Press, 1994.
Zimmerman, Warren. *Origins of a Catastrophe.* New York: Times Books, 1996.
Zubok, Vladislav, and Constantine Pleshakov. *Inside the Kremlin's Cold War.* Cambridge: Harvard University Press, 1996.

AMERICAN POLICY IN EAST ASIA

Armacost, Michael H. *Friends or Rivals?* New York: Columbia University Press, 1996.
Berman, Larry. *Lyndon Johnson's War.* New York: Norton, 1989.
Bernstein, Richard, and Ross H. Munro. *The Coming Conflict with China.* New York: Knopf, 1997.
Buckley, Roger. *U.S.-Japan Alliance Diplomacy, 1945–1990.* New York: Cambridge University Press, 1992.
Cheung, Gordon C. K. *Market Liberalism.* New Brunswick, N.J.: Transaction Publishers, 1998.
Cossa, Ralph A. *Restructuring the U.S.–Japan Alliance.* Washington, D.C.: CSIS Press, 1997.
Cumings, Bruce. *Korea's Place in the Sun.* New York: Norton, 1997.
DiLeo, David L. *George Ball, Vietnam, and the Rethinking of Containment.* Chapel Hill: University of North Carolina Press, 1991.
Dower, John. *Japan in Peace and War.* New York: New Press, 1994.
Dulles, Foster R. *American Foreign Policy toward Communist China.* New York: Crowell, 1972.
Fallows, James. *Looking at the Sun.* New York: Pantheon, 1994.
Frankel, Jeffrey A., and Miles Kahler, eds. *Regionalism and Rivalry.* Chicago: University of Chicago Press, 1993.
Gardner, Lloyd C., and Ted Gittinger, eds. *Vietnam: The Early Decisions.* Austin: University of Texas Press, 1997.
Gelb, Leslie, and Richard K. Betts. *The Irony of Vietnam.* Washington, D.C.: Brookings, 1979.
Gelb, Leslie, et al. *The Pentagon Papers.* New York: Bantam Books, 1971.
Green, Michael J., and Patrick M. Cronin, eds. *The U.S.–Japan Alliance.* New York: Council on Foreign Relations Press, 1999.
Halberstam, David. *The Best and the Brightest.* New York: Random House, 1969.
Herring, George C. *America's Longest War.* 2d ed. New York: Wiley, 1988.
___. *LBJ and Vietnam.* Austin: University of Texas Press, 1994.

Hunt, Michael H. *Lyndon Johnson's War.* New York: Hill and Wang, 1996.
Karnow, Stanley C. *In Our Image.* New York: Ballentine Books, 1989.
___. *Vietnam.* New York: Viking Press, 1983.
Kattenburg, Paul. *The Vietnam Trauma in American Foreign Policy, 1945–1975.* New Brunswick: Transaction Books, 1980.
Lind, Michael. *Vietnam, the Necessary War.* New York: Free Press, 1999.
Logevall, Frederik. *Choosing War.* Berkeley: University of California Press, 1999.
Metzger, Thomas A., and Ramon H. Myers, eds. *Greater China and U.S. Foreign Policy.* Stanford: Hoover Institution Press, 1996.
Sheehan, Neil. *A Bright Shining Lie.* New York: Random House, 1988.
Sigal, Leon V. *Disarming Strangers.* Princeton: Princeton University Press, 1998.
Spanier, John W. *The Truman-MacArthur Controversy and the Korean War.* Rev. ed. New York: Norton, 1965.
Tow, William T. *Encountering the Dominant Player.* New York: Columbia University Press, 1991.
Wainstock, Dennis D. *Truman, MacArthur, and the Korean War.* Westport, Conn.: Greenwood Press, 1999.
Williams, William Appleman, et al., eds., *America in Vietnam.* Garden City, N.Y.: Anchor Books, 1975.

AMERICAN POLICY IN THE MIDDLE EAST AND SOUTHERN ASIA

Bill, James A. *The Eagle and the Lion.* New Haven: Yale University Press, 1988.
Brands, H. W. *Into the Labyrinth.* New York: McGraw Hill, 1994.
Cohen, Roger, and Claudio Gati. *In The Eyes of the Storm.* New York: Farrar, Straus and Giroux, 1991.
Cordesman, Anthony H. *Perilous Prospects.* Boulder: Westview Press, 1996.
Friedman, Thomas L. *From Beirut to Jerusalem.* New York: Anchor Books, 1989.
Gasiorowski, Mark J. *U.S. Foreign Policy and the Shah.* Ithaca: Cornell University Press, 1991.
Gendzier, Irene L. *Notes from the Minefield.* New York: Columbia University Press, 1997.
Gerges, Fawaz A. *America and Political Islam.* New York: Cambridge University Press, 1999.
Graham-Brown, Sarah. *Sanctioning Saddam.* New York: St. Martin's Press, 1999.
Hunter, Shireen T. *The Future of Islam and the West.* Westport, Conn.: Praeger, 1998.
Jentleson, Bruce W. *With Friends Like These.* New York: Norton, 1994.
Kux, Dennis. *India and the United States.* Washington, D.C.: National Defense University Press, 1993.
Lenczowski, George. *American Presidents and the Middle East.* Durham: Duke University Press, 1990.
Lesch, David W., ed. *The Middle East and the United States.* 2d ed. Boulder: Westview Press, 1999.
McMahon, Robert J. *The Cold War on the Periphery.* New York: Columbia University Press, 1994.
Quandt, William. *Camp David.* Washington, D.C.: Brookings, 1986.
___. *Peace Process.* Washington, D.C.: Brookings, 1993.
Renshon, Stanley A., ed. *The Political Psychology of the Gulf War.* Pittsburgh: University of Pittsburgh Press, 1993.
Roger, Louis, and Owen Roger, eds. *Suez 1956.* New York: Oxford, 1989.
Rubin, Barry. *Revolution until Victory?* Cambridge: Harvard University Press, 1994.
Safran, Nadav. *Intifada.* New York: Simon and Schuster, 1989.
___. *Israel: The Embattled Ally.* Cambridge: Harvard University Press, 1978.
___. *Saudi Arabia: The Ceaseless Quest for Security.* Cambridge: Harvard University Press, 1985.

Sick, Gary. *All Fall Down.* New York: Penguin Books, 1986.
Sifry, Micah L., and Christopher Cerf, eds. *The Gulf War Reader.* New York: Random House, 1991.
Tessler, Mark. *A History of the Israeli-Palestinian Conflict.* Bloomington: Indiana University Press, 1994.

AMERICAN POLICY IN AFRICA

Alinghaus, Bruce E., ed. *Arms for Africa.* Lexington, Mass.: Lexington Books, 1983.
Anstee, Margaret Joan. *Orphan of the Cold War.* New York: St. Martin's Press, 1996.
Bender, Gerald, James Coleman, and Richard Sklar, eds. *African Crisis Areas and U.S. Foreign Policy.* Berkeley: University of California Press, 1985.
Clarke, Walter, and Jeffrey Herbst, eds. *Learning from Somalia.* Boulder: Westview Press, 1997.
Dickson, David A. *United States Foreign Policy toward Sub-Saharan Africa.* Lanham, Md.: University Press of America, 1985.
Giliomee, Hermann, and Lawrence Schlemmer. *From Apartheid to Nation Building.* New York: Oxford University Press, 1990.
Jackson, Henry F. *From the Congo to Soweto.* New York: Morrow, 1982.
Kelly, Sean. *America's Tyrant.* Washington, D.C.: American University Press, 1993.
Layachi, Azzedine. *The United States and North Africa.* New York: Praeger, 1990.
Packenham, Robert A. *Liberal America and the Third World.* Princeton: Princeton University Press, 1973.
Schraeder, Peter J. *United States Foreign Policy toward Africa.* New York: Cambridge University Press, 1994.
Stevenson, Jonathan. *Losing Mogadishu.* Annapolis, Md.: Naval Institute Press, 1995.

AMERICAN POLICY IN LATIN AMERICA

Blasier, Cole. *The Hovering Giant.* Rev. ed. Pittsburgh: University of Pittsburgh Press, 1985.
Coatsworth, John H. *Central America and the United States.* New York: Twayne Publishers, 1994.
Dinges, John. *Our Man in Panama.* New York: Random House, 1990.
Domíguez, Jorge I. *To Make a World Safe for Revolution.* Cambridge: Harvard University Press, 1989.
Draper, Theodore. *The Dominican Revolt.* New York: Commentary, 1968.
Gutman, Roy. *Banana Diplomacy.* New York: Simon and Schuster, 1988.
Hufbauer, Gary Clyde, and Jeffrey J. Schott. *Western Hemisphere Economic Integration.* Washington, D.C.: Institute for International Economics, 1994.
Huggins, Martha K. *Political Policing.* Durham: Duke University Press, 1998.
Immerman, Robert H. *The CIA in Guatemala: The Foreign Policy of Intervention.* Austin: University of Texas Press, 1982.
Kagan, Robert. *A Twilight Struggle.* New York: Free Press, 1996.
LaFeber, Walter. *Inevitable Revolutions.* New York: Norton, 1983.
Lake, Anthony. *Somoza Falling.* Boston: Houghton Mifflin, 1989.
___. *The "Tar Baby" Option.* New York: Columbia University Press, 1976.
LeoGrande, William M. *Our Own Backyard.* Chapel Hill: University of North Carolina Press, 1998.
Lowenthal, Abraham F., ed. *Exporting Democracy.* Baltimore: Johns Hopkins University Press, 1991.
___. *Partners in Conflict.* Baltimore: Johns Hopkins University Press, 1987.
Maingot, Anthony P. *The United States and the Caribbean.* Boulder: Westview Press, 1996.
Marcella, Gabriel. *Warriors in Peacetime.* Portland: Frank Cass, 1994.

Morley, Morris H. *Imperial State and Revolution.* New York: Cambridge University Press, 1987.

Pastor, Robert A. *Condemned to Repetition.* Princeton: Princeton University Press, 1987.

___. *Whirlpool.* Princeton: Princeton University Press, 1993.

Rabe, Stephen G. *Eisenhower and Latin America.* Chapel Hill: University of North Carolina Press, 1988.

Schlesinger, Stephen, and Stephen Kinzer. *Bitter Fruit.* Garden City, N.Y.: Anchor Books, 1982.

Schoultz, Lars. *Beneath the United States.* Cambridge: Harvard University Press, 1998.

Shacochis, Bob. *The Immaculate Invasion.* New York: Viking, 1999.

Shafer, Michael D. *Deadly Paradigms.* Princeton: Princeton University Press, 1988.

Sigmund, Paul. *The Overthrow of Allende and the Politics of Chile.* Pittsburgh: University of Pittsburgh Press, 1977.

Smith, Peter H. *Talons of the Eagle.* 2d. ed. New York: Oxford University Press, 2000.

Suchliki, Jaime. *Cuba.* New York: Brassey's, 1990.

Walker, Thomas W., ed. *Reagan versus the Sandinistas.* Boulder: Westview Press, 1987.

AMERICA AND THE INTERNATIONAL POLITICAL ECONOMY

Baldwin, David A. *Economic Statecraft.* Princeton: Princeton University Press, 1985.

Bhagwati, Jagdish. *The World Trading System at Risk.* Princeton: Princeton University Press, 1991.

Bhagwati, Jagdish, and Hugh T. Patrick, eds. *Aggressive Unilateralism.* Ann Arbor: University of Michigan Press, 1990.

Block, Fred. *Origins of International Economic Disorder.* Berkeley: University of California Press, 1977.

Buchanan, Patrick J. *The Great Betrayal.* Boston: Little, Brown, 1998.

Destler, I. M. *American Trade Politics.* 2d ed. Washington, D.C.: Twentieth Century Fund, 1992.

___. *Making Foreign Economic Policy.* Washington, D.C.: Brookings, 1980.

Gertcher, Frank L., and William Weide. *The Political Economy of National Defense.* Boulder: Westview Press, 1987.

Gilpin, Robert. *The Challenge of Global Capitalism.* Princeton: Princeton University Press, 2000.

___. *The Political Economy of International Relations.* Princeton: Princeton University Press, 1987.

Haass, Richard, ed. *Economic Sanctions and American Diplomacy.* New York: Council on Foreign Relations Press, 1998.

Hall, Peter A., ed. *The Political Power of Economic Ideas.* Princeton: Princeton University Press, 1989.

Hoekman, Bernard, and Michel Kostecki. *The Political Economy of the World Trading System.* New York: Oxford University Press, 1996.

Hook, Steven W. *National Interest and Foreign Aid.* Boulder: Lynne Rienner, 1995.

Hook, Steven W., ed. *Foreign Aid toward the Millennium.* Boulder: Lynne Rienner, 1996.

Kapstein, Ethan B. *Governing the Global Economy.* Cambridge: Harvard University Press, 1994.

___. *The Political Economy of National Security.* New York: McGraw-Hill, 1992.

Krasner, Stephen D. *Defending the National Interest.* Princeton: Princeton University Press, 1978.

___. *Structural Conflict.* Berkeley: University of California Press, 1985.

Kunz, Diane B. *Butter and Guns.* New York: Free Press, 1997.

Lewis, Arthur. *The Evolution of the International Economic Order.* Princeton: Princeton University Press, 1978.

Luttwak, Edward. *Turbo-Capitalism.* New York: HarperCollins, 1999.
Maren, Michael. *The Road to Hell.* New York: Free Press, 1997.
O'Hanlon, Michael, and Carol Graham, *A Half Penny on the Federal Dollar.* Washington, D.C.: Brookings, 1997.
Pollard, Robert A. *Economic Security and the Origins of the Cold War, 1945–1950.* New York: Columbia University Press, 1985.
Reich, Robert. *The Work of Nations.* New York: Vintage, 1992.
Rothstein, Robert. *The Weak in the World of the Strong.* New York: Columbia University Press, 1977.
Spero, Joan, and Jeffrey A. Hart. *The Politics of International Economic Relations.* 5th ed. New York: St. Martin's Press, 1997.
Tucker, Robert. *Inequality of Nations.* New York: Basic Books, 1977.
Tulchin, Martin, and Susan Tulchin. *Buying into America.* New York: Times Books, 1988.
Zakaria, Fareed. *From Wealth to Power.* Princeton: Princeton University Press, 1998.

DOMESTIC POLITICS AND AMERICAN FOREIGN POLICY

Allison, Graham T., and Philip Zelikow. *Essence of Decision.* 2d ed. New York: Longman, 1999.
Alterman, Eric. *Who Speaks for America?* Ithaca: Cornell University Press, 1998.
Barnet, Richard J. *The Rockets' Red Glare.* New York: Touchstone, 1990.
Blechman, Barry. *The Politics of National Security.* New York: Oxford University Press, 1990.
Caldwell, Daniel. *The Dynamics of Domestic Politics and Arms Control.* Columbia: University of South Carolina Press, 1991.
Charles-Philippe, David. *Foreign Policy Failure in the White House.* Lanham, Md.: University Press of America, 1994.
Crabb, Cecil V., Jr., and Pat M. Holt. *Invitation to Struggle.* 4th ed. Washington, D.C.: CQ Press, 1992.
Crabb, Cecil V., Jr., et al. *Congress and the Foreign Policy Process.* Baton Rouge: Louisiana State University Press, 2000.
Darling, Arthur B. *The Central Intelligence Agency.* University Park: Pennsylvania State University Press, 1990.
Destler, I. M., Leslie H. Gelb, and Anthony Lake. *Our Own Worst Enemy.* New York: Simon and Schuster, 1984.
Dumbrell, John. *The Making of U.S. Foreign Policy.* New York: Manchester University Press, 1990.
Foyle, Douglas C. *Counting the Public In.* New York: Columbia University Press, 1999.
Halperin, Morton H. *Bureaucratic Politics and Foreign Policy.* Washington, D.C.: Brookings, 1974.
Haney, Patrick J. *Organizing for Foreign Policy Crises.* Ann Arbor: University of Michigan Press, 1997.
Henkin, Louis. *Foreign Affairs and the Constitution.* New York: Norton, 1972.
Hinckley, Barbara. *Less than Meets the Eye.* Chicago: University of Chicago Press, 1994.
Hughes, Barry B. *The Domestic Context of American Foreign Policy.* San Francisco: W. H. Freeman, 1978.
Hulnick, Arthur. *Fixing the Spy Machine.* Westport, Conn.: Praeger, 1999.
Janis, Irving L. *Groupthink.* 2d ed. Boston: Houghton Mifflin, 1983.
Jeffreys-Jones, Rhodri. *The CIA and American Diplomacy.* New Haven: Yale University Press, 1989.
Jervis, Robert, and Jack Snyder, eds. *Dominos and Bandwagons.* New York: Oxford University Press, 1991.
Johnson, Loch K. *America's Secret Power.* New York: Oxford University Press, 1989.

Kull, Steven, and I. M. Destler. *Misreading the Public.* Washington, D.C.: Brookings, 1999.
Lindsay, James M. *Congress and the Politics of U.S. Foreign Policy.* Baltimore: Johns Hopkins University Press, 1994.
Lowenthal, Mark M. *Intelligence: From Secrets to Policy.* Washington, D.C.: CQ Press, 1999.
Mann, Thomas E., ed. *A Question of Balance.* Washington, D.C.: Brookings, 1990.
May, Christopher. *In the Name of War.* Cambridge: Harvard University Press, 1989.
Mermin, Jonathan. *Debating War and Peace.* Princeton: Princeton University Press, 1999.
Nathan, James A., and James K. Oliver. *Foreign Policy Making and the American Political System.* 2d ed. Boston: Little, Brown, 1987.
Nutter, John J. *The CIA's Black Ops.* Amherst, N.Y.: Prometheus Books, 2000.
Pastor, Robert A. *Congress and the Politics of U.S. Foreign Economic Policy.* Berkeley: University of California Press, 1980.
Richelson, Jeffrey T. *The U.S. Intelligence Community.* Cambridge: Ballinger, 1985.
Ripley, Randall B., and James Lindsay. *Congress Resurgent.* Ann Arbor: University of Michigan Press, 1993.
Rosati, Jerel A. *The Carter Administration's Quest for Global Community.* Columbia: University of South Carolina Press, 1987.
___. *The Politics of U.S. Foreign Policy.* 2d ed. Fort Worth: Harcourt Brace Jovanovich, 1999.
Rubin, Barry. *Secrets of State.* New York: Oxford University Press, 1985.
Shuman, Howard E., and Walter R. Thomas. *The Constitution and National Security.* Washington, D.C.: National Defense University Press, 1990.
Silverstein, Gordon. *Imbalance of Powers.* New York: Oxford University Press, 1997.
Sobel, Richard, ed. *Public Opinion in U.S. Foreign Policy.* Lanham, Md.: Rowman and Littlefield, 1993.
Stearns, Monteagle. *Talking to Strangers.* Princeton: Princeton University Press, 1996.
Sutter, Robert G. *U.S. Policy toward China: An Introduction to the Role of Interest Groups.* Lanham, Md.: Rowman and Littlefield, 1998.
Tivnan, Edward. *The Lobby.* New York: Simon and Schuster, 1987.
Tucker, Robert H., Charles B. Keely, and Linda Wrigley, eds. *Immigration and U.S. Foreign Policy.* Boulder: Westview Press, 1990.
Wittkopf, Eugene R. *Faces of Internationalism.* Durham: Duke University Press, 1990.
Zegart, Amy B. *Flawed by Design: The Evolution of the CIA, JCS, and NSC.* Stanford: Stanford University Press, 1999.

MEMOIRS AND BIOGRAPHIES OF AMERICAN LEADERS

Acheson, Dean. *Present at the Creation.* New York: Norton, 1969.
Ambrose, Stephen E. *Eisenhower.* 2 vols. New York: Simon and Schuster, 1983 and 1984.
___. *Nixon.* New York: Simon and Schuster, 1992.
Andrianopoulos, Gerry A. *Kissinger and Brzezinski.* New York: St. Martin's Press, 1991.
Baker, James A., III. *The Politics of Diplomacy.* New York: Putnam, 1995.
Bill, James A. *George Ball.* New Haven: Yale University Press, 1997.
Blackman, Ann. *Seasons of Her Life: A Biography of Madeleine Korbel Albright.* New York: Scribner's, 1998.
Brands, H. W. *The Wages of Globalism.* New York: Oxford University Press, 1994.
Brinkley, Douglas, ed. *Dean Acheson and the Making of U.S. Foreign Policy.* New York: St. Martin's Press, 1993.
Brown, Harold. *Thinking about National Security.* Boulder: Westview Press, 1983.
Brzezinski, Zbigniew. *Power and Principle.* New York: Farrar, Straus and Giroux, 1983.
Bullock, Alan. *Hitler and Stalin.* New York: Knopf, 1992.
Bundy, McGeorge. *Danger and Survival.* New York: Random House, 1988.
Bush, George H. W., and Brent Scowcroft. *A World Transformed.* New York: Knopf, 1998.

Cannon, Lou. *Reagan.* New York: Random House, 1981.
Carter, Jimmy. *Keeping Faith.* New York: Bantam Books, 1982.
Chace, James. *Acheson.* New York: Simon and Schuster, 1998.
Christopher, Warren. *In the Stream of History.* Stanford: Stanford University Press, 1998.
Dallek, Robert. *Franklin D. Roosevelt and American Foreign Policy, 1932–1945.* New York: Oxford University Press, 1979.
Eisenhower, Dwight D. *Mandate for Change.* New York: New American Library, 1965.
___. *Waging Peace.* New York: Doubleday, 1965.
Feis, Herbert. *Churchill, Roosevelt, Stalin.* Princeton: Princeton University Press, 1957.
Ferrell, Robert H. *George C. Marshall.* New York: Cooper Square Publishers, 1966.
Gates, Robert M. *From the Shadows.* New York: Simon and Schuster, 1996.
Guhin, Michael. *John Foster Dulles.* New York: Columbia University Press, 1972.
Immerman, Richard H. *John Foster Dulles and the Diplomacy of the Cold War.* Princeton: Princeton University Press, 1990.
Isaacson, Walter. *Kissinger.* New York: Simon and Schuster, 1992.
Isaacson, Walter, and Evan Thomas. *The Wise Men.* New York: Simon and Schuster, 1986.
Johnson, Lyndon B. *The Vantage Point.* New York: Popular Library, 1971.
Kalb, Marvin, and Bernard Kalb. *Kissinger.* Boston: Little, Brown, 1974.
Kearns, Doris. *Lyndon Johnson and the American Dream.* New York: Harper and Row, 1976.
Kennan, George F. *Memoirs.* Boston: Little, Brown, 1967.
Kennedy, Robert F. *Thirteen Days.* New York: Norton, 1971.
Kissinger, Henry A. *The White House Years.* Boston: Little, Brown, 1979.
___. *Years of Upheaval.* Boston: Little, Brown, 1982.
Knock, Thomas J. *To End All Wars: Woodrow Wilson and the Quest for a New World Order.* New York: Oxford University Press, 1992.
McCullough, David. *Truman.* New York: Simon and Schuster, 1992.
McFarlane, Robert C., with Zofia Smardz. *Special Trust.* New York: Cadell and Davies, 1994.
McLellan, David S. *Cyrus Vance.* Totowa, N.J.: Rowman and Allanheld, 1985.
Miscamble, Wilson D. *George F. Kennan and the Making of American Foreign Policy, 1947–1950.* Princeton: Princeton University Press, 1992.
Nixon, Richard. *RN.* New York: Grosset and Dunlap, 1978.
Parmet, Herbert S. *Eisenhower and the American Crusades.* New York: Macmillan, 1972.
Pogue, Forrest C. *George C. Marshall.* New York: Viking Press, 1987.
Rusk, Dean, as told to Richard Rusk. *As I Saw It.* New York: Norton, 1990.
Schlesinger, Arthur M., Jr. *A Thousand Days.* New York: Crest Books, 1967.
Schulzinger, Robert D. *Henry Kissinger.* New York: Columbia University Press, 1989.
Sherwood, Robert E. *Roosevelt and Hopkins.* New York: Harper, 1948.
Smith, Gaddis. *Dean Acheson.* New York: Cooper Square Publishers, 1972.
Sorensen, Theodore C. *Kennedy.* New York: Bantam Books, 1966.
Stoessinger, John. *Henry Kissinger.* New York: Norton, 1976.
Truman, Harry S. *Memoirs.* 2 vols. New York: New American Library, 1965.
Vance, Cyrus. *Hard Choices.* New York: Simon and Schuster, 1982.
Weinberger, Caspar W. *Fighting for Peace.* New York: Warner, 1990.

Select Web Sites

The following Web sites may be useful to students of American foreign policy—either as supplements to this text or as resources for research projects. This list is by no means exhaustive. It can, however, provide a gateway to related sites and sources of information. Each URL should be preceded by http://.

U.S. GOVERNMENT: EXECUTIVE BRANCH

White House (www.whitehouse.gov)
Central Intelligence Agency (www.cia.gov)
Department of Commerce (www.doc.gov)
Department of Defense (www.defenselink.mil)
    Defense Intelligence Agency (www.dia.mil)
    Joint Chiefs of Staff (www.dtic.mil/jcs)
    U.S. Army (www.army.mil)
    U.S. Navy (www.navy.mil)
    U.S. Air Force (www.af.mil)
    U.S. Marine Corps (www.usmc.mil)
    North Atlantic Treaty Organization (www.nato.int)
Department of Labor (www.dol.gov)
Department of State (www.state.gov)
    U.S. Agency for International Development (www.info.usaid.gov)
    U.S. Arms Control and Disarmament Agency (www.acda.gov)
    U.S. Information Agency (www.usinfo.state.gov)
National Security Agency (www.nsa.gov)
U.S. Trade Representative (www.ustr.gov)
U.S. Mission to the United Nations (www.un.int/usa)

U.S. GOVERNMENT: LEGISLATIVE BRANCH

Congressional Budget Office (www.cbo.gov)
Library of Congress (www.loc.gov)
    Congressional Research Service (www.loc.gov/crsinfo)
U.S. House of Representatives (www.house.gov)
    International Relations Committee (www.house.gov/international_relations)
    National Security Committee (www.house.gov/hasc)
U.S. Senate (www.senate.gov)
    Foreign Relations Committee (www.senate.gov/~foreign)
    Armed Services Committee (www.senate.gov/~armed_services)

U.S. GOVERNMENT: JUDICIAL BRANCH

U.S. Supreme Court (www.uscourts.gov)
U.S. Court of International Trade (www.uscit.gov)

INTERNATIONAL GOVERNMENTAL ORGANIZATIONS

Asia-Pacific Economic Cooperation (www.apecsec.org.sg)
Association of South East Asian Nations (www.aseansec.org)
European Union (www.europa.eu.int)
International Court of Justice (www.icj-cij.org)
International Finance Corporation (www.ifc.org)
International Labor Organization (www.ilo.org)
International Monetary Fund (www.imf.org)
Organization of American States (www.oas.org)
Organization for Economic Cooperation and Development (www.oecd.org)
Organization of Petroleum Exporting Countries (www.opec.org)
United Nations (www.unsystem.org)
World Bank (www.worldbank.org)
World Trade Organization (www.wto.org)

INTERNATIONAL NONGOVERNMENTAL ORGANIZATIONS

AFL–CIO (www.aflcio.org)
American Israel Public Affairs Committee (www.aipac.org)
Amnesty International (www.amnesty.org)
Corporate Watch (www.corpwatch.org)
Freedom House (www.freedomhouse.org)
GreenNet (www.gn.apc.org)
Greenpeace (www.greenpeace.org)
Human Rights Watch (www.hrw.org)
International Chamber of Commerce (www.iccwbo.org)
International Committee of the Red Cross (www.icrc.org)
Public Citizen (www.citizen.org)
Sierra Club (www.sierraclub.org)
Stockholm International Peace Research Institute (www.sipri.se)
World Wildlife Fund (www.wwf.org)

THINK TANKS AND FOUNDATIONS

American Enterprise Institute (www.aei.org)
Brookings Institution (www.brookings.org)
CATO Institute (www.cato.org)
Close Up Foundation (www.closeup.org)
Council on Foreign Relations (www.cfr.org)
Economic Policy Institute (www.epinet.org)
Federation of American Scientists (www.fas.org)
Global Policy Forum (www.globalpolicy.org)
Heritage Foundation (www.heritage.org)
National Science Foundation (www.nsf.gov)
Overseas Development Council (www.odc.org)
RAND (www.rand.org)
United States Institute of Peace (www.usip.org)

ILLUSTRATION CREDITS AND ACKNOWLEDGMENTS

Page 1	Radu Sigheti, Reuters
8	National Archives
24	National Archives
42	AP/Wide World Photos
52	National Archives
77	Library of Congress
88	Corbis/Bettmann-UPI
114	AP/Wide World Photos
122	National Archives
137	LBJ Library
149	UPI/Bettmann
155	AP/Wide World Photos
175	White House
197	AP/Wide World Photos
201	Reagan Presidential Library
220	AP/Wide World Photos
232	Reuters
249	Reuters
261	R. Michael Jenkins, Congressional Quarterly
286	R. Michael Jenkins, Congressional Quarterly
290	Patrick de Noirmont, Reuters
297	Reuters
319	Arnd Wiegmann, Reuters
335	Dragan Kujundzic, Reuters
350	Andy Clark, Reuters
354	Scott J. Ferrell, Congressional Quarterly

Index